Why Do You Need This New Edition?

The fifth edition of *A Sequence for Academic Writing* represents a major revision that freshens examples, clarifies and expands instruction, and generally makes the text more adaptable and accessible.

New model papers

- A new example critique in Chapter 2 is based on Charles Krauthammer's "The Moon We Left Behind," an argument against the cancellation of the manned lunar program.
- A new model explanatory synthesis in Chapter 3 introduces readers to the Space Elevator, a plan (considered feasible by NASA) to lift objects to Earth orbit along a thin nanotube ribbon.
- A new model analysis in Chapter 5 applies a classic theory of rumor propagation to a widespread rumor: that travelers in foreign lands were being drugged and surgically deprived of their kidneys.

Updates to other chapters

- Using airport pat-downs as an example, the model argument synthesis in Chapter 4 now shows how the issue of individual privacy vs. public safety will follow students off campus, into the wider world.
- Chapter 5, on analysis, has been almost completely reorganized and rewritten.
- Chapter 7 (Locating, Mining, and Citing Sources) now includes the 2010 APA and 2009 MLA guidelines. Discussion of the Research Question has been expanded, as has coverage of formulating effective search queries, avoiding plagiarism in the digital age, and "fair use" of digital sources.

PEARSON

A Sequence for Academic Writing

FIFTH EDITION

Laurence Behrens
University of California, Santa Barbara

Leonard J. Rosen
Bentley University

Boston   Columbus   Indianapolis   New York   San Francisco   Upper Saddle River
Amsterdam   Cape Town   Dubai   London   Madrid   Milan   Munich   Paris
Montréal   Toronto   Delhi   Mexico City   São Paulo   Sydney   Hong Kong
Seoul   Singapore   Taipei   Tokyo

Executive Editor: Suzanne Phelps Chambers
Senior Marketing Manager: Sandra McGuire
Senior Supplements Editor: Donna Campion
Production Manager: Savoula Amanatidis
Project Coordination, Text Design, and Electronic Page Makeup: Integra
    Software Services, Inc.
Cover Design Manager: Wendy Ann Fredericks
Cover Designer: Nancy Sacks
Cover Art: *Synchopation III*, © Gil Mayers/SuperStock
Photo Researcher: Poyee Oster
Senior Manufacturing Buyer: Roy L. Pickering, Jr.
Printer and Binder: Edwards Brothers, Inc.
Cover Printer: Lehigh-Phoenix Color Corporation–Hagerstown

This title is restricted to sales and distribution in North America only.

For permission to use copyrighted material, grateful acknowledgment is made to the copyright holders on pp. 339–343, which are hereby made part of this copyright page.

Library of Congress Cataloging-in-Publication Data
Behrens, Laurence.
    A sequence for academic writing/Laurence Behrens, Leonard J. Rosen.—5th ed.
        p. cm.
    Includes bibliographical references and index.
    ISBN-13: 978-0-205-17288-7
    ISBN-10: 0-205-17288-1
    1. English language—Rhetoric.   2. Academic writing.   I. Rosen, Leonard J.
        II. Title.
    PE1408.B46926 2011
    808'042—dc22
                                                            2011010721

10 9 8 7 6 5 4 3 2—EDW—15 14 13 12

ISBN-13: 978-0-205-17288-7
ISBN-10:   0-205-17288-1

A Sequence for Academic Writing evolved out of another of our texts, *Writing and Reading Across the Curriculum (WRAC)*. Through eleven editions over the last thirty years, *WRAC* has helped more than a million students prepare for the writing to be done well beyond the freshman composition course. *WRAC* features a rhetoric in which students are introduced to the core skills of summary, critique, synthesis, and analysis, and a reader that presents readings in the disciplines to which students can apply the skills learned in the earlier chapters.

Because the skills of summary, critique, synthesis, and analysis are so central to academic thinking and writing, many instructors—both those teaching writing across the curriculum and those using other approaches to composition instruction—have found *WRAC* a highly useful introduction to college-level writing. We therefore adapted the rhetoric portion of *WRAC*, creating a separate book that instructors can use apart from any additional reading content they choose to incorporate into their writing courses. *A Sequence for Academic Writing* is both an adaptation of *WRAC* and an expansion: It includes chapters, sections, and additional writing assignments not found in the parent text.

WHAT'S NEW IN THIS EDITION?

The fifth edition of *A Sequence for Academic Writing* represents a significant revision of the previous edition.

- The model student critique, explanatory synthesis, and analysis in Chapters 2, 3, and 5, respectively, have been replaced with papers on new subjects. The new example critique is based on Charles Krauthammer's "The Moon We Left Behind," an argument against the cancellation of the manned lunar program. The new model explanatory synthesis in Chapter 3 introduces readers to the Space Elevator, a plan (considered feasible by NASA) to lift objects to Earth orbit along a thin nanotube ribbon. The synthesis builds on several articles on the subject in the chapter itself (as well as on other sources) and explains the physics of the space elevator, obstacles to building the elevator, and possible consequences of building—positive and negative. The new model analysis in Chapter 5 applies a classic theory of rumor propagation to a particular rumor that some years ago went "viral" with the aid of the Internet and raised fears of travelers in foreign lands being drugged and surgically deprived of their kidneys.

- The model argument synthesis in Chapter 4 has been revised to show a current example—airport security pat-downs—of how the issue of individual privacy vs. public safety will follow students off campus, into the wider world.

- Chapter 5, on analysis, has been almost completely reorganized and rewritten.

- Chapter 7 (Locating, Mining, and Citing Sources) now includes coverage of the 2010 APA guidelines to citation format along with the 2009 Modern Language Association guidelines—changes that reflect the latest editions of the MLA and APA manuals. Discussion of the Research Question has been expanded, along with coverage formulating effective search queries, avoiding plagiarism in the digital age, and "fair use" of digital sources.

Thus the fifth edition of *A Sequence for Academic Writing* represents a major revision that freshens examples, clarifies and expands instruction, and generally makes more adaptable and accessible a text that, we are told, has helped introduce students to source-based writing in a variety of academic settings. As ever, we rely on the criticism of colleagues to improve our work, and we invite you to contact the publisher with suggested revisions.

ORGANIZATION AND KEY FEATURES

We proceed through a sequence from Summary, Paraphrase, and Quotation to Critical Reading and Critique, to Explanatory Synthesis and Argument Synthesis, to Analysis. Students will find in Chapter 6 a discussion of the writing process that is reinforced throughout the text. Chapter 7, Locating, Mining, and Citing Sources, introduces students to the tools and techniques they will need in order to apply the skills learned earlier to sources they gather themselves when conducting research.

The book ends with a controlled research assignment in Chapter 8, Practicing Academic Writing. We make a special effort in all chapters to address the issue of plagiarism and have added a new section on the topic in Chapter 7. Both there and in Chapter 1, we offer techniques for steering well clear of plagiarism, at the same time encouraging students to live up to the highest ethical standards.

Key features in *A Sequence for Academic Writing* include *boxes*, which sum up important concepts in each chapter; brief writing *exercises*, which prompt individual and group activities; *writing assignments*, which encourage students to practice the skills they learn in each chapter; and *model papers*, which provide example responses to writing assignments discussed in the text.

While we are keenly aware of the overlapping nature of the skills on which we focus, and while we could endlessly debate an appropriate order in which to cover these skills, a book is necessarily linear. We have chosen the sequence that makes the most sense to us. Teachers should feel free to use these chapters in whatever order they decide is most useful to their individual aims and philosophies. Understanding the material in a later chapter does not, in most cases, depend on students' having read material in the earlier chapters.

SUPPLEMENTS

Instructor's Manual

The *Instructor's Manual (IM)* provides sample syllabi and assignment ideas for traditional and Web-based courses. Each IM chapter opens with a summary of the chapter in the student text, followed by specific instruction on that chapter's focus. Writing/Critical Thinking Activities offer additional exercises that make use of Internet sources, and Revision Activities are also provided for Chapters 1 to 8. In addition, each IM chapter provides extensive lists of Web source material for both students and instructors.

MyCompLab

PEARSON
mycomplab

MyCompLab provides multimedia resources for students and teachers in one easy-to-use site. In this site, students will find guided assistance through each step of the writing process; interactive tutorials and videos that illustrate key concepts; over thirty model documents from across the curriculum; *Exchange*, Pearson's online peer-review program; the "Avoiding Plagiarism" tutorial; diagnostic grammar tests and thousands of practice questions; and *Research Navigator*^{TM}, a database with thousands of magazines and academic journals, the subject-search archive of the *New York Times*, "Link Library," library guides, and more. Learn more about MyCompLab at **http://www.mycomplab.com.**

ACKNOWLEDGMENTS

We would like to thank the following reviewers for their help in the preparation of this text: Elizabeth Baines, Truckee Meadows Community College; Patricia Baldwin, Pitt Community College; Sherri Brouillette, Millersville University; Bryce Campbell, Victor Valley College; Margaret L. Clark, Florida Community College at Jacksonville; Diane Z. De Bella, University of Colorado; Grey Glau, Arizona State University; Pat Hartman, Cleveland State University; Wendy Hayden, University of Maryland; Randall McClure, Minnesota State University–Mankato; Jamil Mustafa, Lewis University; and Deborah Richey, Owens Community College. We would also like to thank reviewers of previous editions of this text: Cora Agatucci, Central Oregon Community College; Bruce Closser, Andrews University; Clinton R. Gardner, Salt Lake Community College; Margaret Graham, Iowa State University; Susanmarie Harrington, Indiana University and Purdue University Indianapolis; Georgina Hill, Western Michigan University; Jane M. Kinney, Valdosta State University; Susan E. Knutson, University of Minnesota–Twin Cities; Cathy Leaker, North Carolina State University; Kate Miller, Central Michigan University; Lyle W. Morgan, Pittsburg State University; Joan Perkins,

University of Hawaii; Catherine Quick, Stephen F. Austin State University; Emily Rogers, University of Illinois–Urbana Champaign; Amanda McGuire Rzicznek, Bowling Green State University; William Scott Simkins, University of Southern Mississippi; Doug Swartz, Indiana University Northwest; Marcy Taylor, Central Michigan University; Zach Waggoner, Western Illinois University; Heidemarie Z. Weidner, Tennessee Technological University; Betty R. Youngkin, The University of Dayton; and Terry Meyers Zawacki, George Mason University. We are also grateful to UCSB librarian Lucia Snowhill for helping us update the reference sources in Chapter 7.

Thanks to Lynn Huddon, the editor who first suggested that we undertake *A Sequence for Academic Writing,* and who has now moved on to other projects. Suzanne Phelps Chambers, our current editor, has been a wellspring of energy and good ideas, and we thank her for ongoing contributions to the book. Thanks also to editorial assistant Laney Whitt for her many kindnesses during manuscript preparation and to Martha Beyerlein, whose meticulous coordination of the production process saved our sanity. We are also grateful to our copyeditor, Elizabeth Jahaske; our proofreader, Amy Handy; and to Savoula Amanatidis, production manager, for careful and attentive handling of the production process. Each has contributed mightily to this project, and we extend our warmest appreciation.

LAURENCE BEHRENS
LEONARD J. ROSEN

NOTE TO THE STUDENT

In your sociology class, you are assigned to write a paper on the role of peer groups in influencing attitudes toward smoking. Your professor expects you to read some of the literature on the subject as well as to conduct interviews with members of such groups. For an environmental studies course, you must write a paper on how one or more industrial plants in a particular area have been affecting the local ecosystem. In your film studies class, you must select a contemporary filmmaker—you are trying to decide between Quentin Tarantino and Guillermo Del Toro—and examine how at least three of his films demonstrate a distinctive point of view.

These writing assignments are typical of those you will undertake during your college years. In fact, such assignments are also common in professional life: for instance, scientists writing environmental impact statements, social scientists writing accounts of their research for professional journals, and film critics showing how the latest effort by a filmmaker fits into the general body of his or her work.

Core Skills

To succeed in such assignments, you will need to develop and hone particular skills in critical reading, thinking, and writing. You must develop—not necessarily in this order—the abilities to

- read and accurately *summarize* a selection of material on your subject;
- determine the quality and relevance of your sources through a process of *critical reading* and assessment;
- *synthesize* different sources by discovering the relationships among them and showing how these relationships produce insights about the subject under discussion;
- *analyze* objects or phenomena by applying particular perspectives and theories;
- develop effective techniques for (1) discovering and using pertinent, authoritative information and ideas and (2) presenting the results of your work in generally accepted disciplinary formats.

A Sequence for Academic Writing will help you to meet these goals. In conversations with faculty across the curriculum, time and again we have been struck by the shared desire to see students thinking and writing in subject-appropriate ways. Psychology, biology, and engineering teachers want their students to think, talk, and write like psychologists, biologists, and engineers. We set out, therefore, to learn the strategies writers use to enter conversations in their respective disciplines; and we discovered that four readily learned strategies—summary, critique, synthesis, and analysis—provide the basis for the great majority of writing in freshman- through senior-level courses, and in courses across disciplines. We therefore made these skills the centerpiece of instruction in this book.

Applications Beyond College

While summary, critique, synthesis, and analysis are primary critical thinking and writing skills practiced throughout the university, these skills are also crucial to the work you will do in your life beyond the university. You will write e-mails, letters, and reports that will explain and persuade; you will evaluate the work of others; you will be expected to gather multiple viewpoints on a topic and to digest these viewpoints (that is, to summarize each and to synthesize all into a coherent whole); you will be called on to conduct close analyses in order to learn how things work or what their constituent parts may be. In sum, the skills you gain in learning how to summarize, evaluate, synthesize, and analyze will serve you well both in college and beyond.

Part One ■ *Structures*

1 ■ Summary, Paraphrase, and Quotation

■ WHAT IS A SUMMARY?

The best way to demonstrate that you understand the information and the ideas in any piece of writing is to compose an accurate and clearly written summary of that piece. By a *summary* we mean a *brief restatement, in your own words, of the content of a passage* (a group of paragraphs, a chapter, an article, a book). This restatement should focus on the *central idea* of the passage. The briefest of summaries (one or two sentences) will do no more than this. A longer, more complete summary will indicate, in condensed form, the main points in the passage that support or explain the central idea. It will reflect the order in which these points are presented and the emphasis given to them. It may even include some important examples from the passage. But it will not include minor details. It will not repeat points simply for the purpose of emphasis. And it will not contain any of your own opinions or conclusions. A good summary, therefore, has three central qualities: *brevity, completeness,* and *objectivity.*

■ CAN A SUMMARY BE OBJECTIVE?

Objectivity could be difficult to achieve in a summary. By definition, writing a summary requires you to select some aspects of the original and leave out others. Since deciding what to select and what to leave out calls for your personal judgment, your summary really is a work of interpretation. And, certainly, your interpretation of a passage may differ from another person's.

One factor affecting the nature and quality of your interpretation is your *prior knowledge* of the subject. For example, if you're attempting to summarize an anthropological article and you're a novice in that field, then your summary of the article will likely differ from that of your professor, who has spent twenty years studying this particular area and whose judgment about what is more or less significant is undoubtedly more reliable than your own. By the same token, your personal or professional *frame of reference* may also affect your interpretation. A union representative and a management representative attempting to summarize the latest management offer would probably come up with two very different accounts. Still, we believe that in most cases it's possible to produce a reasonably objective summary of a passage if you make a conscious, good-faith effort to be unbiased and to prevent your own feelings on the subject from coloring your account of the author's text.

■ USING THE SUMMARY

In some quarters, the summary has a bad reputation—and with reason. Summaries are often provided by writers as substitutes for analyses. As students, many of us have summarized books that we were supposed to *review critically*. All the same, the summary does have a place in respectable college work. First, writing a summary is an excellent way to understand what you read. This in itself is an important goal of academic study. If you don't understand your source material, chances are you won't be able to refer to it usefully in a paper. Summaries help you understand what you read because they force you to put the text into your own words. Practice with writing summaries also develops your general writing habits, because a good summary, like any other piece of good writing, is clear, coherent, and accurate.

Where Do We Find Written Summaries?

Here are just a few of the types of writing that involve summary:

ACADEMIC WRITING

- **Critique papers** summarize material in order to critique it.
- **Synthesis papers** summarize to show relationships between sources.
- **Analysis papers** summarize theoretical perspectives before applying them.
- **Research papers:** note-taking and reporting research require summary.
- **Literature reviews:** overviews of work are presented in brief summaries.
- **Argument papers** summarize evidence and opposing arguments.
- **Essay exams** demonstrate understanding of course materials through summary.

WORKPLACE WRITING

- **Policy briefs** condense complex public policy.
- **Business plans** summarize costs, relevant environmental impacts, and other important matters.
- **Memos, letters, and reports** summarize procedures, meetings, product assessments, expenditures, and more.
- **Medical charts** record patient data in summarized form.
- **Legal briefs** summarize relevant facts and arguments of cases.

Second, summaries are useful to your readers. Let's say you're writing a paper about the McCarthy era in the United States, and in part of that paper you want to discuss Arthur Miller's *The Crucible* as a dramatic treatment of the subject. A summary of the plot would be helpful to a reader who hasn't seen or read—or who doesn't remember—the play. Or perhaps you're writing a paper about the politics of recent American military interventions. If your reader isn't likely to be familiar with American actions in Kosovo and Afghanistan, it would be a good idea to summarize these events at some early point in the paper. In many cases (an exam, for instance), you can use a summary to demonstrate your knowledge of what your professor already knows; when writing a paper, you can use a summary to inform your professor about some relatively unfamiliar source.

Third, summaries are required frequently in college-level writing. For example, on a psychology midterm, you may be asked to explain Carl Jung's theory of the collective unconscious and to show how it differs from Sigmund Freud's theory of the personal unconscious. You may have read about Jung's theory in your textbook or in a supplementary article, or your instructor may have outlined it in her lecture. You can best demonstrate your understanding of it by summarizing it. Then you'll proceed to contrast it with Freud's theory—which, of course, you must also summarize.

■ THE READING PROCESS

It may seem to you that being able to tell (or retell) in summary form exactly what a passage says is a skill that ought to be taken for granted in anyone who can read at high school level. Unfortunately, this is not so: For all kinds of reasons, people don't always read carefully. In fact, it's probably safe to say that usually they don't. Either they read so inattentively that they skip over words, phrases, or even whole sentences, or, if they do see the words in front of them, they see them without registering their significance.

When a reader fails to pick up the meaning and implications of a sentence or two, usually there's no real harm done. (An exception: You could lose credit on an exam or paper because you failed to read or to realize the significance of a crucial direction by your instructor.) But over longer stretches—the paragraph, the section, the article, or the chapter—inattentive or haphazard reading interferes with your goals as a reader: to perceive the shape of the argument, to grasp the central idea, to determine the main points that compose it, to relate the parts of the whole, and to note key examples. This kind of reading takes a lot more energy and determination than casual reading. But in the long run it's an energy-saving method because it enables you to retain the content of the material and to draw upon that content in your own responses. In other words, it allows you to develop an accurate and coherent written discussion that goes beyond summary.

Critical Reading for Summary

- *Examine the context.* Note the credentials, occupation, and publications of the author. Identify the source in which the piece originally appeared. This information helps illuminate the author's perspective on the topic he or she is addressing.

- *Note the title and subtitle.* Some titles are straightforward; the meanings of others become clearer as you read. In either case, titles typically identify the topic being addressed and often reveal the author's attitude toward that topic.

- *Identify the main point.* Whether a piece of writing contains a thesis statement in the first few paragraphs or builds its main point without stating it up front, look at the entire piece to arrive at an understanding of the overall point being made.

- *Identify the subordinate points.* Notice the smaller subpoints that make up the main point, and make sure you understand how they relate to the main point. If a particular subpoint doesn't clearly relate to the main point you've identified, you may need to modify your understanding of the main point.

- *Break the reading into sections.* Notice which paragraphs make up a piece's introduction, body, and conclusion. Break up the body paragraphs into sections that address the writer's various subpoints.

- *Distinguish between points, examples, and counterarguments.* Critical reading requires careful attention to what a writer is *doing* as well as what he or she is *saying*. When a writer quotes someone else, or relays an example of something, ask yourself why this is being done. What point is the example supporting? Is another source being quoted as support for a point or as a counterargument that the writer sets out to address?

- *Watch for transitions within and between paragraphs.* In order to follow the logic of a piece of writing, as well as to distinguish between points, examples, and counterarguments, pay attention to the transitional words and phrases writers use. Transitions function like road signs, preparing the reader for what's next.

- *Read actively and recursively.* Don't treat reading as a passive, linear progression through a text. Instead, read as though you are engaged in a dialogue with the writer: Ask questions of the text as you read, make notes in the margin, underline key ideas in pencil, put question or exclamation marks next to passages that confuse or excite you. Go back to earlier points once you finish a reading, stop during your reading to recap what's come so far, and move back and forth through a text.

■ HOW TO WRITE SUMMARIES

Every article you read will present its own challenge as you work to summarize it. As you'll discover, saying in a few words what has taken someone else a great many can be difficult. But like any other skill, the ability to summarize improves with practice. Here are a few pointers to get you started. They represent possible stages, or steps, in the process of writing a summary. These pointers are not meant to be ironclad rules; rather, they are designed to encourage habits of thinking that will allow you to vary your technique as the situation demands.

Guidelines for Writing Summaries

- *Read the passage carefully.* Determine its structure. Identify the author's purpose in writing. (This will help you distinguish between more important and less important information.) Make a note in the margin when you get confused or when you think something is important; highlight or underline points sparingly, if at all.

- *Reread.* This time divide the passage into sections or stages of thought. The author's use of paragraphing will often be a useful guide. *Label,* on the passage itself, each section or stage of thought. *Underline* key ideas and terms. Write notes in the margin.

- *Write one-sentence summaries,* on a separate sheet of paper, of each stage of thought.

- *Write a thesis—a one- or two-sentence summary of the entire passage.* The thesis should express the central idea of the passage, as you have determined it from the preceding steps. You may find it useful to follow the approach of most newspaper stories—naming the *what, who, why, where, when,* and *how* of the matter. For persuasive passages, summarize in a sentence the author's conclusion. For descriptive passages, indicate the subject of the description and its key feature(s). *Note:* In some cases, *a suitable thesis statement may already be in the original passage.* If so, you may want to quote it directly in your summary.

- *Write the first draft of your summary* by (1) combining the thesis with your list of one-sentence summaries or (2) combining the thesis with one-sentence summaries *plus* significant details from the passage. In either case, eliminate repetition and less important information. Disregard minor details or generalize them (e.g., Bill Clinton and George W. Bush might be generalized as "recent presidents"). Use as few words as possible to convey the main ideas.

(continues)

> • *Check your summary against the original passage* and make what-
> ever adjustments are necessary for accuracy and completeness.
>
> • *Revise your summary,* inserting transitional words and phrases where
> necessary to ensure coherence. Check for style. *Avoid a series of short,*
> *choppy sentences.* Combine sentences for a smooth, logical flow of
> ideas. Check for grammatical correctness, punctuation, and spelling.

■ DEMONSTRATION: SUMMARY

To demonstrate these points at work, let's go through the process of summarizing a passage of expository material—that is, writing that is meant to inform
and/or persuade. Read the following selection carefully. Try to identify its
parts and understand how they work together to create an overall statement.

WILL YOUR JOB BE EXPORTED?
Alan S. Blinder

Alan S. Blinder is the Gordon S. Rentschler Memorial Professor of Economics at Princeton
University. He has served as vice chairman of the Federal Reserve Board and was a mem-
ber of President Clinton's original Council of Economic Advisers.

The great conservative political philosopher Edmund Burke, who probably would
not have been a reader of *The American Prospect,* once observed, "You can never
plan the future by the past."[*] But when it comes to preparing the American workforce for the jobs of the future, we may be doing just that.

For about a quarter-century, demand for labor appears to have shifted toward
the college-educated and away from high school graduates and dropouts. This
shift, most economists believe, is the primary (though not the sole) reason for rising
income inequality, and there is no end in sight. Economists refer to this phenomenon
by an antiseptic name: skill-biased technical progress. In plain English, it means that
the labor market has turned ferociously against the low skilled and the uneducated.

In a progressive society, such a worrisome social phenomenon might elicit
some strong policy responses, such as more compensatory education, stepped-up
efforts at retraining, reinforcement (rather than shredding) of the social safety net,
and so on. You don't fight the market's valuation of skills; you try to mitigate its more
deleterious effects. We did a bit of this in the United States in the 1990s, by raising
the minimum wage and expanding the Earned Income Tax Credit.[†] Combined with

---

[*]Edmund Burke (1729–1797) was a conservative British statesman, philosopher, and author.
The American Prospect, in which "Will Your Job Be Exported?" first appeared in the November
2006 issue, describes itself as "an authoritative magazine of liberal ideas."
[†]The Earned Income Tax Credit, an anti-poverty measure enacted by Congress in 1975 and
revised in the 1980s and 1990s, provides a credit against federal income taxes for any filer who
claims a dependent child.

tight labor markets, these measures improved things for the average worker. But in this decade, little or no mitigation has been attempted. Social Darwinism has come roaring back.*

With one big exception: We have expended considerable efforts to keep more young people in school longer (e.g., reducing high-school dropouts and sending more kids to college) and to improve the quality of schooling (e.g., via charter schools and No Child Left Behind†). Success in these domains may have been modest, but not for lack of trying. You don't have to remind Americans that education is important; the need for educational reform is etched into the public consciousness. Indeed, many people view education as the silver bullet. On hearing the question "How do we best prepare the American workforce of the future?" many Americans react reflexively with: "Get more kids to study science and math, and send more of them to college."

5   Which brings me to the future. As I argued in a recent article in *Foreign Affairs* magazine, the greatest problem for the next generation of American workers may not be lack of education, but rather "offshoring"—the movement of jobs overseas, especially to countries with much lower wages, such as India and China. Manufacturing jobs have been migrating overseas for decades. But the new wave of offshoring, of *service* jobs, is something different.

Traditionally, we think of service jobs as being largely immune to foreign competition. After all, you can't get your hair cut by a barber or your broken arm set by a doctor in a distant land. But stunning advances in communication technology, plus the emergence of a vast new labor pool in Asia and Eastern Europe, are changing that picture radically, subjecting millions of presumed-safe domestic service jobs to foreign competition. And it is not necessary actually to move jobs to low-wage countries in order to restrain wage increases; the mere threat of offshoring can put a damper on wages.

Service-sector offshoring is a minor phenomenon so far, Lou Dobbs notwithstanding; probably well under 1 percent of U.S. service jobs have been outsourced.** But I believe that service-sector offshoring will eventually exceed manufacturing-sector offshoring by a hefty margin—for three main reasons. The first is simple arithmetic: There are vastly more service jobs than manufacturing jobs in the United States (and in other rich countries). Second, the technological advances that have made service-sector offshoring possible will continue and accelerate, so the range of services that can be moved offshore will increase ineluctably. Third, the

---

*Social Darwinism, a largely discredited philosophy dating from the Victorian era and espoused by Herbert Spenser, asserts that Charles Darwin's observations on natural selection apply to human societies. Social Darwinists argue that the poor are less fit to survive than the wealthy and should, through a natural process of adaptation, be allowed to die out.
†Charter schools are public schools with specialized missions to operate outside of regulations that some feel restrict creativity and performance in traditional school settings. The No Child Left Behind Act of 2001 (NCLB) mandates standards-based education for all schools receiving federal funding. Both the charter schools movement and NCLB can be understood as efforts to improve public education.
**Lou Dobbs, a conservative columnist and former political commentator for CNN, is well known for his anti-immigration views.

number of (e.g., Indian and Chinese) workers capable of performing service jobs offshore seems certain to grow, perhaps exponentially.

I do not mean to paint a bleak picture here. Ever since Adam Smith and David Ricardo, economists have explained and extolled the gains in living standards that derive from international trade.* Those arguments are just as valid for trade in services as for trade in goods. There really *are* net gains to the United States from expanding service-sector trade with India, China, and the rest. The offshoring problem is not about the adverse nature of what economists call the economy's eventual equilibrium. Rather, it is about the so-called transition—the ride from here to there. That ride, which could take a generation or more, may be bumpy. And during the long adjustment period, many U.S. wages could face downward pressure.

Thus far, only American manufacturing workers and a few low-end service workers (e.g., call-center operators) have been competing, at least potentially, with millions of people in faraway lands eager to work for what seems a pittance by U.S. standards. But offshoring is no longer limited to low-end service jobs. Computer code can be written overseas and e-mailed back to the United States. So can your tax return and lots of legal work, provided you do not insist on face-to-face contact with the accountant or lawyer. In writing and editing this article, I communicated with the editors and staff of *The American Prospect* only by telephone and e-mail. Why couldn't they (or I, for that matter) have been in India? The possibilities are, if not endless, at least vast.

10   What distinguishes the jobs that cannot be offshored from the ones that can? The crucial distinction is not—and this is the central point of this essay—the required levels of skill and education. These attributes have been critical to labor-market success in the past, but may be less so in the future. Instead, the new critical distinction may be that some services either require personal delivery (e.g., driving a taxi and brain surgery) or are seriously degraded when delivered electronically (e.g., college teaching—at least, I hope!), while other jobs (e.g., call centers and keyboard data entry) are not. Call the first category personal services and the second category impersonal services. With this terminology, I have three main points to make about preparing our workforce for the brave, new world of the future.

First, we need to think about, plan, and redesign our educational system with the crucial distinction between personal service jobs and impersonal service jobs in mind. Many of the impersonal service jobs will migrate offshore, but the personal service jobs will stay here.

Second, the line that divides personal services from impersonal services will move in only one direction over time, as technological progress makes it possible to deliver an ever-increasing array of services electronically.

Third, the novel distinction between personal and impersonal jobs is quite different from, and appears essentially unrelated to, the traditional distinction between jobs that do and do not require high levels of education.

---

*Adam Smith (1723–1790), Scottish author of *An Inquiry into the Nature and Causes of the Wealth of Nations* (1776), established the foundations of modern economics. David Ricardo (1772–1823) was a British businessman, statesman, and economist who founded the classical school of economics and is best known for his studies of monetary policy.

For example, it is easy to offshore working in a call center, typing transcripts, writing computer code, and reading X-rays. The first two require little education; the last two require quite a lot. On the other hand, it is either impossible or very difficult to offshore janitorial services, fast-food restaurant service, college teaching, and open-heart surgery. Again, the first two occupations require little or no education, while the last two require a great deal. There seems to be little or no correlation between educational requirements (the old concern) and how "offshorable" jobs are (the new one).

15   If so, the implications could be startling. A generation from now, civil engineers (who must be physically present) may be in greater demand in the United States than computer engineers (who don't). Similarly, there might be more divorce lawyers (not offshorable) than tax lawyers (partly offshorable). More imaginatively, electricians might earn more than computer programmers. I am not predicting any of this; lots of things influence relative demands and supplies for different types of labor. But it all seems within the realm of the possible as technology continues to enhance the offshorability of even highly skilled occupations. What does seem highly likely is that the relative demand for labor in the United States will shift away from impersonal services and toward personal services, and this shift will look quite different from the familiar story of skill-biased technical progress. So Burke's warning is worth heeding.

I am *not* suggesting that education will become a handicap in the job market of the future. On the contrary, to the extent that education raises productivity and that better-educated workers are more adaptable and/or more creative, a wage premium for higher education should remain. Thus, it still makes sense to send more of America's youth to college. But, over the next generation, the kind of education our young people receive may prove to be more important than how much education they receive. In that sense, a college degree may lose its exalted "silver bullet" status.

Looking back over the past 25 years, "stay in school longer" was excellent advice for success in the labor market. But looking forward over the next 25 years, more subtle occupational advice may be needed. "Prepare yourself for a high-end personal service occupation that is not offshorable" is a more nuanced message than "stay in school." But it may prove to be more useful. And many non-offshorable jobs—such as carpenters, electricians, and plumbers—do not require college education.

The hard question is how to make this more subtle advice concrete and actionable. The children entering America's educational system today, at age 5, will emerge into a very different labor market when they leave it. Given gestation periods of 13 to 17 years and more, educators and policy-makers need to be thinking now about the kinds of training and skills that will best prepare these children for their future working lives. Specifically, it is essential to educate America's youth for the jobs that will actually be available in America 20 to 30 years from now, not for the jobs that will have moved offshore.

Some of the personal service jobs that will remain in the United States will be very high-end (doctors), others will be less glamorous though well paid (plumbers), and some will be "dead end" (janitor). We need to think long and hard about the types of skills that best prepare people to deliver high-end personal services, and how to teach those skills in our elementary and high schools. I am not an education specialist, but it strikes me that, for example, the central thrust of No Child Left Behind is pushing the nation in exactly the wrong direction. I am all for accountability. But the nation's school system will not build the creative, flexible, people-oriented workforce we will need in the future by drilling kids incessantly with rote preparation for standardized tests in the vain hope that they will perform as well as memory chips.

20   Starting in the elementary schools, we need to develop our youngsters' imaginations and people skills as well as their "reading, writing, and 'rithmetic." Remember that kindergarten grade for "works and plays well with others"? It may become increasingly important in a world of personally delivered services. Such training probably needs to be continued and made more sophisticated in the secondary schools, where, for example, good communications skills need to be developed.

More vocational education is probably also in order. After all, nurses, carpenters, and plumbers are already scarce, and we'll likely need more of them in the future. Much vocational training now takes place in community colleges; and they, too, need to adapt their curricula to the job market of the future.

While it is probably still true that we should send more kids to college and increase the number who study science, math, and engineering, we need to focus on training more college students for the high-end jobs that are unlikely to move offshore, and on developing a creative workforce that will keep America incubating and developing new processes, new products, and entirely new industries. Offshoring is, after all, mostly about following and copying. America needs to lead and innovate instead, just as we have in the past.

Educational reform is not the whole story, of course. I suggested at the outset, for example, that we needed to repair our tattered social safety net and turn it into a retraining trampoline that bounces displaced workers back into productive employment. But many low-end personal service jobs cannot be turned into more attractive jobs simply by more training—think about janitors, fast-food workers, and nurse's aides, for example. Running a tight labor market would help such workers, as would a higher minimum wage, an expanded Earned Income Tax Credit, universal health insurance, and the like.

Moving up the skill ladder, employment is concentrated in the public or quasi-public sector in a number of service occupations. Teachers and health-care workers are two prominent examples. In such cases, government policy can influence wages and working conditions directly by upgrading the structure and pay of such jobs—developing more professional early-childhood teachers and fewer casual daycare workers for example—as long as the taxpayer is willing to foot the bill. Similarly, some service jobs such as registered nurses are in short supply mainly because we are not training enough qualified personnel. Here, too, public policy can help by widening the pipeline to allow more workers through. So there are a variety of policy levers that might do some good—if we are willing to pull them.

25   But all that said, education is still the right place to start. Indeed, it is much more than that because the educational system affects the entire population and because no other institution is nearly as important when it comes to preparing our

youth for the world of work. As the first industrial revolution took hold, America radically transformed (and democratized) its educational system to meet the new demands of an industrial society. We may need to do something like that again. There is a great deal at stake here. If we get this one wrong, the next generation will pay dearly. But if we get it (close to) right, the gains from trade promise coming generations a prosperous future.

The somewhat inchoate challenge posed here—preparing more young Americans for personal service jobs—brings to mind one of my favorite Churchill quotations: "You can always count on Americans to do the right thing—after they've tried everything else." It is time to start trying.

Read, Reread, Highlight

Let's consider our recommended pointers for writing a summary.

As you reread the passage, note in the margins of the essay important points, shifts in thought, and questions you may have. Consider the essay's significance as a whole and its stages of thought. What does it say? How is it organized? How does each part of the passage fit into the whole? What do all these points add up to?

Here is how several paragraphs from the middle of Blinder's article might look after you have marked the main ideas by highlighting and by marginal notations.

Offshored service jobs will eclipse lost manufacturing jobs—3 reasons

Service-sector offshoring is a minor phenomenon so far, Lou Dobbs notwithstanding; probably well under 1 percent of U.S. service jobs have been outsourced. But I believe that service-sector offshoring will eventually exceed manufacturing-sector offshoring by a hefty margin—for three main reasons. The first is simple arithmetic: There are vastly more service jobs than manufacturing jobs in the United States (and in other rich countries). Second, the technological advances that have made service-sector offshoring possible will continue and accelerate, so the range of services that can be moved offshore will increase ineluctably. Third, the number of (e.g., Indian and Chinese) workers capable of performing service jobs offshore seems certain to grow, perhaps exponentially.

Long-term economy will be ok. Short-to-middle term will be "bumpy"

I do not mean to paint a bleak picture here. Ever since Adam Smith and David Ricardo, economists have explained and extolled the gains in living standards that derive from international trade. Those arguments are just as valid for trade in services as for trade in goods. There really are net gains to the United States from expanding service-sector trade with India, China, and the rest. The offshoring problem is not about the adverse nature of what economists call the economy's eventual equilibrium. Rather, it is about the so-called transition—the ride from here to there. That ride, which could take a generation or more, may be bumpy.

And during the long adjustment period, many U.S. wages could face downward pressure.

Thus far, only American manufacturing workers and a few low-end service workers (e.g., call-center operators) have been competing, at least potentially, with millions of people in faraway lands eager to work for what seems a pittance by U.S. standards. But offshoring is no longer limited to low-end service jobs. Computer code can be written overseas and e-mailed back to the United States. So can your tax return and lots of legal work, provided you do not insist on face-to-face contact with the accountant or lawyer. In writing and editing this article, I communicated with the editors and staff of *The American Prospect* only by telephone and e-mail. Why couldn't they (or I, for that matter) have been in India? The possibilities are, if not endless, at least vast.

What distinguishes the jobs that cannot be offshored from the ones that can? The crucial distinction is not—and this is the central point of this essay—the required levels of skill and education. These attributes have been critical to labor-market success in the past, but may be less so in the future. Instead, the new critical distinction may be that some services either require personal delivery (e.g., driving a taxi and brain surgery) or are seriously degraded when delivered electronically (e.g., college teaching—at least, I hope!), while other jobs (e.g., call centers and keyboard data entry) are not. Call the first category personal services and the second category impersonal services. With this terminology, I have three main points to make about preparing our workforce for the brave, new world of the future.

First, we need to think about, plan, and redesign our educational system with the crucial distinction between personal service jobs and impersonal service jobs in mind. Many of the impersonal service jobs will migrate offshore, but the personal service jobs will stay here.

Second, the line that divides personal services from impersonal services will move in only one direction over time, as technological progress makes it possible to deliver an ever-increasing array of services electronically.

Third, the novel distinction between personal and impersonal jobs is quite different from, and appears essentially unrelated to, the traditional distinction between jobs that do and do not require high levels of education.

Marginal notes:

High-end jobs to be lost

B's main point: Key distinction: Personal service jobs stay; impersonal jobs go

3 points re: prep of future workforce

Movement: impersonal → personal

Level of ed. not related to future job security

Divide into Stages of Thought

When a selection doesn't contain sections with thematic headings, as is the case with "Will Your Job Be Exported?", how do you determine where one stage of thought ends and the next one begins? Assuming that what you have read is coherent and unified, this should not be difficult. (When a selection is unified, all of its parts pertain to the main subject; when a selection is coherent, the parts follow one another in logical order.) Look particularly for transitional sentences at the beginning of paragraphs. Such sentences generally work in one or both of two ways: (1) they summarize what has come before; (2) they set the stage for what is to follow.

Look at the sentences that open paragraphs 5 and 10: "Which brings me to the future" and "What distinguishes the jobs that cannot be offshored from the ones that can?" In both cases Blinder makes a clear announcement. Grammatically speaking, "Which brings me to the future" is a fragment, not a sentence. Experienced writers will use fragments on occasion to good effect, as in this case. The fragment clearly has the sense of a complete thought: the pronoun "which" refers readers to the content of the preceding paragraphs, asking readers to summarize that content and then, with the predicate "brings me to the future," to move forward into the next part of the article. Similarly, the question "What distinguishes the jobs that cannot be offshored from the ones that can?" implicitly asks readers to recall an important distinction just made (the definitions of offshorable and non-offshorable jobs) and then clearly moves readers forward to new, related content. As you can see, the openings of paragraphs 5 and 10 announce new sections in the article.

Each section of an article generally takes several paragraphs to develop. Between paragraphs, and almost certainly between sections of an article, you will usually find transitions that help you understand what you have just read and what you are about to read. For articles that have no subheadings, try writing your own section headings in the margins as you take notes. Blinder's article can be divided into five sections.

> **Section 1:** *Recent past: education of workers important*—For twenty-five years, the labor market has rewarded workers with higher levels of education (paragraphs 1–4).

> **Section 2:** *Future: ed level won't always matter—workers in service sector will lose jobs offshore*—Once thought immune to outsourcing, even highly trained service workers will lose jobs to overseas competition (paragraphs 5–9).

> **Section 3:** *Which service jobs at highest risk?* Personal service workers are safe; impersonal service workers, both highly educated and not, will see jobs offshored (paragraphs 10–15).

> **Section 4:** *Educating the future workforce*—Emphasizing the kind, not amount, of education will help to prepare workers for jobs of the future (paragraphs 16–22).

> **Section 5:** *Needed policy reforms*—Government can improve conditions for low-end service workers and expand opportunities for higher-end service workers; start with education (paragraphs 23–26).

Write a Brief Summary of Each Stage of Thought

The purpose of this step is to wean yourself from the language of the original passage, so that you are not tied to it when writing the summary. Here are brief summaries, one for each stage of thought in "Will Your Job Be Exported?"

Section 1: Recent past: education of workers important (paragraphs 1–4).

> For the past twenty-five years, the greater a worker's skill or level of education, the better and more stable the job.

Section 2: Future: ed level won't always matter—workers in service sector will lose jobs offshore (paragraphs 5–9).

> Advances in technology have brought to the service sector the same pressures that forced so many manufacturing jobs offshore to China and India. The rate of offshoring in the service sector will accelerate and "eventually exceed" job losses in manufacturing, says Blinder, and jobs requiring both relatively little education (like call-center staffing) and extensive education (like software development) will be lost to workers overseas.

Section 3: Which service jobs at highest risk? (paragraphs 10–15).

> While "personal services" workers (like barbers and surgeons) will be relatively safe from offshoring because their work requires close physical proximity to customers, "impersonal services" workers (like call-center operators and radiologists), regardless of their skill or education, will be at risk because their work can be completed remotely without loss of quality and then delivered via phone or computer. Blinder believes that "the relative demand for labor in the United States will [probably] shift away from impersonal services and toward personal services."

Section 4: Educating the future workforce (paragraphs 16–22).

> Blinder advises young people to plan for "a high-end personal service occupation that is not offshorable." He also urges educators to prepare the future workforce by anticipating the needs of a personal services economy and redesigning classroom instruction and vocational training accordingly.

Section 5: Needed policy reforms (paragraphs 23–26).

> Blinder urges the government to develop policies that will improve wages and conditions for low-wage personal service workers (like janitors); to encourage more low-wage workers (like daycare providers) to retrain and take on better jobs; and to increase opportunities for professional and vocational training in high-demand areas (like nursing and carpentry).

Write a Thesis: A Brief Summary of the Entire Passage

The thesis is the most general statement of a summary (or any other type of academic writing). It is the statement that announces the paper's subject and the claim that you or—in the case of a summary—another author will be making about that subject. Every paragraph of a paper illuminates the thesis by providing supporting detail or explanation. The relationship of these paragraphs to the thesis is analogous to the relationship of the sentences within a paragraph to the topic sentence. Both the thesis and the topic sentences are general statements (the thesis being the more general) that are followed by systematically arranged details.

To ensure clarity for the reader, *the first sentence of your summary should begin with the author's thesis, regardless of where it appears in the article itself.* An author may locate her thesis at the beginning of her work, in which case the thesis operates as a general principle from which details of the presentation follow. This is called a *deductive* organization: thesis first, supporting details second. Alternatively, an author may locate his thesis at the end of the work, in which case the author begins with specific details and builds toward a more general conclusion, or thesis. This is called an *inductive* organization. And, as you might expect, an author might locate the thesis anywhere between beginning and end, at whatever point it seems best positioned.*

A thesis consists of a subject and an assertion about that subject. How can we go about fashioning an adequate thesis for a summary of Blinder's article? Probably no two versions of Blinder's thesis statement would be worded identically, but it is fair to say that any reasonable thesis will indicate that Blinder's subject is the future loss to offshoring of American jobs in the service sector—that part of the economy that delivers services to consumers, from low end (e.g., janitorial services) to high end (e.g., neurosurgery). How does Blinder view the situation? How secure will service jobs be if Blinder's distinction between personal and impersonal services is valid? Looking back over our section summaries, we find that Blinder insists on three points: (1) that education and skill matter less than they once did in determining job quality and security; (2) that the distinction between personal and impersonal services will increasingly determine which jobs remain and which are offshored; and (3) that the distinction between personal and impersonal has implications for the future of both education and public policy.

Does Blinder make a statement anywhere in this passage that pulls all this together? Examine paragraph 10 and you will find his thesis—two sentences that answer his question about which jobs will and will not be sent offshore: "The crucial distinction is not—and this is the central point of this essay—the required levels of skill and education.... Instead, the new critical distinction may be that some services either require personal delivery (e.g., driving a taxi

---

*Blinder positions his thesis midway through his five-section article. He opens the selection by discussing the role of education in the labor market during the past twenty-five years (Section 1, pars. 1–4). He continues by summarizing an earlier article on the ways in which service jobs are following manufacturing jobs offshore (Section 2, pars. 5–9). He then presents a two-sentence thesis in answer to the question that opens paragraph 10: "What distinguishes the jobs that cannot be offshored from the ones that can?" The remainder of the article either develops this thesis (Section 3, pars. 10–15) or follows its implications for education (Section 4, pars. 16–22) and public policy (Section 5, pars. 23–26).

and brain surgery) or are seriously degraded when delivered electronically (e.g., college teaching—at least, I hope!), while other jobs (e.g., call centers and keyboard data entry) are not."

You may have learned that a thesis statement must be expressed in a single sentence. We would offer a slight rewording of this generally sound advice and say that a thesis statement must be *expressible* in a single sentence. For reasons of emphasis or style, a writer might choose to distribute a thesis across two or more sentences. Certainly, the sense of Blinder's thesis can take the form of a single statement: "The critical distinction is X, not Y." For reasons largely of emphasis, he divides his thesis into two sentences—in fact, separating these sentences with another sentence that explains the first part of the thesis: "These attributes [that is, skill and education] have been critical to labor-market success in the past, but may be less so in the future."

Here is a one-sentence version of Blinder's two-sentence thesis:

> The quality and security of future jobs in America's service sector will be determined by how "offshorable" those jobs are.

Notice that the statement anticipates a summary of the *entire* article: both the discussion leading up to Blinder's thesis and his discussion after. To clarify for our readers the fact that this idea is Blinder's and not ours, we might qualify the thesis as follows:

> In "Will Your Job Be Exported?" economist Alan S. Blinder argues that the quality and security of future jobs in America's service sector will be determined by how "offshorable" those jobs are.

The first sentence of a summary is crucially important, for it orients readers by letting them know what to expect in the coming paragraphs. In the example above, the sentence refers directly to an article, its author, and the thesis for the upcoming summary. The author and title reference could also be indicated in the summary's title (if this were a freestanding summary), in which case their mention could be dropped from the thesis statement. And lest you become frustrated too quickly with how much effort it takes to come up with this crucial sentence, keep in mind that writing an acceptable thesis for a summary takes time. In this case, it took three drafts, roughly ten minutes, to compose a thesis and another few minutes of fine-tuning after a draft of the entire summary was completed. The thesis needed revision because the first draft was vague; the second draft was improved but too specific on a secondary point; the third draft was more complete but too general on a key point:

> **Draft 1:** We must begin now to train young people for high-quality personal service jobs.
>
> (Vague. The question of why we should begin training isn't clear, nor is the phrase "high-quality personal service jobs." Define this term or make it more general.)

Draft 2: Alan S. Blinder argues that unlike in the past, the quality and security of future American jobs will not be determined by skill level or education but rather by how "offshorable" those jobs are.

(*Better, but the reference to "skill level or education" is secondary to Blinder's main point about offshorable jobs.*)

Draft 3: In "Will Your Job Be Exported?" economist Alan S. Blinder argues that the quality and security of future jobs will be determined by how "offshorable" those jobs are.

(*Close—but not "all" jobs. Blinder specifies which types of jobs are "offshorable."*)

Final Draft: In "Will Your Job Be Exported?" economist Alan S. Blinder argues that the quality and security of future jobs in America's service sector will be determined by how "offshorable" those jobs are.

Write the First Draft of the Summary

Let's consider two possible summaries of Blinder's article: (1) a short summary, combining a thesis with brief section summaries, and (2) a longer summary, combining thesis, brief section summaries, and some carefully chosen details. Again, keep in mind that you are reading final versions; each of the following summaries is the result of at least two full drafts. Highlighting indicates transitions added to smooth the flow of the summary.

Summary 1: Combine Thesis Sentence with Brief Section Summaries

In "Will Your Job Be Exported?" economist Alan S. Blinder argues that the quality and security of future jobs in America's service sector will be determined by how "offshorable" those jobs are. For the past twenty-five years, the greater a worker's skill or level of education, the better and more stable the job. No longer. Advances in technology have brought to the service sector the same pressures that forced so many manufacturing jobs offshore to China and India. The rate of offshoring in the service sector will accelerate, and jobs requiring both relatively little education (like call-center staffing) and extensive education (like software development) will increasingly be lost to workers overseas.

These losses will "eventually exceed" losses in manufacturing, but not all services jobs are equally at risk. While "personal services" workers (like barbers and surgeons) will be relatively safe from offshoring because their work requires close physical proximity to customers, "impersonal services" workers (like call-center operators and radiologists), regardless of their skill or education, will be at risk because their work can be completed remotely without loss of quality and then delivered via phone or computer. "[T]he relative demand for labor in the United States will [probably] shift away from impersonal services and toward personal services."

Blinder recommends three courses of action: He advises young people to plan for "a high-end personal service occupation that is not offshorable."

He urges educators to prepare the future workforce by anticipating the needs of a personal services economy and redesigning classroom instruction and vocational training accordingly. Finally, he urges the government to adopt policies that will improve existing personal services jobs by increasing wages for low-wage workers; retraining workers to take on better jobs; and increasing opportunities in high-demand, well-paid areas like nursing and carpentry. Ultimately, Blinder wants America to prepare a new generation to "lead and innovate" in an economy that will continue exporting jobs that require "following and copying."

The Strategy of the Shorter Summary

This short summary consists essentially of a restatement of Blinder's thesis plus the section summaries, modified or expanded a little for stylistic purposes. You'll recall that Blinder locates his thesis midway through the article, in paragraph 10. But note that this model summary *begins* with a restatement of his thesis. Notice also the relative weight given to the section summaries within the model. Blinder's main point, his "critical distinction" between personal and impersonal services jobs, is summarized in paragraph 2 of the model. The other paragraphs combine summaries of relatively less important (that is, supporting or explanatory) material. Paragraph 1 combines summaries of the article's Sections 1 and 2; paragraph 3 combines summaries of Sections 4 and 5.

Between the thesis and the section summaries, notice the insertion of three (highlighted) transitions. The first—a fragment (*No longer*)—bridges the first paragraph's summaries of Sections 1 and 2 of Blinder's article. The second transition links a point Blinder makes in his Section 2 (*Losses in the service sector will "eventually exceed" losses in manufacturing*) with an introduction to the key point he will make in Section 3 (*Not all service jobs are equally at risk*). The third transition (*Blinder recommends three courses of action*) bridges the summary of Blinder's Section 3 to summaries of Sections 4 and 5. Each transition, then, links sections of the whole: each casts the reader back to recall points just made; each casts the reader forward by announcing related points about to be made. Our model ends with a summary of Blinder's motivation for writing, the sense of which is implied by the section summaries but nowhere made explicit.

Summary 2: Combine Thesis Sentence, Section Summaries, and Carefully Chosen Details

The thesis and brief section summaries could also be used as the outline for a more detailed summary. However, most of the details in the passage won't be necessary in a summary. It isn't necessary even in a longer summary of this passage to discuss all of Blinder's examples of jobs that are more or less likely to be sent offshore. It would be appropriate, though, to mention one example of such a job; to review his reasons for thinking "that service-sector offshoring will eventually exceed manufacturing-sector offshoring by a hefty margin"; and to expand on his point that a college education in itself will no longer ensure job security.

None of these details appeared in the first summary; but in a longer summary, a few carefully selected details might be desirable for clarity. How do you decide which details to include? First, working with Blinder's point that one's job type (personal services vs. impersonal services) will matter more for future job quality and security than did the once highly regarded "silver bullet" of education, you may want to cite some of the most persuasive evidence supporting this idea. For example, you could explore why some highly paid physicians, like radiologists, might find themselves competing for jobs with lower-paid physicians overseas. Further, your expanded summary might reflect the relative weight Blinder gives to education (seven paragraphs, the longest of the article's five sections).

You won't always know which details to include and which to exclude. Developing good judgment in comprehending and summarizing texts is largely a matter of reading skill and prior knowledge (see p. 2). Consider the analogy of the seasoned mechanic who can pinpoint an engine problem by simply listening to a characteristic sound that to a less-experienced person is just noise. Or consider the chess player who can plot three separate winning strategies from a board position that to a novice looks like a hopeless jumble. In the same way, the more practiced a reader you are, the more knowledgeable you will become about the subject and the better able you will be to make critical distinctions between elements of greater and lesser importance. In the meantime, read as carefully as you can and use your own best judgment as to how to present your material.

Here's one version of a completed summary with carefully chosen details. Note that we have highlighted phrases and sentences added to the original, briefer summary.

> In "Will Your Job Be Exported?" economist Alan S. Blinder argues that the quality and security of future jobs in America's service sector will be determined by how "offshorable" those jobs are. For the past twenty-five years, the greater a worker's skill or level of education, the better and more stable the job. Americans have long regarded education as the "silver bullet" that could propel motivated people to better jobs and a better life. No longer. Advances in technology have brought to the service sector the same pressures that forced so many manufacturing jobs offshore to China and India. The rate of offshoring in the service sector will accelerate, says Blinder, and jobs requiring both relatively little education (like call-center staffing) and extensive education (like software development) will increasingly be lost to workers overseas.
>
> Blinder expects that job losses in the service sector will "eventually exceed" losses in manufacturing, for three reasons. Developed countries have more service jobs than manufacturing jobs; as technology speeds

communications, more service jobs will be offshorable; and the numbers of qualified offshore workers is increasing. Service jobs lost to foreign competition may cause a "bumpy" period as the global economy sorts out what work gets done where, by whom. In time, as the global economy finds its "eventual equilibrium," offshoring will benefit the United States; but the consequences in the meantime may be painful for many.

That pain will not be shared equally by all service workers, however. While "personal service" workers (like barbers and surgeons) will be relatively safe from offshoring because their work requires close physical proximity to customers, "impersonal service" workers (like audio transcribers and radiologists), regardless of their skill or education, will be at risk because their work can be completed remotely without loss of quality and then delivered via phone or computer. In the coming decades, says Blinder, "the relative demand for labor in the United States will [probably] shift away from impersonal services and toward personal services." This shift will be influenced by the desire to keep good jobs in the United States while exporting jobs that require "following and copying." Highly trained computer coders will face the same pressures of outsourcing as relatively untrained call-center attendants. A tax attorney whose work requires no face-to-face interaction with clients may see her work migrate overseas while a divorce attorney, who must interact with clients on a case-by-case basis, may face no such competition. Same educations, different outcomes: what determines their fates in a global economy is the nature of their work (that is, personal vs. impersonal), not their level of education.

Based on this analysis, Blinder recommends three courses of action: First, he advises young people to plan for "a high-end personal service occupation that is not offshorable." Many good jobs, like carpentry and plumbing, will not require a college degree. Next, Blinder urges educators to prepare the future workforce by anticipating the needs of a personal services economy and redesigning classroom instruction and vocational training accordingly. These efforts should begin in elementary school and develop imagination and interpersonal skills rather than capacities for rote memorization. Finally, Blinder urges the government to develop policies that will improve wages and conditions for low-wage personal services workers (like janitors); to encourage more low-wage workers (like daycare providers) to retrain and take on better service jobs; and to increase opportunities for professional and vocational training for workers in high-demand services areas (like nurses and electricians). Ultimately, Blinder wants America to prepare a new generation of workers who will "lead and innovate...just as we have in the past."

The Strategy of the Longer Summary

Compared to the first, briefer summary, this effort (seventy percent longer than the first) includes Blinder's reasons for suggesting that job losses in the services sector will exceed losses in manufacturing. It emphasizes Blinder's point that job type (personal vs. impersonal services), not a worker's education level, will ensure job security. It includes Blinder's point that offshoring in the service sector is part of a larger global economy seeking "equilibrium." And it offers more on Blinder's thoughts concerning the education of future workers.

The final two of our suggested steps for writing summaries are (1) to check your summary against the original passage, making sure that you have included all the important ideas, and (2) to revise so that the summary reads smoothly and coherently. The structure of this summary generally reflects the structure of the original article—with one significant departure, as noted earlier. Blinder uses a modified inductive approach, stating his thesis midway through the article. The summary, however, states the thesis immediately, then proceeds deductively to develop that thesis.

■ HOW LONG SHOULD A SUMMARY BE?

The length of a summary depends both on the length of the original passage and on the use to which the summary will be put. If you are summarizing an entire article, a good rule of thumb is that your summary should be no longer than one-fourth the length of the original passage. Of course, if you were summarizing an entire chapter or even an entire book, it would have to be much shorter than that. The longer summary above is one-quarter the length of Alan Blinder's original. Although it shouldn't be very much longer, you have seen (pp. 18–19) that it could be quite a bit shorter.

The length as well as the content of the summary also depends on the *purpose* to which it will be put. Let's suppose you decided to use Blinder's piece in a paper that deals with the loss of manufacturing jobs in the United States and the rise of the service economy. In this case, in an effort to explain the complexities of the service economy to your readers, you might summarize *only* Blinder's core distinction between jobs in personal services and impersonal services, likely mentioning that jobs in the latter category are at risk of offshoring. If, instead, you were writing a paper in which you argued that the forces of globalization will eventually collapse the world's economies into a single, global economy, you would likely give less attention to Blinder's distinction between personal and impersonal services. More to the point might be his observation that highly skilled, highly educated workers in the United States are now finding themselves competing with qualified, lower-wage workers in China and India. Thus, depending on your purpose, you would summarize either selected portions of a source or an entire source. We will see this process more fully demonstrated in the upcoming chapters on syntheses.

Exercise 1.1

Individual and Collaborative Summary Practice

Turn to Chapter 2 and read Damon Beres's opinion piece in the *Washington Square News* (the New York University student newspaper): "The Common App Fallacy" (pp. 79–80). Follow the steps for writing summaries outlined above—read, underline, and divide into stages of thought. Write a one- or two-sentence summary of each stage of thought in Beres's essay. Then gather in groups of three or four classmates and compare your summary sentences. Discuss the differences in your sentences, and come to some consensus about the divisions in Beres's stages of thought—and the ways in which to best sum them up.

As a group, write a one- or two-sentence thesis statement summing up the entire passage. You could go even further, and, using your individual summary sentences—or the versions of them your group revised—put together a brief summary of Beres's essay. Model your work on the brief summary of Blinder's article, on pages 18–19.

■ SUMMARIZING FIGURES AND TABLES

In your reading in the sciences and social sciences, you will often find data and concepts presented in nontext forms—as figures and tables. Such visual devices offer a snapshot, a pictorial overview of material that is more quickly and clearly communicated in graphic form than as a series of (often complicated) sentences. Note that in essence, figures and tables are themselves summaries. The writer uses a graph, which in an article or book is labeled as a numbered "figure," and presents the quantitative results of research as points on a line or a bar or as sections ("slices") of a pie. Pie charts show relative proportions, or percentages. Graphs, especially effective in showing patterns, relate one variable to another: for instance, income to years of education, or sales figures of a product over a period of three years.

Writers regularly draw on graphs, charts, and tables to provide information or to offer evidence for points they are arguing. Consider the following passage from an op-ed article by Michael Klare arguing that the United States and China should cooperate, rather than compete, in order to supply their future energy needs:

> In 2007, according to Energy Department figures, the United States consumed about 21 million barrels of oil a day, nearly three times as much as China. Even more significant, we imported 13 million barrels every day, a vastly greater amount than China's import tally. So, although it is indeed true that Chinese and American consumers are competing for access to overseas supplies, thereby edging up prices, American consumption still sets the pace in international oil markets.
>
> The reality is that as far as the current run-up in gasoline prices is concerned, other factors are more to blame: shrinking oil output from such key producers as Mexico, Russia and Venezuela; internal violence in Iraq and Nigeria; refinery inadequacies in the U.S. and elsewhere; speculative stockpiling by global oil brokers, and so on. These conditions are likely to persist for the foreseeable future, so prices will remain high.

Peer into the future, however, and the China factor starts looming much larger.

With its roaring economy and millions of newly affluent consumers—many of whom are now buying their first automobiles—China is rapidly catching up with the United States in its net oil intake. According to the most recent projections, Chinese petroleum consumption is expected to jump from 8 million barrels a day in 2008 to an estimated 12 million in 2020 and to 16 million in 2030. American consumption will also climb, but not as much, reaching an estimated 27 million barrels a day in 2030. In terms of oil imports, moreover, the gap will grow even smaller. Chinese imports are projected to hit 10.8 million barrels a day in 2030, compared with 16.4 million for the United States. Clearly, the Sino-American competition for foreign oil supplies will grow ever more intense with every passing year.*

A good deal of the data Klare provides in this passage likely came from graphs, charts, and tables.

In the following pages, we present four figures and a table from various sources, all related to the world's rising oil consumption and its dwindling supply.

Bar Graphs

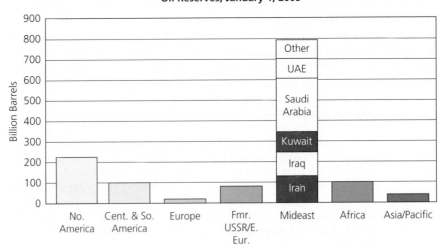

■ Figure 1.1   World Oil Reserves by Region, January 1, 2005[†]

---

*Michael T. Klare, "The U.S. and China are over a Barrel," *Los Angeles Times* 28 Apr. 2008: 17. Klare is professor of peace and world security studies at Hampshire College and the author of *Rising Powers, Shrinking Planet: The New Geopolitics of Energy.*
[†]*Oil and Gas Journal* 1 Jan. 2005. <http://www.eia.doe.gov/pub/oil_gas/petroleum/analysis_publications/oil_market_basics/sup_image_reserves.htm>.

Figure 1.1 is a bar graph indicating the world's known oil reserves as of January 2005. The vertical axis of this graph indicates the number of barrels, in billions, estimated to be available. The horizontal axis indicates various regions of the world. The vertical bar above each region indicates the number of billions of barrels. Note that the bar indicating the largest available supplies, the Mideast, is subdivided into the nations of that region in control of the largest oil reserves.

Here is a summary of the information presented in Figure 1.1:

> As of January 1, 2005, the Middle East had by far the largest quantities of oil reserves in the world, almost 800 billion barrels. North America, the region with the next highest oil reserves, has slightly more than a quarter of this quantity, just over 200 billion barrels. Central and South America and Africa come next, each with about 100 billion barrels. Russia and Eastern Europe have slightly less than this quantity. Compared to these oil-rich regions, Asia and the Pacific region and Europe have relatively minimal amounts. Within the Middle East region, Saudi Arabia has the largest oil reserves, about 250 billion barrels. This one country therefore has more oil than any other entire region in the world. Iran, Iraq, and Kuwait each have at least 100 million barrels of oil. Each of these countries, therefore, has at least as much in oil reserves as all of the African countries or all of the Central and South American countries combined.

Figure 1.2 (next page), another bar graph, indicates the number of years (from 2003—the "zero" point on the horizontal axis) until the midpoint of depletion of national oil reserves for fifteen countries. Note that this graph features bars stretching in opposite directions: The bars to the left indicate negative values; the bars to the right indicate positive values. Thus, Norway will have used up half of its total oil reserves by 2008, five years after the date the chart was prepared. Canada, by contrast, reached the midpoint of its depletion about eight years *before* 2003.

Exercise 1.2

Summarizing Graphs

Write a brief summary of the data in Figure 1.2. Use our summary of Figure 1.1 as a model.

Pie Charts

Bar graphs are useful for visually comparing numerical quantities. Pie charts, on the other hand, are useful for visually comparing percentages of a whole. The pie represents the whole; the individual slices represent the relative sizes of the parts. Figure 1.3 is a pie chart indicating the relative oil

Time to Depletion Midpoint of Oil Reserves, 2003 (Years)

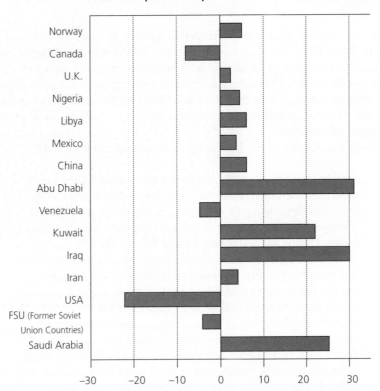

Figure 1.2   This graph illustrates the number of years to the midpoint of the depletion of oil reserves for various major oil-producing nations in 2003. A negative value means that the midpoint was in the past. The only countries a significant distance from their midpoints are the major Middle East producers.*

The Oil Consumption Pie, 2007

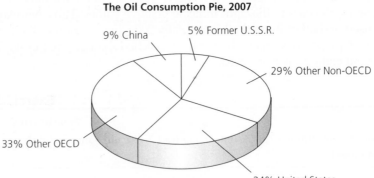

■ Figure 1.3   The Oil Consumption Pie†

---

*The Hubbert Peak for World Oil. Chart updated 2003. <http://www.oilcrisis.com/summary.htm>.
†Association for the Study of Peak Oil and Gas—U.S.A. <http://www.aspo-usa.com/index.php?option=com_content&task=view&id=298&Itemid=91>.

consumption of various regions of the world in 2007. Each slice represents a percentage of the world's total oil consumption.

In this chart, OECD stands for the Organization for Economic Cooperation and Development.* Note that only two of the five pie slices represent individual countries: the United States (an OECD country) and China. Two additional slices represent "other OECD countries" and "other Non–OECD countries" (i.e., countries other than China and the former USSR, which are separately represented in the chart). Finally, note that the "former USSR" slice indicates Russia and Eastern European countries—such as Bulgaria, Romania, and Estonia—that are not presently members of the OECD (as are Hungary and Poland).

Exercise 1.3

Summarizing Pie Charts

Write a brief summary of the data in Figure 1.3. Use our summary of Figure 1.1 (or your summary of Figure 1.2) as a model.

Line Graphs

Line graphs are useful for showing trends over a period of time. Usually, the horizontal axis indicates years, months, or shorter periods, and the vertical axis indicates a quantity: dollars, barrels, personnel, sales, anything that can be counted. The line running from left to right indicates the changing values, over a given period, of the object of measurement. Frequently, a line graph will feature multiple lines (perhaps in different colors, perhaps some solid, others dotted, etc.), each indicating a separate variable to be measured. Thus, a line graph could show the changing approval ratings of several presidential candidates over the course of a campaign season. Or it could indicate the number of iPhones vs. BlackBerrys sold in a given year.

The line graph shown in Figure 1.4 indicates the changes in several U.S. oil consumption variables, over time: (1) total oil demand (in millions of barrels per day), (2) oil consumption demand for transportation alone, and (3) domestic oil production. Note that because the graph was produced in

---

*The OECD is a Paris-based international group, founded in 1961, that collects and analyzes economic data. According to its Web site <http://www.oecd.org>, "[I]ts mission [is] to help…member countries to achieve sustainable economic growth and employment and to raise the standard of living in member countries while maintaining financial stability…[and contributing] to the development of the world economy." OECD countries, democracies with market economies, include Australia, Austria, Belgium, Canada, the Czech Republic, Denmark, Finland, France, Germany, Greece, Hungary, Iceland, Ireland, Italy, Japan, Korea, Luxembourg, Mexico, the Netherlands, New Zealand, Norway, Poland, the Slovak Republic, Spain, Switzerland, Sweden, Turkey, the United Kingdom, and the United States.

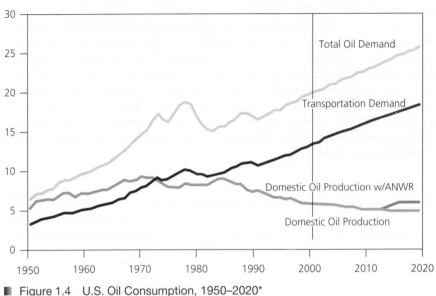

U.S. Oil Consumption, 1950–2020 (million barrels per day)

■ Figure 1.4   U.S. Oil Consumption, 1950–2020*

2001, the fifty-year period before that indicates historical data; the twenty-year period following is a projection based on estimates. Note also that somewhere around 2015, the domestic oil production line splits in two: The upper range indicates the level of oil production if Alaskan oil reserves are included; the lower range indicates domestic production without this particular resource.

Exercise 1.4

Summarizing Line Graphs

Write a brief summary of the key data in Figure 1.4. Use our summary of Figure 1.1 (or your summary of Figure 1.2) as a model.

Tables

A table presents numerical data in rows and columns for quick reference. If the writer chooses, tabular information can be converted to graphic information. Charts and graphs are preferable when the writer wants to emphasize a pattern or relationship; tables are preferable when the writer wants to emphasize numbers. While the previous charts and graphs represented

*Energy Information Administration (EIA), Annual Energy Outlook, 2001: "Potential Oil Production from the Coastal Plain of ANWR [Arctic National Wildlife Refuge [ANWR]]," EIR Reserves and Production Division. <http://energy.senate.gov/legislation/energybill/charts/chart8.pdf>.

a relatively small number of factors (regions or countries, quantities of oil produced or consumed in a given year or over a period of time), Table 1.1 breaks down oil production into numerous countries, organized by region.* Note that since production is represented in thousands of barrels daily, each number should be multiplied by 1000. The number at the upper left corner of page 30, 8295, therefore represents the 8,295,000 barrels a day produced by the United States in 1996. "Total World" production that year (p. 32, lower left) was 69,931,000 barrels per day.

A table may contain so much data that you would not want to summarize *all* of it for a particular paper. In this case, you would summarize the *part* of a table that you find useful. Here is a summary drawn from the information from Table 1.1 focusing just on the North American and Middle Eastern sections. Notice that the summary requires the writer to read closely and discern which information is significant. The table reports raw data and does not speak for itself. At the end of the summary the writer, using information not only from this table but also from Figure 1.4, "U.S. Oil Consumption, 1950–2020," draws her own conclusions:

> In 1996, the United States produced 8.3 million barrels of oil daily, or 89% of Saudi Arabia's production of 9.3 million barrels. By 2006, the United States was producing less than 7 million barrels, or 62% of Saudi Arabia's 11 million barrels. If we compare by region, the figures are only marginally more favorable to Americans. In 1996, the countries of North America produced 68% of the oil produced by the countries of the Middle East. Ten years later, that 68% had declined to 54%. Though the years between 1996 and 2006 have seen ups and downs in oil production by both regions, the overall trend is clear: North American production is falling and Middle East production is rising. Further, North American production is falling primarily because of declines in U.S. production; generally, Canadian and Mexican production have seen small but steady rises. Canada, for example, was producing about 2.5 million barrels of oil in 1996 and just over 3 million barrels in 2006. But this half-million-barrel rise was dwarfed by the 1.5-million-barrel rise in production by Saudi Arabia during that same period. The implications are clear: far from being self-sufficient in oil production, the United States is becoming less self-sufficient every year and is becoming ever more dependent for its petroleum supplies on a region whose political stability and reliability as a petroleum source are in serious question.

---

*"British Petroleum Statistical Review of World Energy 2006: Oil Production." British Petroleum. 2007. <http://www.bp.com/liveassets/bp_internet/gloablbp/globalbp_uk_english/ reports_and_publications/statistical_energy_review_2007/STAGING/local_assets/downloads/ pdf/table_of_world_oil_production_2007.pdf>

Table 1.1 Oil Production by Country, 1996–2006*

Producer	Thousands of barrels daily											Change: 2006 over 2005	2006 share of total
	1996	1997	1998	1999	2000	2001	2002	2003	2004	2005	2006		
USA	8295	8269	8011	7731	7733	7669	7626	7400	7228	6895	6871	−0.5%	8.0%
Canada	2480	2588	2672	2604	2721	2677	2858	3004	3085	3041	3147	4.4%	3.9%
Mexico	3277	3410	3499	3343	3450	3560	3585	3789	3824	3760	3683	−2.1%	4.7%
Total North America	14,052	14,267	14,182	13,678	13,904	13,906	14,069	14,193	14,137	13,695	13,700	0.1%	16.5%
Argentina	823	877	890	847	819	830	818	806	754	725	716	−1.3%	0.9%
Brazil	807	868	1003	1133	1268	1337	1499	1555	1542	1715	1809	5.5%	2.3%
Colombia	635	667	775	838	711	627	601	564	551	554	558	0.7%	0.7%
Ecuador	393	397	385	383	409	416	401	427	535	541	545	0.7%	0.7%
Peru	121	120	116	107	100	98	98	92	94	111	116	3.5%	0.1%
Trinidad & Tobago	141	135	134	141	138	135	155	164	152	171	174	1.5%	0.2%
Venezuela	3137	3321	3480	3126	3239	3142	2895	2554	2907	2937	2824	−3.9%	3.7%
Other S. & Cent. America	102	108	125	124	130	137	152	153	144	142	140	−1.7%	0.2%
Total S. & Cent. America	6159	6493	6908	6699	6813	6722	6619	6314	6680	6897	6881	−0.4%	8.8%
Azerbaijan	183	182	231	279	282	301	311	313	315	452	654	44.9%	0.8%
Denmark	208	230	238	299	363	348	371	368	390	377	342	−9.3%	0.4%
Italy	104	114	108	96	88	79	106	107	105	117	111	−5.6%	0.1%
Kazakhstan	474	536	537	631	744	836	1018	1111	1297	1356	1426	5.6%	1.7%
Norway	3232	3280	3138	3139	3346	3418	3333	3264	3188	2969	2778	−6.9%	3.3%
Romania	142	141	137	133	131	130	127	123	119	114	105	−8.0%	0.1%
Russian Federation	6114	6227	6169	6178	6536	7056	7698	8544	9287	9552	9769	2.2%	12.3%
Turkmenistan	90	108	129	143	144	162	182	202	193	192	163	−15.2%	0.2%
United Kingdom	2735	2702	2807	2909	2667	2476	2463	2257	2028	1809	1636	−9.6%	2.0%
Uzbekistan	174	182	191	191	177	171	171	166	152	126	125	−0.7%	0.1%
Other Europe & Eurasia	546	524	506	474	465	465	501	509	496	469	454	−2.9%	0.5%
Total Europe & Eurasia	14,003	14,226	14,190	14,473	14,943	15,444	16,281	16,965	17,570	17,533	17,563	0.2%	21.6%

Table 1.1 (continued)

Producer	Thousands of barrels daily											Change: 2006 over 2005	2006 share of total
	1996	1997	1998	1999	2000	2001	2002	2003	2004	2005	2006		
Iran	3759	3776	3855	3603	3818	3794	3543	4183	4248	4268	4343	1.2%	5.4%
Iraq	580	1166	2121	2610	2614	2523	2116	1344	2030	1833	1999	9.0%	2.5%
Kuwait	2129	2137	2232	2085	2206	2148	1995	2329	2482	2643	2704	2.4%	3.4%
Oman	897	909	905	911	959	961	900	824	756	779	743	-4.6%	0.9%
Qatar	568	719	747	797	855	854	783	917	990	1045	1133	8.1%	1.3%
Saudi Arabia	9299	9482	9502	8853	9491	9209	8928	10,164	10,638	11,114	10,859	-2.3%	13.1%
Syria	586	577	576	579	548	581	548	527	495	458	417	-8.9%	0.5%
United Arab Emirates	2438	2567	2643	2511	2626	2534	2324	2611	2656	2751	2969	7.3%	3.5%
Yemen	357	375	380	405	450	455	457	448	420	426	390	-8.7%	0.5%
Other Middle East	50	50	49	48	48	47	48	48	48	34	32	-7.7%	**
Total Middle East	**20,662**	**21,758**	**23,010**	**22,402**	**23,614**	**23,107**	**21,642**	**23,395**	**24,764**	**25,352**	**25,589**	**0.7%**	**31.2%**
Algeria	1386	1421	1461	1515	1578	1562	1680	1852	1946	2016	2005	-0.3%	2.2%
Angola	716	741	731	745	746	742	905	862	976	1233	1409	14.3%	1.8%
Cameroon	110	124	105	95	88	81	75	68	62	58	63	8.6%	0.1%
Chad	–	–	–	–	–	–	–	24	168	173	153	-11.7%	0.2%
Rep. of Congo (Brazzaville)	200	225	264	266	254	234	231	215	216	246	262	6.7%	0.3%
Egypt	894	873	857	827	781	758	751	749	721	696	678	-2.5%	0.8%
Equatorial Guinea	17	62	85	96	117	173	215	247	343	356	358	0.6%	0.5%
Gabon	365	364	337	340	327	301	295	240	235	234	232	-0.9%	0.3%
Libya	1452	1491	1480	1425	1475	1427	1375	1485	1624	1751	1835	4.2%	2.2%
Nigeria	2145	2316	2167	2066	2155	2274	2103	2263	2502	2580	2460	-4.9%	3.0%
Sudan	5	9	12	63	174	211	233	255	325	355	397	11.8%	0.5%
Tunisia	89	81	83	84	78	71	75	68	72	74	69	-7.1%	0.1%
Other Africa	62	64	63	56	56	53	63	71	75	72	68	-5.3%	0.1%

(continued)

Table 1.1 (continued)

Producer	Thousands of barrels daily											Change: 2006 over 2005	2006 share of total
	1996	1997	1998	1999	2000	2001	2002	2003	2004	2005	2006		
Total Africa	7441	7770	7644	7579	7830	7887	8001	8398	9263	9846	9990	1.4%	12.1%
Australia	619	669	644	625	809	733	731	624	541	554	544	−2.1%	0.6%
Brunei	165	163	157	182	193	203	210	214	210	206	221	7.1%	0.3%
China	3170	3211	3212	3213	3252	3306	3346	3401	3481	3627	3684	1.6%	4.7%
India	778	800	787	788	780	780	801	798	816	784	807	3.1%	1.0%
Indonesia	1680	1557	1520	1408	1456	1389	1288	1183	1152	1129	1071	−5.3%	1.3%
Malaysia	773	777	779	737	735	719	757	776	793	767	747	−3.1%	0.9%
Thailand	105	126	130	140	176	191	204	236	223	265	286	8.7%	0.3%
Vietnam	179	205	245	296	328	350	354	364	427	398	367	−8.0%	0.5%
Other Asia Pacific	245	229	217	218	200	195	193	195	186	197	215	8.0%	0.3%
Total Asia Pacific	7615	7737	7692	7608	7928	7866	7884	7791	7829	7926	7941	0.1%	9.7%
TOTAL WORLD	69,931	72,251	73,626	72,439	75,033	74,932	74,496	77,056	80,244	81,250	81,663	0.4%	100.0%
of which:													
European Union 25	3325	3304	3407	3542	3355	3147	3203	2995	2774	2535	2306	−9.0%	2.8%
OECD	21,355	21,660	21,492	21,095	21,514	21,297	21,422	21,156	20,716	19,825	19,398	−2.2%	23.3%
OPEC	28,472	29,953	31,207	29,999	31,512	30,857	29,031	30,884	33,175	34,068	34,202	0.2%	41.7%
Non-OPEC†	34,288	34,925	35,028	34,887	35,507	35,415	35,933	35,673	35,661	35,343	35,162	−0.5%	43.0%
Former Soviet Union	7171	7374	7391	7552	8014	8660	9533	10,499	11,407	11,840	12,299	3.9%	15.3%

*Includes crude oil, shale oil, oil sands and NGLs (the liquid content of natural gas where this is recovered separately). Excludes liquid fuels from other sources such as biomass and coal derivatives.
** Less than 0.05%
† Excludes Former Soviet Union.

Note: Annual changes and shares of total are calculated using million tons per annum figures.

32

Exercise 1.5

Summarizing Tables

Focus on other data in Table 1.1 and write a brief summary of your own. Or locate another table on the general topic of oil production or consumption and summarize part or all of its data. Suggestion: "Oil Production and Consumption Country Comparison Table" from the World Factbook <http://education.yahoo.com/reference/factbook/countrycompare/oil/1a.html>.

■ PARAPHRASE

In certain cases, you may want to *paraphrase* rather than summarize material. Writing a paraphrase is similar to writing a summary: It involves recasting a passage into your own words, so it requires your complete understanding of the material. The difference is that while a summary is a shortened version of the original, the paraphrase is approximately the same length as the original.

Why write a paraphrase when you can quote the original? You may decide to offer a paraphrase of material written in language that is dense, abstract, archaic, or possibly confusing.

Let's consider some examples. If you were investigating the ethical concerns relating to the practice of in vitro fertilization, you might conclude that you should read some medical literature. You might reasonably want to hear from the doctors who are themselves developing, performing, and questioning the procedures that you are researching. In professional journals and bulletins, physicians write to one another, not to the general public. They use specialized language. If you wanted to refer to the following technically complex selection, you might need to write a paraphrase.

> [I]t is not only an improvement in the success-rate that participating research scientists hope for but, rather, developments in new fields of research in in-vitro gene diagnosis and in certain circumstances gene therapy. In view of this, the French expert J. F. Mattei has asked the following question: "Are we forced to accept that in vitro fertilization will become one of the most compelling methods of genetic diagnosis?" Evidently, by the introduction of a new law in France and Sweden (1994), this acceptance (albeit with certain restrictions) has already occurred prior to the application of in vitro fertilization reaching a technically mature and clinically applicable phase. This may seem astonishing in view of the question placed by the above-quoted French expert: the idea of embryo production so as to withhold one or two embryos before implantation presupposes a definite "attitude towards eugenics." And to destroy an embryo merely because of its genetic characteristics could signify the reduction of a human life to the sum of its genes. Mattei asks: "In face of a molecular judgment on our lives, is there no possibility for appeal? Will the diagnosis of inherited

> monogenetic illnesses soon be extended to genetic predisposition for
> multi-factorial illnesses?"*

Like most literature intended for physicians, the language of this selection is somewhat forbidding to nonspecialists, who will have trouble with
phrases such as "predisposition for multi-factorial illnesses." As a courtesy
to your readers and in an effort to maintain a consistent tone and level in
your essay, you could paraphrase this paragraph from a medical newsletter.
First, of course, you must understand the meaning of the passage, perhaps no
small task. But, having read the material carefully (and consulted a dictionary), you might prepare a paraphrase like this one:

> Writing in *Biomedical Ethics,* Dietmar Mieth reports that fertility
> specialists today want not only to improve the success rates of their
> procedures but also to diagnose and repair genetic problems before
> they implant fertilized eggs. Because the result of the in vitro process
> is often more fertilized eggs than can be used in a procedure, doctors
> may examine test-tube embryos for genetic defects and "withhold one
> or two" before implanting them. The practice of selectively implant-
> ing embryos raises concerns about eugenics and the rights of rejected
> embryos. On what genetic grounds will specialists distinguish flawed
> from healthy embryos and make a decision whether or not to implant?
> The appearance of single genes linked directly to specific, or "mono-
> genetic," illnesses could be grounds for destroying an embryo. More
> complicated would be genes that predispose people to an illness but
> in no way guarantee the onset of that illness. Would these genes,
> which are only one factor in "multi-factorial illnesses," also be labeled
> undesirable and lead to embryo destruction? Advances in fertility
> science raise difficult questions. Already, even before techniques of
> genetic diagnosis are fully developed, legislatures are writing laws
> governing the practices of fertility clinics.

We begin our paraphrase with the same "not only/but also" logic of
the original's first sentence, introducing the concepts of genetic diagnosis
and therapy. The next four sentences in the original introduce concerns of
a "French expert." Rather than quote Mieth quoting the expert, and immediately mentioning new laws in France and Sweden, we decided (first) to
explain that in vitro fertilization procedures can give rise to more embryos
than needed. We reasoned that nonmedical readers would appreciate our
making explicit the background knowledge that the author assumes other
physicians possess. Then we quote Mieth briefly ("withhold one or two"
embryos) to provide some flavor of the original. We maintain focus on the
ethical questions and wait until the end of the paraphrase before mentioning

---

*Dietmar Mieth, "In Vitro Fertilization: From Medical Reproduction to Genetic Diagnosis,"
Biomedical Ethics: Newsletter of the European Network for Biomedical Ethics 1.1 (1996): 45.

the laws to which Mieth refers. Our paraphrase is roughly the same length as the original, and it conveys the author's concerns about eugenics. As you can see, the paraphrase requires a writer to make decisions about the presentation of material. In many, if not most, cases, you will need to do more than simply "translate" from the original, sentence by sentence, to write your paraphrase.

When you come across a passage that you don't understand, the temptation is to skip over it. Resist this temptation! Use a paraphrase as a tool for explaining to yourself the main ideas of a difficult passage. By translating another writer's language into your own, you clarify what you understand and pinpoint what you don't. The paraphrase therefore becomes a tool for learning the subject.

The following pointers will help you write paraphrases.

How to Write Paraphrases

- Make sure that you understand the source passage.
- Substitute your own words for those of the source passage; look for synonyms that carry the same meaning as the original words.
- Rearrange your own sentences so that they read smoothly. Sentence structure, even sentence order, in the paraphrase need not be based on that of the original. A good paraphrase, like a good summary, should stand by itself.

Paraphrases are generally about the same length as (and sometimes shorter than) the passages on which they are based. But sometimes clarity requires that a paraphrase be longer than a tightly compacted source passage. For example, suppose you wanted to paraphrase this statement by Sigmund Freud:

> We have found out that the distortion in dreams which hinders our understanding of them is due to the activities of a censorship, directed against the unacceptable, unconscious wish-impulses.

If you were to paraphrase this statement (the first sentence in the Tenth Lecture of his *General Introduction to Psychoanalysis*), you might come up with something like this:

> It is difficult to understand dreams because they contain distortions. Freud believed that these distortions arise from our internal censor, which attempts to suppress unconscious and forbidden desires.

Essentially, this paraphrase does little more than break up one sentence into two and somewhat rearrange the sentence structure for clarity.

Like summaries, then, paraphrases are useful devices, both in helping you to understand source material and in enabling you to convey the essence of this source material to your readers. When would you choose to write a summary instead of a paraphrase (or vice versa)? The answer depends on your purpose in presenting the source material. As we've said, summaries are generally based on articles (or sections of articles) or books. Paraphrases are generally based on particularly difficult (or important) paragraphs or sentences. You would seldom paraphrase a long passage, or summarize a short one, unless there were particularly good reasons for doing so. (A lawyer might want to paraphrase several pages of legal language so that his or her client, who is not a lawyer, could understand it.) The purpose of a summary is generally to save your reader time by presenting him or her with a brief version of a lengthy source. The purpose of a paraphrase is generally to clarify a short passage that might otherwise be unclear. Whether you summarize or paraphrase may also depend on the importance of your source. A particularly important source—if it is not too long—may rate a paraphrase. If it is less important, or peripheral to your central argument, you may write a summary instead. And, of course, you may choose to summarize only part of your source—the part that is most relevant to the point you are making.

Exercise 1.6

Paraphrasing

Locate and photocopy three relatively complex, but brief, passages from readings currently assigned in your other courses. Paraphrase these passages, making the language more readable and understandable. Attach the photocopies to the paraphrases.

■ QUOTATIONS

A *quotation* records the exact language used by someone in speech or writing. A *summary,* in contrast, is a brief restatement in your own words of what someone else has said or written. And a *paraphrase* is also a restatement, although one that is often as long as the original source. Any paper in which you draw upon sources will rely heavily on quotation, summary, and paraphrase. How do you choose among the three?

Remember that the papers you write should be your own—for the most part: your own language and certainly your own thesis, your own inferences, and your own conclusion. It follows that references to your source materials should be written primarily as summaries and paraphrases, both of which are built on restatement, not quotation. You will use summaries when you need a *brief* restatement, and paraphrases, which provide more explicit detail than summaries, when you need to follow the development of a source closely. When you quote too much, you risk losing ownership of your work: More easily than you might think, your voice can be drowned out by the voices of those you've quoted. So *use quotation sparingly,* as you would a pungent spice.

Nevertheless, quoting just the right source at the right time can significantly improve your papers. The trick is to know when and how to use quotations.

Quotations can be direct or indirect. A *direct* quotation is one in which you record precisely the language of another. An *indirect* quotation is one in which you report what someone has said without repeating the words exactly as spoken (or written):

Direct quotation: Franklin D. Roosevelt said, "The only thing we have to fear is fear itself."

Indirect quotation: Franklin D. Roosevelt said that we have nothing to fear but fear itself.

The language in a direct quotation, which is indicated by a pair of quotation marks (" "), must be faithful to the wording of the original passage. When using an indirect quotation, you have the liberty of changing words (although not changing meaning). For both direct and indirect quotations, *you must credit your sources,* naming them either in (or close to) the sentence that includes the quotation or in a parenthetical citation. (See Chapter 7, pp. 281–302, for specific rules on citing sources properly.)

Choosing Quotations

You'll find that using quotations can be particularly helpful in several situations.

Quoting Memorable Language

You should quote when the source material is worded so eloquently or powerfully that to summarize or paraphrase it would be to sacrifice much of the impact and significance of the meaning. Here, for example, is the historian John Keegan describing how France, Germany, Austria, and Russia slid inexorably in 1914 into the cataclysm of World War I:

> In the event, the states of Europe proceeded, as if in a dead march and a dialogue of the deaf, to the destruction of their continent and its civilization.

No paraphrase could do justice to the power of Keegan's words as they appear in his book *The First World War* (1998). You would certainly want to quote them in any paper dealing with the origins of this conflict.

When to Quote

- Use quotations when another writer's language is particularly memorable and will add interest and liveliness to your paper.
- Use quotations when another writer's language is so clear and economical that to make the same point in your own words would, by comparison, be ineffective.
- Use quotations when you want the solid reputation of a source to lend authority and credibility to your own writing.

Quoting Clear and Concise Language

You should quote a source when its language is particularly clear and economical—when your language, by contrast, would be wordy. Read this passage from a biology text by Patricia Curtis:

> The honeybee colony, which usually has a population of 30,000 to 40,000 workers, differs from that of the bumblebee and many other social bees or wasps in that it survives the winter. This means that the bees must stay warm despite the cold. Like other bees, the isolated honeybee cannot fly if the temperature falls below 10°C (50°F) and cannot walk if the temperature is below 7°C (45°F). Within the wintering hive, bees maintain their temperature by clustering together in a dense ball; the lower the temperature, the denser the cluster. The clustered bees produce heat by constant muscular movements of their wings, legs, and abdomens. In very cold weather, the bees on the outside of the cluster keep moving toward the center, while those in the core of the cluster move to the colder outside periphery. The entire cluster moves slowly about on the combs, eating the stored honey from the combs as it moves.*

A summary of this paragraph might read:

> Honeybees, unlike many other varieties of bee, are able to live through the winter by "clustering together in a dense ball" for body warmth.

A paraphrase of the same passage would be considerably more detailed:

> Honeybees, unlike many other varieties of bee (such as bumblebees), are able to live through the winter. The 30,000 to 40,000 bees within a honeybee hive could not, individually, move about in cold winter temperatures. But when "clustering together in a dense ball," the bees generate heat by constantly moving their body parts. The cluster also moves slowly about the hive, those on the periphery of the cluster moving into the center, those in the center moving to the

---

*Patricia Curtis, "Winter Organization," *Biology,* 2nd ed. (New York: Worth, 1976): 822–23.

periphery, and all eating honey stored in the combs. This nutrition, in addition to the heat generated by the cluster, enables the honeybee to survive the cold winter months.

In both the summary and the paraphrase we've quoted Curtis's "clustering together in a dense ball," a phrase that lies at the heart of her description of wintering honeybees. For us to describe this clustering in any language other than Curtis's would be pointless when her description is admirably brief and precise.

Quoting Authoritative Language

You should use quotations that lend authority to your work. When quoting an expert or a prominent political, artistic, or historical figure, you elevate your own work by placing it in esteemed company. Quote respected figures to establish background information in a paper, and your readers will tend to perceive that information as reliable. Quote the opinions of respected figures to endorse a statement that you've made, and your statement becomes more credible to your readers. Here, in a discussion of space flight, the writer David Chandler refers to a physicist and a physicist-astronaut:

> A few scientists—notably James Van Allen, discoverer of the Earth's radiation belts—have decried the expense of the manned space program and called for an almost exclusive concentration on unmanned scientific exploration instead, saying this would be far more cost-effective.
>
> Other space scientists dispute that idea. Joseph Allen, physicist and former shuttle astronaut, says, "It seems to be argued that one takes away from the other. But before there was a manned space program, the funding on space science was zero. Now it's about $500 million a year."

In the first paragraph Chandler has either summarized or used an indirect quotation to incorporate remarks made by James Van Allen into the discussion on space flight. In the second paragraph, Chandler directly quotes Joseph Allen. Both quotations, indirect and direct, lend authority and legitimacy to the article, for both James Van Allen and Joseph Allen are experts on the subject of space flight. Note that Chandler provides brief but effective biographies of his sources, identifying each one, so that their qualifications to speak on the subject are known to all:

James Van Allen, *discoverer of the Earth's radiation belts...*

Joseph Allen, *physicist and former shuttle astronaut...*

The phrases in italics are *appositives*. Their function is to rename the nouns they follow by providing explicit, identifying detail. Any information about a person that can be expressed in the following sentence pattern can be made into an appositive phrase:

James Van Allen is the *discoverer of the Earth's radiation belts.*

He has decried the expense of the manned space program.

Sentence with an appositive:

James Van Allen, *discoverer of the Earth's radiation belts,* has decried the expense of the manned space program.

Appositives (in the example above, "discoverer of the Earth's radiation belts") efficiently incorporate identifying information about the authors you quote, while adding variety to the structure of your sentences.

Incorporating Quotations into Your Sentences

Quoting Only the Part of a Sentence or Paragraph That You Need

We've said that a writer selects passages for quotation that are especially vivid, memorable, concise, or authoritative. Now put these principles into practice. Suppose that while conducting research on college sports, you've come across the following, written by Robert Hutchins, former president of the University of Chicago:

> If athleticism is bad for students, players, alumni, and the public, it is even worse for the colleges and universities themselves. They want to be educational institutions, but they can't. The story of the famous halfback whose only regret, when he bade his coach farewell, was that he hadn't learned to read and write is probably exaggerated. But we must admit that pressure from trustees, graduates, "friends," presidents, and even professors has tended to relax academic standards. These gentry often overlook the fact that a college should not be interested in a fullback who is a half-wit. Recruiting, subsidizing and the double educational standard cannot exist without the knowledge and the tacit approval, at least, of the colleges and universities themselves. Certain institutions encourage susceptible professors to be nice to athletes now admitted by paying them for serving as "faculty representatives" on the college athletic board.*

Suppose that in this paragraph you find a gem, a sentence with striking language that will enliven your discussion:

> These gentry often overlook the fact that a college should not be interested in a fullback who is a half-wit.

Incorporating the Quotation into the Flow of Your Own Sentence

Once you've selected the passage you want to quote, you need to work the material into your paper in as natural and fluid a manner as possible. Here's how we would quote Hutchins:

> Robert Hutchins, former president of the University of Chicago, asserts that "a college should not be interested in a fullback who is a half-wit."

---

*Robert Hutchins, "Gate Receipts and Glory," *Saturday Evening Post* 3 Dec. 1983: 38.

Note that we've used an appositive to identify Hutchins. And we've used only the part of the paragraph—a single clause—that we thought memorable enough to quote directly.

Avoiding Freestanding Quotations

A quoted sentence should never stand by itself, as in the following example:

> Various people associated with the university admit that the pressures of athleticism have caused a relaxation of standards. "These gentry often overlook the fact that a college should not be interested in a fullback who is a half-wit." But this kind of thinking is bad for the university and even worse for the athletes.

Even if it were followed by a parenthetical citation, a freestanding quotation would be jarring to the reader. You need to introduce the quotation with a *signal phrase* that attributes the source, not in a parenthetical citation but in some other part of the sentence—beginning, middle, or end. Thus, you could write:

> As Robert Hutchins notes, "These gentry often overlook the fact that a college should not be interested in a fullback who is a half-wit."

Here's a variation with the signal phrase in the middle:

> "These gentry," asserts Robert Hutchins, "often overlook the fact that a college should not be interested in a fullback who is a half-wit."

Another alternative is to introduce a sentence-long quotation with a colon:

> But Robert Hutchins disagrees: "These gentry often overlook the fact that a college should not be interested in a fullback who is a half-wit."

Use colons also to introduce indented quotations (as when we introduce long quotations in this chapter).

When attributing sources in signal phrases, try to vary the standard *states, writes, says,* and so on. Stronger verbs you might consider are: *asserts, argues, maintains, insists, asks,* and even *wonders.*

Exercise 1.7

Incorporating Quotations

Return to the article (pp. 7–12) by Alan S. Blinder, "Will Your Job Be Exported?" Find sentences that you think make interesting points. Imagine you want to use these points in a paper you're writing on job prospects in the twenty-first century. Write five different sentences that use a variety of the techniques discussed thus far to incorporate whole sentences as well as phrases from Blinder's article.

Using Ellipses

Using quotations becomes somewhat complicated when you want to quote the beginning and end of a passage but not its middle. Here's part of a paragraph from Thoreau's *Walden:*

> To read well, that is to read true books in a true spirit, is a noble exercise, and one that will task the reader more than any exercise which the customs of the day esteem. It requires a training such as the athletes underwent, the steady intention almost of the whole life to this object. Books must be read as deliberately and reservedly as they were written.*

And here is how we can use this material in a quotation:

> Reading well is hard work, writes Henry David Thoreau in *Walden,* "that will task the reader more than any exercise which the customs of the day esteem.... Books must be read as deliberately and reservedly as they were written."

Whenever you quote a sentence but delete words from it, as we have done above, indicate this deletion to the reader with three spaced periods—called an "ellipsis"—in the sentence at the point of deletion. The rationale for using an ellipsis mark is that a direct quotation must be reproduced *exactly* as it was written or spoken. When writers delete or change any part of the quoted material, readers must be alerted so they don't think the changes were part of the original. When deleting an entire sentence or sentences from a quoted paragraph, as in the example above, end the sentence you have quoted with a period, place the ellipsis, and continue the quotation.

If you are deleting the middle of a single sentence, use an ellipsis in place of the deleted words:

> "To read well...is a noble exercise, and one that will task the reader more than any exercise which the customs of the day esteem."

If you are deleting material from the end of one sentence through to the beginning of another sentence, add a sentence period before the ellipsis:

> "It requires a training such as the athletes underwent.... Books must be read as deliberately and reservedly as they were written."

If you begin your quotation of an author in the middle of his or her sentence, you need not indicate deleted words with an ellipsis. Be sure, however, that the syntax of the quotation fits smoothly with the syntax of your sentence:

> Reading "is a noble exercise," writes Henry David Thoreau.

---

*Henry David Thoreau, *Walden* (New York: Signet Classic, 1960): 72.

Using Brackets to Add or Substitute Words

Use brackets whenever you need to add or substitute words in a quoted sentence. The brackets indicate to the reader a word or phrase that does not appear in the original passage but that you have inserted to prevent confusion. For example, when a pronoun's antecedent would be unclear to readers, delete the pronoun from the sentence and substitute an identifying word or phrase in brackets. When you make such a substitution, no ellipsis mark is needed. Assume that you wish to quote either of the underlined sentences in the following passage by Jane Yolen:

> Golden Press's *Walt Disney's Cinderella* set the new pattern for America's Cinderella. This book's text is coy and condescending. (Sample: "And her best friends of all were—guess who—the mice!") The illustrations are poor cartoons. And Cinderella herself is a disaster. She cowers as her sisters rip her homemade ball gown to shreds. (Not even homemade by Cinderella, but by the mice and birds.) <u>She answers her stepmother with whines and pleadings. She is a sorry excuse for a heroine, pitiable and useless.</u> She cannot perform even a simple action to save herself, though she is warned by her friends, the mice. She does not hear them because she is "off in a world of dreams." Cinderella begs, she whimpers, and at last has to be rescued by—guess who—the mice!*

In quoting one of these sentences, you would need to identify to whom the pronoun *she* refers. You can do this inside the quotation by using brackets:

> Jane Yolen believes that "[Cinderella] is a sorry excuse for a heroine, pitiable and useless."

When the pronoun begins the sentence to be quoted, you can identify the pronoun outside the quotation and begin quoting your source one word later:

> Jane Yolen believes that in the Golden Press version, Cinderella "is a sorry excuse for a heroine, pitiable and useless."

When to Summarize, Paraphrase, and Quote

SUMMARIZE:

- To present main points of a lengthy passage (article or book)
- To condense peripheral points necessary to discussion

(continues)

---

*Jane Yolen, "America's 'Cinderella,'" *Children's Literature in Education* 8 (1977): 22.

> **PARAPHRASE:**
> - To clarify a short passage
> - To emphasize main points
>
> **QUOTE:**
> - To capture another writer's particularly memorable language
> - To capture another writer's clearly and economically stated language
> - To lend authority and credibility to your own writing

Here's another example of a case where the pronoun needing identification occurs in the middle of the sentence to be quoted. Newspaper reporters must use brackets when quoting a source, who in an interview might say this:

> After the fire they did not return to the station house for three hours.

If the reporter wants to use this sentence in an article, he or she needs to identify the pronoun:

> An official from City Hall, speaking on the condition that he not be identified, said, "After the fire [the officers] did not return to the station house for three hours."

You will also need to add bracketed information to a quoted sentence when a reference essential to the sentence's meaning is implied but not stated directly. Read the following paragraph from Walter Isaacson's biography of Albert Einstein, *Einstein: His Life and Universe:*

> Newton had bequeathed to Einstein a universe in which time had an absolute existence that tick-tocked along independent of objects and observers, and in which space likewise had an absolute existence. Gravity was thought to be a force that masses exerted on one another rather mysteriously across empty space. <u>Within this framework, objects obeyed mechanical laws that had proved remarkably accurate—almost perfect—in explaining everything from the orbits of the planets, to the diffusion of gases, to the jiggling of molecules, to the propagation of sound (though not light) waves.</u>

If you wanted to quote only the underlined sentence above, you would need to provide readers with a bracketed explanation; otherwise, the phrase "this framework" would be unclear. Here is how you would manage the quotation:

> According to Walter Isaacson, Newton's universe was extremely regular and predictable:
>
>> Within this framework [that time and space exist independently of their observation and that gravity results from masses exerting a remote

attraction on one another], objects obeyed mechanical laws that had proved remarkably accurate—almost perfect—in explaining everything from the orbits of the planets, to the diffusion of gases, to the jiggling of molecules, to the propagation of sound (though not light) waves. (223)

Incorporating Quotations into Your Sentences

- **Quote only the part of a sentence or paragraph that you need.** Use no more of the writer's language than necessary to make or reinforce your point.

- **Incorporate the quotation into the flow of your own sentence.** The quotation must fit, both syntactically and stylistically, into your surrounding language.

- **Avoid freestanding quotations.** A quoted sentence should never stand by itself. Use a *signal phrase*—at the beginning, the middle, or the end of the sentence—to attribute the source of the quotation.

- **Use ellipsis marks.** Indicate deleted language in the middle of a quoted sentence with ellipsis marks. Deleted language at the beginning or end of a sentence generally does not require ellipsis marks.

- **Use brackets to add or substitute words.** Use brackets to add or substitute words in a quoted sentence when the meaning of the quotation would otherwise be unclear—for example, when the antecedent of a quoted pronoun is ambiguous.

Exercise 1.8

Using Brackets

Write your own sentences incorporating the following quotations. Use brackets to clarify information that isn't clear outside its original context—and refer to the original sources to remind yourself of this context.

From the David Chandler paragraph on James Van Allen (pp. 39–40):

   a.   Other space scientists *dispute that idea.*

   b.   Now *it's about $500 million a year.*

From the Jane Yolen excerpt on Cinderella (p. 43):

   a.   *This book's* text is coy and condescending.

   b.   *She* cannot perform even a simple action to save herself, though she is warned by her friends, the mice.

   c.   She does not hear *them* because she is "off in a world of dreams."

Remember that when you quote the work of another, you are obligated to credit—or cite—the author's work properly; otherwise, you may be guilty of plagiarism. See pages 281–302 for guidance on citing sources.

■ AVOIDING PLAGIARISM

Plagiarism is generally defined as the attempt to pass off the work of another as one's own. Whether born out of calculation or desperation, plagiarism is the least tolerated offense in the academic world. The fact that most plagiarism is unintentional—arising from an ignorance of the conventions rather than deceitfulness—makes no difference to many professors.

The ease of cutting and pasting whole blocks of text from Web sources into one's own paper makes it tempting for some to take the easy way out and avoid doing their own research and writing. But, apart from the serious ethical issues involved, the same technology that makes such acts possible also makes it possible for instructors to detect them. Software marketed to instructors allows them to conduct Web searches, using suspicious phrases as keywords. The results often provide irrefutable evidence of plagiarism.

Of course, plagiarism is not confined to students. Recent years have seen a number of high-profile cases—some of them reaching the front pages of newspapers—of well-known scholars who were shown to have copied passages from sources into their own book manuscripts, without proper attribution. In some cases, the scholars maintained that these appropriations were simply a matter of carelessness, that in the press and volume of work, they had lost track of which words were theirs and which were the words of their sources. But such excuses sounded hollow: These careless acts inevitably embarrassed the scholars professionally, tarnished their otherwise fine work and reputations, and disappointed their many admirers.

You can avoid plagiarism and charges of plagiarism by following the basic rules provided on page 47.

Following is a passage from an article by Richard Rovere on Senator Joseph P. McCarthy, along with several student versions of the ideas represented.

> McCarthy never seemed to believe in himself or in anything he had said. He knew that Communists were not in charge of American foreign policy. He knew that they weren't running the United States Army. He knew that he had spent five years looking for Communists in the government and that—although some must certainly have been there, since Communists had turned up in practically every other major government in the world—he hadn't come up with even one.*

---

*Richard Rovere, "The Most Gifted and Successful Demagogue This Country Has Ever Known," *New York Times Magazine*, 30 Apr. 1967.

One student version of this passage reads:

> McCarthy never believed in himself or in anything he had said. He knew that Communists were not in charge of American foreign policy and weren't running the United States Army. He knew that he had spent five years looking for Communists in the government, and although there must certainly have been some there, since Communists were in practically every other major government in the world, he hadn't come up with even one.

Clearly, this is intentional plagiarism. The student has copied the original passage almost word for word.

Here is another version of the same passage:

> McCarthy knew that Communists were not running foreign policy or the Army. He also knew that although there must have been some Communists in the government, he hadn't found a single one, even though he had spent five years looking.

This student has attempted to put the ideas into her own words, but both the wording and the sentence structure are so heavily dependent on the original passage that even if it *were* cited, most professors would consider it plagiarism.

In the following version, the student has sufficiently changed the wording and sentence structure, and she uses a *signal phrase* (a phrase used to introduce a quotation or paraphrase, signaling to the reader that the words to follow come from someone else) to properly credit the information to Rovere, so that there is no question of plagiarism:

> According to Richard Rovere, McCarthy was fully aware that Communists were running neither the government nor the Army. He also knew that he hadn't found a single Communist in government, even after a lengthy search (192).

And although this is not a matter of plagiarism, as noted above, it's essential to quote accurately. You are not permitted to change any part of a quotation or to omit any part of it without using brackets or ellipses.

Rules for Avoiding Plagiarism

- Cite *all* quoted material and *all* summarized and paraphrased material, unless the information is common knowledge (e.g., the Civil War was fought from 1861 to 1865).
- Make sure that both the *wording* and the *sentence structure* of your summaries and paraphrases are substantially your own.

WRITING ASSIGNMENT: SUMMARY

Read "The Political Genius of Abraham Lincoln" by Doris Kearns Goodwin. (This selection by the Pulitzer Prize–winning historian is from her 2005 book *Team of Rivals: The Political Genius of Abraham Lincoln*.) Write a summary of the passage, following the directions in this chapter for dividing the article into sections, for writing a one-sentence summary of each section, and then for joining section summaries with a thesis. Prepare for the summary by making notes in the margins. You may find it useful to recall that well-written pieces, like Goodwin's, often telegraph clues to their own structure as a device for assisting readers. Such clues can be helpful when preparing a summary. Your finished product should be the result of two or more drafts.

Note: Additional summary assignments will be found in Chapter 8, "Practicing Academic Writing," focusing on the changing landscape of jobs in a global economy.

THE POLITICAL GENIUS OF ABRAHAM LINCOLN

Doris Kearns Goodwin*

Doris Kearns Goodwin won the Pulitzer Prize in history for No Ordinary Time. *She is the author of* Wait Till Next Year, The Fitzgeralds and the Kennedys, *and* Lyndon Johnson and the American Dream.

In 1876, the celebrated orator Frederick Douglass dedicated a monument in Washington, D.C., erected by black Americans to honor Abraham Lincoln. The former slave told his audience that "there is little necessity on this occasion to speak at length and critically of this great and good man, and of his high mission in the world. That ground has been fully occupied.... The whole field of fact and fancy has been gleaned and garnered. Any man can say things that are true of Abraham Lincoln, but no man can say anything that is new of Abraham Lincoln."

Speaking only eleven years after Lincoln's death, Douglass was too close to assess the fascination that this plain and complex, shrewd and transparent, tender and iron-willed leader would hold for generations of Americans. In the nearly two hundred years since his birth, countless historians and writers have uncovered new documents, provided fresh insights, and developed an ever-deepening understanding of our sixteenth president.

In my own effort to illuminate the character and career of Abraham Lincoln, I have coupled the account of his life with the stories of the remarkable men who were his rivals for the 1860 Republican presidential nomination—New York senator William H. Seward, Ohio governor Salmon P. Chase, and Missouri's distinguished elder statesman Edward Bates.

---

*Doris Kearns Goodwin, *Team of Rivals: The Political Genius of Abraham Lincoln* (New York: Simon and Schuster, 2005): v–viii.

Taken together, the lives of these four men give us a picture of the path taken by ambitious young men in the North who came of age in the early decades of the nineteenth century. All four studied law, became distinguished orators, entered politics, and opposed the spread of slavery. Their upward climb was one followed by many thousands who left the small towns of their birth to seek opportunity and adventure in the rapidly growing cities of a dynamic, expanding America.

5   Just as a hologram is created through the interference of light from separate sources, so the lives and impressions of those who companioned Lincoln give us a clearer and more dimensional picture of the president himself. Lincoln's barren childhood, his lack of schooling, his relationships with male friends, his complicated marriage, the nature of his ambition, and his ruminations about death can be analyzed more clearly when he is placed side by side with his three contemporaries.

When Lincoln won the nomination, each of his celebrated rivals believed the wrong man had been chosen. Ralph Waldo Emerson recalled his first reception of the news that the "comparatively unknown name of Lincoln" had been selected: "we heard the result coldly and sadly. It seemed too rash, on a purely local reputation, to build so grave a trust in such anxious times."

Lincoln seemed to have come from nowhere—a backwoods lawyer who had served one undistinguished term in the House of Representatives and had lost two consecutive contests for the U.S. Senate. Contemporaries and historians alike have attributed his surprising nomination to chance—the fact that he came from the battleground state of Illinois and stood in the center of his party. The comparative perspective suggests a different interpretation. When viewed against the failed efforts of his rivals, it is clear that Lincoln won the nomination because he was shrewdest and canniest of them all. More accustomed to relying upon himself to shape events, he took the greatest control of the process leading up to the nomination, displaying a fierce ambition, an exceptional political acumen, and a wide range of emotional strengths, forged in the crucible of personal hardship, that took his unsuspecting rivals by surprise.

That Lincoln, after winning the presidency, made the unprecedented decision to incorporate his eminent rivals into his political family, the cabinet, was evidence of a profound self-confidence and a first indication of what would prove to others a most unexpected greatness. Seward became secretary of state, Chase secretary of the treasury, and Bates attorney general. The remaining top posts Lincoln offered to three former Democrats whose stories also inhabit these pages—Gideon Welles, Lincoln's "Neptune," was made secretary of the navy, Montgomery Blair became post-master general, and Edwin M. Stanton, Lincoln's "Mars," eventually became secretary of war. Every member of this administration was better known, better educated, and more experienced in public life than Lincoln. Their presence in the cabinet might have threatened to eclipse the obscure prairie lawyer from Springfield.

It soon became clear, however, that Abraham Lincoln would emerge the undisputed captain of this most unusual cabinet, truly a team of rivals. The powerful competitors who had originally disdained Lincoln became colleagues who helped him steer the country through its darkest days. Seward was the first to appreciate Lincoln's remarkable talents, quickly realizing the futility of his plan to relegate the president to a figurehead role. In the months that followed, Seward would become Lincoln's closest friend and advisor in the administration. Though Bates initially viewed Lincoln as a well-meaning but incompetent administrator, he eventually concluded that the president was an unmatched leader, "very near being a perfect man." Edwin Stanton, who had treated Lincoln with contempt at their initial acquaintance, developed a great respect for the commander in chief and was unable to control his tears for weeks after the president's death. Even Chase, whose restless ambition for the presidency was never realized, at last acknowledged that Lincoln had outmaneuvered him.

10   This, then, is a story of Lincoln's political genius revealed through his extraordinary array of personal qualities that enabled him to form friendships with men who had previously opposed him; to repair injured feelings that, left untended, might have escalated into permanent hostility; to assume responsibility for the failures of subordinates; to share credit with ease; and to learn from mistakes. He possessed an acute understanding of the sources of power inherent in the presidency, an unparalleled ability to keep his governing coalition intact, a tough-minded appreciation of the need to protect his presidential prerogatives, and a masterful sense of timing. His success in dealing with the strong egos of the men in his cabinet suggests that in the hands of a truly great politician the qualities we generally associate with decency and morality—kindness, sensitivity, compassion, honesty, and empathy—can also be impressive political resources.

Critical Reading and Critique ■ 2

■ CRITICAL READING

When writing papers in college, you are often called on to respond critically to source materials. Critical reading requires the abilities to both summarize and evaluate a presentation. As you have seen in Chapter 1, a *summary* is a brief restatement in your own words of the content of a passage. An *evaluation* is a more ambitious undertaking. In your college work, you read to gain and *use* new information. But because sources are not equally valid or equally useful, you must learn to distinguish critically among them by evaluating them.

There is no ready-made formula for determining validity. Critical reading and its written equivalent—the *critique*—require discernment, sensitivity, imagination, knowledge of the subject, and above all, willingness to become involved in what you read. These skills are developed only through repeated practice. But you must begin somewhere, and so we recommend you start by posing two broad questions about passages, articles, and books that you read: (1) To what extent does the author succeed in his or her purpose? (2) To what extent do you agree with the author?

Question 1: To What Extent Does the Author Succeed in His or Her Purpose?

All critical reading *begins with an accurate summary.* Before attempting an evaluation, you must be able to locate an author's thesis and identify the selection's content and structure. You must understand the author's *purpose.* Authors write to inform, to persuade, and to entertain. A given piece may be primarily *informative* (a summary of the research on cloning), primarily *persuasive* (an argument on what the government should do to alleviate homelessness), or primarily *entertaining* (a play about the frustrations of young lovers). Or it may be all three (as in John Steinbeck's novel *The Grapes of Wrath,* about migrant workers during the Great Depression). Sometimes authors are not fully conscious of their purpose. Sometimes their purpose changes as they write. Also, multiple purposes can overlap: A piece of writing may need to inform the reader about an issue in order to make a persuasive point. But if the finished piece is coherent, it will have a primary reason for having been written, and it should be apparent that the author is attempting primarily to inform, persuade, or entertain a particular audience. To identify this primary reason—this purpose—is your first job as a critical reader. Your next job is to determine how successful the author has been in achieving this objective.

Where Do We Find Written Critiques?

Here are just a few of the types of writing that involve critique:

ACADEMIC WRITING

- **Research papers** critique sources in order to establish their usefulness.
- **Position papers** stake out a position by critiquing other positions.
- **Book reviews** combine summary with critique.
- **Essay exams** demonstrate understanding of course material by critiquing it.

WORKPLACE WRITING

- **Legal briefs and legal arguments** critique previous arguments made or anticipated by opposing counsel.
- **Business plans and proposals** critique other less cost-effective, efficient, or reasonable approaches.
- **Policy briefs** communicate strengths and weaknesses of policies and legislation through critique.

As a critical reader, you bring various criteria, or standards of judgment, to bear when you read pieces intended to inform, persuade, or entertain.

Writing to Inform

A piece intended to inform will provide definitions, describe or report on a process, recount a story, give historical background, and/or provide facts and figures. An informational piece responds to questions such as:

What (or who) is _____?

How does _____ work?

What is the controversy or problem about?

What happened?

How and why did it happen?

What were the results?

What are the arguments for and against _____?

To the extent that an author answers these and related questions and that the answers are a matter of verifiable record (you could check for accuracy if you had the time and inclination), the selection is intended to inform.

Having identified such an intention, you can organize your response by considering three other criteria: accuracy, significance, and fair interpretation of information.

Evaluating Informative Writing

Accuracy of Information   If you are going to use any of the information presented, you must be satisfied that it is trustworthy. One of your responsibilities as a critical reader, then, is to find out if the information is accurate. This means you should check facts against other sources. Government publications are often good resources for verifying facts about political legislation, population data, crime statistics, and the like. You can also search key terms in library databases and on the Web. Since material on the Web is essentially self-published, however, you must be especially vigilant in assessing its legitimacy. A wealth of useful information is now available on the Internet—as are distorted "facts," unsupported opinion, and hidden agendas.

Significance of Information   One useful question that you can put to a reading is "So what?" In the case of selections that attempt to inform, you may reasonably wonder whether the information makes a difference. What can the reader gain from this information? How is knowledge advanced by the publication of this material? Is the information of importance to you or to others in a particular audience? Why or why not?

Fair Interpretation of Information   At times you will read reports whose sole purpose is to relate raw data or information. In these cases, you will build your response on Question 1, introduced on page 51: To what extent does the author succeed in his or her purpose? More frequently, once an author has presented information, he or she will attempt to evaluate or interpret it—which is only reasonable, since information that has not been evaluated or interpreted is of little use. One of your tasks as a critical reader is to make a distinction between the author's presentation of facts and figures and his or her attempts to evaluate them. Watch for shifts from straightforward descriptions of factual information ("20 percent of the population") to assertions about what this information means ("a *mere* 20 percent of the population"), what its implications are, and so on. Pay attention to whether the logic with which the author connects interpretation with facts is sound. You may find that the information is valuable but the interpretation is not. Perhaps the author's conclusions are not justified. Could you offer a contrary explanation for the same facts? Does more information need to be gathered before firm conclusions can be drawn? Why?

Writing to Persuade

Writing is frequently intended to persuade—that is, to influence the reader's thinking. To make a persuasive case, the writer must begin with an assertion that is arguable, some statement about which reasonable people could disagree. Such an assertion, when it serves as the essential organizing principle of the article or book, is called a *thesis*. Here are two examples:

> Because they do not speak English, many children in this affluent land are being denied their fundamental right to equal educational opportunity.

> Bilingual education, which has been stridently promoted by a small group of activists with their own agenda, is detrimental to the very students it is supposed to serve.

Thesis statements such as these—and the subsequent assertions used to help support them—represent conclusions that authors have drawn as a result of researching and thinking about an issue. You go through the same process yourself when you write persuasive papers or critiques. And just as you are entitled to evaluate critically the assertions of authors you read, so your professors—and other students—are entitled to evaluate *your* assertions, whether they be written arguments or comments made in class discussion.

Keep in mind that writers organize arguments by arranging evidence to support one conclusion and to oppose (or dismiss) another. You can assess the validity of an argument and its conclusion by determining whether the author has (1) clearly defined key terms, (2) used information fairly, and (3) argued logically and not fallaciously (see pp. 58–62).

Exercise 2.1

Informative and Persuasive Thesis Statements

With a partner from your class, identify at least one informative and one persuasive thesis statement from two passages of your own choosing. Photocopy these passages and highlight the statements you have selected.

As an alternative, and also working with a partner, write one informative and one persuasive thesis statement for *three* of the topics listed in the last paragraph of this exercise. For example, for the topic of prayer in schools, your informative thesis statement could read:

> Both advocates and opponents of school prayer frame their position as a matter of freedom.

Your persuasive thesis statement might be worded:

> As long as schools don't dictate what kinds of prayers students should say, then school prayer should be allowed and even encouraged.

> Don't worry about taking a position that you agree with or feel you could support; this exercise doesn't require that you write an essay. The topics:

school prayer

gun control

immigration

stem cell research

grammar instruction in English class

violent lyrics in music

teaching computer skills in primary schools

curfews in college dormitories

course registration procedures

Evaluating Persuasive Writing

Read the argument that follows on the cancellation of the National Aeronautics and Space Administration's lunar program. We will illustrate our discussion on defining terms, using information fairly, and arguing logically by referring to Charles Krauthammer's argument, which appeared as an op-ed in the *Washington Post* on July 17, 2009. The model critique that follows these illustrations will be based on this same argument.

THE MOON WE LEFT BEHIND
Charles Krauthammer

Michael Crichton once wrote that if you told a physicist in 1899 that within a hundred years humankind would, among other wonders (nukes, commercial airlines), "travel to the moon, and then lose interest...the physicist would almost certainly pronounce you mad." In 2000, I quoted these lines expressing Crichton's incredulity at America's abandonment of the moon. It is now 2009 and the moon recedes ever further.

Next week marks the 40th anniversary of the first moon landing. We say we will return in 2020. But that promise was made by a previous president, and this president [Obama] has defined himself as the antimatter to George Bush. Moreover, for all of Barack Obama's Kennedyesque qualities, he has expressed none of Kennedy's enthusiasm for human space exploration.

So with the Apollo moon program long gone, and with Constellation,* its supposed successor, still little more than a hope, we remain in retreat from space. Astonishing. After countless millennia of gazing and dreaming, we finally got off the ground at Kitty Hawk in 1903. Within 66 years, a nanosecond in human history, we'd landed on the moon. Then five more landings, 10 more moonwalkers and, in the decades since, nothing.

To be more precise: almost 40 years spent in low Earth orbit studying, well, zero-G nausea and sundry cosmic mysteries. We've done it with the most beautiful, intricate, complicated—and ultimately, hopelessly impractical—machine ever built by man: the space shuttle. We turned this magnificent bird into a truck for hauling goods and people to a tinkertoy we call the international space station, itself created in a fit of post-Cold War internationalist absentmindedness as a place where people of differing nationality can sing "Kumbaya" while weightless.

---

*Constellation was a NASA human spaceflight program designed to develop post–space shuttle vehicles capable of traveling to the moon and perhaps to Mars. Authorized in 2005, the program was canceled by President Obama in 2010.

5   The shuttle is now too dangerous, too fragile and too expensive. Seven more flights and then it is retired, going—like the Spruce Goose* and the Concorde†— into the Museum of Things Too Beautiful and Complicated to Survive.

America's manned space program is in shambles. Fourteen months from today, for the first time since 1962, the United States will be incapable not just of sending a man to the moon but of sending anyone into Earth orbit. We'll be totally grounded. We'll have to beg a ride from the Russians or perhaps even the Chinese.

So what, you say? Don't we have problems here on Earth? Oh, please. Poverty and disease and social ills will always be with us. If we'd waited for them to be rectified before venturing out, we'd still be living in caves.

Yes, we have a financial crisis. No one's asking for a crash Manhattan Project. All we need is sufficient funding from the hundreds of billions being showered from Washington—"stimulus" monies that, unlike Eisenhower's interstate highway system or Kennedy's Apollo program, will leave behind not a trace on our country or our consciousness—to build Constellation and get us back to Earth orbit and the moon a half-century after the original landing.

Why do it? It's not for practicality. We didn't go to the moon to spin off cooling suits and freeze-dried fruit. Any technological return is a bonus, not a reason. We go for the wonder and glory of it. Or, to put it less grandly, for its immense possibilities. We choose to do such things, said JFK, "not because they are easy, but because they are hard." And when you do such magnificently hard things—send sailing a Ferdinand Magellan or a Neil Armstrong—you open new human possibility in ways utterly unpredictable.

10   The greatest example? Who could have predicted that the moon voyages would create the most potent impetus to—and symbol of—environmental consciousness here on Earth: Earthrise, the now iconic Blue Planet photograph brought back by Apollo 8?

Ironically, that new consciousness about the uniqueness and fragility of Earth focused contemporary imagination away from space and back to Earth. We are now deep into that hyper-terrestrial phase, the age of iPod and Facebook, of social networking and eco-consciousness.

But look up from your BlackBerry one night. That is the moon. On it are exactly 12 sets of human footprints—untouched, unchanged, abandoned. For the first time in history, the moon is not just a mystery and a muse, but a nightly rebuke. A vigorous young president once summoned us to this new frontier, calling the voyage "the most hazardous and dangerous and greatest adventure on which man has ever embarked." And so we did it. We came. We saw. Then we retreated.

How could we?

---

*Spruce Goose was the informal name bestowed by critics on the H4 Hercules, a heavy transport aircraft designed and built during World War II by the Hughes Aircraft Company. Built almost entirely of birch (not spruce) because of wartime restrictions on war materials, the aircraft boasted the largest height and wingspan of any aircraft in history. Only one prototype was built, and the aircraft made only one flight, on November 2, 1947. It is currently housed at the Evergreen Aviation Museum in McMinnville, Oregon.

†Admired for its elegant design as well as its speed, the Concorde was a supersonic passenger airliner built by a British-French consortium. It was first flown in 1969, entered service in 1976 (with regular flights to and from London, Paris, Washington, and New York), and was retired in 2003, a casualty of economic pressures. Only twenty Concordes were built.

Critical Reading Practice

Look back at the Critical Reading for Summary box on page 5 of Chapter 1. Use each of the guidelines listed there to examine the essay by Charles Krauthammer. Note in the margins of the selection, or on a separate sheet of paper, the essay's main point, subpoints, and use of examples.

Persuasive Strategies

Clearly Defined Terms The validity of an argument depends to some degree on how carefully an author has defined key terms. Take the assertion, for example, that American society must be grounded in "family values." Just what do people who use this phrase mean by it? The validity of their argument depends on whether they and their readers agree on a definition of "family values"—as well as what it means to be "grounded in" family values. If an author writes that in the recent past, "America's elites accepted as a matter of course that a free society can sustain itself only through virtue and temperance in the people,"* readers need to know what exactly the author means by "elites" and by "virtue and temperance" before they can assess the validity of the argument. In such cases, the success of the argument—its ability to persuade—hinges on the definition of a term. So, in responding to an argument, be sure you (and the author) are clear on what exactly is being argued. Unless you are, no informed response is possible.

Note that in addition to their *denotative* meaning (their specific or literal meaning), many words carry a *connotative* meaning (their suggestive, associative, or emotional meaning). For example, the denotative meaning of "home" is simply the house or apartment where one lives. But the connotative meaning—with its associations of family, belongingness, refuge, safety, and familiarity—adds a significant emotional component to this literal meaning. (See more on connotation in "Emotionally Loaded Terms," pp. 58–59.)

In the course of his argument, Krauthammer writes of "America's abandonment of the moon" and of the fact that we have "retreated" from lunar exploration. Consider the words "abandon" and "retreat." What do these words mean to you? Look them up in a dictionary for precise definitions (note all possible meanings provided). In what contexts are we most likely to see these words used? What emotional meaning and significance do they generally carry? For example, what do we usually think of people who abandon a marriage or military units that retreat? To what extent does it appear to you that Krauthammer is using these words in accordance with one or more of their dictionary definitions, their denotations? To what extent does the force of his argument also depend upon the power of these words' connotative meanings?

*Charles Murray, "The Coming White Underclass," *Wall Street Journal,* October 20, 1993.

When writing a paper, you will need to decide, like Krauthammer, which terms to define and which you can assume the reader will define in the same way you do. As the writer of a critique, you should identify and discuss any undefined or ambiguous term that might give rise to confusion.

Fair Use of Information   Information is used as evidence in support of arguments. When you encounter such evidence, ask yourself two questions: (1) "Is the information accurate and up to date?" At least a portion of an argument becomes invalid when the information used to support it is wrong or stale. (2) "Has the author cited *representative* information?" The evidence used in an argument must be presented in a spirit of fair play. An author is less than ethical when he presents only the evidence favoring his own views even though he is well aware that contrary evidence exists. For instance, it would be dishonest to argue that an economic recession is imminent and to cite only indicators of economic downturn while ignoring and failing to cite contrary (positive) evidence.

"The Moon We Left Behind" is not an information-heavy essay. The success of the piece turns on the author's powers of persuasion, not on his use of facts and figures. Krauthammer does, however, offer some key facts relating to Project Apollo and the fact that President Obama was not inclined to back a NASA-operated lunar-landing program. And, in fact, Krauthammer's fears were confirmed in February 2010, about six months after he wrote "The Moon We Left Behind," when the president canceled NASA's plans for further manned space exploration flights in favor of government support for commercial space operations.

Logical Argumentation: Avoiding Logical Fallacies

At some point, you'll need to respond to the logic of the argument itself. To be convincing, an argument should be governed by principles of *logic*— clear and orderly thinking. This does *not* mean that an argument cannot be biased. A biased argument—that is, an argument weighted toward one point of view and against others, which is in fact the nature of argument— may be valid as long as it is logically sound.

Let's examine several types of faulty thinking and logical fallacies you will need to watch for.

Emotionally Loaded Terms   Writers sometimes attempt to sway readers by using emotionally charged words. Words with positive connotations (e.g., "family values") are intended to sway readers to the author's point of view; words with negative connotations (e.g., "paying the price") try to sway readers away from an opposing point of view. The fact that an author uses emotionally loaded terms does not necessarily invalidate an argument. Emotional appeals are perfectly legitimate and time-honored modes of persuasion. But in academic writing, which is grounded in logical argumentation, they should not be the *only* means of persuasion. You should be sensitive to *how* emotionally loaded terms are being used. In particular, are they being used deceptively or to hide the essential facts?

We've already noted Krauthammer's use of the emotionally loaded terms "abandonment" and "retreat" when referring to the end of the manned space program. Notice also his use of the term "Kumbaya" in the sentence declaring that the international space station was "created in a fit of post-Cold War internationalist absentmindedness as a place where people of differing nationality can sing 'Kumbaya' while weightless." "Kumbaya" is an African-American spiritual dating from the 1930s, often sung by scouts around campfires. Jeffrey Weiss reports on the dual connotations of this word: "The song was originally associated with human and spiritual unity, closeness and compassion, and it still is, but more recently it is also cited or alluded to in satirical, sarcastic or even cynical ways that suggest blind or false moralizing, hypocrisy, or naively optimistic views of the world and human nature."* Is Krauthammer drawing upon the emotional power of the original meaning or upon the more recent significance of this term? How does his particular use of "Kumbaya" strengthen (or weaken) his argument? What appears to be the difference in his mind between the value of the international space station and the value of returning to the moon? As someone evaluating the essay, you should be alert to this appeal to your emotions and then judge whether or not the appeal is fair and convincing. Above all, you should not let an emotional appeal blind you to shortcomings of logic, ambiguously defined terms, or a misuse of facts.

Ad Hominem Argument In an *ad hominem* argument, the writer rejects opposing views by attacking the person who holds them. By calling opponents names, an author avoids the issue. Consider this excerpt from a political speech:

> I could more easily accept my opponent's plan to increase revenues by collecting on delinquent tax bills if he had paid more than a hundred dollars in state taxes in each of the past three years. But the fact is, he's a millionaire with a millionaire's tax shelters. This man hasn't paid a wooden nickel for the state services he and his family depend on. So I ask you: Is *he* the one to be talking about taxes to *us?*

It could well be that the opponent has paid virtually no state taxes for three years; but this fact has nothing to do with, and is used as a ploy to divert attention from, the merits of a specific proposal for increasing revenues. The proposal is lost in the attack against the man himself, an attack that violates principles of logic. Writers (and speakers) should make their points by citing evidence in support of their views and by challenging contrary evidence.

In "The Moon We Left Behind," Krauthammer's only individual target is President Obama. While he does, at several points, unfavorably compare Obama to Kennedy, he does not do so in an *ad hominem* way. That is, he attacks

---

*Jeffery Weiss, "'Kumbaya': How did a sweet simple song become a mocking metaphor?" *Dallas Morning News.* 12 Nov. 2006.

Obama less for his personal qualities than for his policy decision to close down NASA's manned space program. At most, he laments that Obama "has expressed none of Kennedy's enthusiasm for human space exploration."

Faulty Cause and Effect   The fact that one event precedes another in time does not mean that the first event has caused the second. An example: Fish begin dying by the thousands in a lake near your hometown. An environmental group immediately cites chemical dumping by several manufacturing plants as the cause. But other causes are possible: A disease might have affected the fish; the growth of algae might have contributed to the deaths; or acid rain might be a factor. The origins of an event are usually complex and are not always traceable to a single cause. So you must carefully examine cause-and-effect reasoning when you find a writer using it. In Latin, this fallacy is known as *post hoc, ergo propter hoc* ("after this, therefore because of this").

Toward the end of "The Moon We Left Behind," Krauthammer declares that having turned our "imagination away from space and back to Earth...[w]e are now deep into that hyper-terrestrial phase, the age of iPod and Facebook, of social networking and eco-consciousness." He appears here to be suggesting a pattern of cause and effect: that as a people, we are no longer looking outward but, rather, turning inward; and this shift in our attention and focus has resulted in—or at least is a significant cause of—the death of the manned space program. Questions for a critique might include the following: (1) To what extent do you agree with Krauthammer's premise that we live in an inward-looking, rather than an outward-looking, age and that it is fair to call our present historical period "the age of iPod and Facebook"? (2) To what extent do you agree that because we may live in such an age, the space program no longer enjoys broad public or political support?

Either/Or Reasoning   Either/or reasoning also results from an unwillingness to recognize complexity. If in analyzing a problem an author artificially restricts the range of possible solutions by offering only two courses of action, and then rejects the one that he opposes, he cannot logically argue that the remaining course of action, which he favors, is therefore the only one that makes sense. Usually, several other options (at least) are possible. For whatever reason, the author has chosen to overlook them. As an example,

Tone

Tone refers to the overall emotional effect produced by a writer's choice of language. Writers might use especially emphatic words to create a tone: A film reviewer might refer to a "magnificent performance," or a columnist might criticize "sleazeball politics."

(continues)

These are extreme examples of tone; tone can also be more subtle, particularly if the writer makes a special effort *not* to inject emotion into the writing. As we indicated in the section on emotionally loaded terms, the fact that a writer's tone is highly emotional does not necessarily mean that the writer's argument is invalid. Conversely, a neutral tone does not ensure an argument's validity.

Many instructors discourage student writing that projects a highly emotional tone, considering it inappropriate for academic or preprofessional work. (One sure sign of emotion: the exclamation mark, which should be used sparingly.)

suppose you are reading a selection on genetic engineering in which the author builds an argument on the basis of the following:

> Research in gene splicing is at a crossroads: Either scientists will be carefully monitored by civil authorities and their efforts limited to acceptable applications, such as disease control; or, lacking regulatory guidelines, scientists will set their own ethical standards and begin programs in embryonic manipulation that, however well intended, exceed the proper limits of human knowledge.

Certainly, other possibilities for genetic engineering exist beyond the two mentioned here. But the author limits debate by establishing an either/or choice. Such a limitation is artificial and does not allow for complexity. As a critical reader, you need to be on the alert for reasoning based on restrictive, either/or alternatives.

Hasty Generalization   Writers are guilty of hasty generalization when they draw their conclusions from too little evidence or from unrepresentative evidence. To argue that scientists should not proceed with the Human Genome Project because a recent editorial urged that the project be abandoned is to make a hasty generalization. That lone editorial may be unrepresentative of the views of most individuals—both scientists and laypeople—who have studied and written about the matter. To argue that one should never obey authority because Stanley Milgram's Yale University experiments in the 1960s showed the dangers of obedience is to ignore the fact that Milgram's experiments were concerned primarily with obedience to *immoral* authority. The experimental situation was unrepresentative of most routine demands for obedience—for example, to obey a parental rule or to comply with a summons for jury duty—and a conclusion about the malevolence of all authority would be a hasty generalization.

False Analogy   Comparing one person, event, or issue to another may be illuminating, but it can also be confusing or misleading. Differences between the two may be more significant than their similarities, and conclusions drawn from one may not necessarily apply to the other. A candidate for governor or president who argues that her experience as CEO of a major business would make her effective in governing a state or the country is assuming an analogy between the business and the political/civic worlds that does not hold up to examination. Most businesses are hierarchical, or top down: when a CEO issues an order, he or she can expect it to be carried out without argument. But governors and presidents command only their own executive branches. They cannot issue orders to independent legislatures or courts (much less private citizens); they can only attempt to persuade. In this case the implied analogy fails to convince the thoughtful reader or listener.

Begging the Question   To beg the question is to assume as proven fact the very thesis being argued. To assert, for example, that America does not need a new health care delivery system because America currently has the best health care in the world does not prove anything: It merely repeats the claim in different—and equally unproven—words. This fallacy is also known as *circular reasoning*.

Non Sequitur   *Non sequitur* is Latin for "it does not follow"; the term is used to describe a conclusion that does not logically follow from the premise. "Since minorities have made such great strides in the past few decades," a writer may argue, "we no longer need affirmative action programs." Aside from the fact that the premise itself is arguable (*have* minorities made such great strides?), it does not follow that because minorities *may* have made great strides, there is no further need for affirmative action programs.

Oversimplification   Be alert for writers who offer easy solutions to complicated problems. "America's economy will be strong again if we all 'buy American,'" a politician may argue. But the problems of America's economy are complex and cannot be solved by a slogan or a simple change in buying habits. Likewise, a writer who argues that we should ban genetic engineering assumes that simple solutions ("just say no") will be sufficient to deal with the complex moral dilemmas raised by this new technology.

Exercise 2.3

Understanding Logical Fallacies

Make a list of the nine logical fallacies discussed in the preceding section. Briefly define each one in your own words. Then, in a group of three or four classmates, review your definitions and the examples we've provided for each logical fallacy. Collaborate with your group to find or invent additional examples for each of the fallacies. Compare your examples with those generated by the other groups in your class.

Writing to Entertain

Authors write not only to inform and persuade but also to entertain. One response to entertainment is a hearty laugh, but it is possible to entertain without encouraging laughter: A good book or play or poem may prompt you to reflect, grow wistful, become elated, get angry. Laughter is only one of many possible reactions. Like a response to an informative piece or an argument, your response to an essay, poem, story, play, novel, or film should be precisely stated and carefully developed. Ask yourself some of the following questions (you won't have space to explore all of them, but try to consider the most important ones):

- Did I care for the portrayal of a certain character?
- Did that character (or a group of characters united by occupation, age, ethnicity, etc.) seem overly sentimental, for example, or heroic?
- Did his adversaries seem too villainous or stupid?
- Were the situations believable?
- Was the action interesting or merely formulaic?
- Was the theme developed subtly or powerfully, or did the work come across as preachy or unconvincing?
- Did the action at the end of the work follow plausibly from what had come before? Was the language fresh and incisive or stale and predictable?

Explain as specifically as possible what elements of the work seemed effective or ineffective and why. Offer an overall assessment, elaborating on your views.

Question 2: To What Extent Do You Agree with the Author?

A critical evaluation consists of two parts. The first part, just discussed, assesses the accuracy and effectiveness of an argument in terms of the author's logic and use of evidence. The second part, discussed here, responds to the argument—that is, agrees or disagrees with it.

Identify Points of Agreement and Disagreement

Be precise in identifying where you agree and disagree with an author. State as clearly as possible what *you* believe, in relation to what the author believes, as presented in the piece. Whether you agree enthusiastically, agree with reservations, or disagree, you can organize your reactions in two parts:

- Summarize the author's position.
- State your own position and explain why you believe as you do. The elaboration, in effect, becomes an argument itself, and this is true regardless of the position you take.

Any opinion that you express is effective to the extent you support it by supplying evidence from your reading (which should be properly cited), your observation, or your personal experience. Without such evidence, opinions cannot be authoritative. "I thought the article on inflation was lousy." Or: "It was terrific." Why? "I just thought so, that's all." Such opinions have no value because the criticism is imprecise: The critic has taken neither the time to read the article carefully nor the time to carefully explore his or her own reactions.

Exercise 2.4

Exploring Your Viewpoints—in Three Paragraphs

Go to a Web site that presents short persuasive essays on current social issues, such as reason.com, opinion-pages.org, drudgereport.com, or Speakout.com. Or go to an Internet search engine like Google or Bing and type in a social issue together with the word "articles," "editorials," or "opinion," and see what you find. Locate a selection on a topic of interest that takes a clear, argumentative position. Print out the selection on which you choose to focus.

- Write one paragraph summarizing the author's key argument.
- Write two paragraphs articulating your agreement or disagreement with the author. (Devote each paragraph to a *single* point of agreement or disagreement.)

Be sure to explain why you think or feel the way you do and, wherever possible, cite relevant evidence—from your reading, experience, or observation.

Explore the Reasons for Agreement and Disagreement: Evaluate Assumptions

One way of elaborating your reactions to a reading is to explore the underlying *reasons* for agreement and disagreement. Your reactions are based largely on assumptions that you hold and how those assumptions compare with the author's. An *assumption* is a fundamental statement about the world and its operations that you take to be true. Often, a writer will express an assumption directly, as in this example:

> #1 One of government's most important functions is to raise and spend tax revenues on projects that improve the housing, medical, and nutritional needs of its citizens.

In this instance, the writer's claim is a direct expression of a fundamental belief about how the world, or some part of it, should work. The argumentative claim *is* the assumption. Just as often, an argument and its underlying assumption are not identical. In these cases, the assumption is some other statement that is implied by the argumentative claim—as in this example:

> #2 Human spaceflight is a waste of public money.

The logic of this second statement rests on an unstated assumption relating to the word *waste*. What, in this writer's view, is a *waste* of money? What is an effective or justified use? In order to agree or not with statement #2, a critical reader must know what assumption(s) it rests on. A good candidate for such an assumption would be statement #1. That is, a person who believes statement #1 about how governments ought to raise and spend money could well make statement #2. This may not be the only assumption underlying statement #2, but it could well be one of them.

Inferring and Implying Assumptions

Infer and *imply* are keywords relating to hidden, or unstated, assumptions; you should be clear on their meanings. A critical reader *infers* what is hidden in a statement and, through that inference, brings what is hidden into the open for examination. Thus, the critical reader infers from statement #2 on human spaceflight the writer's assumption (statement #1) on how governments should spend money. At the same time, the writer of statement #2 *implies* (hints at but does not state directly) an assumption about how governments should spend money. There will be times when writers make statements and are unaware of their own assumptions.

Assumptions provide the foundation on which entire presentations are built. You may find an author's assumptions invalid—that is, not supported by factual evidence. You may disagree with value-based assumptions underlying an author's position—for instance, what constitutes "good" or "correct" behavior. In both cases, you may well disagree with the conclusions that follow from these assumptions. Alternatively, when you find that your own assumptions are contradicted by actual experience, you may be forced to conclude that certain of your fundamental beliefs about the world and how it works were mistaken.

An Example of Hidden Assumptions from the World of Finance

An interesting example of an assumption fatally colliding with reality was revealed during a recent congressional investigation into the financial meltdown of late 2008 precipitated by the collapse of the home mortgage market—itself precipitated, many believed, by an insufficiently regulated banking and financial system run amuck. During his testimony before the House Oversight Committee in October of that year, former Federal Reserve chairman Alan Greenspan was grilled by committee chairman Henry Waxman (D-CA) about his "ideology"—essentially an assumption or set of assumptions that become a governing principle. (In the following transcript, you can substitute the word "assumption" for "ideology.")

Greenspan responded, "I do have an ideology. My judgment is that free, competitive markets are by far the unrivaled way to organize economies. We have tried regulation; none meaningfully worked." Greenspan defined an ideology as "a conceptual framework [for] the way people deal with reality. Everyone has one. You have to. To exist, you need an ideology." And he pointed out that the assumptions on which he and the Federal Reserve operated were supported by "the best banking lawyers in the business...and an outside counsel of expert professionals to advise on regulatory matters."

Greenspan then admitted that in light of the economic disaster engulfing the nation, he had found a "flaw" in his ideology—that actual experience had violated some of his fundamental beliefs. The testimony continues:

> Chairman Waxman: You found a flaw?
>
> Mr. Greenspan: I found a flaw in the model that I perceived is the critical functioning structure that defines how the world works, so to speak.
>
> Chairman Waxman: In other words, you found that your view of the world, your ideology, was not right, it was not working.
>
> Mr. Greenspan: Precisely. That's precisely the reason I was shocked, because I had been going for 40 years or more with very considerable evidence that it was working exceptionally well.*

The lesson? All the research, expertise, and logical argumentation in the world will fail if the premise (assumption, ideology) on which it is based turns out to be "flawed."

How do you determine the validity of assumptions once you have identified them? In the absence of more scientific criteria, you start by considering how well the author's assumptions stack up against your own experience, observations, reading, and values—while remaining honestly aware of the limits of your own personal knowledge.

Readers will want to examine the assumption at the heart of Krauthammer's essay: that continuing NASA's manned space program and, in particular, the program to return human beings to the moon, is a worthwhile enterprise. The writer of the critique that follows questions this assumption. But you may not: you may instead fully support such a program. That's your decision, perhaps made even *before* you read Krauthammer's essay, perhaps as a *result* of having read it. What you must do as a critical reader is to recognize assumptions, whether they are stated or not. You should spell

---

*United States. Cong. House Committee on Oversight and Government Reform. *The Financial Crisis and the Role of Federal Regulators.* 110th Cong., 2nd sess. Washington: GPO, 2008.

them out and then accept or reject them. Ultimately, your agreement or disagreement with an author will rest on your agreement or disagreement with that author's assumptions.

■ CRITIQUE

In Chapter 1 we focused on summary—the condensed presentation of ideas from another source. Summary is fundamental to much of academic writing because such writing relies so heavily on the works of others for the support of its claims. It's not going too far to say that summarizing is the critical thinking skill from which a majority of academic writing builds. However, most academic thinking and writing goes beyond summary. Generally, we use summary to restate our understanding of things we see or read. We then put that summary to use. In academic writing, one typical use of summary is as a prelude to critique.

A *critique* is a *formalized, critical reading of a passage*. It is also a personal response; but writing a critique is considerably more rigorous than saying that a movie is "great," or a book is "fascinating," or "I didn't like it." These are all responses, and, as such, they're a valid, even essential, part of your understanding of what you see and read. But such responses don't illuminate the subject—even for you—if you haven't explained how you arrived at your conclusions.

Your task in writing a critique is to turn your critical reading of a passage into a systematic evaluation in order to deepen your reader's (and your own) understanding of that passage. When you read a selection to critique, determine the following:

- What an author says
- How well the points are made
- What assumptions underlie the argument
- What issues are overlooked
- What implications can be drawn from such an analysis

When you write a critique, positive or negative, include the following:

- A fair and accurate summary of the passage
- Information and ideas from other sources (your reading or your personal experience and observations) if you think these are pertinent
- A statement of your agreement or disagreement with the author, backed by specific examples and clear logic
- A clear statement of your own assumptions

Remember that you bring to bear on any subject an entire set of assumptions about the world. Stated or not, these assumptions underlie every evaluative comment you make. You therefore have an obligation, both to the reader and to yourself, to clarify your standards by making your assumptions explicit. Not only do your readers stand to gain by your forthrightness, but you do as well. The process of writing a critical assessment forces you to examine your own knowledge, beliefs, and assumptions. Ultimately, the critique is a way of learning about yourself—yet another example of the ways in which writing is useful as a tool for critical thinking.

How to Write Critiques

You may find it useful to organize a critique into five sections: introduction, summary, assessment of the presentation (on its own terms), your response to the presentation, and conclusion.

The box on pages 68–69 offers guidelines for writing critiques. These guidelines do not constitute a rigid formula. Most professional authors write critiques that do not follow the structure outlined here. Until you are more confident and practiced in writing critiques, however, we suggest you follow these guidelines. They are meant not to restrict you, but rather to provide a workable sequence for writing critiques until a more fully developed set of experiences and authorial instincts are available to guide you.

Guidelines for Writing Critiques

- *Introduce.* Introduce both the passage under analysis and the author. State the author's main argument and the point(s) you intend to make about it.

  Provide background material to help your readers understand the relevance or appeal of the passage. This background material might include one or more of the following: an explanation of why the subject is of current interest; a reference to a possible controversy surrounding the subject of the passage or the passage itself; biographical information about the author; an account of the circumstances under which the passage was written; a reference to the intended audience of the passage.

- *Summarize.* Summarize the author's main points, making sure to state the author's purpose for writing.

- *Assess the presentation.* Evaluate the validity of the author's presentation, distinct from your points of agreement or disagreement. Comment on the author's success in achieving his or her purpose by reviewing three or four specific points. You might base your review on one or more of the following criteria:

  Is the information accurate?

  Is the information significant?

  Has the author defined terms clearly?

  Has the author used and interpreted information fairly?

  Has the author argued logically?

(continues)

- *Respond to the presentation.* Now it is your turn to respond to the author's views. With which views do you agree? With which do you disagree? Discuss your reasons for agreement and disagreement, when possible tying these reasons to assumptions—both the author's and your own. Where necessary, draw on outside sources to support your ideas.

- *Conclude.* State your conclusions about the overall validity of the piece—your assessment of the author's success at achieving his or her aims and your reactions to the author's views. Remind the reader of the weaknesses and strengths of the passage.

■ DEMONSTRATION: CRITIQUE

The critique that follows is based on Charles Krauthammer's op-ed piece "The Moon We Left Behind" (pp. 55–56), which we have already begun to examine. In this formal critique, you will see that it is possible to agree with an author's main point, at least provisionally, yet disagree with other elements of the argument. Critiquing a different selection, you could just as easily accept the author's facts and figures but reject the conclusion he draws from them. As long as you carefully articulate the author's assumptions and your own, explaining in some detail your agreement and disagreement, the critique is yours to take in whatever direction you see fit.

Let's summarize the preceding sections by returning to the core questions that guide critical reading. You will see how, when applied to Charles Krauthammer's argument, they help to set up a critique.

To What Extent Does the Author Succeed in His or Her Purpose?

To answer this question, you will need to know the author's purpose. Krauthammer wrote "The Moon We Left Behind" to persuade his audience that manned space flight must be supported. He makes his case in three ways: (1) he attacks the Obama administration's decision to "retreat" from the moon—i.e., to end NASA's manned space program; (2) he argues for the continuation of this program; and (3) he rebuts criticisms of the program. He aims to achieve this purpose by unfavorably comparing President Obama to President Kennedy, who challenged the nation to put a man on the moon within a decade; by arguing that we should return to the moon for "the wonder and glory of it"; and by challenging the claims that (a) we need first to fix the problems on earth and that (b) we can't afford such a program. One of the main tasks of the writer of a critique of Krauthammer is to explain the extent to which Krauthammer has achieved his purpose.

To What Extent Do You Agree with the Author?
Evaluate Assumptions

Krauthammer's argument rests upon two assumptions: (1) it is an essential characteristic of humankind to explore—and going to the moon was a great and worthwhile example of exploration; and (2) inspiring deeds are worth our expense and sacrifice—and thus continuing NASA's manned program and returning to the moon is worth our time, effort, and money. One who critiques Krauthammer must determine the extent to which she or he shares these assumptions. The writer of the model critique does, in fact, share Krauthammer's first assumption while expressing doubt about the second.

One must also determine the persuasiveness of Krauthammer's arguments for returning to the moon, as well as the persuasiveness of his counterarguments to those who claim this program is too impractical and too expensive. The writer of the model critique believes that Krauthammer's arguments are generally persuasive, even (in the conclusion) judging them "compelling." On the other hand, the critique ends on a neutral note—taking into account the problems with Krauthammer's arguments.

Remember that you don't need to agree with an author to believe that he or she has succeeded in his or her purpose. You may well admire how cogently and forcefully an author has argued without necessarily accepting her position. Conversely, you may agree with a particular author while acknowledging that he has not made a very strong case—and perhaps has even made a flawed one—for his point of view. For example, you may heartily approve of the point Krauthammer is making—that the United States should return to the moon. At the same time, you may find problematic the substance of his arguments and/or his strategy for arguing, particularly the dismissive manner in which he refers to the U.S. efforts in space over the last forty years:

> To be more precise: almost 40 years spent in low Earth orbit studying, well, zero-G nausea and sundry cosmic mysteries. We've done it with the most beautiful, intricate, complicated—and ultimately, hopelessly impractical—machine ever built by man: the space shuttle. We turned this magnificent bird into a truck for hauling goods and people to a tinkertoy we call the international space station....

Perhaps you support Krauthammer's position but find his sarcasm distasteful. That said, these two major questions for critical analysis (whether or not the author has been successful in his purpose and the extent to which you agree with the author's assumptions and arguments) are related. You will typically conclude that an author whose arguments have failed to persuade you has not succeeded in her purpose.

The selections you are likely to critique will be those, like Krauthammer's, that argue a specific position. Indeed, every argument you read is an invitation to agree or disagree. It remains only for you to speak up and justify your own position.

MODEL CRITIQUE

Andrew Harlan

Professor Rose Humphreys

Writing 2

11 January 2011

A Critique of Charles Krauthammer's

"The Moon We Left Behind"

(1)   In his 1961 State of the Union address, President John F. Kennedy issued a stirring challenge: "that this nation should commit itself to achieving the goal, before this decade is out, of landing a man on the Moon and returning him safely to the Earth." At the time, Kennedy's proposal seemed like science fiction. Even the scientists and engineers of the National Aeronautics and Space Administration (NASA) who were tasked with the job didn't know how to meet Kennedy's goal. Spurred, however, partly by a unified national purpose and partly by competition with the Soviet Union, which had beaten the United States into space with the first artificial satellite in 1957, the Apollo program to land men on the moon was launched. On July 20, 1969 Kennedy's challenge was met when Apollo 11 astronauts Neil Armstrong and Buzz Aldrin landed their lunar module on the Sea of Tranquility.

(2)   During the next few years, five more Apollo flights landed on the moon. In all, twelve Americans walked on the lunar surface; some even rode on a 4-wheeled "Rover," a kind of lunar dune buggy. But in December 1972 the Apollo program was cancelled. Since that time, some 40 years ago, humans have frequently returned to space, but none have returned to the moon. In February 2010 President Obama ended NASA's moon program, transferring responsibility for manned space exploration to private industry and re-focusing the government's resources on technological development and innovation. The administration had signaled its intentions earlier, in 2009. In July of that year, in an apparent attempt to rouse public opinion against the President's revised priorities for space exploration, Charles Krauthammer wrote "The Moon We Left Behind." It is these revised priorities that are the

focus of his op-ed piece, a lament for the end of lunar exploration and a powerful, if flawed, critique of the administration's decision.

(3)   Trained as a doctor and a psychiatrist, Charles Krauthammer is a prominent conservative columnist who has won the Pulitzer Prize for his political commentary. Krauthammer begins and ends his op-ed with expressions of dismay and anger at "America's abandonment of the moon." He unfavorably compares the current president, Barack Obama, with the "vigorous young" John F. Kennedy, in terms of their support for manned space exploration. It is inconceivable to Krauthammer that a program that achieved such technical glories and fired the imaginations of millions in so short a span of time has fallen into such decline.

(4)   Krauthammer anticipates the objections to his plea to keep America competitive in manned space exploration and to return to the moon. We have problems enough on earth, critics will argue. His answer: "If we waited to solve these perennial problems before continuing human progress, we'd still be living in caves." Concerning the expense of continuing the space program, Krauthammer argues that a fraction of the funds being "showered" on the government's stimulus programs (some $1 trillion) would be sufficient to support a viable space program. And as for practicality, he dismisses the idea that we need a practical reason to return to the moon. "We go," he argues, "for the wonder and glory of it. Or, to put it less grandly, for its immense possibilities." Ultimately, Krauthammer urges us to turn away from our mundane preoccupations and look up at the moon where humans once walked. How could Americans have gone so far, he asks, only to retreat?

(5)   In this opinion piece, Charles Krauthammer offers a powerful, inspiring defense of the American manned space program; and it's hard not to agree with him that our voyages to the moon captured the imagination and admiration of the world and set a new standard for scientific and technical achievement. Ever since that historic day in July 1969, people have been asking, "If we can land a man on the moon, why can't we [fill in your favorite social or political challenge]?" In a way, the fact that going to the

Harlan 3

moon was not especially practical made the achievement even more admirable: we went not for gain but rather to explore the unknown, to show what
human beings, working cooperatively and exercising their powers of reason
and their genius in design and engineering, can accomplish when sufficiently challenged. "We go," Krauthammer reminds us, "for the wonder and
glory of it...for its immense possibilities."

6   And what's wrong with that? For a relatively brief historical moment,
Americans, and indeed the peoples of the world, came together in pride and
anticipation as Apollo 11 sped toward the moon and, days later, as the lunar module descended to the surface. People collectively held their breaths
after an oxygen tank explosion disabled Apollo 13 on the way to the moon
and as the astronauts and Mission Control guided the spacecraft to a safe
return. A renewed moon program might similarly help to reduce divisions
among people—or at least among Americans—and highlight the reality
that we are all residents of the same planet, with more common interests
(such as protecting the environment) than is often apparent from our perennial conflicts. Krauthammer's praise of lunar exploration and its benefits
is so stirring that many who do not accept his conclusions may share his
disappointment and indignation at its demise.

7   "The Moon We Left Behind" may actually underestimate the practical
aspects of moon travel. "Any technological return," Krauthammer writes,
"is a bonus, not a reason." But so many valuable bonuses have emerged
from space flight and space exploration that the practical offshoots of lunar
exploration may in fact be a valid reason to return to the moon. For instance,
the technology developed from the special requirements of space travel has
found application in health and medicine (breast cancer detection, laser angi-
oplasty), industrial productivity and manufacturing technology, public safety
(radiation hazard detectors, emergency rescue cutters), and transportation
(studless winter tires, advanced lubricants, aids to school bus design) ("NASA
Spinoffs"). A renewed moon program would also be practical in providing a
huge employment stimulus to the economy. According to the NASA Langley

Harlan 4

Research Center, "At its peak, the Apollo program employed 400,000 people and required the support of over 20,000 industrial firms and universities" ("Apollo Program"). Returning to the moon would create comparable numbers of jobs in aerospace engineering, computer engineering, biology, general engineering, and meteorology, along with hosts of support jobs, from accounting to food service to office automation specialists ("NASA Occupations").

⑧   Krauthammer's emotional call may be stirring, but he dismisses too quickly some of the practical arguments against a renewed moon program. He appears to assume a degree of political will and public support for further lunar exploration that simply does not exist today. First, public support may be lacking—for legitimate reasons. It is not as if with a renewed lunar program we would be pushing boundaries and exploring the unknown: we would not be *going* to the moon; we would be *returning* to the moon. A significant percentage of the public, after considering the matter, may reasonably conclude: "Been there, done that." They may think, correctly or not, that we should set our sights elsewhere rather than collecting more moon rocks or taking additional stunning photographs from the lunar surface. Whatever practical benefits can be derived from going to the moon, many (if not all) have already been achieved. It would not be at all unreasonable for the public, even a public that supports NASA funding, to say, "Let's move on to other goals."

⑨   Second, Krauthammer's argument that poverty and disease and social ills will always be with us is politically flawed. This country faces financial pressures more serious than those at any other time since the Great Depression; and real, painful choices are being made by federal, state, and local officials about how to spend diminished tax dollars. The "vigorous young" JFK, launching the moon program during a time of expansion and prosperity, faced no such restrictions. Krauthammer's dismissal of ongoing poverty and other social ills is not likely to persuade elected representatives who are shuttering libraries, closing fire stations, ending unemployment benefits, and curtailing medical services. Nor will a public that is enduring these cuts be impressed by Krauthammer's call to "wonder and glory." Accurately or not, the public is likely to see the matter in terms of choices between a re-funded lunar program (nice, but optional) and renewed jobless benefits (essential). Not many politicians, in such distressed times, would be willing to go on record by voting for "nice" over "essential"—not if they wanted to keep their jobs.

(10) Finally, it's surprising—and philosophically inconsistent—for a conservative like Krauthammer, who believes in a smaller, less free-spending government, to be complaining about the withdrawal of massive government support for a renewed moon program. After all, the government hasn't banned moon travel; it has simply turned over such projects to private industry. If lunar exploration and other space flights appear commercially viable, there's nothing to prevent private companies and corporations from pursuing their own programs.

(11) In "The Moon We Left Behind," Charles Krauthammer stirs the emotions with his call for the United States to return to the moon; and, in terms of practical spinoffs, such a return could benefit this country in many ways. Krauthammer's argument is compelling, even if he too easily discounts the financial and political problems that will pose real obstacles to a renewed lunar program. Ultimately, what one thinks of Krauthammer's call to renew moon exploration depends on how one defines the human enterprise and the purpose of collective agreement and collective effort— what we call "government." To what extent should this purpose be to solve problems in the here and now? To what extent should it be to inquire and to push against the boundaries for the sake of discovery and exploration, to learn more about who we are and about the nature of our universe? There have always been competing demands on national budgets and more than enough problems to justify spending every tax dollar on problems of poverty, social justice, crime, education, national security, and the like. Krauthammer argues that if we are to remain true to our spirit of inquiry, we cannot ignore the investigation of space because scientific and technological progress is also a human responsibility. He argues that we can—indeed, we must—do both: look to our needs here at home and also dream and explore. But the public may not find his argument convincing.

Harlan 6

Works Cited

"Apollo Program." *Apollo Program HSF*. National Aeronautics and Space
    Administration, 2 July 2009. Web. 16 Sept. 2010.

Harwood, William. "Obama Kills Moon Program, Endorses Commercial Space."
    Spaceflight Now. Spaceflight Now, 1 Feb. 2010. Web. 13 Sept. 2010.

Kennedy, John F. "Rice University Speech." 12 Sept. 1962. *Public Papers
    of the Presidents of the United States*. Vol. 1., 1962. 669–70. Print.

---. "Special Message to the Congress on Urgent National Needs." *John F.
    Kennedy Presidential Library and Museum*. John F. Kennedy Presiden-
    tial Library and Museum, 25 May 1961. Web. 14 Sept. 2010.

Krauthammer, Charles. "The Moon We Left Behind." *Washington Post*
    17 July 2009: A17. Print.

"NASA Occupations." *Nasajobsoccupations*. National Aeronautics and
    Space Administration, 28 July 2009. Web. 12 Sept. 2010.

"NASA Spinoffs: Bringing Space Down to Earth." *The Ultimate Space Place*.
    National Aeronautics and Space Administration, 2 Feb. 2004. Web.
    18 Sept. 2010.

Exercise 2.5

Informal Critique of the Model Critique

Before reading our analysis of this model critique, write your own informal
response to it. What are its strengths and weaknesses? To what extent does
the critique follow the general Guidelines for Writing Critiques that we outlined on pages 68–69? To the extent that it varies from the guidelines, speculate on why. Jot down ideas for a critique that takes a different approach to
Krauthammer's op-ed.

■ Critical Reading for Critique

- *Use the tips from Critical Reading for Summary on page 5.* Remember to examine the context; note the title and subtitle; identify the
  main point; identify the subpoints; break the reading into sections;

(continues)

distinguish between points, examples, and counterarguments; watch for transitions within and between paragraphs; and read actively.

- *Establish the writer's primary purpose in writing.* Is the piece meant primarily to inform, persuade, or entertain?
- *Evaluate informative writing. Use these criteria (among others):*
  Accuracy of information
  Significance of information
  Fair interpretation of information
- *Evaluate persuasive writing. Use these criteria (among others):*
  Clear definition of terms
  Fair use and interpretation of information
  Logical reasoning
- *Evaluate writing that entertains. Use these criteria (among others):*
  Interesting characters
  Believable action, plot, and situations
  Communication of theme
  Use of language
- *Decide whether you agree or disagree with the writer's ideas, position, or message.* Once you have determined the extent to which an author has achieved his or her purpose, clarify your position in relation to the writer's.

The Strategy of the Critique

- Paragraphs 1 and 2 of the model critique introduce the topic. They provide a context by way of a historical review of America's lunar-exploration program from 1962 to 1972, leading up to the president's decision to scrub plans for a return to the moon. The two-paragraph introduction also provides a context for Krauthammer's—and the world's—admiration for the stunning achievement of the Apollo program. The second paragraph ends with the thesis of the critique, the writer's overall assessment of Krauthammer's essay.

- Paragraphs 3–4 introduce Krauthammer and summarize his arguments.

  - Paragraph 3 provides biographical information about Krauthammer and describes his disappointment and indignation at "America's abandonment of the moon."
  - Paragraph 4 treats Krauthammer's anticipated objections to the continuation of the manned space program and rebuttals to these objections.

- Paragraphs 5, 6, and 7 support Krauthammer's argument.
    - Paragraphs 5 and 6 begin the writer's evaluation, focusing on the reasons that Krauthammer finds so much to admire in the lunar-exploration program. Most notably: it was a stunning technological achievement that brought the people of the world together (if only briefly). The writer shares this admiration.
    - Paragraph 7 indirectly supports Krauthammer by pointing out that even though he downplays the practical benefits of lunar exploration, the space program has yielded numerous practical technological spinoffs.
- Paragraphs 8–10 focus on the problems with Krauthammer's argument.
    - In paragraph 8, the writer points out that there is little public support for returning to the moon, a goal that many people will see as already accomplished and impractical for the immediate future.
    - Paragraph 9 argues that Krauthammer underestimates the degree to which an electorate worried about skyrocketing deficits and high unemployment would object to taxpayer dollars being used to finance huge government spending on a renewed lunar program.
    - Paragraph 10 points out how surprising it is that a conservative like Krauthammer would advocate a government-financed manned space program when the same goal could be accomplished by private enterprise.
- Paragraph 11 concludes the critique, summing up the chief strengths and weaknesses of Krauthammer's argument and pointing out that readers' positions will be determined by their views on the "human enterprise" and the purpose of government. How do we balance our "human responsibility" for the expansion of knowledge and technology with the competing claims of education, poverty, crime, and national security?

WRITING ASSIGNMENT: CRITIQUE

Read and then write a critique of "The Common App Fallacy," in which a columnist for New York University's *Washington Square News* argues against the wisdom of using the Common Application in the college application process. You might read such an essay in your own college newspaper; here is your opportunity to respond. The piece originally appeared in the *Washington Square News* on January 22, 2008.

Before reading, review the tips presented in the Critical Reading for Critique box (pp. 76–77). When you're ready to write your critique, start by jotting down notes in response to the tips for critical reading and the earlier discussions of evaluating writing in this chapter. What assumptions does Damon Beres make? Review the logical fallacies on pages 58–62, and identify any that appear in the essay. Work out your ideas on paper, perhaps producing an outline. Then write a rough draft of your critique. Review the reading and revise your rough draft at least once before considering it finished. You may want to look ahead to Chapter 6, "Writing as a Process," to help guide you through writing your critique.

For an additional exercise in writing critiques, see Chapter 8, a practice chapter that assembles readings on the topic of the changing nature of jobs in a global economy. You will have the opportunity to write a critique that you then place into a larger argument.

THE COMMON APP FALLACY

Damon Beres

It's a small miracle that I'm able to have this column for you today. No, I'm not a victim of crippling arthritis, nor did my sticky laptop keyboard give me carpal tunnel syndrome. Rather, it dawned on me that I was one of over 11,000 chosen from a pool of nearly 34,000 students, as the Office of Undergraduate Admissions reports, to join New York University's freshman class last year. If I were a smarter man, I'd start playing the lottery.

Truth is, college applications are a crapshoot in this day and age. My friends back home, with GPAs that resemble the population of China and extracurriculars that make Jimmy Carter look like a lazy old coot, are getting shut out of the Ivies, shut out of their "targets," and, well, shut out of everywhere. At this rate, it seems the only thing most of them will be getting into is antidepressants.

Colleges nationwide, from Yale University to the University of South Carolina, have been reporting substantial increases in applications for years now. Part of that is good, as that probably means that more kids are interested in pursuing higher education. The downside, of course, is that many aren't getting into the schools they want or deserve.

In order to counter this, students apply to as many schools as they can, spitting applications out like bitter saliva. The average from people I've talked to seems to be around 10, though many that I know have applied to upward of 16. What they don't seem to realize is that hedging their bets like this is only making things worse for everyone. Schools have a larger, more competitive application pool to pick from, and kids are taking spots at universities that they may, in fact, have little to no interest in.

5   It's not their fault, though; universities, the College Board, and worst of all, the Common Application are encouraging this dance. The College Board makes it easy to blast those precious SAT scores out to every college under the sun, provided mommy and daddy's credit card isn't maxed out, while the Common Application makes shuttling apps to any number of schools a simple process of point-and-click. With such tools at their disposal, and knowing that the competition will make full use of them, how could any student resist mass applications?

As the nation's top "dream school," as reported by the *Princeton Review* (and why not? We've had Olsens, an Osment and that little girl from *Matilda*), NYU is in a prime position to affect the application process. Harvard caused quite a stir when it got rid of early admissions, so why won't NYU's admissions department do something similar and become a nationwide trendsetter?

It's simple, really: Get rid of the Common Application. Besides pulling in easy money from application fees, what benefit does it provide? New York University is already a competitive institution, a school that's more than able to play in the big leagues, so it certainly doesn't need the extra applicants that the Common App brings in. The more universities that can shake faith in the Common App, the better; it's a cheap, money-making scheme that homogenizes applicants and schools alike. A supplemental essay or two for each school—essays that can easily be adapted from essays for other schools—certainly can't make up for a personalized, unique application that shows a serious interest in the school. It's troubling that nearly 100 universities, including the likes of Dartmouth, Northwestern and Yale, are Common App–exclusive, as it indicates that the college application process has turned from an individualized search for the right place into a cold, sterile business. NYU has a reputation, so why doesn't it use it?

Maybe it has to be a joint endeavor. Maybe high school students should actually care about their applications, which might mean taking the time to search for a handful of schools that they feel are perfect fits. Maybe the College Board and Common App should go all-out with their greed and charge more to send out scores and applications to discourage students from sending them out with reckless abandon. Maybe it doesn't all have to be such a crapshoot.

For the class of 2011, Williams College accepted 1,194 students out of 6,448. Massachusetts Institute of Technology accepted 1,553 out of 12,445. Brown University accepted 2,683 out of 19,059. Princeton University accepted 1,838 out of 18,942. I have about a one-in-five chance of winning on a "Crazy Cash" scratch-off ticket. Shouldn't students have a better chance at getting into college?

Explanatory Synthesis

■ WHAT IS A SYNTHESIS?

A *synthesis* is a written discussion that draws on two or more sources. It follows that your ability to write syntheses depends on your ability to infer relationships among sources like these:

- Essays
- Fiction
- Interviews

- Articles
- Lectures
- Visual media

This process is nothing new for you because you infer relationships all the time—say, between something you've read in the newspaper and something you've seen for yourself, or between the teaching styles of your favorite and least favorite instructors. In fact, if you've written research papers, you've already written syntheses.

In a *synthesis,* you make explicit the relationships that you have inferred among separate sources.

Summary and Critique as a Basis for Synthesis

The skills you've already learned and practiced in the previous two chapters will be vital in writing syntheses. Before you're in a position to draw relationships between two or more sources, you must understand what those sources say; you must be able to *summarize* those sources. Readers will frequently benefit from at least partial summaries of sources in your synthesis essays. At the same time, you must go beyond summary to make judgments—judgments based on your *critical reading* of your sources: what conclusions you've drawn about the quality and validity of these sources, whether you agree or disagree with the points made in your sources, and why you agree or disagree.

Inference as a Basis for Synthesis:
Moving Beyond Summary and Critique

In a synthesis, you go beyond the critique of individual sources to determine the relationships among them. Is the information in source B, for example, an extended illustration of the generalizations in source A? Would it be useful to compare and contrast source C with source B? Having read and considered sources A, B, and C, can you infer something else—in other words, D (not a source, but your own idea)?

Because a synthesis is based on two or more sources, you will need to be selective when choosing information from each. It would be neither possible nor desirable, for instance, to discuss in a ten-page paper on the American Civil War every point that the authors of two books make about their subject. What you as a writer must do is select from each source the ideas and information that best allow you to achieve your purpose.

■ PURPOSE

Your purpose in reading source materials and then drawing on them to write your own material is often reflected in the wording of an assignment. For instance, consider the following assignments on the Civil War:

American History: Evaluate the author's treatment of the origins of the Civil War.

Economics: Argue the following proposition, in light of your readings: "The Civil War was fought not for reasons of moral principle but for reasons of economic necessity."

Government: Prepare a report on the effects of the Civil War on Southern politics at the state level between 1870 and 1917. Focus on one state.

Mass Communications: Discuss how the use of photography during the Civil War may have affected the perceptions of the war by Northerners living in industrial cities.

Literature: Select two Southern writers of the twentieth century whose work you believe was influenced by the divisive effects of the Civil War. Discuss the ways this influence is apparent in a novel or a group of short stories written by each author. The works should not be *about* the Civil War.

Applied Technology: Compare and contrast the technology of warfare available in the 1860s with the technology available a century earlier.

Each of these assignments creates a particular purpose for writing. Having located sources relevant to your topic, you would select for possible use in a paper only the parts of those sources that helped you in fulfilling this purpose. And how you used those parts—how you related them to other material from other sources—would also depend on your purpose.

Example: Same Sources, Different Uses

If you were working on the government assignment, you might draw on the same source as a student working on the literature assignment by referring to Robert Penn Warren's novel *All the King's Men*, about Louisiana politics in the early part of the twentieth century. But because the purposes of the two

---

■ **Where Do We Find Written Syntheses?**

Here are just a few of the types of writing that involve synthesis:

ACADEMIC WRITING

- **Analysis papers** synthesize and apply several related theoretical approaches.
- **Research papers** synthesize multiple sources.
- **Argument papers** synthesize different points into a coherent claim or position.
- **Essay exams** demonstrate understanding of course material through comparing and contrasting theories, viewpoints, or approaches in a particular field.

WORKPLACE WRITING

- **Newspaper and magazine articles** synthesize primary and secondary sources.
- **Position papers and policy briefs** compare and contrast solutions for solving problems.
- **Business plans** synthesize ideas and proposals into one coherent plan.
- **Memos and letters** synthesize multiple ideas, events, and proposals into concise form.
- **Web sites** synthesize information from various sources to present in Web pages and related links.

---

assignments are different, you and the other student would make different uses of this source. The parts or aspects of the novel that you find worthy of detailed analysis might be mentioned only in passing—or not at all—by the other student.

■ USING YOUR SOURCES

Your purpose determines not only what parts of your sources you will use but also how you will relate those parts to one another. Since the very essence of synthesis is the combining of information and ideas, you must have some basis on which to combine them. *Some relationships among the material in your sources must make them worth synthesizing.* It follows that the better able you are to discover such relationships, the better able you will be to use your sources in writing syntheses. Notice that the mass communications assignment requires you to draw a *cause-and-effect* relationship between photographs of the war and Northerners' perceptions of the war. The applied technology assignment requires you to *compare and contrast* state-of-the-art weapons technology in the eighteenth and nineteenth centuries. The economics assignment requires you to *argue* a proposition. In each case, *your purpose will determine how you relate your source materials to one another.*

Consider some other examples. You may be asked on an exam question or in the instructions for a paper to *describe* two or three approaches to prison reform during the past decade. You may be asked to *compare and contrast* one country's approach to imprisonment with another's. You may be asked to *develop an argument* of your own on this subject, based on your reading. Sometimes (when you are not given a specific assignment) you determine your own purpose: You are interested in exploring a particular subject; you are interested in making a case for one approach or another. In any event, your purpose shapes your essay. Your purpose determines which sources you research, which ones you use, which parts of them you use, at which points in your paper you use them, and in what manner you relate them to one another.

■ TYPES OF SYNTHESES: EXPLANATORY AND ARGUMENT

In this and the next chapter we categorize syntheses into two main types: *explanatory* and *argument*. The easiest way to recognize the difference between the two types may be to consider the difference between a news article and an editorial on the same subject. For the most part, we'd say that the main purpose of the news article is to convey *information,* and that the main purpose of the editorial is to convey *opinion* or *interpretation*. Of course, this distinction is much too simplified: News articles often convey opinion or bias, sometimes subtly, sometimes openly; and editorials often convey unbiased information along with opinion. But as a practical matter we can generally agree on the distinction between a news article that primarily conveys information and an editorial that primarily conveys opinion. You should be able to observe this distinction in the selections shown here as Explanation and Argument.

Explanation: News Article from the New York Times

WHILE WARNING ABOUT FAT, U.S. PUSHES CHEESE SALES

By Michael Moss

November 6, 2010

Domino's Pizza was hurting early last year. Domestic sales had fallen, and a survey of big pizza chain customers left the company tied for the worst tasting pies.

Then help arrived from an organization called Dairy Management. It teamed up with Domino's to develop a new line of pizzas with 40 percent more cheese, and proceeded to devise and pay for a $12 million marketing campaign.

Consumers devoured the cheesier pizza, and sales soared by double digits. "This partnership is clearly working," Brandon Solano, the Domino's vice president for brand innovation, said in a statement to The New York Times.

But as healthy as this pizza has been for Domino's, one slice contains as much as two-thirds of a day's maximum recommended amount of saturated fat, which has been linked to heart disease and is high in calories.

5   And Dairy Management, which has made cheese its cause, is not a private business consultant. It is a marketing creation of the United States Department of Agriculture—the same agency at the center of a federal anti-obesity drive that discourages over-consumption of some of the very foods Dairy Management is vigorously promoting....

Argument: Editorial from the Boston Globe

GOT TOO MUCH CHEESE?

By Derrick Z. Jackson

November 9, 2010

...The chief executive of Dairy Management, Thomas Gallagher,... declined to be interviewed by the [New York] Times, but in a column last year in a trade publication, he wrote, "More cheese on pizza equals more cheese sales. In fact, if every pizza included one more ounce of cheese, we would see an additional 250 million pounds of cheese annually."

Emboldened by its success with cheese, Dairy Management is now reportedly working on bamboozling the public that chocolate milk is a sports recovery drink and persuading children to eat green beans by slathering them with cheese.

A year ago, at a joint press conference held by the USDA, the National Dairy Council and the National Football League to promote exercise, Gallagher said, "Child nutrition, particularly in schools, has been a cornerstone of the National Dairy Council for nearly a century. The program centers on youth taking the lead in changing the school environment."

The truth makes this a galling proclamation. Despite all the nutrition initiatives launched by the Obama administration, the cornerstone of federal policy continues to clog the nation's arteries, making a mockery of programs boasting how youth can take the lead. What is a cornerstone for the USDA is a gravestone for nutrition.

We'll say, for the sake of convenience, that the news article *explains* the contradictory messages on nutrition that the federal government is communicating and that the editorial *argues* that the contradiction is damaging. This important distinction between explanation and argument extends beyond the news to other materials you might consult while doing research. Consider a second set of passages:

What Are Genetically Modified (GM) Foods?

GENETICALLY MODIFIED FOODS AND ORGANISMS
The United States Department of Energy

November 5, 2008

Combining genes from different organisms is known as recombinant DNA technology, and the resulting organism is said to be "genetically modified," "genetically engineered," or "transgenic." GM products (current or those in development) include medicines and vaccines, foods and food ingredients, feeds, and fibers.

Locating genes for important traits—such as those conferring insect resistance or desired nutrients—is one of the most limiting steps in the process. However, genome sequencing and discovery programs for hundreds of organisms are generating detailed maps along with data-analyzing technologies to understand and use them.

In 2006, 252 million acres of transgenic crops were planted in 22 countries by 10.3 million farmers. The majority of these crops were herbicide- and insect-resistant soybeans, corn, cotton, canola, and alfalfa. Other crops grown commercially or field-tested are a sweet potato resistant to a virus that could decimate most of the African harvest, rice with increased iron and vitamins that may alleviate chronic malnutrition in Asian countries, and a variety of plants able to survive weather extremes.

On the horizon are bananas that produce human vaccines against infectious diseases such as hepatitis B; fish that mature more quickly; cows that are resistant to bovine spongiform encephalopathy (mad cow disease); fruit and nut trees that yield years earlier, and plants that produce new plastics with unique properties.

WHY A GM FREEZE?
The GM Freeze Campaign

November 11, 2010

Genetic modification in food and farming raises many fundamental environmental, social, health and ethical concerns. There is increasing evidence of contamination of conventional crops and wild plants, and potential damage to wildlife. The effects on human health of eating these foods remain uncertain and some scientists are calling for much more rigorous safety testing. It is clear that further research into all these issues is vital. Furthermore the public has not been properly involved in decision making processes, despite strong public support for the precautionary approach to GM in the [United Kingdom] and the [European Union].

Much more time is needed to assess the need for and implications of using genetic modification in food and farming, in particular the increasing control of corporations who rely on patents to secure their future markets.

Both of these passages deal with the topic of genetically modified (GM) foods. The first is excerpted from a largely informational Web site published by the U.S. Department of Energy, which oversees the Human Genome Project, the government's ongoing effort to map gene sequences and apply that knowledge. We say the DOE account is "largely informational" because readers can find a great deal of information here about genetically modified foods. At the same time, however, the DOE explanation is subtly biased in favor of genetic modification: note the absence of any language raising questions about the ethics or safety of GM foods; note also the use of terms like "desired nutrients" and "insect resistance"—with their positive connotations. The DOE examples show GM foods in a favorable light, and the passage as a whole assumes the value and importance of genetic manipulation.

As we see in the second passage, however, that assumption is not shared by all. Excerpted from a Web site advocating a freeze on genetically modified crops, the second passage primarily argues against the ethics and safety of such manipulation, calling for more study before modified crops are released widely into the environment. At the same time, the selection provides potentially important explanatory materials: (1) the claim that there is "increasing evidence of contamination of conventional crops and wild plants, and potential damage to wildlife"; (2) the claim that corporations control GM crops, and potentially the food supply, through patents. We can easily and quickly confirm these claims through research; if confirmed, the information—which is nested in a primarily argumentative piece—could prove useful in a paper on GM foods.

So while it is fair to say that most writing can be broadly categorized as explanatory or argumentative, understand that in practice, many of the materials you read will be a mix: *primarily* one or the other but not altogether one or the other. It will be your job as an alert, critical reader to determine when authors are explaining or arguing—sometimes in the same sentence.

For instance, you might read the following in a magazine article: "The use of goats to manufacture anti-clotting proteins for humans in their milk sets a dangerous precedent." Perhaps you did not know that scientists have genetically manipulated goats (by inserting human genes) to create medicines. That much of the statement is factual. It is explanatory. Whether or not this fact "sets a dangerous precedent" is an argument. You could agree or not with the argument; but your views would not change the fact about the genetic manipulation of farm animals. Even within a single sentence, then, you must be alert to distinguishing between explanation and argument.

■ HOW TO WRITE SYNTHESES

Although writing syntheses can't be reduced to a lockstep method, it should help you to follow the guidelines listed in the box below.

In this chapter we'll focus on explanatory syntheses. In the next chapter, we'll discuss the argument synthesis.

Guidelines for Writing Syntheses

- *Consider your purpose in writing.* What are you trying to accomplish in your paper? How will this purpose shape the way you approach your sources?

- *Select and carefully read your sources* according to your purpose. Then reread the passages, mentally summarizing each. Identify those aspects or parts of your sources that will help you fulfill your purpose. When rereading, *label* or *underline* the sources' main ideas, key terms, and any details you want to use in the synthesis.

- *Take notes on your reading.* In addition to labeling or underlining key points in the readings, you might write brief one- or two-sentence summaries of each source. This will help you in formulating your thesis statement and in choosing and organizing your sources later.

- *Formulate a thesis.* Your thesis is the main idea that you want to present in your synthesis. It should be expressed as a complete sentence. You might do some predrafting about the ideas discussed in the readings in order to help you work out a thesis. If you've written one-sentence summaries of the readings, looking over the summaries will help you to brainstorm connections between readings and to devise a thesis.

  When you write your synthesis drafts, you will need to consider where your thesis fits in your paper. Sometimes the thesis is the first sentence, but more often it is *the final sentence of the first paragraph.* If you are writing an *inductively arranged* synthesis (see p. 147), the thesis sentence may not appear until the final paragraphs.

- *Decide how you will use your source material.* How will the information and the ideas in the passages help you fulfill your purpose?

- *Develop an organizational plan,* according to your thesis. How will you arrange your material? It is not necessary to prepare a formal outline. But you should have some plan that will indicate the order in which you will present your material and the relationships among your sources.

- *Draft the topic sentences for the main sections.* This is an optional step, but you may find it a helpful transition from organizational plan to first draft.

- *Write the first draft* of your synthesis, following your organizational plan. Be flexible with your plan, however. Frequently, you will use an outline to get started. As you write, you may discover new ideas and make room for them by adjusting the outline. When this happens, reread your work frequently, making sure that your thesis still accounts for what follows and that what follows still logically supports your thesis.

(continues)

- *Document your sources.* You must do this by crediting sources within the body of the synthesis—citing the author's last name and the page number from which the point was taken—and then providing full citation information in a list of "Works Cited" at the end. Don't open yourself to charges of plagiarism! (See pp. 46–47.)

- *Revise your synthesis,* inserting transitional words and phrases where necessary. Make sure that the synthesis reads smoothly, logically, and clearly from beginning to end. Check for grammatical correctness, punctuation, and spelling.

Note: The writing of syntheses is a recursive process, and you should accept a certain amount of backtracking and reformulating as inevitable. For instance, in developing an organizational plan (Step 6 of the procedure), you may discover a gap in your presentation that will send you scrambling for another source—back to Step 2. You may find that formulating a thesis and making inferences among sources occur simultaneously; indeed, inferences are often made before a thesis is formulated. Our recommendations for writing syntheses will give you a structure that will get you started. But be flexible in your approach; expect discontinuity and, if possible, be assured that through backtracking and reformulating, you will produce a coherent, well-crafted paper.

■ THE EXPLANATORY SYNTHESIS

Many of the papers you write in college will be more or less explanatory in nature. An explanation helps readers understand a topic. Writers explain when they divide a subject into its component parts and present them to the reader in a clear and orderly fashion. Explanations may entail descriptions that re-create in words some object, place, emotion, event, sequence of events, or state of affairs.

- As a student reporter, you may need to explain an event—to relate when, where, and how it took place.

- In a science lab, you would observe the conditions and results of an experiment and record them for review by others.

- In a political science course, you might review research on a particular subject—say, the complexities underlying the debate over gay marriage—and then present the results of your research to your professor and the members of your class.

Your job in writing an explanatory paper—or in writing the explanatory portion of an argumentative paper—is not to argue a particular point, but rather *to present the facts in a reasonably objective manner.* Of course, explanatory papers, like other academic papers, should be based on a thesis (see pp. 99–100). But the purpose of a thesis in an explanatory paper is less to advance a particular opinion than to focus the various facts contained in the paper.

■ DEMONSTRATION: EXPLANATORY SYNTHESIS—GOING UP? AN ELEVATOR RIDE TO SPACE

To illustrate how the process of synthesis works, we'll begin with a number of short extracts from several articles on the same subject.

Suppose you were writing a paper on an intriguing idea you came across in a magazine: a space elevator—a machine that would lift objects into earth orbit, and beyond, not by blasting them free of earth's gravity using rockets but by lifting them in ways similar to (but also different from) the way elevators on earth lift people and material in tall buildings. Once considered a fancy of science fiction, the idea has received serious attention among scientists and even NASA. In fact, an elevator to space could be built relatively soon.

Fascinated by the possibility of an elevator to space being built in your lifetime, you decide to conduct some research with the goal of *explaining* what you discover to interested classmates.

Exercise 3.1

Exploring the Topic

Read the selections that follow on the subject of space elevators. Before continuing with the discussion after the selections, write a page or two of responses. You might imagine the ways an elevator to space might change you and, more broadly, the economy, the military, and international relations. What do you imagine will concern some people about a space elevator? What do you think might be of interest to journalists, the military, politicians, businesspeople, entertainers, artists?

In the following pages we present excerpts from the kinds of source materials you might locate during the research process.

Note: To save space and for the purpose of demonstration, we offer excerpts from four sources only; a full list of sources appears in the "Works Cited" of the model synthesis on pages 119–120. In preparing your paper, of course, you would draw on the entire articles from which these extracts were taken. (The discussion of how these passages can form the basis of an explanatory synthesis resumes on p. 98.)

THE HISTORY OF THE SPACE ELEVATOR

P.K. Aravind

P. K. Aravind teaches in the Department of Physics at the Worcester Polytechnic Institute, Worcester, Massachusetts. The following is excerpted from "The Physics of the Space Elevator" in The American Journal of Physics *(May 2007).*

I. Introduction

A space elevator is a tall tower rising from a point on the Earth's equator to a height well above a geostationary orbit,* where it terminates in a counterweight (see Fig. 1a). Although the idea of such a structure is quite old, it is only within the last decade or so that it has attracted serious scientific attention. NASA commissioned some studies of the elevator in the 1990s that concluded that it would be feasible to build one and use it to transport payload cheaply into space and also to launch spacecraft on voyages to other planets.[1] Partly as a result of this study, a private organization called Liftport[2] was formed in 2003 with the goal of constructing a space elevator and enlisting the support of universities, research labs, and businesses that might have an interest in this venture. Liftport's website features a timer that counts down the seconds to the opening of its elevator on 12 April 2018. Whether that happens or not, the space elevator represents an application of classical mechanics to an engineering project on a gargantuan scale that would have an enormous impact on humanity if it is realized. As such, it is well worth studying and thinking about for all the possibilities it has to offer.

This article explains the basic mechanical principles underlying the construction of the space elevator and discusses some of its principal applications. It should be accessible to anyone who has had a course in undergraduate mechanics and could help give students in such a course a feeling for some of the contemporary applications of mechanics. Before discussing the physics of the space elevator, we recall some of the more interesting facts of its history. The earliest mention of anything like the elevator seems to have been in the book of Genesis, which talks of an attempt by an ancient civilization to build a tower to heaven—the "Tower of Babel"—that came to naught because of a breakdown of communication between the participants. In more recent times the concept of the space elevator was first proposed by the Russian physicist Konstantin Tsiolkovsky in 1895 and then again by the Leningrad engineer, Yuri Artsutanov, in 1960.[3] The concept was rediscovered by the American engineer, Jerome Pearson,[4] in 1975. In 1978 Arthur Clarke brought the idea to the attention of the general public through his novel *Fountains of Paradise*[5] and at about the same time Charles Sheffield, a physicist, wrote a novel[6] centered on the same concept. Despite this publicity, the idea of the elevator did not really catch on among scientists because an analysis of its structure showed that no known material was strong enough to build it.

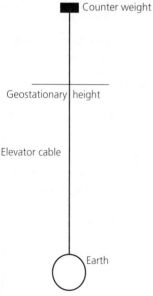

Figure 1a

*Geostationary orbit, also referred to as geostationary earth orbit (or GEO), marks the altitude above the earth's equator (22,236 miles) at which a satellite will rotate at the same speed as the earth itself and, thus, appear to remain motionless in the sky.

This pessimism was largely neutralized by the discovery of carbon nanotubes in 1991.[7] Carbon nanotubes, which are essentially rolled up sheets of graphite, have a tensile strength greatly exceeding that of any other known material. Their high tensile strength, combined with their relatively low density, makes nanotubes an excellent construction material for a space elevator and led to a resurgence of interest in the concept.

Notes

1. See the story "Audacious and outrageous: Space elevators" at http://science.nasa .gov/headlines/y2000/ast07sep_1.htm.
2. Liftport, http://www.liftport.com/.
3. K. E. Tsiolkowskii, *Dreams of Earth and Sky* 1895, reissue, Athena Books, Barcelona-Singapore, 2004. Y. Artsutanov, "V Kosmos na Elektrovoze" "To the cosmos by electric train" Komsomolskaya Pravda, 31 July 1960.
4. J. Pearson, "The orbital tower: A spacecraft launcher using the Earth's rotational energy," Acta Astronaut. **2,** 785–799 1975.
5. Arthur C. Clarke, *Fountains of Paradise* Harcourt Bruce Jovanovich, New York, 1978.
6. Charles Sheffield, *The Web Between the Worlds* Baen, Simon and Schuster, Riverdale, NY, 2001.
7. S. Iijima, "Helical microtubules of graphitic carbon," Nature London **354,** 56–58 1991.

APPLICATIONS OF THE SPACE ELEVATOR
Bradley C. Edwards

Bradley Edwards, Director of Research for the Institute for Scientific Research (ISR), is the best-known advocate of the space elevator. Rejected as a young man from the astronaut corps due to health concerns, he earned an advanced degree in physics and worked at the Los Alamos National Laboratory on projects related to space technologies. The selection that follows is excerpted from a 2003 report (The Space Elevator: National Institute for Advanced Concepts Phase II Report) *prepared on the completion of a grant from NASA.*

Every development must have some value to be worth doing. In the case of the space elevator there are both short and long-term applications.... The immediate first use of the space elevator is deployment of Earth-orbiting satellites for telecommunications, military, Earth monitoring, etc....

The traditional markets the space elevator will address include:

- Telecommunications
- Remote sensing
- Department of Defense

The U.S. satellite launch market is expected to be at 110 launches per year when we enter the market.[1]

However, we plan to extend this traditional base and target smaller institutions who are interested in space activities—clients who, until now, have been unable to afford it. The new markets we will encourage and target include:

- Solar Energy Satellites (clean, limitless power from space)
- Space-System Test-Bed (universities, aerospace)
- Environmental Assessment (pollution, global change)
- Agricultural Assessment (crop analysis, forestry)
- Private Communications Systems (corporate)
- National Systems (developing countries)
- Medical Therapy (aging, physical handicaps, chronic pain)
- Entertainment / Advertising (sponsorships, remote video adventures)
- Space Manufacturing (biomedical, crystal, electronics)
- Asteroid Detection (global security)
- Basic Research (biomedical, commercial production, university programs)
- Private Tracking Systems (Earth transportation inventory, surveillance)
- Space Debris Removal (International environmental)
- Exploratory Mining Claims (robotic extraction)
- Tourism / Communities (hotels, vacations, medical convalescence)

We expect solar power satellites to be one of the major markets to develop when we become operational and have begun dialogs with [British Petroleum] Solar about launch requirements and interest. Solar power satellites consist of square miles of solar arrays that collect solar power and then beam the power back to Earth for terrestrial consumption. Megawatt systems will have masses of several thousand tons[2] and will provide power at competitive rates to fossil fuels, without pollution, if launch costs get below $500/lb....

5   Another market we expect to emerge is solar system exploration and development. Initially this would be unmanned but a manned segment, based on the Mars Direct (Zubrin) scenario, could emerge early after elevator operations begin. The exploration market would include:

- Exploratory and mining claims missions to asteroids, Mars, Moon, and Venus
- Science-based, university and private sponsored missions
- In-situ resource production on Mars and Moon
- Large mapping probes for Mars and the asteroids
- Near-Earth object catastrophic impact studies from space

The exploration market would be expected to consist of only a few lifts a year within two years of operations but each mission would be a larger one and produce substantial media attention. In the long-term, such practices will increase our revenue as manned activities in space grow.

Another market to consider in the coming decades is space tourism. We may encourage tourism early on with day-long joyrides to space and later possibly lease a ribbon for long-term, hotels in space. Such activities will produce positive public perception and broaden the long-term market. In a recent survey by Zogby International it was found that "7% of affluent (people) would pay

$20 million for 2-week orbital flight; 19% would pay $100,000 for 15-minute sub-orbital flight." These numbers indicate a possible future market that could be tapped as well.

Notes
1. Zogby International
2. NASA and ESA studies

GOING UP
Brad Lemley

The following excerpt appeared in the July 2004 issue of Discover *magazine.*

The key to conquering the solar system is inside a black plastic briefcase on Brad Edwards's desk. Without ceremony, he pops open the case to reveal it: a piece of black ribbon about a foot long and a half-inch wide, stretched across a steel frame.

Huh? No glowing infinite-energy orb, no antigravity disk, just a hunk of tape with black fibers. "This came off a five-kilometer-long spool," says Edwards, tapping it with his index finger. "The technology is moving along quickly."

The ribbon is a piece of carbon-nanotube composite. In as little as 15 years, Edwards says, a version that's three feet wide and thinner than the page you are reading could be anchored to a platform 1,200 miles off the coast of Ecuador and stretch upward 62,000 miles into deep space, kept taut by the centripetal force provided by Earth's rotation. The expensive, dangerous business of rocketing people and cargo into space would become obsolete as elevators climb the ribbon and hoist occupants to any height they fancy: low, for space tourism; geosynchronous, for communications satellites; or high, where Earth's rotation would help fling spacecraft to the moon, Mars, or beyond. Edwards contends that a space elevator could drop payload costs to $100 a pound versus the space shuttle's $10,000. And it would cost as little as $6 billion to build—less than half what Boston spent on the Big Dig highway project.

Science fiction writers, beginning with Arthur C. Clarke in

Ocean-based platform for a space elevator

his 1979 novel, *The Fountains of Paradise,* and a few engineers have kicked around fantastic notions of a space elevator for years. But Edwards's proposal—laid out in a two-year $500,000 study funded by the NASA Institute for Advanced Concepts—strikes those familiar with it as surprisingly practical. "Brad really put the pieces together," says Patricia Russell, associate director of the institute. "Everyone is intrigued. He brought it into the realm of reality."

5   "It's the most detailed proposal I have seen so far. I was delighted with the simplicity of it," says David Smitherman, technical manager of the advanced projects office at NASA's Marshall Space Flight Center. "A lot of us feel that it's worth pursuing."

Still, there's many a slip between speculative space proposals and the messy real world. The space shuttle, to name one example, was originally projected to cost $5.5 million per launch; the actual cost is more than 70 times as much. The International Space Station's cost may turn out to be 10 times its original $8 billion estimate. While NASA takes the space elevator seriously, the idea is officially just one of dozens of advanced concepts jostling for tight funding, and it was conspicuously absent from President Bush's January 14 [2004] address, in which he laid out plans for returning to the moon by 2020, followed by a manned mission to Mars.

So the United States does not appear to be in a mad rush to build an elevator to heaven anytime soon. On the other hand, for reasons Edwards makes abundantly clear, the United States cannot afford to dither around for decades with his proposal. "The first entity to build a space elevator will own space," he says. And after several hours spent listening to Edwards explain just how and why that is so, one comes away persuaded that he is probably right.

Climber

Ascent vehicles will vary in size, configuration, and power, depending on function. All will climb via tractorlike treads that pinch the ribbon like the wringers of an old-fashioned washing machine. Power for the motors will come from photovoltaic cells on the climbers' undersides that are energized by a laser beamed

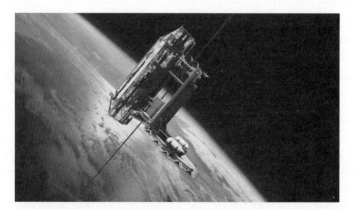

Space elevator in earth orbit showing tether and laser power beam

up from the anchor station. At least two additional lasers will be located else-where in case clouds block the anchor station's beam.

Counterweight

A deployment booster, carried aloft in pieces by a vehicle such as the space shut-tle and assembled in low Earth orbit, will unfurl two thin strips of ribbon stretching from Earth to deep space. Once the strips are anchored to a site on Earth, 230 unmanned climbers will "zip" together and widen the strips. Those climbers will then remain permanently at the far end of the ribbon, just below the deployment booster, to serve as a counterweight.

WHY WE NEED A SPACE ELEVATOR

Cathy Swan and Peter Swan

Cathy Swan (Southwest Analytic Network) and Peter Swan (Teaching Science and Tech-nology) are Arizona-based science writers. The following is excerpted from their article in Space Policy *published in 2006.*

Why build the space elevator? Because we must! The human spirit and the hu-man condition have a rare opportunity as we enter the 21st century to leapfrog current limitations. Early lunar-mission photography gave humanity a tremen-dous boost as we recognized the Earth as a "Big Blue Marble" where borders were invisible. According to Kofi Annan, [former] Secretary General of the United Nations:

> When one of the early missions produced the first photographs of the Earth taken from space, it revealed a planet without national borders, a fragile orb dependent on a delicate web of resources and ecosystems, a single sphere that is the common home for all of humanity [2, p. 15].

This realization energizes the space elevator "why" discussion:

- The human spirit should not have restrictions;
- Chemical rockets cannot effectively move humanity beyond low-Earth orbit (LEO);
- A space option will enable solutions to some of humanity's problems through extraterrestrial missions.

Expansion of the human spirit

Thanks to technology we now have the opportunity to take a space option. Such an option would help solve Earth's problems by making available resources from extra-planetary sources. It would change humanity's view from a planetary one to that of a solar system full of vistas.

The space option has opened up alternatives not well understood in the 20th century. With it, the human race can see beyond the limitations of a single world and expand beyond L[ow] E[arth] O[rbit]. The operation of a single, and then multiple, space elevators will provide an important tool for rescuing humanity from the limitations of a single world with expanding populations and limited resources. This is because it will allow us to avoid the use of dangerous and expensive chemical propulsion.

The failure of chemical rocket engines to stimulate economic growth in space

The first 50 years of space exploration were all based upon the chemistry of rocket engines. This phenomenal reach of humanity into the galaxy enabled communications satellites, major storm warning systems, footsteps on the Moon, investigations of Mars by surface rovers and countless other successes. The tremendous cost of launch, just to get into space, has driven our choices of what has been and will in future be accomplished. The costs of the Space Shuttle after 2005 will be beyond comprehension when one takes the budget for the years remaining (2005–2010)* and divides it by the number of launches remaining. This simple calculation shows a cost of greater than $2 billion per launch. Less expensive standard launches exist, such as Ariane, Atlas V, Delta IV, Proton, and Sea Launch. But even the new launches that advertise low cost through commercial processes cost tens of millions of dollars when placing large payloads into space. The reality is that the cost to launch a chemical rocket will never be inexpensive because we "throw it away." Even "reusable" rockets throw away over 80% of the mass at the launch pad as consumed fuel.

5   The issue with chemical rockets is that it takes roughly 94% (depending upon the launch vehicle) of the launch mass on the pad to raise the altitude of the payload satellite to 300km and raise the velocity to 7.9 km/s (17,600 mph). Some 80% of the mass at the pad is chemical fuel to be consumed—leaving 20% for "motors, propellant tanks, propellant pumps, support structures, guidance and control systems, recovery systems, and finally, payload." [3, p. 4]. The need for a thrust to weight ratio of greater than one at the pad and the tremendous problem of gravity and drag ensures that the chemical rocket answer is not, and will not become, cost-effective as an infrastructure to the stars. The problem is simple and will not be solved by single-stage to orbit or re-usable rockets; chemical rockets require consumption of 94% of initial launch mass. The infrastructure does not remain for the next launch. A space elevator will change the equation with an infrastructure that is maintained and re-used over the lifetime of the project. Just imagine an infrastructure to deliver objects into space for $100/kg!

The following analogy puts this chemical rocket quandary into perspective. An American buys a car from Japan. The car is shipped by car carrier across the Pacific [to be truly analogous, the car carrier ship must only load around 6% of the mass of the ship...as payload (cars), well below its capacity]. The car is off-loaded in Los Angeles. The car carrier ship is then sunk near Catalina Island. The question is: how much would the new car cost if we used the chemical launch/satellite model of economics? The answer does not bear thinking about.

• • •

---

*NASA's shuttle fleet was retired in 2011.

Developing a Vision

Pursuit of a mega-project requires technical knowledge, funding, political support, and management skills; however, one critical component which will increase the probability of success is an exciting vision to pull the program together and drive it forward. The development of a vision is an extremely complex task. It should be done with an initial cadre of people trying to determine the best way to lead with a concept, idea or thrust. The establishment of a vision is critical to constant forward motion for the team. It should be accomplished early in the development cycle, before the establishment of any hard requirements. The sooner the better.

During the 60s and 70s, millions dreamed of traveling to space. There are many more who dream of a better life and a good future for their children. Many of these people fear that their dreams will not come true. Fear and hope are powerful drivers. The Apollo program was driven by fear of losing to the USSR* and hope of a new space age with all its benefits. For the space elevator the same type of visions exist that motivated Columbus, the transcontinental railway builders and the interstate highway systems planners: creating easy access to new worlds, facilitating new discoveries and presenting endless horizons for our future. The space elevator will give us a road to limitless opportunities and a path through the limitations.

---

*The Union of Soviet Socialist Republics, or Soviet Union, was founded through a socialist revolution in 1922 and dissolved in 1991. After World War II, the Soviet Union became the chief political and military rival of the United States, with which it competed for influence and advantage both around the globe and in space. The Soviets launched the first artificial satellite, Sputnik, in 1957. In response, the United States accelerated its own efforts to reach space, culminating in the Apollo program, which landed Neil Armstrong and Buzz Aldrin on the moon on July 20, 1969.

Consider Your Purpose

We asked a student, Sheldon Kearney, to read these four selections and to use them (and others) as sources in an explanatory paper on the space elevator. (We also asked him to write additional comments describing the process of developing his ideas into a draft.) His paper (the final version begins on p. 112) drew on seventeen selections on space elevator technology. How did he—how would you—go about synthesizing the sources?

First, remember that before considering the *how*, you must consider the *why*. In other words, what is your *purpose* in synthesizing these sources? You might use them for a paper dealing with a broader issue: the commercialization of space, for instance. If this were your purpose, any sources on the space elevator would likely be used in only one section devoted to cost-effective options for lifting materials from earth into zero gravity. Because such a broader paper would consider topics other than the space elevator (for instance, a discussion of business opportunities in earth orbit or of possible legal problems among companies operating in space), it would need to draw on sources unrelated to space elevators.

For a business or finance course, you might search for sources that would help you present options for private and government funding of space elevators. The sources gathered by Sheldon Kearney could help explain the technology; but, again, you would need to find other sources to investigate the advantages and disadvantages of public versus private funding or types of private funding. Your overall intention would still be explanatory; yet your focus and your selection of sources would need to broaden from what a space elevator is (the focus of his present paper) to a consideration of the ways in which different classes of investors could pay for actual construction. *Your purpose in writing, then, governs your choice of sources.*

Assume that your goal is to write an explanation of space elevators: a *synthesis* that will explain what the elevator is, how it works, its pros and cons, and why advocates believe it should be built. As part of a larger paper, this explanation would be relatively brief. But if your intention is to explain in greater detail, for an audience of nonspecialists, the basics of space elevator technology and the challenges we can expect with its development, then you will write a paper much like the one Kearney has, the development of which you'll follow in the coming pages. The goal: to present information but not advance a particular opinion or slant on the subject.

Exercise 3.2

Critical Reading for Synthesis

Review the four readings on space elevators and list the ways they explain the technology, address potential advantages and disadvantages, and identify obstacles to construction. Make your list as specific and detailed as you can. Assign a source to each item on the list.

Formulate a Thesis

The difference between a purpose and a thesis is primarily a difference of focus. Your purpose provides direction to your research and gives a focus to your paper. Your thesis sharpens this focus by narrowing it and formulating it in the words of a single declarative statement. (Chapter 6 has more on formulating thesis statements.)

Since Kearney's purpose in this case was to synthesize source material with little or no comment, his thesis would be the most obvious statement he could make about the relationship among the source readings. By "obvious" we mean a statement that is broad enough to encompass the main points of all the readings. Taken as a whole, what do they *mean*? Here Kearney describes the process he followed in coming up with a thesis for his explanatory synthesis:

> I began my writing process by looking over all the readings and noting the main point of each reading in a sentence on a piece of paper.
> Then I reviewed all of these points and identified the patterns in the readings. These I recorded underneath my list of main points: All the readings focus on the space elevator: definition, construction, technical

obstacles, uses, potential problems. The readings explain a technology that has significant business, military, and environmental implications.

Looking over these points, I drafted what I thought was a preliminary thesis. This thesis summed up for me the information I found in my sources:

> Building a space elevator has garnered the attention of NASA, the U.S. Air Force, foreign nations, private industry, and scientists alike as a feasible and cost effective means of reaching into space.

This was a true statement, the basis of my first draft. What ended up happening, though (I realized this even before my instructor read the draft and commented), was that my supposed thesis wasn't a thesis at all. Instead, I had written a statement that allowed me to write a series of summaries and bullet points and call that a paper. So this first effort was not successful, although one good thing happened: in my conclusion, when I forced myself to sum up, I wrote a sentence that looked more like an organizing thesis statement:

> The development of the space elevator will undoubtedly become a microcosm of the human spirit, for better and for worse.

This statement seemed more promising, and my instructor suggested I use this as my thesis. But the more I thought about "microcosm of the human spirit," the more nervous I got about explaining what the "human spirit" is. That seemed to me too large a project. I figured that might be a trap, so I used a different thesis for my second draft:

> Building the space elevator could lead to innovation and exploration; but there could be problems—caused both by technology and by people—that could derail the project.

This version of the thesis allowed me to write more of a synthesis, to get a conversation going with the sources. After I wrote a second draft, I revised the thesis again. This time, I wanted to hint more directly at the types of problems we could expect. I introduced "earth-bound conflicts" to suggest that the familiar battles we fight down here could easily follow us into space:

> If built, the space elevator would likely promote a new era of innovation and exploration. But one can just as easily imagine progress being compromised by familiar, earth-bound conflicts.

I added "if built" to plant a question that would prepare readers for a discussion of obstacles to constructing the elevator. Originally this thesis was one sentence, but it was long and I split it into two.

Decide How You Will Use Your Source Material

To begin, you will need to summarize your sources—or, at least, be *able* to summarize them. That is, the first step to any synthesis is understanding what your sources say. But because you are synthesizing *ideas* rather than sources, you will have to be more selective than if you were writing a simple summary. In your synthesis, you will not use *all* the ideas and information in every source, only the ones related to your thesis. Some sources might be summarized in their entirety; others, only in part. Look over your earlier notes or sentences discussing the topics covered in the readings, and refer back to the readings themselves. Focusing on the more subtle elements of the issues addressed by the authors, expand your earlier summary sentences. Write brief phrases in the margin of the sources, underline key phrases or sentences, or take notes on a separate sheet of paper or in a word processing file or electronic data-filing program. Decide how your sources can help you achieve your purpose and support your thesis.

For example, how might you use a diagram to explain the basic physics of the space elevator? How would you present a discussion of possible obstacles to the elevator's construction or likely advantages to the country, or business, that builds the first elevators? How much would you discuss political or military challenges?

Develop an Organizational Plan

An organizational plan is your map for presenting material to the reader. What material will you present? To find out, examine your thesis. Do the content and structure of the thesis (that is, the number and order of assertions) suggest an organizational plan for the paper? For example, consider Kearney's revised thesis:

> If built, the space elevator would likely promote a new era of innovation and exploration. But one can just as easily imagine progress being compromised by familiar, earth-bound conflicts.

Without knowing anything about space elevators, a reader of this thesis could reasonably expect the following:

- Definition of the space elevator: What is it? How does it work?
- "If built"—what are the obstacles to building a space elevator?
- What innovations?
- What explorations?
- What problems ("conflicts") on earth would jeopardize construction and use of a space elevator?

Study your thesis, and let it help suggest an organization. Expect to devote at least one paragraph of your paper to developing each section that your thesis promises. Having examined the thesis closely and identified likely sections, think through the possibilities of arrangement. Ask yourself: What information does the reader need to understand first? How do I build on this first section—what block of information will follow? Think of each section in relation to others until you have placed them all and have worked your way through to a plan for the whole paper.

Bear in mind that any one paper can be written—successfully—according to a variety of plans. Your job before beginning your first draft is to explore possibilities. Sketch a series of rough outlines:

- Arrange and rearrange your paper's likely sections until you develop a plan that both enhances the reader's understanding and achieves your objectives as a writer.

- Think carefully about the logical order of your points: Does one idea or point lead to the next?

- If not, can you find a more logical place for the point, or are you just not clearly articulating the connections between the ideas?

Your final paper may well deviate from your final sketch; in the act of writing you may discover the need to explore new material, to omit planned material, to refocus or to reorder your entire presentation. Just the same, a well-conceived organizational plan will encourage you to begin writing a draft.

Summary Statements

In notes describing the process of organizing his material, Kearney refers to all the sources he used, including the four excerpted in this chapter.

> In reviewing my sources and writing summary statements, I detected four main groupings of information:
>
> - The technology for building a space elevator is almost here. Only one major obstacle remains: building a strong enough tether.
> - Several sources explained what the space elevator is and how it could change our world.
> - Another grouping of articles discussed the advantages of the elevator and why we need it.
> - A slightly different combination of articles presented technical challenges and also problems that might arise among nations, such as competition.
>
> I tried to group some of these topics into categories that would have a logical order. What I first wanted to communicate was the sense that the technical obstacles to building a space elevator have been (or soon will be) solved or, in theory, at least, are solvable.
>
> Early in the paper, likely in the paragraph after the introduction, I figured I should explain exactly what a space elevator is.
>
> I would then need to explain the technical challenges—mainly centered on the tether and, possibly, power issues. After covering the technical challenges, I could follow with the challenges that people could pose (based largely on competition and security needs).
>
> I also wanted to give a sense that there's considerable reason for optimism about the space elevator. It's a great idea; but, typically, people could

get in the way of their own best interests and defeat the project before it ever got off the ground.

I returned to my thesis and began to think about a structure for the paper.

> Building the space elevator could lead to innovation and exploration; but there could be problems—caused both by technology and by people— that could derail the project.

Based on his thesis, Kearney developed an outline for an eight-paragraph paper, including introduction and conclusion:

1. Introduction: The space elevator <u>can</u> be built a lot sooner than we think.
2. The basic physics of a space elevator is not that difficult to understand.
3. The key to the elevator's success is making a strong tether. Scientists believe they have found a suitable material in carbon nanotubes.
4. Weather and space junk pose threats to the elevator; but these potential problems are solvable with strategic placement of the elevator and sophisticated monitoring systems.
5. Powering the elevator will be a challenge, but one likely source is electricity collected by solar panels and beamed to the climber.
6. Space elevators promise important potential benefits: cost of transporting materials to space will be drastically reduced; industries, including tourism, would take advantage of a zero- gravity environment; and more.
7. Among the potential human-based (as opposed to technology-based) problems to building a space elevator: a new space race; wars to prevent one country from gaining strategic advantage over others, ownership, and access.
8. A space elevator could be inspiring and could usher in a new era of exploration.

Write the Topic Sentences

Writing draft versions of topic sentences (an optional step) will get you started on each main idea of your synthesis and will help give you the sense of direction you need to proceed. Here are Kearney's draft topic sentences for sections, based on the thesis and organizational plan he developed. Note that when read in sequence following the thesis, these sentences give an idea of the logical progression of the essay as a whole.

- A space elevator is exactly what it sounds like.
- A space elevator is not a standard elevator, but a rope—or tether—with a counterweight at the far end kept in place by centrifugal force extending 60,000 miles into space.

- There already exists a single material strong enough to act as a tether for the space elevator, carbon nanotubes.
- Because the space elevator would reach from Earth through our atmosphere and into space, it would face a variety of threats to the integrity of its tether.
- Delivering power to the climbers is also a major point of consideration.
- The ability of a space elevator to lift extremely heavy loads from Earth into space is beneficial for a number of reasons.
- Ownership, as any homeowner can tell you, comes with immense responsibly; and ownership of a technology that could change the world economy would almost certainly create huge challenges.
- The ambition to build a tower so high it would scrape the heavens is an idea stretching back as far as the story of the Tower of Babel.

Organize a Synthesis by Idea, Not by Source

A synthesis is a blending of sources organized by *ideas*. The following rough sketches suggest how to organize and how *not* to organize a synthesis. The sketches assume you have read seven sources on a topic, sources A–G.

INCORRECT: ORGANIZING BY SOURCE + SUMMARY

Thesis

Summary of source A in support of the thesis.

Summary of source B in support of the thesis.

Summary of source C in support of the thesis.

(Etc.)

Conclusion

This is *not* a synthesis because it does not blend sources. Each source stands alone as an independent summary. No dialogue among sources is possible.

CORRECT: ORGANIZING BY IDEA

Thesis

First idea: Refer to and discuss *parts* of sources (perhaps A, C, F) in support of the thesis.

Second idea: Refer to and discuss *parts* of sources (perhaps B, D) in support of the thesis.

(continues)

> Third idea: Refer to and discuss *parts* of sources (perhaps A, E, G) in support of the thesis.
>
> (Etc.)
>
> Conclusion
>
> This *is* a synthesis because the writer blends and creates a dialogue among sources in support of an idea. Each organizing idea, which can be a paragraph or group of related paragraphs, in turn supports the thesis.

Write Your Synthesis

Here is the first draft of Kearney's explanatory synthesis. Thesis and topic sentences are highlighted. Modern Language Association (MLA) documentation style, explained in Chapter 7, is followed throughout.

Alongside this first draft we have included comments and suggestions for revision from Kearney's instructor. For purposes of demonstration, these comments are likely to be more comprehensive than the selective comments provided by most instructors.

■ EXPLANATORY SYNTHESIS: FIRST DRAFT

Sheldon Kearney

Professor Leslie Davis

Technology and Culture

October 1, 2010

The Space Elevator

(1)   A space elevator is exactly what it sounds like: an elevator reaching into space. And though some thirty years ago the notion of a such an elevator was little more than science fiction, today, building a space elevator has garnered the attention of NASA, the U.S. Air Force, foreign nations, private industry, and scientists alike as a feasible and cost-effective means of reaching into space.

(2)   A space elevator is not a standard elevator, but a rope—or tether—with a counterweight at the far end kept in place by centrifugal force extending 60,000 miles into space (citation needed). The rotation of the earth combined with the weight and size of the tether would keep the line taught. As ___notes, imagine a rope hanging down from the earth rather than extending up (citation needed). Rather than having a counterweight moving cargo up and down the tether, as in a conventional elevator, a space elevator would make use of mechanical climbers to move cargo into and down from space. (Image needed for this?)

(3)   There already is a material strong enough to act as a tether for the space elevator, carbon nanotubes.

Title and Paragraph 1

Your title could be more interesting and imaginative. Your first paragraph has no organizing statement, no thesis. Devise a statement—or find one in the draft (see your last paragraph—"microcosm of the human spirit")—that can create a map for your readers. Finally, expand the first paragraph and make it an interesting (fascinating?) transition into the world of space elevators.

Paragraph 2

Consider using an image to help readers understand what a space elevator is and how it works. Also consider using an analogy—what is the space elevator like that readers would understand?

Kearney 2

Discovered in 1991 by Sumio Iijima, carbon nanotubes have been tested in labs to be X times
stronger and X times lighter than steel (get stats).
In theory the production of a carbon nanotube ribbon only a meter wide and millimeters thick would
be strong enough to act as the space elevator's
tether. "Small quantities of some nanotubes have
been made that are sufficiently strong enough to
be used in a space elevator," though the scale of
production would need to be drastically increased to
build the tether needed for the space elevator
(Olson interview).

(4)   Threats. Because the space elevator would
reach from Earth through our atmosphere and into
space, there are threats it will face to the integrity
of its tether. Weather conditions such as hurricanes
and lightning pose a threat to the space elevator, as do impacts from Earth-bound objects, i.e.
planes, as well as low earth orbit objects such as
satellites and meteors and orbital debris. These
types of threats have possible solutions. Locating
the space elevator off of the Galapagos Islands in
open water, if possible, minimizes the likelihood of
lightning, wind, and hurricanes damaging the elevator. In this sight, the occurrence of such events
are extremely rare (footnote needed, as well as image provided by Edwards). Furthermore, by attaching the space elevator to a large ocean vessel, such
as a deep water oil platform, it would be possible
to move the tether in the case of severe weather
conditions. The ability to move the space elevator

Paragraph 3

The tether is a crucial component of the space elevator. Any
obstacles to building? Expand
this part of the explanation.

Paragraphs 4 and 5

Reverse the order of paragraphs 4 and 5. "Power" is a
core element of the elevator's
success. A discussion of
"threats" assumes the space
elevator is already functional.
Logically, "power" should
come first.

Kearney 3

is important: NASA estimates that there are some 500,000 objects within the Earth's orbit that could catastrophically damage the space elevator (NASA sight and Edwards).

(5) Delivering power to the climbers is also a major point of consideration. Bringing along the fuel would be prohibitively heavy due to the length of the trip, as would dragging a long power cord. Powering the elevator with laser beams of electricity generated by solar cells on the ground has been proposed by advocates of the space elevator. Lasers powerful enough to be used to fuel the climbers are already commercially available (Olsen interview).

(6) The ability of a space elevator to lift extremely heavy loads from Earth into space is beneficial for a number of reasons. Chemical rockets are only able to carry approximately 6% of their total weight into space as cargo, with the remaining 94% used for fuel to escape the Earth's gravity and launch vehicles (Swan, 2006 2.2). For a space elevator, however, the immense strength of the tether would allow for mechanical climbers to lift extremely heavy loads. There are several obvious advantages to a space elevator:

- As the tether's strength builds over time, there is virtually no limit to the strength and payload capacity of the elevator.
- Inexpensive access to space would quickly permit the development of entirely new space-based industries like tourism and manufacturing.
- The increased ability to place satellites into space would increase the security

Paragraph 6

This paragraph, currently in both sentence and bullet format, needs to be split up and expanded. The cost analysis is an important piece of justifying the space elevator. Expand this discussion and explain the expected savings. Also, as part of justifying a new thesis re: "the human spirit," expand your bulleted list of benefits. Possibly develop a full paragraph for each bullet.

Kearney 4

and amount of digital information needed in the global economy.

- The development of a space elevator could also further act as a launching point for future interplanetary exploration.

(7) Dr. Edwards notes that "the first entity to build a space elevator will own space" (Edwards 2000 needed). In this he is certainly correct. But ownership, as any homeowner can tell you, comes with immense responsibility; and ownership of a technology that could change the world economy would almost certainly create huge challenges (Eric Westling Interview). Key questions to consider:

- Will the creation of one space elevator create a new space race between nations?
- Will one nation's desire to prevent its construction lead to war?
- Who will own the elevator?
- Who will have access to space via the elevator?

(8) The ambition to build a tower so high it would scrape the heavens is an idea stretching back as far as the story of the Tower of Babel. For these ancient builders their ambition was too great and they were punished. The development of the space elevator will undoubtedly become a microcosm of the human spirit, for better and for worse. A space elevator will inspire untold technological developments and usher in a yet unknown expansion of the human condition as we begin in earnest to explore beyond the confines and limitations of the Earth. Yet, the development of a space elevator will almost certainly act as a lightning rod for international conflict.

Paragraph 7

Similar to the comment re: paragraph 6: split the current paragraph and expand bulleted points. If your paper is to account "for better and for worse" elements of the human spirit (see par. 8), then you need a full discussion of problems associated with the elevator. Presently, only these abbreviated bullets suggest possible problems. Expand—possibly a paragraph for each bullet.

Paragraph 8

You have found your thesis in this paragraph: "The developments...for better and for worse." Consider moving this sentence to the head of the paper and building out the conclusion to discuss the space elevator and "the human spirit."

Revise Your Synthesis: Global, Local, and Surface Revisions

Many writers find it helpful to plan for three types of revision: global, local, and surface.

Global revisions affect the entire paper: the thesis, the type and pattern of evidence employed, and the overall organization. A global revision may also emerge from a change in purpose—say, when a writer realizes that a paper works better as an argument than as an explanation. In this case, Kearney decided to revise globally based on his instructor's suggestion to use a statement from the conclusion as a thesis in the second draft. The immediate consequence of this decision: Kearney realized he needed to expand substantially the discussion of the benefits of the space elevator and also its potential problems. Such an expansion would make good on the promise of his new thesis for the second draft (a reformulation of his "human spirit" statement at the end of the first draft): "Building the space elevator could lead to innovation and exploration; but there could be problems—caused both by technology and by people—that could derail the project."

Local revisions affect paragraphs: topic and transitional sentences; the type of evidence presented within a paragraph; evidence added, modified, or dropped within a paragraph; logical connections from one sentence or set of sentences within a paragraph to another.

Surface revisions deal with sentence style and construction, word choice, and errors of grammar, mechanics, spelling, and citation form.

Revising the First Draft: Highlights

Global

- At present, the paper has no organizing thesis. Consider moving the sentence underlined in the final paragraph to the first paragraph and letting it serve as your thesis for the revision. "Microcosm of the human spirit" is promising because our reach into space does speak to the human spirit.

- Be careful in your conclusion not to move your explanatory synthesis into the territory of argument. The paragraph as written shifts away from your sources to your personal point of view concerning what might happen post-development of a space elevator.

- Expand the bullet points on the benefits and key challenges facing development of the space elevator (paragraphs 6–7). Expanded, each bullet point could become a paragraph. Considered together, these discussions of benefits and challenges could justify your explanatory claim about "microcosm."

- In paragraph 6, explain in more detail the cost advantages of the space elevator. Relatively inexpensive access to space is one of the key benefits.

Local

- Your introduction needs work. Create more of a context for your topic that moves readers to your (new) thesis. The topic is fascinating. Show your fascination to readers! Work as well on your concluding paragraph; assuming you move the underlined statement in that paragraph to your introduction (where it would serve as a thesis), the remaining conclusion will be weak.

- Expand your discussion of power requirements for the elevator (paragraph 5) and move that before your discussion of threats (currently paragraph 4). Logic: a discussion of threats assumes an operational space elevator, one of the requirements of which is a dependable power supply.

- Expand your discussion of the tether in paragraph 3—a key component of the elevator. We need to know more, including obstacles to making the tether.

- Graphic images could be very helpful to your explanation of the space elevator. You consider using them in paragraphs 2 and 4.

- Assuming you expand the paper and justify your explanatory claim about the development of the elevator providing a "microcosm of the human spirit," you could expand your conclusion. What do you mean, exactly, by "human spirit"—and, also, by "for better and for worse"?

Surface

- Avoid weak verbs (see the first sentence of paragraph 5). Revise passive constructions such as "has been proposed by" in paragraph 5 and "were punished" in paragraph 8.

- Avoid constructions like "there is" and "there are" in paragraphs 3 and 4.

- Watch for errors like "taught" vs. "taut" in paragraph 2 and "sight" vs. "site" in paragraph 4.

- Fix grammatical errors—for instance, subject-verb agreement in paragraph 4: "the occurrence of such events "are" or "is"?

Exercise 3.3

Revising the Explanatory Synthesis

Try your hand at creating a final draft of the paper on pages 106–109 by following the revision suggestions above and using your own best judgment about how to improve the first draft. Make global, local, and surface changes. After writing your own version of the paper, compare it to the revised version of our student paper below.

MODEL EXPLANATORY SYNTHESIS

Sheldon Kearney

Professor Leslie Davis

Technology and Culture

October 12, 2010

Going Up? An Elevator Ride to Space

(1) In his 1979 science fiction novel *The Fountains of Paradise*, Arthur C. Clarke introduced his readers to space elevators. While Clarke's idea of a platform that would ride a tether into space (eliminating the need for rockets) was not new, his novel helped focus scientific imaginations on the possibilities. A space elevator is exactly what it sounds like: a platform rising from the ground, not to the top floor of a building but into the weightlessness of earth orbit. It's a real-life Tower of Babel, built to "reach unto heaven" (Gen. 11.4). For thirty years, the elevator has been little more than science fiction hinting at future space tourism, manufacturing in zero gravity, mining of asteroids, abundant solar power beamed to anywhere on earth, and dramatically less expensive inter-planetary travel. Today, however, NASA, the U.S. Air Force, and private industry regard the technology as both feasible and cost-effective. If built, the space elevator would likely promote a new era of innovation and exploration. But one can just as easily imagine progress being compromised by familiar, earthbound conflicts.

(2) The physics of a space elevator should be familiar to any child who has spun a rope with a rock attached to one end: as the arm spins, the rope remains extended to its full length in the air, apparently defying gravity. The rope and the rock stay up because centrifugal force acts to push the weight outward, while the rope keeps the rock from flying off. In the case of a space elevator, instead of the child spinning the weight, it is the earth that's spinning. And instead of a rope perhaps three feet in length extending taut from the child's hand out to the rock, the far end of a space tether would be attached to a weight extending 62,000 miles from earth (Aravind 125–26; Kent 3). Movement up and down the tether would not involve the

use of a counterweight and pulley system, as with terrestrial elevators, but rather a mechanical climber to ferry cargo to and from space.

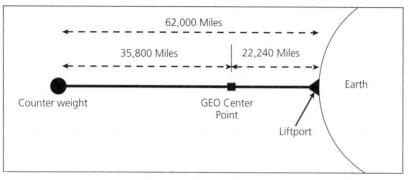

Space Elevator Basic Layout

Figure 1   "The space elevator...is a 1-meter wide tether stretching from the surface of the earth out to a point some 62,000 miles in orbit. The base of the ribbon is attached to a platform on the surface (floating at sea) while the space end of the tether extends past geosynchronous orbit to a counter weight. Lifters...would clamp onto the tether and, using a series of rollers powered by lasers, ascend and descend in order to carry people, material, and cargo to and from orbit." (Kent 3)

When the space elevator was first envisioned, no known material was strong enough to serve as a tether. Then in 1991, Sumio Iijima, a Japanese physicist and materials scientist at Meijo University in Nagoya, discovered the carbon nanotube: "a material that is theoretically one hundred or more times stronger and ten times lighter than steel" (Kent iii). In principle, the production of a carbon nanotube ribbon only a meter wide and millimeters thick would be strong enough to act as the tether for a space elevator. According to Brad Edwards, a former NASA scientist and leading proponent of space elevators, a nanotube strong enough to serve as a tether will soon be available (Interview, NOVA), though the scale of production would have to increase dramatically to achieve the required 62,000 mile length. Because scaling to that extent could create an "unavoidable presence of defects" (Pugno), materials investigation continues. But Edwards is confident enough to predict an operational space elevator by 2031 (Liftport). Production of nanotubes aside, the major obstacles to construction are not

Kearney 3

technical but rather financial (funds must be found to build the elevator); legal (the 62,000 mile tether cannot interfere with existing satellites); and political (interests representing the chemical rocket industry will object to and likely attempt to thwart the elevator) (Edwards, *Phase II* 40).

NASA has been sufficiently intrigued by the concept to join with the Spaceward Foundation in creating "The Space Elevator Games," which awards cash prizes to promising elevator technologies (Shelef). Key modifications to terrestrial elevators have already been designed. For instance, because carrying the fuel necessary to power the elevator platform would render the project as expensive as chemical rockets (which also carry their own fuel), engineers believe that ground-based lasers, powered by the sun, could aim energy beams that would power the mechanical climber. Such lasers are already produced in the United States (LaserMotive).

Figure 2   Ocean-based platform for a space elevator

Kearney 3

Figure 3   Space elevator in earth orbit showing tether and laser power beam
Source: Images created by Alan Chan with permission.

(5)   Because the space elevator would reach from Earth through our atmosphere and into space, the tether would be vulnerable to damage or catastrophic failure from airplanes, space debris, meteors, and violent storms. Impact threats like these also have likely solutions, one being to locate the space elevator in a weather-stable climate—for example, off the Galapagos Islands—in open water, which would minimize the likelihood of damage from lightning or wind (SpaceRef). Attaching the earth-end of the elevator to a large ocean vessel, such as a deep water oil platform, would permit moving a tether threatened by impending collisions with space debris or meteors, which would be tracked by an array of telescopes (Edwards, *Phase I* 5.8; *Phase II* 23).

(6)   At present, NASA and other space agencies around the globe are limited to ferrying relatively small quantities of cargo into space, with dozens of launches needed to build (for example) the international space station. Today, at a per-kilogram cost of $11,000, chemical rockets are able to carry only 6% of their total weight into space as cargo, with the remaining 94% used for fuel to escape the Earth's gravity and to launch vehicles (Swan 2.2). For a space elevator, however, the immense strength of the tether would allow mechanical climbers to lift extremely heavy loads for roughly $100 per kilogram. Edwards estimates that within as few as two years of operation, the elevator could be "capable of supporting a 22 ton

(20,000 kg) climber with a 14 ton (13,000 kg) payload" (*Phase I* 1.4).
He and others estimate the cost of building a space elevator within the
next ten to twenty years to be a tiny fraction of the cost of a trip to Mars
(*Phase 1* 1.8; Lemley).

⑦ The construction of a space elevator could usher in a new era of
exploration and development akin to the reach of the railroad across the
continental United States. In this case, however, not only would the economy of a nation be transformed but also, possibly, the global economy.
With the low-cost lifting of materials into orbit commonplace, the dreams
of science fiction writers could come true, including "mining the asteroid
belt, building zero-G hotels, sailing the solar winds to the moon or Mars,
[and] disposing of our radioactive waste by shooting it into the sun" (Taylor). Inexpensive access to space would quickly permit the development of
entirely new space-based industries. Proposals already exist to use a space
elevator to develop orbiting solar arrays capable of providing cheap, abundant, and clean electrical power to almost anywhere in the world (Edwards,
Phase I 1.7). Such a clean and economically viable energy source made
available to much of the world could decrease dependence on fossil fuels
and the nations that export them (Swan 2.3.1.), which in turn could potentially transform the political and economic landscape here on earth.

⑧ The comparatively inexpensive satellite launches made possible by
a space elevator would secure global data transfer, including communications. A recent study conducted by the University of California, San Diego,
concluded that "the average American consumes about 34 gigabytes of data
and information each day" (Bilton). The invention of the iPhone and other
Web- and video-capable mobile devices as well as the global proliferation
of high-speed Internet in recent years have only increased the need for
secure, fast data transfer. Satellites, along with cell towers and fiber-optic
cables, form the pillars of this transfer. With regular, relatively inexpensive
access to earth orbit provided by a space elevator, military and commercial
interests could have replacement satellites ready for deployment in the

Kearney 6

event of malfunctions (or attack). Sufficient redundancy could be built into these systems to secure the communications and data exchange on which the global economy will increasingly depend.

9 A space elevator could also prove crucial to the success of future interplanetary exploration, since cheap access to space would make manned missions economically feasible. In January 2010 President Obama's proposed federal budget eliminated NASA's Constellation program, which planned for manned missions to the moon within ten years. A working space elevator would significantly reduce the cost of such programs and could make them more attractive in the future. Space agencies would be able to build vehicles on earth, where they are more easily and cheaply assembled, and lift large pieces into space for final assembly.

10 But no one should imagine that the construction of a space elevator will bring only good news or that every predicted benefit will be achieved. The prospect of building a space elevator (like the prospect of building an anti-ballistic missile system) carries with it the potential for fatal misunderstandings and conflicts. For example, a platform in space could provide the builder with enormous military and economic advantages that other nations might find intolerable. We don't need to look much further than the last century to know that nations will launch wars to block rivals from seizing territory that would confer real or perceived advantages. It is not difficult to imagine a scenario in which Russia or China would vigorously protest America's building an elevator capable of creating a military advantage. Even if the United States explained its peaceful intentions, other nations might remain skeptical and, acting out of self-preservation, rush to build their own elevators.

11 And just as nations with nuclear bomb-making capacity strongly discourage other nations from joining that club, one can easily imagine the United States discouraging Iran, for instance, from building a space elevator. Already doubtful of that country's claims for peaceful nuclear development, the United States might also doubt Iran's stated peaceful intentions for a space elevator and move to block its development. The resulting political struggle might look

very much like the current effort to keep Iran from becoming a nuclear state. An alternate scenario: other nations, incapable of building the elevator but not willing to see the United States have one, could launch attacks to disable it. Edwards has already considered the implications of a bomb exploding a mechanical climber and severing the nanotube tether (*Phase II* 38).

(12)   Economic gains, real or perceived, of the nation that builds an elevator could also create problems. Not every nation could afford to build its own elevator. Who, then, would control access? Would poor(er) nations be welcomed to share in the expected bounty? Would the elevator become one more resource that separates nations into haves and have-nots? One can imagine the country that builds and operates the elevator saying to others: "You don't cooperate with us here on earth, so we won't grant you cheap access to space." In this scenario, the elevator could become a political and economic weapon.

(13)   Ninety-eight countries, including the United States and Russia, have signed the Outer Space Treaty, which prohibits the placing of nuclear weapons and other weapons of mass destruction into space and establishes the principle that no country can claim sovereignty of space or celestial bodies beyond earth. The spirit of the agreement is hopeful in being "[i]nspired by the great prospects opening up before mankind as a result of man's entry into outer space" (3); but the agreement is somber as well in recognizing implicitly that nations act in their own interests: "The exploration and use of outer space, including the Moon and other celestial bodies, shall be carried out for the benefit and in the interests of all countries, irrespective of their degree of economic or scientific development, and shall be the province of all mankind" (4). Proponents hope that the nations that build space elevators will adhere to these principles and not seek to make earth orbit the ultimate high ground for economic and military advantage.

(14)   The construction of an elevator to space should excite our collective imaginations; but, human nature being what it is, no one should be surprised if conflicts, along with our hopes, follow the platform into orbit. This is no reason not to pursue research and construction: the elevator and what it makes

Kearney 8

possible could bring great benefits, including pharmaceuticals and exotic materials manufactured in zero gravity, space tourism, endless supplies of renewable energy, secure communications, and a cost-effective platform from which to explore the solar system and beyond. But the space elevator will likely also act as a lightning rod for international competition. In this way, it could well become just another stage on which to play out our quarrels on earth.

Kearney 9

Works Cited

Aravind, P. K. "The Physics of the Space Elevator." *American Journal of Physics* 75.2 (2007): 125–30. PDF file.

The Bible. Introd. and notes by Robert Carroll and Stephen Prickett. Oxford: Oxford UP, 1998. Print. Oxford World's Classics. Authorized King James Vers.

Bilton, Nick. "Part of the Daily American Diet, 34 Gigabytes of Data." *New York Times*. New York Times, 3 Dec. 2009. Web. 14 Sept. 2010.

Clarke, Arthur C. *Fountains of Paradise*. London: V. Gollancz, 1979. Print.

Edwards, Bradley C. Interview. *NOVA: Science Now, Ask the Expert*. PBS, 16 Jan. 2007. Web. 16 Sept. 2010.

---. Interview by Sander Olson. *Nextbigfuture.com*. Lifeboat Foundation, 1 Dec. 2009. Web. 25 Sept. 2010.

---. *The Space Elevator: National Institute for Advanced Concepts Phase I Report*. N.p.: 2000. PDF file.

---. *The Space Elevator: National Institute for Advanced Concepts Phase II Report*. N.p.: 2003. PDF file.

Kent, Jason R. *Getting into Space on a Thread: Space Elevator as Alternative Access to Space*. Maxwell AFB: Air War College, 2007. PDF file.

LaserMotive. Home page. *Lasermotive.com*. LaserMotive, n.d. Web. 14 Sept. 2010.

Kearney 10

Lemley, Brad. "Going Up." *Discovermagazine.com*. Discover Magazine, 25
    July 2004. Web. 12 Sept. 2010.

Liftport. Home page. *Liftport.com*. Liftport, 2003. Web. 20 Sept. 2010.

Kearney 10

Pugno, Nicola M. "On the Strength of the Carbon Nanotube-based Space
    Elevator Cable: From Nanomechanics to Megamechanics." *Journal of
    Physics: Condensed Matter* 18 (2006): 1971–90. PDF file.

Shelef, Ben. "Did You Just Say 'a Space Elevator'?!" *Spaceward.org*.
    Spaceward Foundation, 2008. Web. 18 Sept. 2010.

SpaceRef Interactive. "LiftPort Announces Support of the Space Elevator
    Concept by the National Space Society." *SpaceRef.com*. SpaceRef
    Interactive, 25 June 2003. Web. 12 Sept. 2010.

Swan, Cathy W., and Peter A. Swan. "Why We Need a Space Elevator." *Space
    Policy* 22.2 (2006): 86–91. *Science Direct*. Web. 12 Sept. 2010.

Taylor, Chris. "Space Elevator Entrepreneurs Shoot for the Starts." *CNN.
    com*. Cable News Network, 8 Dec. 2009. Web. 14 Sept. 2010.

United Nations. "Treaty on Principles Governing the Activities of States
    in the Exploration and Use of Outer Space, Including the Moon and
    Other Celestial Bodies." *Treaties and Principles on Outer Space*. New
    York: United Nations, 2002: 3–8. PDF file.

Critical Reading for Synthesis

- *Use the tips from Critical Reading for Summary on page 5.* Remember to examine the context; note the title and subtitle; identify the main point; identify the subpoints; break the reading into sections; distinguish between points, examples, and counterarguments; watch for transitions within and between paragraphs; and read actively and recursively.

- *Establish the writer's primary purpose.* Use some of the guidelines discussed in Chapter 2. Is the piece primarily informative, persuasive, or entertaining? Assess whether the piece achieves its purpose.

(continues)

- ***Read to identify a key idea.*** If you begin reading your source materials with a key idea or topic already in mind, read to identify what your sources have to say about the idea.

- ***Read to discover a key idea.*** If you begin the reading process without a key idea in mind, read to discover a key idea that your sources address.

- ***Read for relationships.*** Regardless of whether you already have a key idea or you are attempting to discover one, your emphasis in reading should be on noting the ways in which the readings relate to each other, to a key idea, and to your purpose in writing the synthesis.

WRITING ASSIGNMENT: THE CHANGING LANDSCAPE OF WORK IN THE TWENTY-FIRST CENTURY

Now we'll give you an opportunity to practice your skills in planning and writing an explanatory synthesis. See Chapter 8, pages 303–338, where we provide nine sources on the way that work will continue to change over the next few decades. Who will be the "winners" and "losers" among American workers? To what extent will education be a factor in your having the career of your choice? Is your job likely to be exported? What forces are changing the shape of employment in business, technology, law, and medicine? Your task in the synthesis will be to understand and present to others less knowledgeable than you the key aspects of the changing landscape of work.

Note that your instructor may want you to complete related assignments in Chapter 8, which ask you to write summaries in preparation for writing a larger explanatory synthesis.

Exercise 3.4

Exploring Online Sources

The online databases available through your school's library, as well as Internet search engines such as Google.com, will yield many sources beyond the ones gathered for you on the topic of "The Changing Landscape of Work in the Twenty-first Century" in Chapter 8. Read the articles on pages 313–338. Then use one or more of your library's databases to conduct an Internet search for additional sources on this topic. You are likely to find more recent sources than those reprinted here. If you end up using any Internet sources for the explanatory synthesis assignment, review our cautionary discussion about using Web-based sources (pp. 265–266).

---

4. Argument Synthesis

■ WHAT IS AN ARGUMENT SYNTHESIS?

An argument is an attempt to persuade a reader or listener that a particular and debatable claim is true. Writers argue in order to establish facts, to make statements of value, and to recommend policies. For instance, answering the question *Why do soldiers sometimes commit atrocities in wartime?* would involve making an argument. To develop this argument, researchers might conduct experiments, interview experts, collect historical evidence, and examine and interpret data. The researchers might then present their findings at professional conferences and in journals and books. The extent to which readers (or listeners) accept these findings will depend on the quality of the supporting evidence and the care with which the researchers have argued their case. What we are calling an argument *synthesis* draws upon evidence from a variety of sources in an attempt to persuade others of the truth or validity of a debatable claim.

By contrast, the explanatory synthesis, as we have seen, is fairly modest in purpose. It emphasizes the sources themselves, not the writer's use of sources to persuade others. The writer of an explanatory synthesis aims to inform, not persuade. Here, for example, is a thesis devised for an explanatory synthesis on the ubiquity of cell phones in contemporary life:

> Cell phones make it possible for us to be always within reach, though many people would prefer *not* to be always within reach.

This thesis summarizes two viewpoints about the impact of cell phones on contemporary life, arguing neither for nor against either viewpoint.

An argument thesis, however, is *persuasive* in purpose. A writer working with the same source material might conceive and support an opposing thesis:

> Cell phones have ruined our ability to be isolated, to be willfully *out of touch* with the rest of the world.

So the thesis for an argument synthesis is a claim about which reasonable people could disagree. It is a claim with which—given the right arguments—your audience might be persuaded to agree. The strategy of your argument synthesis is therefore to find and use convincing *support* for your *claim*.

The Elements of Argument: Claim, Support, and Assumption

One way of looking at an argument is to see it as an interplay of three essential elements: claim, support, and assumption. A *claim* is a proposition or conclusion that you are trying to prove. You prove this claim by using *support* in the form of fact, statistics, or expert opinion. Linking your supporting evidence to your claim is your *assumption* about the subject. This assumption, also called a *warrant* (as we've discussed in Chapter 2), is an underlying belief or principle about some aspect of the world and how it operates. By their nature, assumptions (which are often unstated) tend to be more general than either claims or supporting evidence.

Here are the essential elements of an argument advocating parental restriction of television viewing for high school students:

Claim

> High school students should be restricted to no more than two hours of TV viewing per day.

Support

> An important new study and the testimony of educational specialists reveal that students who watch more than two hours of TV a night have, on average, lower grades than those who watch less TV.

Assumption

> Excessive TV viewing adversely affects academic performance.

As another example, here's an argumentative claim on the topic of computer-mediated communication (CMC)—a term sociologists use to describe online contacts among friends and family:

> CMC threatens to undermine human intimacy, connection, and ultimately community.

Here are the other elements of this argument:

Support

> - People are spending increasing amounts of time in cyberspace: In 1998, the average Internet user spent over four hours per week online, a figure that more than tripled in the last decade.
> - College health officials report that excessive Internet use threatens many college students' academic and psychological well-being.
> - New kinds of relationships fostered on the Internet often pose challenges to pre-existing relationships.

Assumptions

- The communication skills used and the connections formed during Internet contact fundamentally differ from those used and formed during face-to-face contact.
- "Real" connection and a sense of community are sustained by face-to-face contact, not by Internet interactions.

For the most part, arguments should be constructed logically so that assumptions link evidence (supporting facts, statistics, and expert opinions) to claims. As we'll see, however, logic is only one component of effective arguments.

Exercise 4.1

Practicing Claim, Support, and Assumption

Devise two sets of claims, support, and assumptions. First, in response to the example above on computer-mediated communication and relationships, write a one-sentence claim addressing the positive impact (or potentially positive impact) of CMC on relationships—whether you personally agree with the claim or not. Then list the supporting statements on which such a claim might rest, and the assumption that underlies them. Second, write a claim that states your own position on any debatable topic you choose. Again, devise statements of support and relevant assumptions.

The Three Appeals of Argument: *Logos, Ethos, Pathos*

Speakers and writers have never relied on logic alone in advancing and supporting their claims. More than 2000 years ago, the Athenian philosopher and rhetorician Aristotle explained how speakers attempting to persuade others to their point of view could achieve their purpose by relying on one or more *appeals,* which he called *logos, ethos,* and *pathos.*

Since we frequently find these three appeals employed in political argument, we'll use political examples in the following discussion. All three appeals are also used extensively in advertising, legal cases, business documents, and many other types of argument. Bear in mind that in academic writing, the appeal to logic (*logos*) is by far the most commonly used appeal.

Logos

Logos is the rational appeal, the appeal to reason. Academic presentations, including the papers you will write across the curriculum, build almost exclusively on appeals to logic and evidence. If writers and speakers expect to persuade their audiences, they must argue logically and must supply appropriate evidence to support their case. Logical arguments are commonly of two types (often combined): deductive and inductive.

Deductive Reasoning   The *deductive* argument begins with a generalization, then cites a specific case related to that generalization from which
follows a conclusion. An example of a deductive argument may be seen in
President John F. Kennedy's address to the nation in June 1963 on the need
for sweeping civil rights legislation. Kennedy begins with the generalizations that it "ought to be possible...for American students of any color to
attend any public institution they select without having to be backed up
by troops" and that "it ought to be possible for American citizens of any
color to register and vote in a free election without interference or fear of re-
prisal." Kennedy then provides several specific examples (primarily recent
events in Birmingham, Alabama) and statistics to show that this was not the
case. He concludes:

> We face, therefore, a moral crisis as a country and a people. It can-
> not be met by repressive police action. It cannot be left to increased
> demonstrations in the streets. It cannot be quieted by token moves or
> talk. It is time to act in the Congress, in your state and local legislative
> body, and, above all, in all of our daily lives.

Underlying Kennedy's argument is this reasoning:

All Americans should enjoy certain rights. (*assumption*)

Some Americans do not enjoy these rights. (*support*)

We must take action to ensure that all Americans enjoy these rights. (*claim*)

Inductive Reasoning   Another form of logical argumentation is *inductive*
reasoning. A speaker or writer who argues inductively begins not with a
generalization, but with several pieces of specific evidence. The speaker
then draws a conclusion from this evidence. For example, in a debate on gun
control, Senator Robert C. Byrd cited specific examples of rampant crime
involving guns: "I read of young men being viciously murdered for a pair
of sneakers, a leather jacket, or $20." He also offered statistical evidence of
the increasing crime rate: "in 1951, there were 3.2 policemen for every felony
committed in the United States; this year nearly 3.2 felonies will be committed per every police officer." He concluded, "Something has to change. We
have to stop the crimes that are distorting and disrupting the way of life for
so many innocent, law-respecting Americans. The bill that we are debating
today attempts to do just that."

    Senator Edward M. Kennedy also used statistical evidence in arguing
for passage of the Racial Justice Act of 1990, which was designed to ensure that minorities are not disproportionately singled out for the death
penalty. Kennedy pointed out that between 1973 and 1980, 17 defendants
in Fulton County, Georgia, were charged with killing police officers, but
that the only defendant who received the death sentence was a black man.
Kennedy also cited statistics to show that "those who killed whites were
4.3 times more likely to receive the death penalty than were killers of

blacks," and that "in Georgia, blacks who killed whites received the death penalty 16.7 percent of the time, while whites who killed received the death penalty only 4.2 percent of the time."

Maintaining a Critical Perspective   Of course, the mere piling up of evidence does not in itself make the speaker's case. As Donna Cross explains in "Politics: The Art of Bamboozling,"* politicians are very adept at "card-stacking"—lining up evidence in favor of a conclusion without bothering to mention (or barely mentioning) contrary evidence. And statistics can be selected and manipulated to prove anything, as demonstrated in Darrell Huff's landmark book *How to Lie with Statistics* (1954). Moreover, what appears to be a logical argument may in fact be fundamentally flawed. (See Chapter 2 for a discussion of logical fallacies and faulty reasoning strategies.)

On the other hand, the fact that evidence can be distorted, statistics misused, and logic fractured does not mean that these tools of reason should be dismissed. It means only that audiences have to listen and read critically and to question the use of statistics and other evidence.

Exercise 4.2

Using Deductive and Inductive Logic

Choose an issue currently being debated at your school, or a college-related issue about which you are concerned. Write a claim about this issue. Then write two paragraphs addressing your claim—one in which you organize your points deductively (beginning with your claim and following with support) and one in which you organize them inductively (presenting supporting evidence and following with a claim). Possible issues might include college admissions policies, classroom crowding, or grade inflation. Alternatively, you could base your paragraphs on a claim generated in Exercise 4.1.

Ethos

Ethos, or the ethical appeal, is based not on the ethics relating to the subject under discussion, but rather on the ethical status of the person making the argument. A person making an argument must have a certain degree of credibility: That person must be of good character, have sound sense, and be qualified to argue based either on expert experience with the subject matter or on carefully conducted research. Students writing in academic settings establish their appeal to *ethos* by developing presentations that are well organized, carefully reasoned, and thoroughly referenced with source citations. These are the hallmarks of writers and speakers who care deeply about their work. If you care, your audience will care and consider your argument seriously.

Appeals to *ethos* are usually most explicit in political contests. For example, Elizabeth Cervantes Barrón, running for senator as the Peace and

---

*Donna Cross, *Word Abuse: How the Words We Use Use Us* (New York: Coward, 1979).

Freedom candidate, establishes her credibility this way: "I was born and raised in central Los Angeles. I grew up in a multiethnic, multicultural environment where I learned to respect those who were different from me....I am a teacher and am aware of how cutbacks in education have affected our children and our communities." On the other end of the political spectrum, the American Independent gubernatorial candidate Jerry McCready also begins with an ethical appeal: "As a self-employed businessman, I have learned firsthand what it is like to try to make ends meet in an unstable economy being manipulated by out-of-touch politicians." Both candidates are making an appeal to *ethos,* an appeal based on the strength of their personal qualities for the office they seek. Both argue, in effect, "Trust me. My experience makes me a credible, knowledgeable candidate."

L. A. Kauffman is not running for office but writing an article arguing against socialism as an ideology around which to build societies.* To establish his credibility as someone who understands socialism well enough to criticize it meaningfully, Kauffman begins with an appeal to *ethos:* "Until recently, I was executive editor of the journal *Socialist Review.* Before that I worked for the Marxist magazine, *Monthly Review.* My bookshelves are filled with books of Marxist theory, and I even have a picture of Karl Marx up on my wall." Thus, Kauffman establishes his credentials to argue knowledgeably about Marxism.

Exercise 4.3

Using Ethos

Return to the claim you used for Exercise 4.2 and write a paragraph in which you use an appeal to *ethos* to make a case for that claim.

Pathos

Finally, speakers and writers appeal to their audiences by using *pathos,* an appeal to the emotions. Writers in academic settings rely heavily on the force of logic and evidence and rarely make appeals to *pathos.* Beyond academic settings, however, appeals to the emotions are commonplace. Nothing is inherently wrong with using an emotional appeal. Indeed, because emotions often move people far more successfully than reason alone, speakers and writers would be foolish not to use emotion. And it would be a drab, humorless world if human beings were not subject to the sway of feeling as well as reason. The emotional appeal becomes problematic only when it is the *sole* or *primary* basis of the argument.

President Ronald Reagan was a master of emotional appeal. He closed his first Inaugural Address with a reference to the view from the Capitol to the Arlington National Cemetery, where lie thousands of markers of "heroes":

> Under one such marker lies a young man, Martin Treptow, who left his job in a small-town barbershop in 1917 to go to France

---

*L. A. Kauffman, "Socialism: No," *Progressive,* 1 Apr. 1993.

> with the famed Rainbow Division. There, on the western front, he was killed trying to carry a message between battalions under heavy artillery fire. We're told that on his body was found a diary. On the flyleaf under the heading, "My Pledge," he had written these words: "America must win this war. Therefore, I will work, I will save, I will sacrifice, I will endure, I will fight cheerfully and do my utmost, as if the issue of the whole struggle depended on me alone." The crisis we are facing today does not require of us the kind of sacrifice that Martin Treptow and so many thousands of others were called upon to make. It does require, however, our best effort and our willingness to believe in ourselves and to believe in our capacity to perform great deeds, to believe that together with God's help we can and will resolve the problems which now confront us.

Surely, Reagan implies, if Martin Treptow can act so courageously and so selflessly, we can do the same. His logic is somewhat unclear because the connection between Martin Treptow and ordinary Americans of 1981 is rather tenuous (as Reagan concedes); but the emotional power of the heroism of Martin Treptow, whom reporters were sent scurrying to research, carries the argument.

A more recent president, Bill Clinton, also used *pathos*. Addressing an audience of the nation's governors about his welfare plan, Clinton closed his remarks by referring to a conversation he had had with a welfare mother who had gone through the kind of training program Clinton was advocating. Asked by Clinton whether she thought that such training programs should be mandatory, the mother said, "I sure do." Clinton in his remarks explained what she said when he asked her why:

> "Well, because if it wasn't, there would be a lot of people like me home watching the soaps because we don't believe we can make anything of ourselves anymore. So you've got to make it mandatory." And I said, "What's the best thing about having a job?" She said, "When my boy goes to school, and they say, 'What does your mama do for a living?' he can give an answer."

Clinton counts on the emotional power in that anecdote to set up his conclusion: "We must end poverty for Americans who want to work. And we must do it on terms that dignify all of the rest of us, as well as help our country to work better. I need your help, and I think we can do it."

Exercise 4.4

Using Pathos

Return to the claim you used for Exercises 4.2 and 4.3, and write a paragraph in which you use an appeal to *pathos* to argue for that claim.

The Limits of Argument

Our discussion of *ethos* and *pathos* indicates a potentially troubling but undeniable reality: Arguments are not won on the basis of logic and evidence alone. In the real world, arguments don't operate like academic debates. If the purpose of argument is to get people to change their minds or to agree that the writer's or speaker's position on a particular topic is the best available, then the person making the argument must be aware that factors other than evidence and good reasoning come into play when readers or listeners are considering the matter.

These factors involve deep-seated cultural, religious, ethnic, racial, and gender identities, moral preferences, and the effects of personal experiences (either pleasant or unpleasant) that are generally resistant to logic and evidence, however well framed. You could try—using the best available arguments—to convince someone who is pro-life to agree with the pro-choice position (or vice versa). Or you could try to persuade someone who opposes capital punishment to believe that state-endorsed executions are necessary for deterrence (or for any other reason). You might even marshall your evidence and logic to try to persuade someone whose family members have had run-ins with the law that police efforts are directed at protecting the law-abiding.

However, on such emotionally loaded topics, it is extremely difficult, if not impossible, to get people to change their minds because they are so personally invested in their beliefs. As Susan Jacoby, author of *The Age of American Unreason*, notes, "Whether watching television news, consulting political blogs, or (more rarely) reading books, Americans today have become a people in search of validation for opinions that they already hold."*

Fruitful Topics for Argument

The tenacity with which people hold onto longtime beliefs does not mean, however, that they cannot change their minds or that subjects like abortion, capital punishment, gun control, and gay marriage should be off-limits to reasoned debate. It means only that you should be aware of the limits of argument. The most fruitful topics for argument in a freshman composition setting tend to be those on which most people are persuadable, either because they know relatively little about the topic or because deep-rooted cultural, religious, or moral beliefs are not involved. At least initially in your career as a writer of academic papers, it's probably best to avoid "hot-button" topics that are the focus of broader cultural debates, and to focus instead on topics in which *pathos* plays less of a part.

For example, most people are not heavily invested in plug-in hybrid or hydrogen-powered vehicles, so an argument on behalf of the more promising

---

*Susan Jacoby, "Talking to Ourselves: Americans Are Increasingly Close-Minded and Unwilling to Listen to Opposing Views," *Los Angeles Times* 20 Apr. 2008: M10.

technology for the coming decades will not be complicated by deep-seated beliefs. Similarly, most people don't know enough about the mechanics of sleep to have strong opinions on how to deal with sleep deprivation. Your arguments on such topics, therefore, will provide opportunities both to inform your readers or listeners and to persuade them that your arguments, if well reasoned and supported by sound evidence, are at least plausible, if not entirely convincing.

■ DEMONSTRATION: DEVELOPING AN ARGUMENT SYNTHESIS—BALANCING PRIVACY AND SAFETY IN THE WAKE OF VIRGINIA TECH

To demonstrate how to plan and draft an argument synthesis, let's suppose you are taking a course on Law and Society or Political Science or (from the Philosophy Department) Theories of Justice, and you find yourself considering the competing claims of privacy and public safety. The tension between these two highly prized values burst anew into public consciousness in 2007 after a mentally disturbed student at the Virginia Polytechnic Institute shot to death thirty-two fellow students and faculty members and injured seventeen more. Unfortunately, this incident was only the latest in a long history of mass killings at American schools.* It was later revealed that the shooter had a documented history of mental instability, but because of privacy rules, this information was not made available to university officials. Many people demanded to know why this information had not been shared with campus police or other officials so that Virginia Tech could have taken measures to protect members of the university community. Didn't the safety of those who were injured or killed outweigh the privacy of the shooter? At what point, if any, *does* the right to privacy outweigh the right to safety? What *should* the university have done before the killing started? Should federal and state laws on privacy be changed or even abandoned in the wake of this and other similar incidents?

Suppose, in preparing to write a paper on balancing privacy and safety, you located (among others) the following sources:

- *Mass Shootings at Virginia Tech, April 16, 2007: Report of the Review Panel Presented to Governor Kaine, Commonwealth of Virginia,* August 2007 (a report)
- "Laws Limit Schools Even After Alarms" (a newspaper article)

---

*In 1966 a student at the University of Texas at Austin, shooting from the campus clock tower, killed 14 people and wounded 31. In 2006 a man shot and killed five girls at an Amish school in Lancaster, Pennsylvania.

- "Perilous Privacy at Virginia Tech" (an editorial)
- "Colleges Are Watching Troubled Students" (a newspaper article)
- "Campus Stabbing Victim Sues UC Regents" (a newspaper article)
- "Virginia Tech Massacre Has Altered Campus Mental Health Systems" (a newspaper article)
- *The Family Educational Rights and Privacy Act (FERPA)*, sec. 1232g (a federal statute)

　Carefully read these sources (which follow), noting the kinds of evidence—facts, expert opinions, and statistics—you could draw on to develop an *argument synthesis*. Some of these passages are excerpts only; in preparing your paper, you would draw on the entire articles, reports, and book chapters from which these passages were taken. And you would draw on more sources than these in your search for supporting materials (as the writer of the model synthesis has done; see pp. 150–159). But these seven sources provide a good introduction to the subject. Our discussion of how these passages can form the basis of an argument synthesis resumes on page 145.

MASS SHOOTINGS AT VIRGINIA TECH, APRIL 16, 2007

Report of the Review Panel
Presented to Governor Kaine, Commonwealth of Virginia,
August 2007

The following passage leads off the official report of the Virginia Tech shootings by the panel appointed by Virginia Governor Tim Kaine to investigate the incident. The mission of the panel was "to provide an independent, thorough, and objective incident review of this tragic event, including a review of educational laws, policies and institutions, the public safety and health care procedures and responses, and the mental health delivery system." Panel members included the chair, Colonel Gerald Massenghill, former Virginia State Police Superintendent; Tom Ridge, former Director of Homeland Security and former governor of Pennsylvania; Gordon Davies; Dr. Roger L. Depue; Dr. Aradhana A. "Bela" Sood; Judge Diane Strickland; and Carol L. Ellis. The panel's Web site may be found at <http://www.vtreviewpanel.org/panel_info/>.

Summary of Key Findings

On April 16, 2007, Seung Hui Cho, an angry and disturbed student, shot to death 32 students and faculty of Virginia Tech, wounded 17 more, and then killed himself.

　The incident horrified not only Virginians, but people across the United States and throughout the world.

　Tim Kaine, Governor of the Commonwealth of Virginia, immediately appointed a panel to review the events leading up to this tragedy; the handling of the incidents by public safety officials, emergency services providers, and the university; and the services subsequently provided to families, survivors, caregivers, and the community.

The Virginia Tech Review Panel reviewed several separate but related issues in assessing events leading to the mass shootings and their aftermath:

- The life and mental health history of Seung Hui Cho, from early childhood until the weeks before April 16.
- Federal and state laws concerning the privacy of health and education records.
- Cho's purchase of guns and related gun control issues.
- The double homicide at West Ambler Johnston (WAJ) residence hall and the mass shootings at Norris Hall, including the responses of Virginia Tech leadership and the actions of law enforcement officers and emergency responders.
- Emergency medical care immediately following the shootings, both onsite at Virginia Tech and in cooperating hospitals.
- The work of the Office of the Chief Medical Examiner of Virginia.
- The services provided for surviving victims of the shootings and others injured, the families and loved ones of those killed and injured, members of the university community, and caregivers.

5   The panel conducted over 200 interviews and reviewed thousands of pages of records, and reports the following major findings:

1. Cho exhibited signs of mental health problems during his childhood. His middle and high schools responded well to these signs and, with his parents' involvement, provided services to address his issues. He also received private psychiatric treatment and counseling for selective mutism and depression.

    In 1999, after the Columbine shootings, Cho's middle school teachers observed suicidal and homicidal ideations in his writings and recommended psychiatric counseling, which he received. It was at this point that he received medication for a short time. Although Cho's parents were aware that he was troubled at this time, they state they did not specifically know that he thought about homicide shortly after the 1999 Columbine school shootings.

2. During Cho's junior year at Virginia Tech, numerous incidents occurred that were clear warnings of mental instability. Although various individuals and departments within the university knew about each of these incidents, the university did not intervene effectively. No one knew all the information and no one connected all the dots.

3. University officials in the office of Judicial Affairs, Cook Counseling Center, campus police, the Dean of Students, and others explained their failures to communicate with one another or with Cho's parents by noting their belief that such communications are prohibited by the federal laws governing the privacy of health and education records. In reality, federal laws and their state counterparts afford ample leeway to share information in potentially dangerous situations.

4. The Cook Counseling Center and the university's Care Team failed to provide needed support and services to Cho during a period in late 2005 and early

2006. The system failed for lack of resources, incorrect interpretation of privacy laws, and passivity. Records of Cho's minimal treatment at Virginia Tech's Cook Counseling Center are missing.

5. Virginia's mental health laws are flawed and services for mental health users are inadequate. Lack of sufficient resources results in gaps in the mental health system including short term crisis stabilization and comprehensive outpatient services. The involuntary commitment process is challenged by unrealistic time constraints, lack of critical psychiatric data and collateral information, and barriers (perceived or real) to open communications among key professionals.

6. There is widespread confusion about what federal and state privacy laws allow. Also, the federal laws governing records of health care provided in educational settings are not entirely compatible with those governing other health records.

7. Cho purchased two guns in violation of federal law. The fact that in 2005 Cho had been judged to be a danger to himself and ordered to outpatient treatment made him ineligible to purchase a gun under federal law.

8. Virginia is one of only 22 states that report any information about mental health to a federal database used to conduct background checks on would-be gun purchasers. But Virginia law did not clearly require that persons such as Cho—who had been ordered into out-patient treatment but not committed to an institution—be reported to the database. Governor Kaine's executive order to report all persons involuntarily committed for outpatient treatment has temporarily addressed this ambiguity in state law. But a change is needed in the Code of Virginia as well.

9. Some Virginia colleges and universities are uncertain about what they are permitted to do regarding the possession of firearms on campus.

10. On April 16, 2007, the Virginia Tech and Blacksburg police departments responded quickly to the report of shootings at West Ambler Johnston residence hall, as did the Virginia Tech and Blacksburg rescue squads. Their responses were well coordinated.

11. The Virginia Tech police may have erred in prematurely concluding that their initial lead in the double homicide was a good one, or at least in conveying that impression to university officials while continuing their investigation. They did not take sufficient action to deal with what might happen if the initial lead proved erroneous. The police reported to the university emergency Policy Group that the "person of interest" probably was no longer on campus.

12. The VTPD erred in not requesting that the Policy Group issue a campus-wide notification that two persons had been killed and that all students and staff should be cautious and alert.

13. Senior university administrators, acting as the emergency Policy Group, failed to issue an all-campus notification about the WAJ killings until almost 2 hours had elapsed. University practice may have conflicted with written policies.

14. The presence of large numbers of police at WAJ led to a rapid response to the first 9-1-1 call that shooting had begun at Norris Hall.

15. Cho's motives for the WAJ or Norris Hall shootings are unknown to the police or the panel. Cho's writings and videotaped pronouncements do not explain why he struck when and where he did.

16. The police response at Norris Hall was prompt and effective, as was triage and evacuation of the wounded. Evacuation of others in the building could have been implemented with more care.

17. Emergency medical care immediately following the shootings was provided very effectively and timely both onsite and at the hospitals, although providers from different agencies had some difficulty communicating with one another. Communication of accurate information to hospitals standing by to receive the wounded and injured was somewhat deficient early on. An emergency operations center at Virginia Tech could have improved communications.

18. The Office of the Chief Medical Examiner properly discharged the technical aspects of its responsibility (primarily autopsies and identification of the deceased). Communication with families was poorly handled.

19. State systems for rapidly deploying trained professional staff to help families get information, crisis intervention, and referrals to a wide range of resources did not work.

20. The university established a family assistance center at The Inn at Virginia Tech, but it fell short in helping families and others for two reasons: lack of leadership and lack of coordination among service providers. University volunteers stepped in but were not trained or able to answer many questions and guide families to the resources they needed.

21. In order to advance public safety and meet public needs, Virginia's colleges and universities need to work together as a coordinated system of state-supported institutions.

As reflected in the body of the report, the panel has made more than 70 recommendations directed to colleges, universities, mental health providers, law enforcement officials, emergency service providers, lawmakers, and other public officials in Virginia and elsewhere.

LAWS LIMIT SCHOOLS EVEN AFTER ALARMS*

Jeff Gammage and Stacey Burling

This article first appeared in the Philadelphia Inquirer on April 19, 2007, just three days after the Virginia Tech shootings. Inquirer *staff writer Paul Nussbaum contributed to the article.*

If Cho Seung-Hui had been a warning light, he would have been blinking bright red.

---

*Philadelphia Inquirer 19 Apr. 2007: A01.

Two female students complained to campus police that he was stalking them. His poetry was so twisted that his writing professor said she would quit if he weren't removed from her room. Some students found him so menacing that they refused to attend class with him.

Yet Virginia Tech, like other colleges trying to help emotionally troubled students, had little power to force Cho off campus and into treatment.

"We can't even pick up the phone and call their family. They're adults. You have to respect their privacy," said Brenda Ingram-Wallace, director of counseling and chair of the psychology department at Albright College in Reading.

5   In the aftermath of the deadliest shooting in U.S. history, counselors, police authorities, and mental-health professionals say privacy laws prevent colleges from taking strong action regarding students who might be dangerous.

Many at Tech saw Cho as a threat—and shared those fears with authorities. In 2005, after the second stalking complaint, the school obtained a temporary detention order that resulted in Cho undergoing a psychiatric evaluation. But the 23-year-old remained enrolled at the university until the moment he shot himself to death.

Federal laws such as the 1974 Family Educational Rights and Privacy Act (FERPA) and the 1996 Health Insurance Portability and Accountability Act (HIPAA) protect students' right to privacy by banning disclosure of any mental-health problems—even to family members—without a signed waiver.

Patient-therapist confidentiality is crucial, privacy advocates say. Students may shy from treatment for fear of exposure.

FERPA does allow colleges to release information without permission in cases of "health and safety emergencies." But the criteria are so vague, and the potential liability so severe, that administrators say they hesitate to act in any but the most dire circumstances.

10   "The law tends to be protective of individual autonomy rather than getting in there and forcing people to get treatment," said Anthony Rostain, associate professor of psychiatry at the University of Pennsylvania School of Medicine.

Lots of students write violent stories, he noted. How do you distinguish between a future Cho Seung-Hui and a future Quentin Tarantino?*

"This kind of problem happens all the time across college campuses," Rostain said.

The law puts colleges in a tough position, said Dana Fleming, a lawyer with the college and university practice group at Nelson, Kinder, Mousseau & Saturley in Manchester, N.H. Schools may face legal trouble if they try to keep ill students out, if they try to send them home, or if they let them stay.

"No matter which decision they make," she said, "they can find liability on the other end."

15   Colleges can't screen students for mental illnesses during the admissions process because that violates the Americans With Disabilities Act. As a result, schools know which students will need tutoring or want to play soccer, but have no idea who is likely to need mental-health care, Fleming said.

---

*Director, screenwriter, and producer of frequently violent films such as *Reservoir Dogs* (1992), *Pulp Fiction* (1994), and *Kill Bill* (vol. 1, 2003; vol. 2, 2004).

Virginia Tech and most other universities cannot summarily suspend a student. Formal disciplinary charges must be filed and hearings held. Students who initiate a complaint often end up dropping the matter.

Nor can schools expect courts to hospitalize a student involuntarily without solid evidence that he poses a danger to himself or others.

That has left many colleges trying to find creative ways to identify and help troubled students.

At Albright College, administrators recently updated a program where anyone concerned about a student's behavior—a work supervisor, a professor or another student—can fill out a "student alert form."

20   Perhaps friends notice a student has become withdrawn or has stopped showing up for class. If multiple forms arrive concerning the same person, counseling director Ingram-Wallace said, the counseling center investigates by contacting housing officials or by reaching the student via phone or e-mail.

But the choice to speak with a psychological counselor stays with the student. The center can't send a therapist to knock on the student's door, she said.

"On the surface, it sounds like a caring thing to do," she said, but "if they haven't been dangerous to themselves or others, there's no reason to mandate them into any kind of services."

Among students who have been referred to the counseling center, "the responses are mixed," she said. "Some people felt imposed upon."

At St. Lawrence University in Canton, N.Y., every student who visits the health center—even for a head cold—is screened for depression and signs of other mental illness. The effort follows a national study that showed depression rising among college students.

25   If a screening shows someone needs help from the health center, "we literally walk them over there," said Patricia Ellis, director of counseling services.

More than a year before Monday's massacre of 32 students and staff members, Cho was twice accused of stalking female students and taken to a mental-health facility amid fears he was suicidal, police said yesterday.

After the first incident, in November 2005, police referred him to the university disciplinary system. Ed Spencer, Tech's assistant vice president of student affairs, said he could not comment on any proceedings against the gunman because federal law protects students' medical privacy even after death.

The university obtained the detention order after the second stalking complaint, in December 2005. "His insight and judgment are normal," an examiner at the psychiatric hospital concluded.

Yet poet Nikki Giovanni, one of his professors, told CNN that students were so unnerved by Cho's behavior, which included taking cell-phone photos of them in class, that most stopped attending the course. She insisted that he be removed.

30   Lucinda Roy, a codirector of the creative writing program, tutored Cho after that, and tried to get him into counseling. He always refused. Roy sent samples of Cho's writing, with its images of people attacking each other with chain saws, to the campus police, student-affairs office, and other agencies.

PERILOUS PRIVACY AT VIRGINIA TECH

This editorial appeared in the Christian Science Monitor *on September 4, 2007.*

Colleges didn't need last week's report on the Virginia Tech shootings to address a key finding: a faster alert during the crisis may have saved lives. Many colleges have already set blast-notice plans. But here's what needs careful study: the report's conclusions about privacy.

Privacy is a huge issue on campuses. Colleges and universities are dealing with young people who have just become legal adults, but who may still require supervision and even intervention.

That was the case with Seung-Hui Cho, the student who killed 32 people and then himself on April 16. According to the report, which was commissioned by Virginia Gov. Timothy Kaine, this troubled student's behavior raised serious questions about his mental stability while he was at VT, yet no one contacted his parents, and communication about his case broke down among school, law-enforcement, and mental-health officials.

A big reason? A "widespread perception" that privacy laws make it difficult to respond to troubled students, according to the report. But this is "only partly correct."

5   Lack of understanding about federal and state laws is a major obstacle to helping such students, according to the report. The legal complexity, as well as concerns about liability, can easily push teachers, administrators, police, and mental-health workers into a "default" position of withholding information, the report found.

There's no evidence that VT officials consciously decided not to inform Mr. Cho's parents. But the university's lawyer told the panel investigating Cho's case that privacy laws prevent sharing information such as that relating to Cho.

That's simply not true. The report listed several steps that could quite legally have been taken:

The Virginia Tech police, for instance, could have shared with Cho's parents that he was temporarily detained, pending a hearing to commit him involuntarily to a mental-health institution, because that information was public.

And teachers and administrators could have called Cho's parents to notify them of his difficulties, because only student records—not personal observations or conversations—are shielded by the federal privacy law that covers most secondary schools.

10   Notifying Cho's parents was intuitively the right course. Indeed, his middle school contacted his parents to get him help, and they cooperated. His high school also made special arrangements. He improved.

The report points out that the main federal privacy laws that apply to a college student's health and campus records recognize exceptions for information sharing in emergencies that affect public health and safety.

Privacy is a bedrock of American law and values. In a mental-health case, it gives a patient the security to express innermost thoughts, and protects that person from discrimination. But the federal law, at least, does recognize a balance between privacy and public safety, even when colleges can't, or won't.

The report is to be commended for pointing out this disconnect, and for calling for greater clarification of privacy laws and school policies.

Perhaps now, common sense can match up with legal obligations so both privacy and public safety can be served.

COLLEGES ARE WATCHING TROUBLED STUDENTS

Jeffrey McMurray

During the year following the Virginia Tech shootings, many colleges and universities took a hard look at their policies on student privacy and their procedures for monitoring and sharing information about troubled students. This article, by the Associated Press, was first published on March 28, 2008. AP writer Sue Lindsay contributed to this report.

On the agenda: A student who got into a shouting match with a faculty member. Another who harassed a female classmate. Someone found sleeping in a car. And a student who posted a threat against a professor on Facebook.

In a practice adopted at one college after another since the massacre at Virginia Tech, a University of Kentucky committee of deans, administrators, campus police and mental health officials has begun meeting regularly to discuss a watch list of troubled students and decide whether they need professional help or should be sent packing.

These "threat assessment groups" are aimed at heading off the kind of bloodshed seen at Virginia Tech a year ago and at Northern Illinois University last month.

"You've got to be way ahead of the game, so to speak, expect what may be coming. If you're able to identify behaviors early on and get these people assistance, it avoids disruptions in the classrooms and potential violence," said Maj. Joe Monroe, interim police chief at Kentucky.

5   The Kentucky panel, called Students of Concern, held its first meeting last week and will convene at least twice a month to talk about students whose strange or disturbing behavior has come to their attention.

Such committees represent a change in thinking among U.S. college officials, who for a long time were reluctant to share information about students' mental health for fear of violating privacy laws.

"If a student is a danger to himself or others, all the privacy concerns go out the window," said Patricia Terrell, vice president of student affairs, who created the panel.

Terrell shared details of the four discussed cases with The Associated Press on the condition that all names and other identifying information be left out.

Among other things, the panel can order a student into counseling or bar him or her from entering a particular building or talking to a certain person. It can also order a judicial hearing that can lead to suspension or expulsion if the student's offense was a violation of the law or school policy.

10   Although the four cases discussed last week were the ones administrators deemed as needing the most urgent attention, a database listing 26 other student cases has been created, providing fodder for future meetings.

Students are encouraged during their freshman orientation to report suspicious behavior to the dean of students, and university employees all the way down to janitors and cafeteria workers are instructed to tell their supervisors if they see anything.

Virtually every corner of campus is represented in the group's closed-door meetings, including dorm life, academics, counseling, mental health and police.

"If you look back at the Virginia Tech situation, the aftermath, there were several people who knew that student had problems, but because of privacy and different issues, they didn't talk to others about it," said Lee Todd, UK president.

High schools have been doing this sort of thing for years because of shootings, but only since Virginia Tech, when a disturbed student gunman killed 32 people and committed suicide, have colleges begun to follow suit, said Mike Dorn, executive director of Safe Havens International, a leading campus safety firm.

15 "They didn't think it was a real threat to them," Dorn said.

Virginia Tech has added a threat assessment team since the massacre there. Boston University, the University of Utah, the University of Illinois–Chicago and numerous others also have such groups, said Gwendolyn Dungy, executive director of the National Association of Student Personnel Administrators.

Bryan Cloyd, a Virginia Tech accounting professor whose daughter Austin was killed in the rampage, welcomed the stepped-up efforts to monitor troubled students but stressed he doesn't want to turn every college campus into a "police state."

"We can't afford to overreact," Cloyd said, but "we also can't afford to underreact."

Seung-Hui Cho, the Virginia Tech gunman, was ruled a danger to himself in a court hearing in 2005 that resulted from a roommate's call to police after Cho mentioned suicide in an e-mail. He was held overnight at a mental health center off campus and was ordered into outpatient treatment, but he received no follow-up services, despite his sullen, withdrawn behavior and his twisted, violence-filled writings.

20 Mary Bolin-Reece, director of counseling and testing at Kentucky, attends the threat assessment group's meetings but cannot share what she knows or, in most cases, even whether a student has been undergoing counseling. But participants can share information on other possible red flags.

"We always look at, 'Is there a change in the baseline?'" Bolin-Reece said. "The student had previously gotten very good grades, and then there was a drop-off. Something has happened. Is there some shift in their ability to function? If a student is coming to the attention of various parties around the university, we begin to be able to connect the dots."

The University of Kentucky has not had a murder on campus since 1984. Still, the threat-assessment effort has the strong backing of Carol Graham of Fort Carson, Colo., whose son Kevin was a Kentucky student when he committed suicide before leaving for an ROTC summer camp in 2003.

"UK is such a huge university," Graham said. "It's important to know there's a safety net—that people are looking out for each other. With Kevin, his professors thought he was perfect. He'd be an A student. But the people around him were noticing differences."

As for the four cases taken up by the committee: The student who got into an argument with a faculty member—and had also seen a major dip in grades and exhibited poor hygiene—was ordered to meet with the dean of students.

25   The one accused of harassment was referred to a judicial hearing, during which he was expelled from university housing. The student who made the Facebook threat was given a warning. In the case of the student sleeping in a car, a committee member was dispatched to check on the person. No further details were released.

CAMPUS STABBING VICTIM SUES UC REGENTS

Larry Gordon

Student-on-student violence is an all-too-frequent occurrence, and each new case raises questions reminiscent of those raised after the Virginia Tech shooting. The following article about a knife attack at the UCLA campus appeared originally in the Los Angeles Times *on December 8, 2010.*

A mentally ill man's knife attack last year on a fellow UCLA student in a campus chemistry lab is at the center of a legal dispute over a university's responsibility to protect its students from such violence.

The victim of the throat slashing and stabbing on Oct. 8, 2009, is suing her assailant and the University of California regents, alleging in part that school officials and faculty did not respond properly to warnings about his potentially violent behavior. UC has denied any liability in the unprovoked attack, which left Katherine Rosen badly wounded and hospitalized for 10 days after surgery.

Damon Thompson, 21, who admitted to the stabbing, was determined by a Superior Court judge on Nov. 16 to be not guilty by reason of insanity and ordered moved to a psychiatric hospital for an indefinite period. Thompson is expected to remain at Patton State Hospital in San Bernardino County for what his attorney, Robin Berkovitz, said "could be a very long time."

A civil suit against Thompson and the university is scheduled for a hearing in March in Superior Court in Santa Monica. An initial claim sought $20 million in damages, but the current suit does not specify an amount.

5   The case raises similar issues to those posed after the 2007 shooting rampage at Virginia Tech that left 32 students and faculty members dead and [17] others injured. The gunman, a Virginia Tech student who later killed himself, had previously demonstrated bizarre and menacing behavior but was allowed to remain enrolled at the public university.

Most of the Virginia Tech victims' families shared an $11-million settlement from the state, with some funds also going to a nonprofit anti-violence organization. However, two families are proceeding with $10-million lawsuits against the school, alleging that it did not do enough to prevent the shootings and that psychological counseling provided to the gunman before the attack was incompetent.

The Rosen case alleges that, for months before the attack, UCLA officials and professors had received reports of Thompson's "strange, disturbing, erratic, angry, dangerous, threatening and/or paranoid behavior." Thompson allegedly had threatened teachers based on "his irrational belief that other students had taunted and bullied him" so that he would make mistakes in his chemistry experiments, the suit says. But UCLA failed to warn students about Thompson's potentially violent behavior, the victim contends.

Soon after the attack, a UCLA professor told The Times that he had informed campus officials months before the knifing about paranoid and accusatory e-mails that Thompson had sent him. UCLA officials said, however, that Thompson's behavior and messages were not violent before the assault and did not merit expulsion. They said privacy rules prevented them from discussing any treatment or counseling he may have received.

UCLA spokesman Phil Hampton said the university will vigorously contest Rosen's claims.

10   "UCLA believes very strongly that there is no merit to the civil case. The horrific incident resulted from a random act of violence," Hampton said. "And while our hearts go out to the victim and her family for the traumatic experience they endured, the incident could not be foreseen."

In legal papers filed recently, UC attorneys contended that the university should not be held responsible because the attacker was not an employee. "Public universities owe no duty to their students to protect them against criminal acts of third persons," the attorneys wrote. They also argued that public colleges are typically shielded from most liability except for instances involving physical maintenance problems, such as broken steps or walls that could cause injuries.

After the assault, UCLA examined its programs aimed at identifying and assisting students in crisis or who may pose a risk to themselves or others and decided that no major changes were necessary, Hampton said.

In testimony last spring during criminal proceedings against Thompson, Rosen, who was 20 at the time of the attack, described the knife scars she bears on her throat, shoulder, arm, hand and back and the nerve damage that makes it difficult to fully use her left hand and arm. She also said she had experienced nightmares and "general anxiety" since the attack.

Rosen is again taking undergraduate classes at UCLA but has "residual problems, both emotional and physical," said her attorney, Brian Panish. She is "doing everything she can to get better," he added. Rosen declined to be interviewed, the attorney said.

15   Although specifics of the case and applicable state laws differ from the Virginia Tech case, Panish said there is a common theme of schools needing to do more to prevent violence. "The reality is when you send a kid to college, you expect some level of protection," he said.

Prosecutors had sought a life sentence for Thompson, but the reports of three doctors concluded that he was mentally ill. Thompson could one day leave the hospital if doctors determine that he has regained his sanity, but a court hearing would be held before any such decision, court officials said.

Berkovitz, the defense attorney, said the insanity finding and hospitalization were the appropriate result in the case.

However, Deputy Dist. Atty. Kevin Halligan, who handled the case, said he remains troubled by the possibility of Thompson's release. He noted that Rosen was close to death after the attack.

"One of my biggest concerns is the safety of the public and that he could get out and this happens again," Halligan said.

VIRGINIA TECH MASSACRE HAS ALTERED CAMPUS MENTAL HEALTH SYSTEMS

This article, prepared by the Associated Press, is representative of numerous reports of how college administrators across the nation responded to the Virginia Tech killings. Many schools reviewed their existing policies on student privacy and communication and instituted new procedures. The article appeared in the Los Angeles Times *on April 14, 2008.*

The rampage carried out nearly a year ago by a Virginia Tech student who slipped through the mental health system has changed how American colleges reach out to troubled students.

Administrators are pushing students harder to get help, looking more aggressively for signs of trouble and urging faculty to speak up when they have concerns. Counselors say the changes are sending even more students their way, which is both welcome and a challenge, given that many still lack the resources to handle their growing workloads.

Behind those changes, colleges have edged away in the last year from decades-old practices that made student privacy paramount. Now, they are more likely to err on the side of sharing information—with the police, for instance, and parents—if there is any possible threat to community safety. But even some who say the changes are appropriate worry it could discourage students from seeking treatment.

Concerns also linger that the response to shooters like Seung-hui Cho at Virginia Tech and Steven Kazmierczak, who killed five others at Northern Illinois University, has focused excessively on boosting the capacity of campus police to respond to rare events. Such reforms may be worthwhile, but they don't address how to prevent such a tragedy in the first place.

5   It was last April 16, just after 7 a.m., that Cho killed two students in a Virginia Tech dormitory, the start of a shooting spree that continued in a classroom building and eventually claimed 33 lives, including his own.

Cho's behavior and writing had alarmed professors and administrators, as well as the campus police, and he had been put through a commitment hearing where he was found to be potentially dangerous. But when an off-campus psychiatrist sent him back to the school for outpatient treatment, there was no follow-up to ensure that he got it.

People who work every day in the campus mental health field—counselors, lawyers, advocates and students at colleges around the country—say they have seen three major types of change since the Cho shootings:

Faculty are speaking up more about students who worry them. That's accelerating a trend of more demand for mental health services that was already under way before the Virginia Tech shootings.

Professors "have a really heightened level of fear and concern from the behavior that goes on around them," said Ben Locke, assistant director of the counseling center at Penn State University.

10 David Wallace, director of counseling at the University of Central Florida, said teachers are paying closer attention to violent material in writing assignments—warning bells that had worried Cho's professors.

"Now people are wondering, 'Is this something that could be more ominous?'" he said. "Are we talking about the Stephen Kings of the future or about somebody who's seriously thinking about doing something harmful?"

The downside is officials may be hypersensitive to any eccentricity. Says Susan Davis, an attorney who works in student affairs at the University of Virginia: "There's no question there's some hysteria and there's some things we don't need to see."

Changes are being made to privacy policies. In Virginia, a measure signed into law Wednesday by Gov. Tim Kaine requires colleges to bring parents into the loop when dependent students may be a danger to themselves or others.

Even before Virginia Tech, Cornell University had begun treating students as dependents of their parents unless told otherwise—an aggressive legal strategy that gives the school more leeway to contact parents with concerns without students' permission.

15 In Washington, meanwhile, federal officials are trying to clarify privacy guidelines so faculty won't hesitate to report potential threats.

"Nobody's throwing privacy out the window, but we are coming out of an era when individual rights were paramount on college campuses," said Brett Sokolow, who advises colleges on risk management. "What colleges are struggling with now is a better balance of those individual rights and community protections."

The big change since the Virginia Tech shootings, legal experts say, is colleges have shed some of their fear of violating the federal Family Educational Rights and Privacy Act.

Many faculty hadn't realized that the law applies only to educational records, not observations of classroom behavior, or that it contains numerous exceptions.

The stigma of mental illness, in some cases, has grown. "In general, the attention to campus mental health was desperately needed," said Alison Malmon, founder of the national Active Minds group. But some of the debate, she added, "has turned in a direction that does not necessarily support students."

20 All the talk of "threat assessments" and better-trained campus SWAT teams, she said, has distracted the public from the fact that the mentally ill rarely commit violence—especially against others.

"I know that, for many students, it made them feel more stigmatized," Malmon said. "It made them more likely to keep their mental health history silent."

Sokolow, the risk consultant for colleges, estimated in the aftermath of the Virginia Tech and NIU shootings, the schools he works with spent $25 on police and communications for every $1 on mental health. Only recently has he seen a shift.

"Campuses come to me, they want me to help them start behavioral intervention systems," Sokolow said. "Then they go to the president to get the money and, oh, well, the money went into the door locks."

Phone messaging systems and security are nice, he said, but "there is nothing about text-messaging that is going to prevent violence."

THE FAMILY EDUCATIONAL RIGHTS AND PRIVACY ACT (FERPA)

United States Code
Title 20. Education
CHAPTER 31. General Provisions Concerning Education
§ 1232g. Family Educational and Privacy Rights

Following are excerpts from the Family Educational Rights and Privacy Act (FERPA), *the federal law enacted in 1974 that governs restrictions on the release of student educational records. FERPA provides for the withholding of federal funds to educational institutions that violate its provisions, and it is the federal guarantor of the privacy rights of post-secondary students.*

(1) (A) No funds shall be made available under any applicable program to any educational agency or institution which has a policy of denying, or which effectively prevents, the parents of students who are or have been in attendance at a school of such agency or at such institution, as the case may be, the right to inspect and review the education records of their children. If any material or document in the education record of a student includes information on more than one student, the parents of one of such students shall have the right to inspect and review only such part of such material or document as relates to such student or to be informed of the specific information contained in such part of such material. Each educational agency or institution shall establish appropriate procedures for the granting of a request by parents for access to the education records of their children within a reasonable period of time, but in no case more than forty-five days after the request has been made....

(C) The first sentence of subparagraph (A) shall not operate to make available to students in institutions of postsecondary education the following materials:

(i) financial records of the parents of the student or any information contained therein;

(ii) confidential letters and statements of recommendation, which were placed in the education records prior to January 1, 1975, if such letters or statements are not used for purposes other than those for which they were specifically intended;

(iii) if the student has signed a waiver of the student's right of access under this subsection in accordance with subparagraph (D), confidential recommendations—

(I)   respecting admission to any educational agency or institution,

(II) respecting an application for employment, and

(III) respecting the receipt of an honor or honorary recognition.

. . . .

(B) The term "education records" does not include—

(i) records of instructional, supervisory, and administrative personnel and educational personnel ancillary thereto which are in the sole possession of the maker thereof and which are not accessible or revealed to any other person except a substitute;

(ii) records maintained by a law enforcement unit of the educational agency or institution that were created by that law enforcement unit for the purpose of law enforcement;

(iii) in the case of persons who are employed by an educational agency or institution but who are not in attendance at such agency or institution, records made and maintained in the normal course of business which relate exclusively to such person in that person's capacity as an employee and are not available for use for any other purpose; or

(iv) records on a student who is eighteen years of age or older, or is attending an institution of postsecondary education, which are made or maintained by a physician, psychiatrist, psychologist, or other recognized professional or paraprofessional acting in his professional or paraprofessional capacity, or assisting in that capacity, and which are made, maintained, or used only in connection with the provision of treatment to the student, and are not available to anyone other than persons providing such treatment, except that such records can be personally reviewed by a physician or other appropriate professional of the student's choice....

(h) Certain disciplinary action information allowable. Nothing in this section shall prohibit an educational agency or institution from—

(1) including appropriate information in the education record of any student concerning disciplinary action taken against such student for conduct that posed a significant risk to the safety or well-being of that student, other students, or other members of the school community; or

(2) disclosing such information to teachers and school officials, including teachers and school officials in other schools, who have legitimate educational interests in the behavior of the student.

Exercise 4.5

Critical Reading for Synthesis

Having read the selections relating to privacy and safety, pages 131–145, write a one-sentence summary of each. On the same page, list two or three topics that you think are common to several of the selections. Beneath each topic, list the authors who have something to say on that topic and briefly note what they have to say. Finally, for each topic, jot down what *you* have to say. Now regard your effort: With each topic you have created a discussion point suitable for inclusion in a paper. (Of course, until you determine the claim of such a paper, you won't know to what end you might put the discussion.) Write a paragraph or two in which you introduce the topic and then conduct a brief conversation among the interested parties (including yourself).

Consider Your Purpose

Your specific purpose in writing an argument synthesis is crucial. What exactly you want to do will affect your claim and how you organize the evidence. Your purpose may be clear to you before you begin research, or it may not emerge until after you have completed your research. Of course, the sooner your purpose is clear to you, the fewer wasted motions you will make. On the other hand, the more you approach research as an exploratory process, the likelier that your conclusions will emerge from the sources themselves rather than from preconceived ideas. Each new writing project will have its own rhythm in this regard. Be flexible in your approach: through some combination of preconceived structures and invigorating discoveries, you will find your way to the source materials that will yield a promising paper.

Let's say that while reading these seven (and additional) sources on the debate about campus safety and student privacy, you share the outrage of many who blamed the university (and the federal privacy laws on which it relied) for not using the available information in a way that might have spared the lives of those who died. Perhaps you also blame the legislators who wrote the privacy laws for being more concerned about the confidentiality of the mental health records of the individual person than with the safety of the larger college population. Perhaps, you conclude, society has gone too far in valuing privacy more than it appears to value safety.

On the other hand, in your own role as a student, perhaps you share the high value placed on the privacy of sensitive information about yourself. After all, one of the functions of higher education is to foster students' independence as they make the transition from adolescence to adulthood. You can understand that many students like yourself might not want their parents or others to know details about academic records or disciplinary measures, much less information about therapy sought and undertaken at school. Historically, in the decades since the university officially stood *in loco parentis*—in place of parents—students have struggled hard to win the same civil liberties and rights (including the right to privacy) of their elders.

Further, you may wonder whether federal privacy laws do in fact forbid the sharing of information about potentially dangerous students when the health and safety of others are at stake. A little research may begin to confirm your doubts whether Virginia Tech officials were really as helpless as they claimed they were.

Your purpose in writing, then, emerges from these kinds of responses to the source materials you find.

Making a Claim: Formulate a Thesis

As we indicated in the introduction to this chapter, one useful way of approaching an argument is to see it as making a *claim*. A claim is a proposition, a conclusion you have made, that you are trying to prove or demonstrate. If your purpose is to argue that we should work to ensure campus safety without enacting restrictive laws that overturn the hard-won privacy rights of students, then that claim (generally expressed in one-sentence form as a *thesis*) is at the heart of your argument. You will draw support from your sources as you argue logically for your claim.

Not every piece of information in a source is useful for supporting a claim. You must read with care and select the opinions, facts, and statistics that best advance your position. You may even find yourself drawing support from sources that make claims entirely different from your own. For example, in researching the subject of student privacy and campus safety, you may come across editorials arguing that in the wake of the Virginia Tech shootings, student privacy rights should be greatly restricted. Perhaps you will find information in these sources to help support your own contrary arguments.

You might use one source as part of a *counterargument*—an argument opposing your own—so that you can demonstrate its weaknesses and, in the process, strengthen your own claim. On the other hand, the author of one of your sources may be so convincing in supporting a claim that you adopt it yourself, either partially or entirely. The point is that *the argument is in your hands*. You must devise it yourself and use your sources in ways that will support the claim you present in your thesis.

You may not want to divulge your thesis until the end of the paper, thereby drawing the reader along toward your conclusion, allowing the thesis to flow naturally out of the argument and the evidence on which it is based. If you do this, you are working *inductively*. Or you may wish to be more direct and (after an introduction) *begin* with your thesis, following the thesis statement with evidence and reasoning to support it. If you do this, you are working *deductively*. In academic papers, deductive arguments are far more common than inductive ones.

Based on your reactions to reading sources—and perhaps also on your own inclinations as a student—you may find yourself essentially in sympathy with the approach to privacy taken by one of the schools covered in your sources, M.I.T. At the same time, you may feel that M.I.T.'s position does not demonstrate sufficient concern for campus safety and that Cornell's position, on the other hand, restricts student privacy too much. Perhaps most important, you conclude that we don't need to change the law because, if correctly interpreted, the law already incorporates a good balance between privacy and safety. After a few tries, you develop this thesis:

> In responding to the Virginia Tech killings, we should resist rolling back federal rules protecting student privacy; for as long as college officials effectively respond to signs of trouble, these rules already provide a workable balance between privacy and public safety.

Decide How You Will Use Your Source Material

Your claim commits you to (1) arguing that student privacy should remain protected, and (2) demonstrating that federal law already strikes a balance between privacy and public safety. The sources (some provided here, some located elsewhere) offer information and ideas—evidence—that will allow you to support your claim. The excerpt from the official report on the Virginia Tech shootings reveals a finding that school officials failed to correctly interpret federal privacy rules and failed to "intervene effectively." The article "Virginia Tech Massacre Has Altered Campus Mental Health Systems" outlines some of the ways that campuses around the country have instituted policy changes regarding troubled students and privacy in the wake of Virginia Tech. And the excerpt from the *Family Educational Rights and Privacy Act (FERPA)*, the federal law, reveals that restrictions on revealing students' confidential information have a crucial exception for "the safety or well-being of…students, or other members of the school community." (These and several other sources not included in this chapter will be cited in the model argument paper.)

Develop an Organizational Plan

Having established your overall purpose and your claim, having developed a thesis (which may change as you write and revise the paper), and having decided how to draw upon your source materials, how do you logically organize your paper? In many cases, a well-written thesis will suggest an organization. Thus, the first part of your paper will deal with the debate over rolling back student privacy. The second part will argue that as long as educational institutions behave proactively—that is, as long as they actively seek to help troubled students and foster campus safety—existing federal rules already preserve a balance between privacy and safety. Sorting through your material and categorizing it by topic and subtopic, you might compose the following outline:

    I. Introduction. Recap Va. Tech shooting. College officials, citing privacy rules, did not act on available info about shooter with history of mental problems.

    II. Federal rules on privacy. Subsequent debate over balance between privacy and campus safety. Pendulum now moving back toward safety. *Thesis.*

    III. Developments in student privacy in recent decades.
        A. Doctrine of *in loco parentis* defines college-student relationship.
        B. Movement away from *in loco parentis* begins in 1960s, in context not only of student rights but also broader civil rights struggles of the period.
        C. FERPA, enacted 1974, establishes new federal rules protecting student privacy.

    IV. Arguments *against* student privacy.
        A. In wake of Virginia Tech, many blame FERPA protections and college officials, believing privacy rights have been taken too far, putting campus community at risk.
        B. Cornell rolls back some FERPA privacy rights.

    V. Arguments *for* student privacy.
        A. M.I.T. strongly defends right to privacy.
        B. Problem is not federal law but incorrect interpretation of federal law. FERPA provides health and safety exceptions. Virginia Tech

officials erred in citing FERPA for not sharing info about shooter earlier.

C. Univ. of Kentucky offers good balance between competing claims of privacy and safety.
1. watch lists of troubled students
2. threat assessment groups
3. open communication among university officials

VI. Conclusion.

A. Virginia Tech incident was an instance of a legal issue students will encounter in the broader world: rights of the individual vs. rights of the larger group.

B. Virginia Tech incident was tragic but should not cause us to over-turn hard-won privacy rights.

C. We should support a more proactive approach to student mental health problems and improve communication between departments.

Formulate an Argument Strategy

The argument that emerges through this outline will build not only on evidence drawn from sources but also on the writer's assumptions. Consider the bare-bones logic of the argument:

> Laws protecting student privacy serve a good purpose. (*assumption*)
>
> If properly interpreted and implemented, federal law as currently written is sufficient both to protect student privacy and to ensure campus safety. (*support*)
>
> We should not change federal law to overturn or restrict student privacy rights. (*claim*)

The crucial point about which reasonable people will disagree is the *assumption* that laws protecting student privacy serve a good purpose. Those who wish to restrict the information made available to parents are likely to agree with this assumption. Those who favor a policy that allows college officials to inform parents of problems without their children's permission are likely to disagree.

Writers can accept or partially accept an opposing assumption by making a *concession*, in the process establishing themselves as reasonable and willing to compromise (see p. 166). David Harrison does exactly this in the following model synthesis when he summarizes the policies of the University of Kentucky. By raising objections to his own position and conceding some validity to them, he blunts the effectiveness of *counterarguments*. Thus, Harrison concedes the absolute requirement for campus safety, but he argues that this requirement can be satisfied as long as campus officials correctly interpret existing federal law and implement proactive procedures aimed at dealing more effectively with troubled students.

The *claim* of the argument about privacy vs. safety is primarily a claim about *policy*, about actions that should (or should not) be taken. An argument can also concern a claim about *facts* (Does X exist? How can we define X? Does X lead to Y?), a claim about *value* (What is X worth?), or a claim about *cause and effect* (Why did X happen?).

The present argument rests to some degree on a dispute about cause and effect. No one disputes that the primary cause of this tragedy was that a disturbed student was not stopped before he killed people. But many have disputed the secondary cause: Did the massacre happen, in part, because federal law prevented officials from sharing crucial information about the disturbed student? Or did it happen, in part, because university officials failed to interpret correctly what they could and could not do under the law? As you read the following paper, observe how these opposing views are woven into the argument.

Draft and Revise Your Synthesis

The final draft of an argument synthesis, based on the outline above, follows. Thesis, transitions, and topic sentences are highlighted; Modern Language Association (MLA) documentation style is used throughout (except in the citing of federal law).

A cautionary note: When writing syntheses, it is all too easy to become careless in properly crediting your sources. Before drafting your paper, always review the section on Avoiding Plagiarism (pp. 46–47).

MODEL ARGUMENT SYNTHESIS

Harrison 1

David Harrison

Professor Shanker

Law and Society I

21 February 2011

Balancing Privacy and Safety

in the Wake of Virginia Tech

(1)   On April 16, 2007, Seung Hui Cho, a mentally ill student at Virginia Polytechnic Institute, shot to death 32 fellow students and faculty members, and injured 17 others, before killing himself. It was the worst mass shooting in U.S. history, and the fact that it took place on a college

Harrison 2

campus lent a special horror to the event. In the days after the tragedy, several facts about Seung Hui Cho came to light. According to the official Virginia State Panel report on the killings, Cho had exhibited signs of mental disturbance, including "suicidal and homicidal ideations" dating back to high school. And during Cho's junior year at Virginia Tech, numerous incidents occurred that provided clear warnings of Cho's mental instability and violent impulses (Virginia Tech Review 1). University administrators, faculty, and officials were aware of these incidents but failed to intervene to prevent the impending tragedy.

(2)   In the search for answers, attention quickly focused on federal rules governing student privacy that Virginia Tech officials said prevented them from communicating effectively with each other or with Cho's parents regarding his troubles. These rules, the officials argued, prohibit the sharing of information concerning students' mental health with parents or other students. The publicity about such restrictions revived an ongoing debate over university policies that balance student privacy against campus safety. In the wake of the Virginia Tech tragedy, the pendulum seems to have swung in favor of safety. In April 2008, Virginia Governor Tim Kaine signed into law a measure requiring colleges to alert parents when dependent students may be a danger to themselves or to others ("Virginia Tech Massacre" 1). Peter Lake, an educator at Stetson University College of Law, predicted that in the wake of Virginia Tech, "people will go in a direction of safety over privacy" (qtd. in Bernstein, "Mother").

(3)   The shootings at Virginia Tech demonstrate, in the most horrifying way, the need for secure college campuses. Nevertheless, privacy remains a crucial right to most Americans—including college students, many of whom for the first time are exercising their prerogatives as adults. Many students who pose no threat to anyone will, and should, object strenuously to university administrators peering into and making judgments about their private lives. Some might be unwilling to seek professional therapy if they know that the records of their counseling sessions might be released to

their parents or to other students. In responding to the Virginia Tech killings, we should resist rolling back federal rules protecting student privacy;
for as long as college officials effectively respond to signs of trouble, these
rules already provide a workable balance between privacy and public safety.

4   In these days of *Facebook* and reality TV, the notion of privacy rights,
particularly for young people, may seem quaint. In fact, a top lawyer for
the search engine *Google* claimed that in the Internet age, young people
just don't care about privacy the way they once did (Cohen A17). Whatever
the changing views of privacy in a wired world, the issue of student privacy
rights is a serious legal matter that must be seen in the context of the
student-college relationship. This relationship has its historical roots in the
doctrine of *in loco parentis,* Latin for "in the place of the parents."
Generally, this doctrine is understood to mean that the college stands in
place of the student's parent or guardian. The college therefore has "a duty
to protect the safety, morals, and welfare of their students, just as parents
are expected to protect their children" (Pollet).

5   Writing of life at the University of Michigan before the 1960s, one
historian observes that "*in loco parentis* comprised an elaborate structure of
written rules and quiet understandings enforced in the trenches by house-
mothers [who] governed much of the what, where, when, and whom of
students' lives, especially women: what to wear to dinner, what time to be
home, where, when, and for how long they might receive visitors" (Tobin).

6   During the 1960s court decisions began to chip away at the doctrine
of *in loco parentis.* These rulings illustrate that the students' rights movement during that era was an integral part of a broader contemporary social
movement for civil rights and liberties. In *Dixon v. Alabama State Board of
Education,* Alabama State College invoked *in loco parentis* to defend its decision to expel six African-American students without due process for par-
ticipating in a lunchroom counter sit-in. Eventually, a federal appeals court
rejected the school's claim to unrestrained power, ruling that students'
constitutional rights did not end once they stepped onto campus (Weigel).

(7)   Students were not just fighting for the right to hold hands in dorm rooms; they were also asserting their rights as the vanguard of a social revolution. As Stetson law professor Robert Bickel notes: "The fall of *in loco parentis* in the 1960s correlated exactly with the rise of student economic power and the rise of student civil rights" (qtd. in Weigel).

(8)   The students' rights movement received a further boost with the Family Educational Rights and Privacy Act (FERPA), signed into law by President Ford in 1974. FERPA barred schools from releasing educational records— including mental health records—without the student's permission. The Act provides some important exceptions: educational records *can* be released in the case of health and safety emergencies or if the student is declared a dependent on his or her parents' tax returns (*Family*).

(9)   In the wake of Virginia Tech, however, many observers pointed the finger of blame at federal restrictions on sharing available mental health information. Also held responsible were the school's officials, who admitted knowing of Cho's mental instability but claimed that FERPA prevented them from doing anything about it. The State of Virginia official report on the killings notes as follows:

> University officials... explained their failures to commu-
> nicate with one another or with Cho's parents by noting
> their belief that such communications are prohibited by
> the federal laws governing the privacy of health and edu-
> cation records. (Virginia Tech Review 2)

(10)   Observers were quick to declare the system broken. "Laws Limit Schools Even after Alarms," trumpeted a headline in the *Philadelphia Inquirer* (Gammage and Burling). Commentators attacked federal privacy law, charging that the pendulum had swung too far away from campus safety. Judging from this letter to the editor of the *Wall Street Journal,* many agreed wholeheartedly: "Parents have a right to know if their child has a serious problem, and they need to know the progress of their child's

schoolwork, especially if they are paying the cost of the education. Anything less than this is criminal" (Guerriero).

(11)   As part of this public clamor, some schools have enacted policies that effectively curtail student privacy in favor of campus safety. For example: after Virginia Tech, Cornell University began assuming that students were dependents of their parents. Exploiting what the *Wall Street Journal* termed a "rarely used legal exception" in FERPA allows Cornell to provide parents with confidential information without students' permission (Bernstein, "Bucking" A9).

(12)   Conversely, the Massachusetts Institute of Technology lies at the opposite end of the spectrum from Cornell in its staunch defense of student privacy. M.I.T. has stuck to its position even in the wake of Virginia Tech, demanding that the mother of a missing M.I.T. student obtain a subpoena in order to access his dorm room and e-mail records. That student was later found dead, an apparent suicide (Bernstein, "Mother"). Even in the face of lawsuits, M.I.T. remains committed to its stance. Its Chancellor explained the school's position this way:

> Privacy is important. . . . Different students will do different things they absolutely don't want their parents to know about. . . . Students expect this kind of safe place where they can address their difficulties, try out lifestyles, and be independent of their parents (qtd. in Bernstein, "Mother").

(13)   One can easily understand how parents would be outraged by the M.I.T. position. No parent would willingly let his or her child enter an environment where that child's safety cannot be assured. Just as the first priority for any government is to protect its citizens, the first priority of an educational institution must be to keep its students safe. But does this responsibility justify rolling back student privacy rights or returning to a more traditional interpretation of *in loco parentis* in the relationship between a university and its students? No, for the simple reason that the choice is a false one.

Harrison 6

(14)   As long as federal privacy laws are properly interpreted and implemented, they do nothing to endanger campus safety. The problem at Virginia Tech was not the federal government's policy; it was the university's
own practices based on a faulty interpretation of that policy. The breakdown began with the failure of Virginia Tech officials to understand federal
privacy laws. Interpreted correctly, these laws would *not* have prohibited
officials from notifying appropriate authorities of Cho's problems. The
Virginia Tech Review Panel report was very clear on this point: "[F]ederal
laws and their state counterparts afford ample leeway to share information
in potentially dangerous situations" (2). FERPA does, in fact, provide for
a "health and safety emergencies" exception; educational records *can* be
released without the student's consent "in connection with an emergency,
[to] appropriate persons if the knowledge of such information is necessary
to protect the health or safety of the student or other person..." (232g (b)
(1) (g-h)). But Virginia Tech administrators did not invoke this important
exception to FERPA's privacy rules. (Nor did they inform students of Cho's
initial murder of two students, according to the Department of Education—
an action that might have averted the thirty other murders (Potter)).

(15)   An editorial in the *Christian Science Monitor* suggested several other
steps that the university could legally have taken, including informing
Cho's parents that he had been briefly committed to a mental health facility, a fact that was public information. The editorial concluded, scornfully,
that "federal law, at least, does recognize a balance between privacy and
public safety, even when colleges can't, or won't" ("Perilous").

(16)   To be fair, such confusion about FERPA's contingencies appears widespread among college officials. For this reason, the U.S. Department of
Education's revised privacy regulations, announced in March 2008 and intended to "clarify" when schools may release student records, are welcome
and necessary. But simply reassuring anxious university officials that they
won't lose federal funds for revealing confidential student records won't be
enough to ensure campus safety. We need far more effective intervention for

troubled students than the kind provided by Virginia Tech, which the Virginia Tech Review Panel blasted for its "lack of resources" and "passivity" (2). Yet effective interventions can be difficult to coordinate, and the consequences of inaction are sadly familiar. Three years after the Virginia Tech shootings, a student sued the University of California Regents because administrators at UCLA had allegedly failed to address the troubling behaviors of another student who later slashed and nearly killed her (Gordon).

(17)   Schools like the University of Kentucky offer a positive example of intervention, demonstrating that colleges can adopt a robust approach to student mental health without infringing on privacy rights. At Kentucky, "threat assessment groups" meet regularly to discuss a "watch list" of troubled students and decide what to do about them (McMurray). These committees emphasize proactiveness and communication—elements that were sorely missing at Virginia Tech. The approach represents a prudent middle ground between the extreme positions of M.I.T. and Cornell.

(18)   This middle ground takes full account of student privacy rights. For example, the University of Kentucky's director of counseling attends the threat assessment group's meetings but draws a clear line at what information she shares—for instance, whether or not a student has been undergoing counseling. Instead, the group looks for other potential red flags, such as a sharp drop-off in grades or difficulty functioning in the campus environment (McMurray). This open communication between university officials will presumably also help with delicate judgments—whether, for example, a student's violent story written for a creative writing class is an indication of mental instability or simply an early work by the next Stephen King ("Virginia Tech Massacre" 1).

(19)   The debate over rights to individual privacy versus public safety is sure to follow students into the wider world because that debate is one instance of a larger issue. The Fourth Amendment protects citizens "against unreasonable searches and seizures." But for more than two centuries, what constitutes *unreasonable* has been vigorously debated in the courts. Such

Harrison 8

arguments are not likely to end any time soon—on or off college campuses.
Consider the recent public controversy over the installation of full body
scanners at U.S. airports and intrusive pat-downs of travelers, measures
taken by the U.S. Department of Homeland Security to foil terrorist threats.
Predictably, many protested what they considered an assault on personal
privacy, complaining that the scanners revealed body parts otherwise hidden by clothing and that the pat-downs amounted to sexual groping. On
September 1, 2010, a civil liberties group even filed a lawsuit to block deployment of the scanners (Electronic). But many others vigorously defended
the Homeland Security measures as essential to ensuring public safety.
According to a *Washington Post*-ABC News poll, "Nearly two-thirds of Americans support the new full-body security-screening machines at the country's
airports, as most say they put higher priority on combating terrorism than
protecting personal privacy" (Cohen and Halsey).

(20)   What happened at Virginia Tech was a tragedy. Few of us can appreciate the grief of the parents of the shooting victims at Virginia Tech, parents
who trusted that their children would be safe and who were devastated
when that faith was betrayed. To these parents, the words of the M.I.T.
chancellor quoted earlier—platitudes about students "try[ing] out lifestyles"
or "address[ing] their difficulties"—must sound hollow. But we must guard
against allowing a few isolated incidents, however tragic, to restrict the
rights of millions of students, the vast majority of whom graduate college
safely and without incident. Schools must not use Virginia Tech as a pretext
to bring back the bad old days of resident assistants snooping on the private
lives of students and infringing on their privacy. That step is the first down
a slippery slope of dictating morality. Both the federal courts and Congress
have rejected that approach and for good reason have established the importance of privacy rights on campus. These rights must be preserved.

(21)   The Virginia Tech shooting does not demonstrate a failure of current
policy, but rather a breakdown in the enforcement of policy. In its wake,
universities have undertaken important modifications to their procedures.

We should support changes that involve a more proactive approach to student mental health and improvements in communication between departments, such as those at the University of Kentucky. Such measures will not only bring confidential help to the troubled students who need it, they will also improve the safety of the larger college community. At the same time, these measures will preserve hard-won privacy rights on campus.

Works Cited

Bernstein, Elizabeth. "Bucking Privacy Concerns, Cornell Acts as Watchdog." *Wall Street Journal* 27 Dec. 2007: A1+. *LexisNexis*. Web. 10 Feb. 2011.

—. "A Mother Takes On MIT." *Wall Street Journal* 20 Sept. 2007: A1. *Lexis-Nexis*. Web. 10 Feb. 2011.

Cohen, Adam. "One Friend Facebook Hasn't Made Yet: Privacy Rights." *New York Times* 18 Feb. 2008: A1+. *Academic Search Complete*. Web. 9 Feb. 2011.

Cohen, Jon, and Ashley Halsey III. "Poll: Nearly Two-thirds of Americans Support Full-Body Scanners at Airports." *Washington Post*. The Washington Post Co., 23 Nov. 2010. Web. 17 Feb. 2011.

Electronic Privacy Information Center v. Dept. of Homeland Security. No. 10-1157. D.C. Cir. of the US. Sept 1, 2010. *epic.org*. Electronic Privacy Information Center, 1 Sept. 2010. Web. 15 Feb. 2011.

Family Educational Rights and Privacy Act (FERPA). 20 U.S.C. §1232g (b) (1) (g–h) (2006). Print.

Gammage, Jeff, and Stacy Burling. "Laws Limit Schools Even after Alarms." *Philadelphia Inquirer* 19 Apr. 2007: A1. *Academic Search Complete*. Web. 10 Feb. 2011.

Harrison 11

Gordon, Larry. "Campus Stabbing Victim Sues UC Regents." *Los Angeles Times* 8 Dec. 2010. *LexisNexis*. Web. 13 Feb. 2011.

Guerriero, Dom. Letter. *Wall Street Journal* 7 Jan. 2008. *LexisNexis*. Web. 11 Feb. 2011.

McMurray, Jeffrey. "Colleges Are Watching Troubled Students." *AP Online*. Associated Press, 28 Mar. 2008. Web. 11 Feb. 2011.

"Perilous Privacy at Virginia Tech." Editorial. *Christian Science Monitor* 4 Sept. 2007: 8. *Academic Search Complete*. Web. 10 Feb. 2011.

Pollet, Susan J. "Is 'In Loco Parentis' at the College Level a Dead Doctrine?" *New York Law Journal* 288 (2002): 4. Print.

Potter, Dena. "Feds: Va. Tech Broke Law in '07 Shooting Response." *Washington Post*. The Washington Post Co., 10 Dec. 2010. Web. 12 Feb. 2011.

Tobin, James. "The Day 'In Loco Parentis' Died." *Michigan Today*. U of Michigan, Nov. 2007. Web. 10 Feb. 2011.

U.S. Constitution: Fourth Amendment. *Findlaw.com*. Thomson Reuters, n.d. Web. 16 Feb. 2011.

"Virginia Tech Massacre Has Altered Campus Mental Health Systems." *Los Angeles Times* 14 Apr. 2008: A1+. *LexisNexis*. Web. 8 Feb. 2011.

Virginia Tech Review Panel. *Mass Shootings at Virginia Tech, April 16, 2007: Report of the Virginia Tech Review Panel Presented to Timothy M. Kaine, Governor, Commonwealth of Virginia*. Arlington, VA: n.p., 2007. Print.

Weigel, David. "Welcome to the Fun-Free University: The Return of *In Loco Parentis* Is Killing Student Freedom." *Reasononline*. Reason Magazine, Oct. 2004. Web. 7 Feb. 2011.

The Strategy of the Argument Synthesis

In his argument synthesis, Harrison attempts to support a *claim*—one that favors laws protecting student privacy while at the same time helping to ensure campus safety—by offering *support* in the form of facts (what campuses such as the University of Kentucky are doing, what Virginia Tech officials did and failed to do) and opinions (testimony of persons on both sides of the issue). However, because Harrison's claim rests on an *assumption* about the value of student privacy laws, its effectiveness depends partially on the extent to which we, as readers, agree with this assumption. (See our discussion of assumptions in Chapter 2, pp. 64–67.) An assumption (sometimes called a warrant) is a generalization or principle about how the world works or should work—a fundamental statement of belief about facts or values. In this case, the underlying assumption is that college students, as emerging adults and as citizens with civil rights, are entitled to keep their educational records private. Harrison makes this assumption explicit. Though you are under no obligation to do so, stating assumptions explicitly will clarify your arguments to readers.

Assumptions are often deeply rooted in people's psyches, sometimes derived from lifelong experiences and observations and not easily changed, even by the most logical of arguments. People who lose loved ones in incidents such as Virginia Tech, or people who believe that the right to safety of the larger campus community outweighs the right of individual student privacy, are not likely to accept the assumption underlying this paper, nor are they likely to accept the support provided by Harrison. But readers with no firm opinion might well be persuaded and could come to agree with him that existing federal law protecting student privacy is sufficient to protect campus safety, provided that campus officials act responsibly.

A discussion of the model argument's paragraphs, along with the argument strategy for each, follows. Note that the paper devotes one paragraph to developing each section of the outline on pages 148–149. Note also that Harrison avoids plagiarism by the careful attribution and quotation of sources.

- **Paragraph 1:** Harrison summarizes the key events of the Virginia Tech killings and establishes that Cho's mental instability was previously known to university officials.

  Argument strategy: Opening with the bare facts of the massacre, Harrison proceeds to lay the basis for the reaction against privacy rules that will be described in the paragraphs to follow. To some extent, Harrison encourages the reader to share the outrage of many in the general public that university officials failed to act to prevent the killings before they started.

- **Paragraph 2:** Harrison now explains the federal rules governing student privacy and discusses the public backlash against such rules and the new law signed by the governor of Virginia restricting privacy at colleges within the state.

  Argument strategy: This paragraph highlights the debate over student privacy—and in particular the sometimes conflicting demands of student privacy and campus safety that will be central to the rest of the paper. Harrison cites both fact (the new Virginia law) and opinion (the quotation by Peter Lake) to develop this paragraph.

- **Paragraph 3:** Harrison further clarifies the two sides of the apparent conflict between privacy and safety, maintaining that both represent important social values but concluding with a thesis that argues for not restricting privacy.

  Argument strategy: For the first time, Harrison reveals his own position on the issue. He starts the paragraph by conceding the need for secure campuses but begins to make the case for privacy (for example, without privacy rules, students might be reluctant to enter therapy). In his thesis he emphasizes that the demands of both privacy and safety can be satisfied because existing federal rules incorporate the necessary balance.

- **Paragraphs 4–7:** These paragraphs constitute the next section of the paper (see outline, pp. 148–149), covering the developments in student privacy over the past few decades. Paragraphs 4 and 5 cover the doctrine of *in loco parentis;* paragraph 6 discusses how court decisions like *Dixon v. Alabama State Board of Education* began to erode this doctrine.

  Argument strategy: This section of the paper establishes the situation that existed on college campuses before the 1960s—and that presumably would exist again were privacy laws to be rolled back. By linking the erosion of the *in loco parentis* doctrine to the civil rights struggle, Harrison attempts to bestow upon pre-1960s college students (especially women), who were "parented" by college administrators, something of the *ethos* of African-Americans fighting for full citizenship during the civil rights era. Essentially, Harrison is making an analogy between the two groups—one that readers may or may not accept.

- **Paragraph 8:** This paragraph on FERPA constitutes the final part of the section of the paper dealing with the evolution of student privacy since before the 1960s. Harrison explains what FERPA is and introduces an exception to its privacy rules that will be more fully developed later in the paper.

  Argument strategy: FERPA is the federal law central to the debate over the balance between privacy and safety, so Harrison introduces it here as the culmination of a series of developments that weakened *in loco parentis* and guaranteed a certain level of student privacy. But since Harrison in his thesis argues that federal law on student privacy already establishes a balance between privacy and safety, he ends the paragraph by referring to the "health and safety" exception, an exception that will become important later in his argument.

- **Paragraphs 9–11:** These paragraphs constitute the section of the paper that covers the arguments *against* student privacy. Paragraph 9 discusses public reaction against both FERPA and Virginia Tech officials, who were accused of being more concerned with privacy than with safety. Paragraph 10 cites anti-privacy sentiments expressed in newspapers. Paragraph 11 explains how, in the wake of Virginia Tech, schools like Cornell have enacted new policies restricting student privacy.

Argument strategy: Harrison sufficiently respects the sentiments of those whose position he opposes to deal at some length with the counterarguments to his thesis. He quotes the official report on the mass shootings to establish that Virginia Tech officials believed that they were acting according to the law. He quotes the writer of an angry letter about parents' right to know without attempting to rebut its arguments. In outlining the newly restrictive Cornell policies on privacy, Harrison also establishes what he considers an extreme reaction to the massacres: essentially gutting student privacy rules. He is therefore setting up one position on the debate that he will later contrast with other positions—those of M.I.T. and the University of Kentucky.

- **Paragraphs 12–16:** These paragraphs constitute the section of the paper devoted to arguments *for* student privacy. Paragraphs 12 and 13 discuss the M.I.T. position on privacy, as expressed by its chancellor. Paragraph 14 refocuses on FERPA and quotes language to demonstrate that existing federal law provides a health and safety exception to the enforcement of privacy rules. Paragraph 15 quotes an editorial supporting this interpretation of FERPA. Paragraph 16 concedes the existence of confusion about federal rules and makes the transition to an argument about the need for more effective action by campus officials to prevent tragedies like the one at Virginia Tech.

  Argument strategy: Because these paragraphs express Harrison's position, as embedded in his thesis, this is the longest segment of the discussion. Paragraphs 12 and 13 discuss the M.I.T. position on student privacy, which (given that school's failure to accommodate even prudent demands for safety) Harrison believes is too extreme. Notice the transition at the end of paragraph 13: conceding that colleges have a responsibility to keep students safe, Harrison poses a question: Does the goal of keeping students safe justify the rolling back of privacy rights? In a pivotal sentence, he responds, "No, for the simple reason that the choice is a false one." Paragraph 14 develops this response and presents the heart of Harrison's argument. Recalling the health and safety exception introduced in paragraph 8, Harrison now explains *why* the choice is false: he quotes the exact language of FERPA to establish that the problem at Virginia Tech was due not to federal law that prevented campus officials from protecting students, but rather to campus officials who *misunderstood* the law.

  Paragraph 15 amplifies Harrison's argument with a reference to an editorial in the *Christian Science Monitor*. Paragraph 16 marks a transition, within this section, to a position (developed in paragraphs 17 and 18) that Harrison believes represents a sensible stance in the debate over campus safety and student privacy. Harrison bolsters his case by citing here, as elsewhere in the paper, the official report on the Virginia Tech killings. The report, prepared by an expert panel that devoted months to investigating the incident, carries considerable weight as evidence in this argument.

- **Paragraphs 17–18:** These paragraphs continue the arguments in favor of Harrison's position. They focus on new policies in practice at the University of Kentucky that offer a "prudent middle ground" in the debate.

  Argument strategy: Having discussed schools such as Cornell and M.I.T., where the reaction to the Virginia Tech killings was inadequate or unsatisfactory, Harrison now outlines a set of policies and procedures in place at the University of Kentucky since April 2007. Following the transition at the end of paragraph 16 on the need for more effective intervention on the part of campus officials, Harrison explains how Kentucky established a promising form of such intervention: watch lists of troubled students, threat assessment groups, and more open communication among university officials. Thus Harrison positions what is happening at the University of Kentucky—as opposed to rollbacks of federal rules—as the most effective way of preventing future killings like those at Virginia Tech. Kentucky therefore becomes a crucial example for Harrison of how to strike a good balance between the demands of student privacy and campus safety.

- **Paragraphs 19–21:** In his conclusion, Harrison both broadens the context of his discussion about Virginia Tech and reiterates points made in the body of the paper. In paragraph 19, he turns from the shooting to the broader world, suggesting that the tension between the individual's right to privacy and the public's right to safety is not unique to college campuses. In paragraph 20 he agrees that what happened at Virginia Tech was a tragedy but maintains that an isolated incident should not become an excuse for rolling back student privacy rights and bringing back "the bad old days" when campus officials took an active, and intrusive, interest in students' private lives. In paragraph 21, Harrison reiterates the position stated in his thesis: that the problem at Virginia Tech was not a restrictive federal policy that handcuffed administrators but a breakdown in enforcement. He concludes on the hopeful note that new policies established since Virginia Tech will both protect student privacy and improve campus safety.

  Argument strategy: The last three paragraphs, the conclusion, provide Harrison with an opportunity both to extend his thinking beyond a single case and to re-emphasize his main points. In paragraph 19, he moves beyond the world of college and broadens the reach of his argument. The final two paragraphs to some degree parallel the structure of the thesis itself. In paragraph 20, Harrison makes a final appeal against rolling back student privacy rights. This appeal parallels the first clause of the thesis ("In responding to the Virginia Tech killings, we should resist rolling back federal rules protecting student privacy"). In paragraph 21, Harrison focuses not on federal law itself but rather on the kind of measures adopted by schools like the University of Kentucky that go beyond mere compliance with federal law—and thereby demonstrate the validity of part two of Harrison's thesis ("As long as college officials effectively respond to signs of trouble, these rules already provide a workable balance between privacy and public safety"). Harrison thus ends a paper on a grim subject with a note that provides some measure of optimism and that attempts to reconcile proponents on both sides of this emotional debate.

Another approach to an argument synthesis based on the same and additional sources could argue (along with some of the sources quoted in the model paper) that safety as a social value should never be outweighed by the right to privacy. Such a position could draw support from other practices in contemporary society—searches at airports, for example—illustrating that most people are willing to give up a certain measure of privacy, as well as convenience, in the interest of the safety of the community. Whatever your approach to a subject, in first *critically examining* the various sources and then *synthesizing* them to support a position about which you feel strongly, you are engaging in the kind of critical thinking that is essential to success in a good deal of academic and professional work.

■ DEVELOPING AND ORGANIZING THE SUPPORT FOR YOUR ARGUMENTS

Experienced writers seem to have an intuitive sense of how to develop and present supporting evidence for their claims; this sense is developed through much hard work and practice. Less experienced writers wonder what to say first, and having decided on that, wonder what to say next. There is no single method of presentation. But the techniques of even the most experienced writers often boil down to a few tried and tested arrangements.

As we've seen in the model synthesis in this chapter, the key to devising effective arguments is to find and use those kinds of support that most persuasively strengthen your claim. Some writers categorize support into two broad types: *evidence* and *motivational appeals.* Evidence, in the form of facts, statistics, and expert testimony, helps make the appeal to reason. Motivational appeals—appeals grounded in emotion and upon the authority of the speaker—are employed to get people to change their minds, to agree with the writer or speaker, or to decide upon a plan of activity.

Following are the most common strategies for using and organizing support for your claims.

Summarize, Paraphrase, and Quote Supporting Evidence

In most of the papers and reports you will write in college and in the professional world, evidence and motivational appeals derive from your summarizing, paraphrasing, and quoting of material in sources that either have been provided to you or that you have independently researched. For example, in paragraph 9 of the model argument synthesis, Harrison uses a long quotation from the Virginia Tech Review Panel report to make the point that college officials believed they were prohibited by federal privacy law from communicating with one another about disturbed students like Cho. You will find another long quotation later in the synthesis and a number of brief quotations woven into sentences throughout. In addition, you will find summaries and paraphrases. In each case, Harrison is careful to cite the source.

Provide Various Types of Evidence and Motivational Appeals

Keep in mind that you can use appeals to both reason and emotion. The appeal to reason is based on evidence that consists of a combination of *facts* and *expert testimony.* The sources by Tobin and Weigel, for example, offer facts about the evolution over the past few decades of the *in loco parentis* doctrine. Bernstein and McMurray interview college administrators at Cornell, M.I.T., and the University of Kentucky who explain the changing policies at those institutions. The model synthesis makes an appeal to emotion by engaging the reader's self-interest: If campuses are to be made more secure from the acts of mentally disturbed persons, then college officials should take a proactive approach to monitoring and intervention.

Use Climactic Order

Climactic order is the arrangement of examples or evidence in order of anticipated impact on the reader, least to greatest. Organize by climactic order when you plan to offer a number of categories or elements of support for your claim. Recognize that some elements will be more important—and likely more persuasive—than others. The basic principle here is that you should *save the most important evidence for the end* because whatever you say last is what readers are likely to remember best. A secondary principle is that whatever you say first is what they are *next* most likely to remember. Therefore, when you have several reasons to offer in support of your claim, an effective argument strategy is to present the second most important, then one or more additional reasons, and finally the most important reason. Paragraphs 7–11 of the model synthesis do exactly this.

Use Logical or Conventional Order

Using a logical or conventional order involves using as a template a pre-established pattern or plan for arguing your case.

- One common pattern is describing or arguing a *problem/solution.* Using this pattern, you begin with an introduction in which you typically define the problem, perhaps explain its origins, then offer one or more solutions, then conclude.

- Another common pattern presents *two sides of a controversy.* Using this pattern, you introduce the controversy and (in an argument synthesis) your own point of view or claim; then you explain the other side's arguments, providing reasons why your point of view should prevail.
- A third common pattern is *comparison-and-contrast.* This pattern is so important that we will discuss it separately in the next section.

The order in which you present elements of an argument is sometimes dictated by the conventions of the discipline in which you are writing. For example, lab reports and experiments in the sciences and social sciences often follow this pattern: *Opening* or *Introduction, Methods and Materials* (of the experiment or study), *Results, Discussion.* Legal arguments often follow the so-called IRAC format: *Issue, Rule, Application, Conclusion.*

Present and Respond to Counterarguments

When developing arguments on a controversial topic, you can effectively use *counterargument* to help support your claims. When you use counterargument, you present an argument *against* your claim and then show that this argument is weak or flawed. The advantage of this technique is that you demonstrate that you are aware of the other side of the argument and that you are prepared to answer it.

Here is how a counterargument is typically developed:

I. Introduction and claim
II. Main opposing argument
III. Refutation of opposing argument
IV. Main positive argument

Use Concession

Concession is a variation of counterargument. As in counterargument, you present an opposing viewpoint, but instead of dismissing that position, you *concede* that it has some validity and even some appeal, although your own position is the more reasonable one. This concession bolsters your standing as a fair-minded person who is not blind to the virtues of the other side. In the model synthesis, Harrison acknowledges the grief and sense of betrayal of the parents of the students who were killed. He concedes that parents have a right to expect that "the first priority of an educational institution must be to keep its students safe." But he insists that this goal of achieving campus safety can be accomplished without rolling back hard-won privacy rights.

Here is an outline for a typical concession argument:

I. Introduction and claim
II. Important opposing argument

III. Concession that this argument has some validity

IV. Positive argument(s) that acknowledge the counterargument and (possibly) incorporate some elements of it

Sometimes, when you are developing a counterargument or concession argument, you may become convinced of the validity of the opposing point of view and change your own views. Don't be afraid of this happening. Writing is a tool for learning. To change your mind because of new evidence is a sign of flexibility and maturity, and your writing can only be the better for it.

Developing and Organizing Support for Your Arguments

- *Summarize, paraphrase, and quote supporting evidence.* Draw on the facts, ideas, and language in your sources.

- *Provide various types of evidence and motivational appeal.*

- *Use climactic order.* Save the most important evidence in support of your argument for the *end*, where it will have the most impact. Use the next most important evidence *first*.

- *Use logical or conventional order.* Use a form of organization appropriate to the topic, such as problem/solution; sides of a controversy; comparison/contrast; or a form of organization appropriate to the academic or professional discipline, such as a report of an experiment or a business plan.

- *Present and respond to counterarguments.* Anticipate and evaluate arguments against your position.

- *Use concession.* Concede that one or more arguments against your position have some validity; re-assert, nonetheless, that your argument is the stronger one.

Avoid Common Fallacies in Developing and Using Support

In Chapter 2, in the section on critical reading, we considered criteria that, as a reader, you may use for evaluating informative and persuasive writing (see pp. 53, 55–62). We discussed how you can assess the accuracy, the significance, and the author's interpretation of the information presented. We also considered the importance in good argument of clearly defined key terms and the pitfalls of emotionally loaded language. Finally, we saw how to recognize such logical fallacies as either/or reasoning, faulty cause-and-effect reasoning, hasty generalization, and false analogy. As a writer, no less than as a critical reader, you need to be aware of these common problems and how to avoid them.

Be aware, also, of your responsibility to cite source materials appropriately. When you quote a source, double- and triple-check that you have done so accurately. When you summarize or paraphrase, take care to use your own language and sentence structures (though you can, of course, also quote within these forms). When you refer to someone else's idea—even if you are not quoting, summarizing, or paraphrasing it—give the source credit. By being ethical about the use of sources, you uphold the highest standards of the academic community.

■ THE COMPARISON-AND-CONTRAST SYNTHESIS

A particularly important type of argument synthesis is built on patterns of comparison and contrast. Techniques of comparison and contrast enable you to examine two subjects (or sources) in terms of one another. When you compare, you consider *similarities.* When you contrast, you consider *differences.* By comparing and contrasting, you perform a multifaceted analysis that often suggests subtleties that otherwise might not have come to your (or your reader's) attention.

To organize a comparison-and-contrast argument, you must carefully read sources in order to discover *significant criteria for analysis.* A *criterion* is a specific point to which both of your authors refer and about which they may agree or disagree. (For example, in a comparative report on compact cars, criteria for *comparison and contrast* might be road handling, fuel economy, and comfort of ride.) The best criteria are those that allow you not only to account for obvious similarities and differences—those concerning the main aspects of your sources or subjects—but also to plumb deeper, exploring subtle yet significant comparisons and contrasts among details or subcomponents, which you can then relate to your overall thesis.

Note that comparison-and-contrast is frequently not an end in itself but serves some larger purpose. Thus, a comparison-and-contrast synthesis may be a component of a paper that is essentially a critique, an explanatory synthesis, an argument synthesis, or an analysis.

Organizing Comparison-and-Contrast Syntheses

Two basic approaches to organizing a comparison-and-contrast synthesis are organization by *source* and organization by *criteria.*

Organizing by Source or Subject

You can organize a comparative synthesis by first summarizing each of your sources or subjects and then discussing the significant similarities and differences between them. Having read the summaries and become familiar with the distinguishing features of each source, your readers will most likely be able to appreciate the more obvious similarities and differences. In the discussion, your task is to consider both the obvious and the subtle comparisons and contrasts, focusing on the most significant—that is, on those that most clearly support your thesis.

Organization by source or subject works best with passages that can be briefly summarized. If the summary of your source or subject becomes too long, your readers might have forgotten the points you made in the first summary when they are reading the second. A comparison-and-contrast synthesis organized by source or subject might proceed like this:

I. Introduce the paper; lead to thesis.

II. Summarize source/subject A by discussing its significant features.

III. Summarize source/subject B by discussing its significant features.

IV. Discuss in a paragraph (or two) the significant points of comparison and contrast between sources or subjects A and B. Alternatively, begin the comparison-contrast in Section III as you introduce source/subject B.

V. Conclude with a paragraph in which you summarize your points and, perhaps, raise and respond to pertinent questions.

Organizing by Criteria

Instead of summarizing entire sources one at a time with the intention of comparing them later, you could discuss two sources simultaneously, examining the views of each author point by point (criterion by criterion), comparing and contrasting these views in the process. The criterion approach is best used when you have a number of points to discuss or when passages or subjects are long and/or complex. A comparison-and-contrast synthesis organized by criteria might look like this:

I. Introduce the paper; lead to thesis.

II. Criterion 1

   A. Discuss what author #1 says about this point. Or present situation #1 in light of this point.

   B. Discuss what author #2 says about this point, comparing and contrasting #2's treatment of the point with #1's. Or present situation #2 in light of this point and explain its differences from situation #1.

III. Criterion 2

   A. Discuss what author #1 says about this point. Or present situation #1 in light of this point.

   B. Discuss what author #2 says about this point, comparing and contrasting #2's treatment of the point with #1's. Or present situation #2 in light of this point and explain its differences from situation #1.

And so on, proceeding criterion by criterion until you have completed your discussion. Be sure to arrange criteria with a clear method; knowing how the discussion of one criterion leads to the next will ensure smooth transitions throughout your paper. End by summarizing your key points and perhaps raising and responding to pertinent questions.

However you organize your comparison-and-contrast synthesis, keep in mind that comparing and contrasting are not ends in themselves. Your discussion should point to a conclusion, an answer to the question "So what— why bother to compare and contrast in the first place?" If your discussion is part of a larger synthesis, point to and support the larger claim. If you write a stand-alone comparison-and-contrast synthesis, though, you must by the final paragraph answer the "Why bother?" question. The model comparison-and-contrast synthesis that follows does exactly this.

Exercise 4.6

Comparing and Contrasting

Review the model argument synthesis (pp. 150–159) for elements of comparison and contrast—specifically those paragraphs concerning how Cornell University, M.I.T., and the University of Kentucky balance student privacy with the parental right to know about the health and welfare of their children.

1. From these paragraphs in the model paper, extract raw information concerning the positions of the three schools on the issue of student privacy and then craft your own brief comparison-and-contrast synthesis. Identify criteria for comparison and contrast, and discuss the positions of each school in relation to these criteria. *Note:* For this exercise, do not concern yourself with parenthetical citation (that is, with identifying your source materials).

2. Write a paragraph or two that traces the development of comparison-and-contrast throughout the model paper. Having discussed the *how* and *where* of this development, discuss the *why*. Answer this question: Why has the writer used comparison-and-contrast? (Hint: It is not an end in itself.) To what use is it put?

A Case for Comparison-and-Contrast: World War I and World War II

Let's see how the principles of comparison-and-contrast can be applied to a response to a final examination question in a course on modern history. Imagine that having attended classes involving lecture and discussion, and having read excerpts from John Keegan's *The First World War* and Tony Judt's *Postwar: A History of Europe Since 1945*, you were presented with this examination question:

> Based on your reading to date, compare and contrast the two world wars in light of any four or five criteria you think significant. Once

you have called careful attention to both similarities and differences, conclude with an observation. What have you learned? What can your comparative analysis teach us?

Comparison-and-Contrast Organized by Criteria

Here is a plan for a response, essentially a comparison-and-contrast synthesis, organized by *criteria* and beginning with the thesis—and the *claim.*

> *Thesis:* In terms of the impact on cities and civilian populations, the military aspects of the two wars in Europe, and their aftermaths, the differences between World War I and World War II considerably outweigh the similarities.
>
>   I. Introduction. World Wars I and II were the most devastating conflicts in history. *Thesis*
>   II. Summary of main similarities: causes, countries involved, battlegrounds, global scope.
> III. First major difference: Physical impact of war.
>   A. WWI was fought mainly in rural battlegrounds.
>   B. In WWII cities were destroyed.
>   IV. Second major difference: Effect on civilians.
>   A. WWI fighting primarily involved soldiers.
>   B. WWII involved not only military but also massive noncombatant casualties: civilian populations were displaced, forced into slave labor, and exterminated.
>   V. Third major difference: Combat operations.
>   A. World War I, in its long middle phase, was characterized by trench warfare.
>   B. During the middle phase of World War II, there was no major military action in Nazi-occupied Western Europe.
>   VI. Fourth major difference: Aftermath.
>   A. Harsh war terms imposed on defeated Germany contributed significantly to the rise of Hitler and World War II.
>   B. Victorious allies helped rebuild West Germany after World War II but allowed Soviets to take over Eastern Europe.
> VII. Conclusion. Since the end of World War II, wars have been far smaller in scope and destructiveness, and warfare has expanded to involve stateless combatants committed to acts of terror.

The following model exam response, a comparison-and-contrast synthesis organized by criteria, is written according to the preceding plan. (Thesis and topic sentences are highlighted.)

MODEL EXAM RESPONSE

(1) World War I (1914-18) and World War II (1939-45) were the most catastrophic and destructive conflicts in human history. For those who believed in the steady but inevitable progress of civilization, it was impossible to imagine that two wars in the first half of the twentieth century could reach levels of barbarity and horror that would outstrip those of any previous era. Historians estimate that more than 22 million people, soldiers and civilians, died in World War I; they estimate that between 40 and 50 million died in World War II. In many ways, these two conflicts were similar: they were fought on many of the same European and Russian battlegrounds, with more or less the same countries on opposing sides. Even many of the same people were involved: Winston Churchill and Adolf Hitler figured in both wars. And the main outcome in each case was the same: total defeat for Germany. However, in terms of the impact on cities and civilian populations, the military aspects of the two wars in Europe, and their aftermaths, the differences between World Wars I and II considerably outweigh the similarities.

(2) The similarities are clear enough. In fact, many historians regard World War II as a continuation—after an intermission of about twenty years—of World War I. One of the main causes of each war was Germany's dissatisfaction and frustration with what it perceived as its diminished place in the world. Hitler launched World War II partly out of revenge for Germany's humiliating defeat in World War I. In each conflict Germany and its allies (the Central Powers in WWI, the Axis in WWII) went to war against France, Great Britain, Russia (the Soviet Union in WWII), and eventually, the United States. Though neither conflict included literally the entire world, the participation of countries not only in Europe but also in the Middle East, the Far East, and the Western hemisphere made both conflicts global in scope. And as indicated earlier, the number of casualties in each war was unprecedented in history, partly because modern technology had

enabled the creation of deadlier weapons—including tanks, heavy artillery, and aircraft—than had ever been used in warfare.

(3)   Despite these similarities, the differences between the two world wars are considerably more significant. One of the most noticeable differences was the physical impact of each war in Europe and in Russia—the western and eastern fronts. The physical destruction of World War I was confined largely to the battlefield. The combat took place almost entirely in the rural areas of Europe and Russia. No major cities were destroyed in the first war; cathedrals, museums, government buildings, urban houses and apartments were left untouched. During the second war, in contrast, almost no city or town of any size emerged unscathed. Rotterdam, Warsaw, London, Minsk, and—when the Allies began their counterattack—almost every major city in Germany and Japan, including Berlin and Tokyo, were flattened. Of course, the physical devastation of the cities created millions of refugees, a phenomenon never experienced in World War I.

(4)   The fact that World War II was fought in the cities as well as on the battlefields meant that the second war had a much greater impact on civilians than did the first war. With few exceptions, the civilians in Europe during WWI were not driven from their homes, forced into slave labor, starved, tortured, or systematically exterminated. But all of these crimes happened routinely during WWII. The Nazi occupation of Europe meant that the civilian populations of France, Belgium, Norway, the Nether-lands, and other conquered lands, along with the industries, railroads, and farms of these countries, were put into the service of the Third Reich. Millions of people from conquered Europe—those who were not sent directly to the death camps—were forcibly transported to Germany and put to work in support of the war effort.

(5)   During both wars, the Germans were fighting on two fronts—the western front in Europe and the eastern front in Russia. But while both wars were characterized by intense military activity during their initial and final phases, the middle and longest phases—at least in Europe—differed considerably.

The middle phase of the First World War was characterized by trench warfare, a relatively static form of military activity in which fronts seldom moved, or moved only a few hundred yards at a time, even after major battles. By contrast, in the years between the German conquest of most of Europe by early 1941 and the Allied invasion of Normandy in mid-1944, there was no major fighting in Nazi-occupied Western Europe. (The land battles then shifted to North Africa and the Soviet Union.)

6   And of course, the two world wars differed in their aftermaths. The most significant consequence of World War I was that the humiliating and costly war reparations imposed on the defeated Germany by the terms of the 1919 Treaty of Versailles made possible the rise of Hitler and thus led directly to World War II. In contrast, after the end of the Second World War in 1945, the Allies helped rebuild West Germany (the portion of a divided Germany that it controlled), transformed the new country into a democracy, and helped make it one of the most thriving economies of the world. But perhaps the most significant difference in the aftermath of each war involved Russia. That country, in a considerably weakened state, pulled out of World War I a year before hostilities ended so that it could consolidate its 1917 Revolution. Russia then withdrew into itself and took no significant part in European affairs until the Nazi invasion of the Soviet Union in 1941. In contrast, it was the Red Army in World War II that was most responsible for the crushing defeat of Germany. In recognition of its efforts and of its enormous sacrifices, the Allies allowed the Soviet Union to take control of the countries of Eastern Europe after the war, leading to fifty years of totalitarian rule—and the Cold War.

7   While the two world wars that devastated much of Europe were similar in that, at least according to some historians, they were the same war interrupted by two decades, and similar in that combatants killed more efficiently than armies throughout history ever had, the differences between the wars were significant. In terms of the physical impact of the fighting, the impact on civilians, the action on the battlefield at mid-war, and the

aftermaths, World Wars I and II differed in ways that matter to us decades later. The wars in Iraq, Afghanistan, and Bosnia have involved an alliance of nations pitted against single nations; but we have not seen, since the two world wars, grand alliances moving vast armies across continents. The destruction implied by such action is almost unthinkable today. Warfare is changing, and "stateless" combatants like Hamas and Al Qaeda wreak destruction of their own. But we may never again see, one hopes, the devastation that follows when multiple nations on opposing sides of a conflict throw millions of soldiers—and civilians—into harm's way.

The Strategy of the Exam Response

The general strategy of this argument is an organization by *criteria.* The writer argues that although the two world wars exhibited some similarities, the differences between the two conflicts were more significant. Note that the writer's thesis doesn't merely state these significant differences; it also presents them in a way that anticipates both the content and the structure of the response to follow.

In argument terms, the *claim* the writer makes is the conclusion that the two global conflicts were significantly different, if superficially similar. The *assumption* is that key differences and similarities are clarified by employing specific criteria: the impact of the wars upon cities and civilian populations and the consequences of the Allied victories. The *support* comes in the form of historical facts regarding the levels of casualties, the scope of destruction, the theaters of conflict, the events following the conclusions of the wars, and so on.

- **Paragraph 1:** The writer begins by commenting on the unprecedented level of destruction of World Wars I and II and concludes with the thesis summarizing the key similarities and differences.
- **Paragraph 2:** The writer summarizes the key similarities in the two wars: the wars' causes, their combatants, their global scope, and the level of destructiveness made possible by modern weaponry.
- **Paragraph 3:** The writer discusses the first of the key differences: the battlegrounds of World War I were largely rural; the battlegrounds of World War II included cities that were targeted and destroyed.
- **Paragraph 4:** The writer discusses the second of the key differences: the impact on civilians. In World War I, civilians were generally spared

from the direct effects of combat; in World War II, civilians were targeted by the Nazis for systematic displacement and destruction.

- **Paragraph 5:** The writer discusses the third key difference: Combat operations during the middle phase of World War I were characterized by static trench warfare. During World War II, in contrast, there were no major combat operations in Nazi-occupied Western Europe during the middle phase of the conflict.

- **Paragraph 6:** The writer focuses on the fourth key difference: the aftermath of the two wars. After World War I, the victors imposed harsh conditions on a defeated Germany, leading to the rise of Hitler and the Second World War. After World War II, the Allies helped Germany rebuild and thrive. However, the Soviet victory in 1945 led to its postwar domination of Eastern Europe.

- **Paragraph 7:** In the conclusion, the writer sums up the key similarities and differences just covered and makes additional comments about the course of more recent wars since World War II. In this way, the writer responds to the questions posed at the end of the assignment: "What have you learned? What can your comparative analysis teach us?"

■ SUMMARY OF SYNTHESIS CHAPTERS

In this chapter and in Chapter 3, we've considered three main types of synthesis: the *explanatory synthesis,* the *argument synthesis,* and the *comparison-and-contrast synthesis.* Although for ease of comprehension we've placed these in separate categories, the types are not mutually exclusive. Argument syntheses often include extended sections of explanation and/or comparison and contrast. Explanations commonly include sections of comparison-and-contrast. Which type of synthesis you choose will depend on your *purpose* and the method that you decide is best suited to achieve this purpose.

If your main purpose is to help your audience understand a particular subject, and in particular to help them understand the essential elements or significance of this subject, then you will be composing an explanatory synthesis. If your main purpose, on the other hand, is to persuade your audience to agree with your viewpoint on a subject, or to change their minds, or to decide on a particular course of action, then you will be composing an argument synthesis. If your purpose is to clarify similarities or differences, you will compose a comparison-and-contrast synthesis—which may be a paper in itself (either an argument or an explanation) or part of a larger paper (again, either an argument or explanation).

In planning and drafting these syntheses, you can draw on a variety of strategies: supporting your claims by summarizing, paraphrasing, and quoting from your sources; using appeals to *logos, pathos,* and *ethos;* and choosing from among strategies such as climactic or conventional order, counterargument, and concession the approach that will best help you to achieve your purpose.

The strategies of synthesis you've practiced in these two chapters will be dealt with again in Chapter 7, where we'll consider a category of synthesis commonly known as the research paper. The research paper involves all of the skills in preparing summary, critique, and synthesis that we've discussed thus far, the main difference being that you won't find the sources needed to write the paper in this particular text. We'll discuss approaches to locating and critically evaluating sources, selecting material from among them to provide support for your claims, and, finally, documenting your sources in standard professional formats.

We turn, now, to analysis, which is another important strategy for academic thinking and writing. Chapter 5, Analysis, will introduce you to a strategy that, like synthesis, draws upon all the strategies you've been practicing as you move through *A Sequence for Academic Writing*.

WRITING ASSIGNMENT: THE CHANGING LANDSCAPE OF WORK IN THE TWENTY-FIRST CENTURY

Now we'll give you an opportunity to practice your skills in planning and writing an argument synthesis. See Chapter 8, pages 313–338, where we provide ten sources on the way that work will continue to change over the next few decades. Who will be the "winners" and "losers" among American workers? To what extent will education be a factor in your having the career of your choice? Is your job likely to be exported? What are some of the forces changing the shape of employment in business, technology, law, and medicine? In the synthesis, your task will be to take a stand in response to one or more of these questions and then to defend your response to readers.

Note that your instructor may assign related assignments for summary, critique, and explanation to help prepare you for writing a larger argument synthesis.

5 ■ Analysis

■ WHAT IS AN ANALYSIS?

An *analysis* is a type of argument in which you study the parts of something—a physical object, a work of art, a person or group of people, an event, a scientific, economic, or sociological phenomenon—to understand how it works, what it means, or why it might be significant. The writer of an analysis uses an analytical tool: a *principle* or *definition* on the basis of which the subject of study can be divided into parts and examined.

Here are excerpts from two analyses of the movie version of L. Frank Baum's *The Wizard of Oz:*

> At the dawn of adolescence, the very time she should start to distance herself from Aunt Em and Uncle Henry, the surrogate parents who raised her on their Kansas farm, Dorothy Gale experiences a hurtful reawakening of her fear that these loved ones will be rudely ripped from her, especially her Aunt (Em—M for Mother!).*

> [*The Wizard of Oz*] was originally written as a political allegory about grass-roots protest. It may seem harder to believe than Emerald City, but the Tin Woodsman is the industrial worker, the Scarecrow [is] the struggling farmer, and the Wizard is the president, who is powerful only as long as he succeeds in deceiving the people.†

As these paragraphs suggest, what you discover through analysis depends entirely on the principle or definition you use to make your insights. Is *The Wizard of Oz* the story of a girl's psychological development, or is it a story about politics? The answer is *both*. In the first example, the psychiatrist Harvey Greenberg applies the principles of his profession and, not surprisingly, sees *The Wizard of Oz* in psychological terms. In the second example, a newspaper reporter applies the political theories of Karl Marx and, again not surprisingly, discovers a story about politics.

Different as they are, these analyses share an important quality: Each is the result of a specific principle or definition used as a tool to divide an object into parts in order to see what it means and how it works. The writer's choice of analytical tool simultaneously creates and limits the possibilities for analysis. Thus, working with the principles of Freud, Harvey Greenberg

---

*Harvey Greenberg, *The Movies on Your Mind* (New York: Dutton, 1975).
†Peter Dreier, "Oz Was Almost Reality," *Cleveland Plain Dealer* 3 Sept. 1989.

sees *The Wizard of Oz* in psychological, not political, terms; working with the theories of Karl Marx, Peter Dreier understands the movie in terms of the economic relationships among the characters. It's as if the writer of an analysis who adopts one analytical tool puts on a pair of glasses and sees an object in a specific way. Another writer, using a different tool (and a different pair of glasses), sees the object differently.

Where Do We Find Written Analyses?

Here are just a few of the types of writing that involve analysis:

ACADEMIC WRITING

- **Experimental and lab reports** analyze the meaning or implications of the study results in the Discussion section.
- **Research papers** analyze information in sources or apply theories to material being reported.
- **Process analyses** break down the steps or stages involved in completing a process.
- **Literary analyses** examine characterization, plot, imagery, or other elements in works of literature.
- **Essay exams** demonstrate understanding of course material by analyzing data using course concepts.

WORKPLACE WRITING

- **Grant proposals** analyze the issues you seek funding for in order to address them.
- **Reviews of the arts** employ dramatic or literary analysis to assess artistic works.
- **Business plans** break down and analyze capital outlays, expenditures, profits, materials, and the like.
- **Medical charts** record analytical thinking and writing in relation to patient symptoms and possible options.
- **Legal briefs** break down and analyze facts of cases and elements of legal precedents and apply legal rulings and precedents to new situations.
- **Case studies** describe and analyze the particulars of a specific medical, social service, advertising, or business case.

You might protest: Are there as many analyses of *The Wizard of Oz* as there are people to read the book or to see the movie? Yes, or at least as many analyses as there are analytical tools. This does not mean that all analyses are equally valid or useful. Each writer must convince the reader using the power of her or his argument. In creating an analytical discussion, the writer must organize a series of related insights using the analytical tool to examine first one part and then another part of the object being studied. To read Harvey Greenberg's essay on *The Wizard of Oz* is to find paragraph after paragraph of related insights—first about Aunt Em, then the Wicked Witch, then Toto, and then the Wizard. All these insights point to Greenberg's single conclusion: that "Dorothy's 'trip' is a marvelous metaphor for the psychological journey every adolescent must make." Without Greenberg's analysis, we would probably not have thought about the movie as a psychological journey. This is precisely the power of an analysis: its ability to reveal objects or events in ways we would not otherwise have considered.

The writer's challenge is to convince readers that (1) the analytical tool being applied is legitimate and well matched to the object being studied; and (2) the analytical tool is being used systematically and insightfully to divide the object into parts and to make a coherent, meaningful statement about these parts and the object as a whole.

■ HOW TO WRITE ANALYSES

Let's consider a more extended example of analysis, one that approaches excessive TV watching as a type of addiction. This analytical passage illustrates the two defining features of the analysis: a statement of an analytical principle or definition and the use of that principle or definition in closely examining an object, behavior, or event. As you read, try to identify these features. An exercise with questions for discussion follows the passage.

THE PLUG-IN DRUG

Marie Winn

This analysis of television viewing as an addictive behavior appeared originally in Marie Winn's book The Plug-In Drug: Television, Computers, and Family Life (2002). *A writer and media critic, Winn has been interested in the effects of television on both individuals and the larger culture. In this passage, she carefully defines the term* addiction *and then applies it systematically to the behavior under study.*

The word "addiction" is often used loosely and wryly in conversation. People will refer to themselves as "mystery-book addicts" or "cookie addicts." E. B. White wrote of his annual surge of interest in gardening: "We are hooked and are making an attempt to kick the habit." Yet nobody really believes that reading mysteries or ordering seeds by catalogue is serious enough to be compared with addictions to heroin or alcohol. In these cases the word "addiction" is used jokingly to denote a tendency to overindulge in some pleasurable activity.

People often refer to being "hooked on TV." Does this, too, fall into the light-hearted category of cookie eating and other pleasures that people pursue with unusual intensity? Or is there a kind of television viewing that falls into the more serious category of destructive addiction?

Not unlike drugs or alcohol, the television experience allows the participant to blot out the real world and enter into a pleasurable and passive mental state. To be sure, other experiences, notably reading, also provide a temporary respite from reality. But it's much easier to stop reading and return to reality than to stop watching television. The entry into another world offered by reading includes an easily accessible return ticket. The entry via television does not. In this way television viewing, for those vulnerable to addiction, is more like drinking or taking drugs—once you start it's hard to stop.

Just as alcoholics are only vaguely aware of their addiction, feeling that they control their drinking more than they really do ("I can cut it out any time I want—I just like to have three or four drinks before dinner"), many people overestimate their control over television watching. Even as they put off other activities to spend hour after hour watching television, they feel they could easily resume living in a different, less passive style. But somehow or other while the television set is present in their homes, it just stays on. With television's easy gratifications available, those other activities seem to take too much effort.

5   A heavy viewer (a college English instructor) observes:

> I find television almost irresistible. When the set is on, I cannot ignore it. I can't turn it off. I feel sapped, will-less, enervated. As I reach out to turn off the set, the strength goes out of my arms. So I sit there for hours and hours.

Self-confessed television addicts often feel they "ought" to do other things—but the fact that they don't read and don't plant their garden or sew or crochet or play games or have conversations means that those activities are no longer as desirable as television viewing. In a way, the lives of heavy viewers are as unbalanced by their television "habit" as drug addicts' or alcoholics' lives. They are living in a holding pattern, as it were, passing up the activities that lead to growth or development or a sense of accomplishment. This is one reason people talk about their television viewing so ruefully, so apologetically. They are aware that it is an unproductive experience, that by any human measure almost any other endeavor is more worthwhile.

It is the adverse effect of television viewing on the lives of so many people that makes it feel like a serious addiction. The television habit distorts the sense of time. It renders other experiences vague and curiously unreal while taking on a greater reality for itself. It weakens relationships by reducing and sometimes eliminating normal opportunities for talking, for communicating.

And yet television does not satisfy, else why would the viewer continue to watch hour after hour, day after day? "The measure of health," wrote the psychiatrist Lawrence Kubie, "is flexibility...and especially the freedom to cease when sated." But heavy television viewers can never be sated with their television experiences. These do not provide the true nourishment that satiation requires, and thus they find that they cannot stop watching.

Reading Critically: Winn

In an analysis, an author first presents the analytical principle in full and then systematically applies parts of the principle to the object or phenomenon under study. In her brief analysis of television viewing, Marie Winn pursues an alternative, though equally effective, strategy by *distributing* parts of her analytical principle across the essay. Locate where Winn defines key elements of addiction. Locate where she uses each element as an analytical lens to examine television viewing as a form of addiction.

What function does paragraph 4 play in the analysis?

In the first two paragraphs, how does Winn create a funnel-like effect that draws readers into the heart of her analysis?

Recall a few television programs that genuinely moved you, educated you, humored you, or stirred you to worthwhile reflection or action. To what extent does Winn's analysis describe your positive experiences as a television viewer? (Consider how Winn might argue that from within an addicted state, a person may feel "humored, moved, or educated" but is in fact—from a sober outsider's point of view—deluded.) If Winn's analysis of television viewing as an addiction does *not* account for your experience, does it follow that her analysis is flawed? Explain.

Locate and Apply an Analytic Tool

The general purpose of all analysis is to enhance one's understanding of the subject under consideration. A good analysis provides a valuable—if sometimes unusual or unexpected—point of view, a way of *seeing*, a way of *interpreting* some phenomenon, person, event, policy, or pattern of behavior that otherwise may appear random or unexplainable. How well the analysis achieves its purpose depends upon the suitability to the subject and the precision of the analytical tools selected and upon the skill with which the writer (or speaker) applies these tools. Each reader must determine for her- or himself whether the analysis enhances understanding or—in the opposite case—is merely confusing or irrelevant. To what extent does it enhance your understanding of *The Wizard of Oz* to view the story in psychological terms? In political terms? To what extent does it enhance your understanding of excessive TV watching to view such behavior as an addiction?

When you are faced with writing an analysis, consider these two general strategies:

• Locate an analytic tool—a principle or definition that makes a general statement about the way something works.

• Systematically apply this principle or definition to the subject under consideration.

Let's more fully consider each of these strategies.

Locate an Analytic Tool

In approaching her subject, Marie Winn finds in the definition of "addiction" a useful principle for making sense of the way some people watch TV. The word "addiction," she notes, "is used jokingly to denote a tendency to overindulge in some pleasurable activity." The question she decides to tackle is whether, in the case of watching TV, such overindulgence is harmless, or whether it is destructive, and thus constitutes an addiction.

Make yourself aware, as both writer and reader, of a tool's strengths and limitations. Pose these questions of the analytical principle and definitions you use:

- Are they accurate?
- Are they well accepted?
- Do you accept them?
- How successfully do they account for or throw light upon the phenomenon under consideration?
- What are the arguments against them?
- What are their limitations?

Since every principle of definition used in an analysis is the end product of an argument, you are entitled—even obligated—to challenge it. If the analytical tool is flawed, the analysis that follows from it will necessarily be flawed.

Some, for example, would question whether addiction is a useful concept to apply to television viewing. First, we usually think of addiction as applying only to substances such as alcohol, nicotine, or drugs (whether legal or illegal). Second, many people think that the word "addiction" carries inappropriate moral connotations: we disapprove of addicts and think that they have only themselves to blame for their condition. For a time, the American Psychiatric Association dropped the word "addiction" from its definitive guide to psychological disorders, the *Diagnostic and Statistical Manual of Mental Disorders* (DSM), in favor of the more neutral term "dependence." (The latest edition of the DSM has returned to the term "addiction.")

On the other hand, "addiction"—also known as "impulse control disorder"—has long been applied to behavior as well as to substances. People are said to be addicted to gambling, to shopping, to eating, to sex, even to hoarding newspapers. The editors of the new DSM are likely to add Internet addiction to the list of impulse control disorders. The term even has national implications: many argue that this country must break its "addiction" to oil. Thus, there is considerable precedent for Winn to argue that excessive TV watching constitutes an addiction.

Apply the Analytic Tool

Having suggested that TV watching may be an addiction, Winn uses established psychological criteria* to identify the chief components of addictive behavior. She then applies each one of them to the behavior under consideration. In doing so, she presents her case that TV is a "plug-in drug"; and her readers are free to evaluate the success and persuasiveness of her analysis.

In the body of her analysis, Winn systematically applies the component elements of addiction to TV watching. Winn does this by identifying the major components of addiction and applying them to television watching. Users—

1. Turn away from the real world.
2. Overestimate how much control they have over their addiction.
3. Lead unbalanced lives and turn away from social activities.
4. Develop a distorted sense of time.
5. Are never satisfied with their use.

Analysis Across the Curriculum

The principle that you select can be a theory as encompassing as the statement that *myths are the enemy of truth*. It can be as modest as the definition of a term such as *addiction* or *comfort*. As you move from one subject area to another, the principles and definitions you use for analysis will change, as these assignments illustrate:

Sociology: Write a paper in which you place yourself in American society by locating both your absolute position and relative rank on each single criterion of social stratification used by Lenski & Lenski. For each criterion, state whether you have attained your social position by yourself or have "inherited" that status from your parents.

Literature: Apply principles of Jungian psychology to Hawthorne's "Young Goodman Brown." In your reading of the story, apply Jung's principles of the *shadow, persona,* and *anima.*

Physics: Use Newton's second law ($F = ma$) to analyze the acceleration of a fixed pulley from which two weights hang: m_1 (.45 kg) and m_2 (.90 kg). Explain in

---

*For example, the Web site AddictionsandRecovery.org., drawing upon the *Diagnostic and Statistical Manual of Mental Disorders* (DSM) criteria, identifies seven components of substance addiction. A person who answers yes to three of the following questions meets the medical definition of addiction: **Tolerance** (increased use of drugs or alcohol increased over time); **Withdrawal** (adverse physical or emotional reactions to not using); **Difficulty controlling your use** (using more than you would like); **Negative consequences** (using even though use negatively affects mood, self-esteem, health, job, or family); **Neglecting or postponing activities** (putting off or reducing social, recreational, work in order to use); **Spending significant time or emotional energy** (spending significant time obtaining, using, concealing, planning, recovering from, or thinking about use); **Desire to cut down.**

a paragraph the principle of Newton's law and your method of applying it to solve the problem. Assume your reader is not comfortable with mathematical explanations: do not use equations in your paragraph.

Finance: Using Guidford C. Babcock's "Concept of Sustainable Growth" [*Financial Analysis* 26 (May–June 1970): 108–14], analyze the stock price appreciation of the XYZ Corporation, figures for which are attached.

The analytical tools to be applied in these assignments must be appropriate to the discipline. Writing in response to the sociology assignment, you would use sociological principles developed by Lenski and Lenski. In your literature class, you would use principles of Jungian psychology; in physics, Newton's second law; and in finance, a particular writer's concept of "sustainable growth." But whatever discipline you are working in, the first part of your analysis will clearly state which (and whose) principles and definitions you are applying. For audiences unfamiliar with these principles, you will need to explain them; if you anticipate objections to their use, you will need to argue that they are legitimate principles capable of helping you conduct the analysis.

Guidelines for Writing Analyses

Unless you are asked to follow a specialized format, especially in the sciences or the social sciences, you can present your analysis as a paper by following the guidelines below. As you move from one class to another, from discipline to discipline, the principles and definitions you use as the basis for your analyses will change, but the following basic components of analysis will remain the same.

- *Create a context for your analysis.* Introduce and summarize for readers the object, event, or behavior to be analyzed. Present a strong case for why an analysis is needed: Give yourself a motivation to write, and give readers a motivation to read. Consider setting out a problem, puzzle, or question to be investigated.

- *Locate an analytic tool: a principle or definition that will form the basis of your analysis.* Plan to devote an early part of your analysis to arguing for the validity of this principle or definition if your audience is not likely to understand it or if they are likely to think that the principle or definition is not valuable.

- *Analyze your topic by applying your selected analytic tool to the topic's component elements.* Systematically apply elements of the analytic tool to parts of the activity or object under study. You can do this by posing specific questions, based on your analytic principle or definition, about the object or phenomenon. Discuss what you find part by part (organized perhaps by question), in clearly defined subsections of the paper.

(continues)

> • *Conclude by stating clearly what is significant about your analysis.* When considering your analytical paper as a whole, what new or interesting insights have you made concerning the object under study? To what extent has your application of the definition or principle helped you to explain how the object works, what it might mean, or why it is significant?

Formulate a Thesis

Like any other thesis, the thesis of an analysis compresses into a single sentence the main idea of your presentation. Some authors omit an explicit thesis statement, preferring to leave the thesis implied. Underlying Winn's analysis, for example, is an implied thesis: "By applying my multipart definition, we can understand television viewing as an addiction." Other authors may take two or perhaps even more sentences to articulate their thesis. But stated or implied, one sentence or more, your thesis must be clearly formulated at least in your own mind if your analysis is to hold together.

The analysis itself, as we have indicated, is a two-part argument. The first part states and establishes your use of a certain principle or definition that serves as your analytic tool. The second part applies specific parts or components of the principle or definition to the topic at hand.

Develop an Organizational Plan

You will benefit enormously in the writing of a first draft if you plan out the logic of your analysis. Turn key elements of your analytical principle or definition into questions, and then develop the paragraph-by-paragraph logic of the paper.

Turning Key Elements of a Principle or a Definition into Questions

Prepare for an analysis by phrasing questions based on the definition or principle you are going to apply, and then directing those questions to the activity or object to be studied. The method is straightforward:

- State as clearly as possible the principle or definition to be applied.
- Divide the principle or definition into its parts.
- Using each part, form a question.

For example, Marie Winn develops a multipart definition of addiction, each part of which is readily turned into a question that she directs at a specific behavior: television viewing. Her analysis of television viewing can be understood as *responses* to each of her analytical questions. Note that in her brief analysis, Winn does not first define addiction and then analyze television viewing. Rather, *as* she defines aspects of addiction, she analyzes television viewing.

Developing the Paragraph-by-Paragraph Logic of Your Paper

The following paragraph from Marie Winn's analysis illustrates the typical logic of a paragraph in an analytical paper:

> Self-confessed television addicts often feel they "ought" to do other things—but the fact that they don't read and don't plant their garden or sew or crochet or play games or have conversations means that those activities are no longer as desirable as television viewing. In a way, the lives of heavy viewers are as unbalanced by their television "habit" as drug addicts' or alcoholics' lives. They are living in a holding pattern, as it were, passing up the activities that lead to growth or development or a sense of accomplishment. This is one reason people talk about their television viewing so ruefully, so apologetically. They are aware that it is an unproductive experience, that by any human measure almost any other endeavor is more worthwhile.

We see in this paragraph the typical logic of an analysis:

- *The writer introduces a specific analytical tool.* Winn refers to one of the established components of addiction: the addictive behavior crowds out and takes precedence over other, more fruitful activities.

- *The writer applies this analytical tool to the object being examined.* Winn points out that people who spend their time watching television "don't read and don't plant their garden or sew or crochet or play games or have conversations...."

- *The writer uses the tool to identify and then examine the significance of some aspect of the subject under discussion.* Having applied the analytic tool to the subject of television viewing, Winn generalizes about the significance of what is revealed: "This is one reason people talk about their television viewing so ruefully, so apologetically. They are aware that it is an unproductive experience, that by any human measure almost any other endeavor is worthwhile."

An analytic paper takes shape when a writer creates a series of such paragraphs, links them with an overall logic, and draws a general conclusion concerning what was learned through the analysis. Here is the logical organization of Marie Winn's analysis:

- **Paragraph 1:** Introduces the word "addiction" and indicates how the term is generally used.

- **Paragraph 2:** Suggests that television watching might be viewed as a "destructive addiction."

- **Paragraph 3:** Discusses the first component of the definition of addiction: an experience that "allows the participant to blot out the real world and enter into a pleasurable and passive mental state." Applies this first component to television viewing.

- **Paragraphs 4 and 5:** Discuss the second component of addiction—the participant has an illusion of control—and apply this to the experience of television viewing.

- **Paragraph 6:** Discusses the third component of addiction—because it requires so much time and emotional energy, the addictive behavior crowds out other, more productive or socially desirable activities—and applies this to the experience of television viewing.

- **Paragraph 7:** Discusses the fourth component of addiction—the negative consequences arising from the behavior—and applies this to the experience of television viewing.

- **Paragraph 8:** Discusses the fifth component of addiction—the participant is never satisfied because the experience is essentially empty—and applies this to the experience of television viewing. Note that in this paragraph, Winn brings in for support a relevant quotation by the psychiatrist Lawrence Kubie.

Draft and Revise Your Analysis

You will usually need at least two drafts to produce a paper that presents your idea clearly. The biggest changes in your paper will typically come between your first and second drafts. No paper that you write, analysis or otherwise will be complete until you revise and refine your single compelling idea—in the case of analysis, your analytical conclusion about what the object, event, or behavior being examined means or how it is significant. You revise and refine by evaluating your first draft, bringing to it many of the same questions you pose when evaluating any piece of writing:

- Are the facts accurate?
- Are my opinions supported by evidence?
- Are the opinions of others authoritative?
- Are my assumptions clearly stated?
- Are key terms clearly defined?
- Is the presentation logical?
- Are all parts of the presentation well developed?
- Are significant opposing points of view presented?

Address these same questions to the first draft of your analysis, and you will have solid information to guide your revision.

Write an Analysis, Not a Summary

The most common error made in writing analyses—an error that is *fatal* to the form—is to present readers with a summary only. For analyses to succeed, you must *apply* a principle or definition and reach a conclusion about the object, event, or behavior you are examining. By definition, a summary (see Chapter 1) includes none of your own conclusions. Summary is naturally a part of analysis; you will need to summarize the object or activity being examined and, depending on the audience's needs, summarize the principle or definition being applied. But in an analysis, you must take the next step and share insights that suggest the meaning or significance of some object, event, or behavior.

Make Your Analysis Systematic

Analyses should give the reader the sense of a systematic, purposeful examination. Marie Winn's analysis illustrates the point: She sets out specific elements of addictive behavior in separate paragraphs and then uses each, within its paragraph, to analyze television viewing. Winn is systematic in her method, and we are never in doubt about her purpose.

Imagine another analysis in which a writer lays out four elements of a definition and then applies only two, without explaining the logic for omitting the others. Or imagine an analysis in which the writer offers a principle for analysis but directs it to only a half or a third of the object being discussed, without providing a rationale for doing so. In both cases the writer fails to deliver on a promise basic to analyses: Once a principle or definition is presented, it should be thoroughly and systematically applied.

Answer the "So What?" Question

An analysis should make readers *want* to read it. It should give readers a sense of getting to the heart of the matter, that what is important in the object or activity under analysis is being laid bare and discussed in revealing ways. If when rereading the first draft of your analysis, you cannot imagine readers saying, "I never thought of _____ this way," then something may be seriously wrong. Reread closely to determine why the paper might leave readers flat and exhausted, as opposed to feeling that they have gained new and important insights. Closely reexamine your own motivations for writing. Have *you* learned anything significant through the analysis? If not, neither will readers, and they will turn away. If you have gained important insights through your analysis, communicate them clearly. At some point, pull together your related insights and say, in effect, "Here's how it all adds up."

Attribute Sources Appropriately

In an analysis, you often work with just a few sources and apply insights from them to some object or phenomenon you want to understand more thoroughly. Because you are not synthesizing large quantities of data, and because the strength of an analysis derives mostly from *your* application of a principle or definition, the opportunities for not appropriately citing sources are diminished. However, take special care to cite and quote, as necessary, those sources that you draw upon throughout the analysis.

Critical Reading for Analysis

- *Read to get a sense of the whole in relation to its parts.* Whether you are clarifying for yourself a principle or a definition to be used in an analysis, or you are reading a text that you will analyze, understand how parts function to create the whole. If a definition or principle consists of parts, use them to organize sections of your analysis. If your goal is to analyze a text, be aware of its structure: Note the title and subtitle; identify the main point and subordinate points and where they are located; break the material into sections.

- *Read to discover relationships within the object being analyzed.* Watch for patterns. When you find them, be alert—for they create an occasion to analyze, to use a principle or definition as a guide in discussing what the patterns may mean.

    In fiction, a pattern might involve responses of characters to events or to each other, the recurrence of certain words or phrasings, images, themes, or turns of plot (to name a few).

    In poetry, a pattern might involve rhyme schemes, rhythm, imagery, figurative or literal language, and more.

The challenge to you as a reader is first to see a pattern (perhaps using a guiding principle or definition to do so) and then to locate other instances of that pattern. Reading carefully in this way prepares you to conduct an analysis.

When *Your* Perspective Guides the Analysis

In some cases a writer's analysis of a phenomenon or a work of art may not result from anything as structured as a principle or a definition. It may instead follow from the writer's cultural or personal outlook, perspective, or interests. Imagine reading a story or observing the lines of a new building and being asked to analyze it—based not on someone else's definition or principle, but on your own. Your analysis of the story might largely be determined by your preference for fast pacing; intrepid, resourceful heroes; and pitiless, black-hearted villains. Among the principles you might use in analyzing the building are your admiration for curved exterior surfaces and the imaginative use of glass.

Analyses in this case continue to probe the parts of things to understand how they work and what they mean. And they continue to be carefully structured, examining one part of a phenomenon at a time. The essential purpose of the analysis, to *reveal*, remains unchanged. This goal distinguishes the analysis from the critique, whose main purpose is to *evaluate* and *assess validity*.

An intriguing example of how shifts in personal perspective over time may affect one's analysis of a particular phenomenon is offered by Terri

Martin Hekker. In 1977 Hekker wrote an op-ed for the *New York Times* viewing traditional marriage from a perspective very different from that of contemporary feminists, who, she felt, valued self-fulfillment through work more than their roles as traditional housewives:

> I come from a long line of women...who never knew they were unfulfilled. I can't testify that they were happy, but they *were* cheerful....They took pride in a clean, comfortable home and satisfaction in serving a good meal because no one had explained to them that the only work worth doing is that for which you get paid.

Hekker's view of the importance of what she calls "housewifery"—the role of the traditional American wife and mother—derived from her own personal standards and ideals, which themselves derived from a cultural perspective that she admitted were no longer in fashion in the late 1970s.

Almost thirty years later (2006), Hekker's perspective had dramatically shifted. Her shattering experiences in the wake of her unexpected divorce had changed her view—and as a result, her analysis—of the status, value, and prospects of the traditional wife:

> Like most loyal wives of our generation, we'd contemplated eventual widowhood but never thought we'd end up divorced....If I had it to do over again, I'd still marry the man I married and have my children....But I would have used the years after my youngest started school to further my education. I could have amassed two doctorates using the time and energy I gave myself to charitable and community causes and been better able to support myself.

Hekker's new analysis of the role of the traditional wife derives from her changed perspective, based on her own experience and the similar experiences of a number of her divorced friends.

If you find yourself writing an analysis guided by your own insights, not by someone else's, then you owe your reader a clear explanation of your guiding principles and the definitions by which you will probe the subject under study. Continue using the Guidelines for Writing Analyses (see pp. 185–186), modifying this advice as you think fit to accommodate your own personal outlook, perspective, or interests. Above all, remember to structure your analysis with care. Proceed systematically and emerge with a clear statement about what the subject means, how it works, or why it might be significant.

■ DEMONSTRATION: ANALYSIS

Linda Shanker wrote the following paper as a first-semester sophomore in response to this assignment from her sociology professor:

> Read Robert H. Knapp's "A Psychology of Rumor" in your course anthology. Use some of Knapp's observations about rumor to examine a

particular rumor that you have read about in your reading during the first few weeks of this course. Write for readers much like yourself: freshmen or sophomores who have taken one course in sociology. Your object in this paper is to draw upon Knapp to shed light on how the particular rumor you select spread so widely and so rapidly.

MODEL ANALYSIS

Linda Shanker

Social Psychology 1

UCLA

17 November 2010

The Case of the Missing Kidney: An Analysis of Rumor

Rumor! What evil can surpass her speed?

In movement she grows mighty, and achieves

strength and dominion as she swifter flies...

[F]oul, whispering lips, and ears, that catch at all...

She can cling

to vile invention and malignant wrong,

or mingle with her word some tidings true.

—Virgil, *The Aeneid* (Book IV, Ch. 8)

1   The phenomenon of rumor has been an object of fascination since ancient times. In his epic poem *The Aeneid,* Virgil noted some insidious truths about rumors: they spread quickly—especially in our own day, by means of phones, TV, e-mail, and Twitter; they can grow in strength and come to dominate conversation with vicious lies; and they are often mixed with a small portion of truth, a toxic combination that provides the rumor with some degree of credibility. In more recent years, sociologists and psychologists have studied various aspects of rumors: why they are such a common feature of any society, how they tie in to our individual and group views of the world, how and why they spread, why people believe them, and finally, how they can be prevented and contained.

(2)   One of the most important studies is Robert H. Knapp's "A Psychology of Rumor," published in 1944. Knapp's article appeared during World War II (during which he was in charge of rumor control for the Massachusetts Committee of Public Safety), and many of his examples are drawn from rumors that sprang up during that conflict; but his analysis of why rumors form and how they work remains just as relevant today. First, Knapp defines rumor as an unverified statement offered about some topic in the hope that others will believe it (22). He proceeds to classify rumors into three basic types: the *pipe-dream or wish rumor,* based on what we would like to happen; the *bogie rumor,* based on our fears and anxieties; and the *wedge-driving or aggression rumor,* based on "dividing groups and destroying loyalties" (23–24). He notes that rumors do not spread randomly through the population, but rather through certain "sub-groups and factions" who are most susceptible to believing them. Rumors spread particularly fast, he notes, when these groups do not trust officials to tell them the truth. Most important, he maintains, "rumors express the underlying hopes, fears, and hostilities of the group" (27).

(3)   Not all rumors gain traction, of course, and Knapp goes on to outline the qualities that make for successful rumors. For example, a good rumor must be "short, simple, and salient." It must be a good story. Qualities that make for a good story include "a humorous twist...striking and aesthetic detail...simplification of plot and circumstances...[and] exaggeration" (29). Knapp explains how the same rumor can take various forms, each individually suited to the groups among which it is circulating: "[n]ames, numbers, and places are typically the most unstable components of any rumor." Successful rumors adapt themselves to the particular circumstances, anxieties, prejudices of the group, and the details change according to the "tide of current swings in public opinion and interest" (30).

(4)   Knapp's insights are valuable in helping us to understand why some contemporary rumors have been so frightening and yet so effective, for instance, the rumor of the missing kidney. One version of this story, current

Shanker 3

in 1992, is recounted by Robert Dingwall, a sociologist at the University of Nottingham in England:

> A woman friend of another customer had a 17-year-old
> son who went to a night club in Nottingham, called the
> Black Orchid, one Friday evening. He did not come home,
> so she called the police, who were not very interested
> because they thought that he had probably picked up a
> girl and gone home with her. He did not come back all
> weekend, but rang his mother from a call box on Monday,
> saying he was unwell. She drove out to pick him up and
> found him slumped on the floor of the call box. He said
> that he had passed out after a drink in the club and
> remembered nothing of the weekend. There was a neat,
> fresh scar on his abdomen. She took him to the Queen's
> Medical Centre, the main emergency hospital in the city,
> where the doctors found that he had had a kidney re-
> moved. The police were called again and showed much
> more interest. A senior officer spoke to the mother and
> said that there was a secret surveillance operation going
> on in this club and others in the same regional chain in
> other East Midlands cities because they had had several
> cases of the same kind and they thought that the organs
> were being removed for sale by an Asian surgeon. (181)

⑤   It is not clear where this rumor originated, though at around this time the missing kidney story had served as the basis of a *Law and Order* episode in 1992 and a Hollywood movie, *The Harvest,* released in 1992. In any event, within a few months the rumor had spread throughout Britain, with the name of the night club and other details varying according to the city where it was circulating. The following year, the story was transplanted to Mexico; a year later it was set in India. In the Indian version, the operation was performed

Shanker 4

on an English woman traveling alone who went to a New Delhi hospital to have an appendectomy. Upon returning to England, she still felt ill, and after she was hospitalized, it was discovered that her appendix was still there but that her kidney had been removed. In subsequent years the rumor spread to the United States, with versions of the story set in Philadelphia, New Orleans, Houston, and Las Vegas. In 1997, the following message, addressed "Dear Friends," was posted on an Internet message board:

> I wish to warn you about a new crime ring that is target-
> ing business travelers. This ring is well organized, well
> funded, has very skilled personnel, and is currently in
> most major cities and recently very active in New Orleans.
> The crime begins when a business traveler goes to a
> lounge for a drink at the end of the work day. A person in
> the bar walks up as they sit alone and offers to buy them
> a drink. The last thing the traveler remembers until they
> wake up in a hotel room bath tub, their body submerged
> to their neck in ice, is sipping that drink. There is a note
> taped to the wall instructing them not to move and to call
> 911. A phone is on a small table next to the bathtub for
> them to call. The business traveler calls 911 who have be-
> come quite familiar with this crime. The business traveler
> is instructed by the 911 operator to very slowly and care-
> fully reach behind them and feel if there is a tube pro-
> truding from their lower back. The business traveler finds
> the tube and answers, "Yes." The 911 operator tells them
> to remain still, having already sent paramedics to help.
> The operator knows that both of the business traveler's
> kidneys have been harvested. This is not a scam or out
> of a science fiction novel, it is real. It is documented and
> confirmable. If you travel or someone close to you travels,
> please be careful. ("You've Got to Be")

Shanker 5

Subsequent posts on this message board supposedly confirmed this story ("Sadly, this is very true"), adding different details.

(6)   Is there any truth to this rumor? None, whatsoever—not in any of its forms. Police and other authorities in various cities have posted strenuous denials of the story in the newspapers, on official Web sites, and in internal correspondence, as have The National Business Travel Association, the American Gem Trade Association, and the Sherwin Williams Co. ("'Stolen' Kidney Myth Circulating"). As reported in the rumor-reporting website Snopes.com, "the National Kidney Foundation has asked any individual who claims to have had his or her kidneys illegally removed to step forward and contact them. So far no one's showed up." The persistence and power of the missing kidney rumor can be more fully understood if we apply four of Knapp's principles of rumor formation and circulation to this particular urban legend: his notion of the "bogie"; the "striking" details that help authenticate a "good story" and that change as the rumor migrates to different populations; the ways a rumor can ride swings of public opinion; and the mingling of falsehood with truth.

(7)   The kidney rumor is first and foremost the perfect example of Knapp's bogie rumor, the rumor that draws its power from our fears and anxieties. One source of anxiety is being alone in a strange place. (Recall the scary folk tales about children lost in the forest, soon to encounter a witch.) These dreaded kidney removals almost always occur when the victim is away from home, out of town or even out of the country. Most of us enjoy traveling, but we may also feel somewhat uneasy in unfamiliar cities. We're not comfortably on our own turf, so we don't quite know our way around; we don't know what to expect of the local population; we don't feel entirely safe, or at least, we feel that some of the locals may resent us and take advantage of us. We can relate to the 17-year-old in the Nottingham nightclub, to the young English woman alone in New Delhi, to the business traveler having a drink in a New Orleans lounge.

(8)   Of course, our worry about being alone in an unfamiliar city is nothing compared to our anxiety about being cut open. Even under the

Shanker 6

best of circumstances (such as to save our lives), no one looks
forward to surgery. The prospect of being drugged, taken to an unknown
facility, and having members of a crime ring remove one of our organs
without our knowledge or consent—as apparently happened to the
various subjects of this rumor—would be our worst nightmare.
It's little wonder that this particular "bogie" man has such a powerful
grip on our hearts.

(9)   Our anxiety about the terrible things that may happen to us in a
strange place may be heightened because of the fear that our fate is just
punishment for the bad things that we have done. In the Nottingham
version of the rumor, the victim "had probably picked up a girl and gone
home with her" (Dingwall 181). Another version of the story features "an
older man picked up by an attractive woman" (Dingwall 182). Still another version of the story is set in Las Vegas, "Sin City, the place where
Bad Things Happen to the Unwary (especially the 'unwary' who were seen
as deservedly having brought it upon themselves, married men intent
upon getting up to some play-for-pay hanky panky" ("You've Got to Be").
As Dingwall notes of this anxiety about a deserved fate, "[t]he moral is
obvious: young people ought to be careful about night clubs, or more
generally, about any activity which takes them out of a circle of family
and friends" (183).

(10)   In addition to being a classic bogie rumor, Knapp would suggest
that the missing kidney rumor persists because its "striking and aesthetic
detail[s]," while false, have the ring of truth and vary from one version to another, making for a "good story" wherever the rumor spreads. Notice that the
story includes the particular names of the bar or nightclub, the medical facility, the hotel; it describes the size and shape of the scar; and it summarizes
the instructions of the 911 operator to see if there is a tube protruding from
the victim's back. (The detail about the bathtub full of ice and the advice to
"call 911" was added to the story around 1995.) As Knapp observes,
"[n]ames, numbers, and places are typically the most unstable components

Shanker 7

of any rumor" (30), and so the particular cities in which the kidney operations are alleged to have been performed, as well as the particular locations
within those cities, changed as the rumor spread. Another changing detail
concerns the chief villains of this story. Knapp notes that rumors adapt themselves to the particular anxieties and prejudices of the group. Many groups
hate or distrust foreigners and so we find different ethnic or racial "villains"
named in different cities. In the Nottingham version of the story, the operation is performed by an "Asian surgeon." The English woman's kidney was
removed by an Indian doctor. In another version of the story, a Kurdish victim of the kidney operation was lured to Britain "with the promise of a job
by a Turkish businessman" ("You've Got to Be").

⑪   Third, Knapp observes that successful rumors "ride the tide of current swings in public opinion and interest" (30). From news reports as
well as medical and police TV dramas, many people are aware that there
is a great demand for organ transplants and that such demand, combined
with a short supply, has given rise to a black market for illegally obtained
organs. When we combine this awareness with stories that appear to provide convincing detail about the medical procedure involved (the "neat
fresh scar," the tube, the name of the hospital), it is not surprising that
many people accept this rumor as truth without question. One Internet
correspondent, who affirmed that "Yes, this does happen" (her sister-in-
law supposedly worked with a woman whose son's neighbor was a victim
of the operation), noted that the only "good" thing about this situation
was that those who performed the procedure were medically trained, used
sterile equipment, made "exact and clean" incisions ("You've Got to Be"),
and in general took measures to avoid complications that might lead to
the death of the patient.

⑫   Finally, this rumor gains credibility because, as Virgil noted, rumor
"mingle[s] with her word some tidings true." Although no documented
case has turned up of a kidney being removed without the victim's knowledge and consent, there have been cases of people lured into selling their

Shanker 8

kidneys and later filing charges because they came to regret their decisions or were unhappy with the size of their payment ("You Got to Be").

⑬   Rumors can destroy reputations, foster distrust of government and other social institutions, and create fear and anxiety about perceived threats from particular groups of outsiders. Writing in the 1940s about rumors hatched during the war years, Knapp developed a powerful theory that helps us understand the persistence of rumors sixty years later. The rumor of the missing kidney, like any rumor, functions much like a mirror held up to society: it reveals anxiety and susceptibility to made-up but seemingly plausible "facts" related to contemporary social concerns. By helping us to understand the deeper structure of rumors, Knapp's theories can help free us from the "domination" and the "Foul, whispering lips" that Virgil observed so accurately 2,000 years ago.

Shanker 9

Works Cited

Dingwall, Robert. "Contemporary Legends, Rumors, and Collective Behavior: Some Neglected Resources for Medical Technology." *Sociology of Health and Illness* 23.2 (2001): 180–202. Print.

Knapp, Robert H. "A Psychology of Rumor." *Public Opinion Quarterly* 8.1 (1944): 22–37. Print.

"'Stolen' Kidney Myth Circulating: Organ Donation Hurt by Story of Kidney Heist." *UNOS*. United Network for Organ Sharing Newsroom Archive, 20 Aug. 1999. Web. 13 June 2010.

Virgil. *The Aeneid*. Trans. Theodore C. Williams. Perseus 4.0. *Perseus Digital Library*. Web. 17 Oct. 2010.

"You've Got to Be Kidneying." *Snopes.com*. Snopes, 12 Mar. 2008. Web. 12 June 2010.

Informal Analysis of the Model Analysis

Before reading our analysis of this model analysis, write your own informal response to the analysis. What are its strengths and weaknesses? To what extent does it follow the general Guidelines for Writing Analyses that we outlined on pages 185–186? What function does each paragraph serve in the analysis as a whole?

The Strategy of the Analysis

- Paragraph 1 creates a context for the analysis by introducing the phenomenon of rumor, indicating that it has been an object of fascination and study from ancient times (the poet Virgil is quoted) to the present.

- Paragraphs 2 and 3 introduce the key principle that will be used to analyze the selected rumor, as explained by Robert H. Knapp in his article "A Psychology of Rumor." The principle includes Knapp's definition of rumor, his classification of rumors into three types, and the qualities that make for a successful rumor.

- Paragraph 4 begins by indicating how Knapp's principles can be used to help us understand how rumor works, and then presents one particular manifestation of the rumor to be analyzed, the rumor of the missing kidney. Much of the paragraph consists of an extended quotation describing one of the original versions of the rumor, set in Nottingham, England.

- Paragraph 5 describes how the missing kidney rumor metamorphosed and spread, first throughout England, and then to other countries, including Mexico, India, and the United States. A second extended quotation describes a version of the rumor set in New Orleans.

- Paragraph 6 explains that the missing kidney rumor has no factual basis, but that its persistence and power can be accounted for by applying Knapp's principles. The final sentence of this paragraph is the thesis of the analysis.

- Paragraph 7 applies the first of Knapp's principles to the missing kidney rumor: it is a bogie rumor that "draws its power from our fears and anxieties." One such fear is that of being alone in an unfamiliar environment.

- Paragraph 8 continues to apply Knapp's principle of the bogie rumor, this time focusing on our fears about being unwillingly operated upon.

- Paragraph 9 discusses another aspect of the bogie rumor, the fear that what happens to us is a form of punishment for our own poor choices or immoral actions.

- Paragraph 10 deals with a second of Knapp's principles, that the "facts" in rumors are constantly changing: names, places, and other details change as the rumor spreads from one city to another, but the reference to specific details lends the rumor a veneer of authenticity.

- Paragraph 11 deals with a third of Knapp's principles: that successful rumors are often based on topics of current public interest—in this case, organ transplants and that, once again, a surface aura of facts makes the rumor appear credible.

- Paragraph 12 returns to Virgil (cited in paragraph 1), who notes that successful rumors also appear credible because they often mix truth with fiction.

- Paragraph 13, concluding the analysis, indicates why it is important to analyze rumor: shedding light on how and why rumors like this one spread may help us to counteract rumors' destructive effects.

WRITING ASSIGNMENT: ANALYSIS

Read the following passage, "A Theory of Human Motivation," by Abraham Maslow. Then write a paper using Maslow's theory as an analytical tool, applying what he says about human motivation to some element of your own reading, knowledge, or personal experience. As a model for your own paper, you may wish to use Linda Shanker's analysis of the missing kidney rumor (with respect to her application of Knapp's principles of rumor formation). More specific suggestions follow the passage.

A THEORY OF HUMAN MOTIVATION
Abraham H. Maslow

Abraham Maslow (1908–1970) was one of the most influential humanistic psychologists of the twentieth century. He earned his PhD at the University of Wisconsin and spent most of his academic career at Brandeis University in Waltham, Massachusetts. Maslow's theories have been widely applied in business, the military, and academia. His books include Motivation and Personality *(1954) and* Toward a Psychology of Being *(1962). This selection is excerpted from an article that first appeared in* Psychological Review 50 *(1943): 371–96.*

The Basic Needs

The "physiological" needs   The needs that are usually taken as the starting point for motivation theory are the so-called physiological drives....

[A]ny of the physiological needs...serve as channels for all sorts of other needs as well. That is to say, the person who thinks he is hungry may actually be seeking more for comfort, or dependence, than for vitamins or proteins. Conversely, it is possible to satisfy the hunger need in part by other activities such as drinking water or smoking cigarettes....

Undoubtedly these physiological needs...exceed all others in power. What this means specifically is, that in the human being who is missing everything in life in an extreme fashion, it is most likely that the major motivation would be the physiological needs rather than any others. A person who is lacking food, safety, love, and esteem would most probably hunger for food more strongly than for anything else.

Obviously a good way to obscure the "higher" motivations, and to get a lopsided view of human capacities and human nature, is to make the organism extremely and chronically hungry or thirsty. Anyone who attempts to make an emergency picture into a typical one, and who will measure all of man's goals and desires by his behavior during extreme physiological deprivation is certainly being blind to many things. It is quite true that man lives by bread alone—when there is no bread. But what happens to man's desires when there is plenty of bread and when his belly is chronically filled?

5   At once other (and "higher") needs emerge and these, rather than physiological hungers, dominate the organism. And when these in turn are satisfied, again new (and still "higher") needs emerge and so on. This is what we mean by saying that the basic human needs are organized into a hierarchy of relative prepotency.

One main implication of this phrasing is that gratification becomes as important a concept as deprivation in motivation theory, for it releases the organism from the domination of a relatively more physiological need, permitting thereby the emergence of other more social goals. The physiological needs, along with their partial goals, when chronically gratified cease to exist as active determinants or organizers of behavior. They now exist only in a potential fashion in the sense that they may emerge again to dominate the organism if they are thwarted. But a want that is satisfied is no longer a want. The organism is dominated and its behavior organized only by unsatisfied needs. If hunger is satisfied, it becomes unimportant in the current dynamics of the individual.

The safety needs   If the physiological needs are relatively well gratified, there then emerges a new set of needs, which we may categorize roughly as the safety needs. All that has been said of the physiological needs is equally true, although in lesser degree, of these desires. The organism may equally well be wholly dominated by them. They may serve as the almost exclusive organizers of behavior, recruiting all the capacities of the organism in their service, and we may then fairly describe the whole organism as a safety-seeking mechanism. Again we may say of the receptors, the effectors, of the intellect and the other capacities that they are primarily safety-seeking tools. Again, as in the hungry man, we find that the dominating goal [is strongly determinant] not only of his current world-outlook and philosophy but also of his philosophy of the future. Practically everything looks less important than safety (even sometimes the physiological needs which being satisfied, are now underestimated). A man, in this state, if it is extreme enough and chronic enough, may be characterized as living almost for safety alone. . . .

The healthy, normal, fortunate adult in our culture is largely satisfied in his safety needs. The peaceful, smoothly running, "good" society ordinarily makes its members feel safe enough from wild animals, extremes of temperature, criminals, assault and murder, tyranny, etc. Therefore, in a very real sense, he no longer has any safety needs as active motivators. Just as a sated man no longer feels hungry a safe man no longer feels endangered. If we wish to see these needs directly and clearly we must turn to neurotic or near-neurotic individuals, and to the economic and social underdogs. In between these extremes, we can perceive the expressions of safety needs only in such phenomena as, for instance, the common preference for a job with tenure and protection, the desire for a savings account, and for insurance of various kinds (medical, dental, unemployment, disability, old age).

Other broader aspects of the attempt to seek safety and stability in the world are seen in the very common preference for familiar rather than unfamiliar things, or for the known rather than the unknown. The tendency to have some religion or world-philosophy that organizes the universe and the men in it into some sort of satisfactorily coherent, meaningful whole is also in part motivated by safety-seeking. Here too we may list science and philosophy in general as partially motivated by the safety needs.

10 *The love needs* If both the physiological and the safety needs are fairly well gratified, then there will emerge the love and affection and belongingness needs, and the whole cycle already described will repeat itself with this new center. Now the person will feel keenly, as never before, the absence of friends, or a sweetheart, or a wife, or children. He will hunger for affectionate relations with people in general, namely, for a place in his group, and he will strive with great intensity to achieve this goal. He will want to attain such a place more than anything else in the world and may even forget that once, when he was hungry he sneered at love....

One thing that must be stressed at this point is that love is not synonymous with sex. Sex may be studied as a purely physiological need. Ordinarily sexual behavior is multi-determined, that is to say, determined not only by sexual but also by other needs, chief among which are the love and affection needs. Also not to be overlooked is the fact that the love needs involve both giving and receiving love.

The esteem needs All people in our society (with a few pathological exceptions) have a need or desire for a stable, firmly based, (usually) high evaluation of themselves, for self-respect, or self-esteem, and for the esteem of others. By firmly based self-esteem, we mean that which is soundly based upon...achievement and respect from others. These needs may be classified into two subsidiary sets. These are, first, the desire for strength, for achievement, for adequacy, for confidence in the face of the world, and for independence and freedom. Secondly, we have what we may call the desire for reputation or prestige (defining it as respect or esteem from other people), recognition, attention, importance or appreciation....

Satisfaction of the self-esteem need leads to feelings of self-confidence, worth, strength, capability and adequacy of being useful and necessary in the world. But thwarting of these needs produces feelings of inferiority, of weakness and of helplessness. These feelings in turn give rise to either basic discouragement or else compensatory or neurotic trends. An appreciation of the necessity of basic self-confidence and an understanding of how helpless people are without it, can be easily gained from a study of severe traumatic neurosis.

The need for self-actualization Even if all these needs are satisfied, we may still often (if not always) expect that a new discontent and restlessness will soon develop, unless the individual is doing what he is fitted for. A musician must make music, an artist must paint, a poet must write, if he is to be ultimately happy. What a man can be, he must be. This need we may call self-actualization.

15   This term...refers to the desire for self-fulfillment, namely, to the tendency for him to become actualized in what he is potentially. This tendency might be phrased as the desire to become more and more what one is, to become everything that one is capable of becoming.

The specific form that these needs will take will of course vary greatly from person to person. In one individual it may take the form of the desire to be an ideal mother, in another it may be expressed athletically, and in still another it may be expressed in painting pictures or in inventions. It is not necessarily a creative urge although in people who have any capacities for creation it will take this form.*

The clear emergence of these needs rests upon prior satisfaction of the physiological, safety, love and esteem needs. We shall call people who are satisfied in these needs, basically satisfied people, and it is from these that we may expect the fullest (and healthiest) creativeness. Since, in our society, basically satisfied people are the exception, we do not know much about self-actualization, either experimentally or clinically. It remains a challenging problem for research....

Further Characteristics of the Basic Needs

The degree of fixity of the hierarchy of basic needs   We have spoken so far as if this hierarchy were a fixed order but actually it is not nearly as rigid as we may have implied. It is true that most of the people with whom we have worked have seemed to have these basic needs in about the order that has been indicated. However, there have been a number of exceptions.

Degrees of relative satisfaction   So far, our theoretical discussion may have given the impression that these five sets of needs are somehow in a step-wise, all-or-none relationship to each other. We have spoken in such terms as the following: "If one need is satisfied, then another emerges." This statement might give the false impression that a need must be satisfied 100 percent before the next need emerges. In actual fact, most members of our society who are normal, are partially satisfied in all their basic needs and partially unsatisfied in all their basic needs at the same time. A more realistic description of the hierarchy would be in terms of decreasing percentages of satisfaction as we go up the hierarchy of prepotency. For instance, if I may assign arbitrary figures for the sake of illustration, it is as if the average citizen is satisfied perhaps 85 percent in his physiological needs, 70 percent in his safety needs, 50 percent in his love needs, 40 percent in his self-esteem needs, and 10 percent in his self-actualization needs.

20   As for the concept of emergence of a new need after satisfaction of the prepotent need, this emergence is not a sudden salutatory phenomenon but rather a gradual emergence by slow degrees from nothingness. For instance, if...need

---

*In another section of his article, Maslow considers the human "desires to know and to understand" as "in part, techniques for the achievement of basic safety in the world" and, in part, "expressions of self-actualization." Maslow also indicates that "freedom of inquiry and expression" are "preconditions of satisfactions of the basic needs."

A is satisfied only 10 percent then need B may not be visible at all. However, as this need A becomes satisfied 25 percent, need B may emerge 5 percent, as need A becomes satisfied 75 percent need B may emerge 90 percent, and so on.

Unconscious character of needs These needs are neither necessarily conscious nor unconscious. On the whole, however, in the average person, they are more often unconscious rather than conscious. It is not necessary at this point to overhaul the tremendous mass of evidence which indicates the crucial importance of unconscious motivation. It would by now be expected...that unconscious motivations would on the whole be rather more important than the conscious motivations. What we have called the basic needs are very often largely unconscious although they may, with suitable techniques, and with sophisticated people, become conscious....

Multiple motivations of behavior These needs must be understood not to be exclusive or single determiners of certain kinds of behavior. An example may be found in any behavior that seems to be physiologically motivated, such as eating, or sexual play or the like. The clinical psychologists have long since found that any behavior may be a channel through which flow various determinants. Or to say it in another way, most behavior is multi-motivated. Within the sphere of motivational determinants any behavior tends to be determined by several or all of the basic needs simultaneously rather than by only one of them. The latter would be more an exception than the former. Eating may be partially for the sake of filling the stomach, and partially for the sake of comfort and amelioration of other needs. One may make love not only for pure sexual release, but also to convince one's self of one's masculinity: or to make a conquest, to feel powerful, or to win more basic affection. As an illustration, I may point out that it would be possible (theoretically if not practically) to analyze a single act of an individual and see in it the expression of his physiological needs, his safety needs, his love needs, his esteem needs and self-actualization.

References

Cannon, W. B. (1932). *Wisdom of the body.* New York: Norton.
Kardiner, A. (1941). *The traumatic neuroses of war.* New York: Hoeber.
Young, P. (1936). *Motivation of behavior.* New York: Wiley.
Young, P. (1941). The experimental analysis of appetite. *Psychology Bulletin, 38,* 129–164.

In his final sentence, Maslow himself points the way to a potentially productive analysis using his hierarchy of needs: "I may point out that it would be possible (theoretically if not practically) to analyze a single act of an individual and see in it the expression of his physiological needs, his safety needs, his love needs, his esteem needs and self-actualization." One way, then, of conceiving your analysis is to choose a single act—yours or anyone else's—and analyze it according to Maslow's system. You might begin by introducing the person and setting a context for the act; introducing Maslow's hierarchy; and proceeding with the analysis itself as you apply one element of the hierarchy at a time. Use each element as a lens through which you examine the act in a new or revealing way. As you conduct your analysis, recall Maslow's caution that single acts will typically have "multiple motivations."

■ ANALYZING VISUAL MEDIA

Some people believe that visual literacy—that is, the ability to "read" and understand artifacts such as painting, architecture, film, and graphic arts (including Web design)—will be as important in the twenty-first century as textual literacy was in earlier times. While this may be a minority view, there's no denying that in this multimedia age, interpreting visual media is a vital skill. And of the various forms of visual media, advertising is perhaps omnipresent.

Scholars in the humanities and social sciences study advertising from a number of angles: In the fields of cultural studies, literary studies, and American studies, scholars interpret the messages of advertisements much as they do the messages and meanings of artifacts from "high culture," such as literature and art. In opposition to high culture, advertisements (along with television shows, films, and the like) are considered "popular culture" (or "pop culture"), and in the past thirty years or so, the study of these highly pervasive and influential works has attracted academic attention. Scholars in the fields of sociology, communications, and anthropology are also interested in studying pop cultural artifacts because they exert such powerful influences on our lives.

Analysis of advertisements has therefore become a fairly common practice in academia. Let's now take the analytical thinking skills we used in analyzing a social situation (the subject of the Shanker paper) and apply them to print advertisements. In this case, rather than lead you through the analytical process, we will show you several advertisements, along with two critical approaches to analyzing advertisements, and then ask you to perform your own analysis of the ads' features, leading to a sense of their overall meaning or significance.

WRITING ASSIGNMENT: ANALYZING VISUAL MEDIA

Three advertisements appear on the following pages. The first was created to promote Fancy Feast cat food; the second was created to promote IKEA products; and the third advertises GE Monogram kitchen appliances. Study the illustrations and the text in the ads. Then read the two selections that follow. The first, Roland Marchand's "The Appeal of the Democracy of Goods," from his 1985 book *Advertising the American Dream*, describes a common theme underlying many advertisements. The second, Dorothy Cohen's "Elements of an Effective Layout," offers a number of guiding principles for assessing the layout of visual elements in print advertising.

Consider these questions as you study each ad:

- What is depicted in the ad's images?
- What is depicted in the ad's text?
- How do text and images relate to each other in creating the ad's meaning?
- How are shading and font styles used?
- How are words and images placed in relation to one another, and how do these spatial relationships create meaning?
- What is the mood—that is, the emotional output—of the ad? How does this mood help create the ad's meaning?
- How does the ad allude to images, ideas, events, or trends from your knowledge of the contemporary world?

Choose one of the advertisements (pp. 208–210) and the passage by *either* Cohen *or* Marchand. Use the principles presented in the passage you have selected to analyze the ad of your choice. Apply the principles of analytical reasoning demonstrated in the analysis by Linda Shanker earlier in this chapter. That is, apply one or more of the principles explained in the article to one of the advertisements. Develop your analysis in a well-organized, well-developed paper.

For a more ambitious version of this paper, you might use *two* or even *three* ads as the subject of your paper. Review the principles of comparison-and-contrast in Chapter 4 (pp. 168–170). And for an even more ambitious assignment, you could perform a complex analysis and apply both Marchand's *and* Cohen's principles to one or more ads. That is, show how (a) the graphic elements of the ad and (b) its underlying message work to create a unified effect on readers, influencing them to want to buy the product(s) advertised.

The best the world has to offer now presents the best of the sea.

New Fancy Feast® Grilled Tuna and Grilled Salmon.

Two exquisite tastes created especially for the fish connoisseur. Perfectly grilled tuna or salmon, delicately basted in a savory broth. Experience the very latest of the very best from Fancy Feast.

Good taste is easy to recognize.®

www.FancyFeast.com

"You know, I don't ask for much. I'll settle for a pair of jeans that fit, a man who can surprise me occasionally with a gift (no, honey, I didn't mean a lawnmower...), kids who don't drink too much soda, friends who don't drink too much wine, a red carpet hairdo... and a new kitchen.
So, how am I supposed to make it happen? Dress up my husband as a handyman? Or dress up myself? Or do you expect me to mortgage the house for a zillion dollars to get a beautiful kitchen that doesn't make my turkey any tastier than before? That's not happening. Huh? What about IKEA? They don't have kitchens do they?"

Is it possible to get a great kitchen at IKEA?

90th FL 10 RMS W VU.   NEW YORK AT YOUR FEET.
$17 MILLION.

SO WHAT'S COOKING IN THE KITCHEN ?

In this unoccupied 90th floor penthouse, there's a
GE Monogram kitchen.
Every other apartment in this, the tallest residential
building in the world, has a GE Monogram kitchen, too.
Interested parties, please contact Mr. Trump personally.

GE Monogram
Visit monogram.com

imagination at work   *GE*

THE APPEAL OF THE DEMOCRACY OF GOODS
Roland Marchand

Roland Marchand is a professor of history at the University of California, Davis. This selection originally appeared in Marchand's 1985 book Advertising the American Dream: Making Way for Modernity, 1920–1940.

As they opened their September 1929 issue, readers of the *Ladies Home Journal* were treated to an account of the care and feeding of young Livingston Ludlow Biddle III, son and heir of the wealthy Biddles of Philadelphia, whose family coat-of-arms graced the upper right-hand corner of the page. Young Master Biddle, mounted on his tricycle, fixed a serious, slightly pouting gaze upon the reader, while the Cream of Wheat Corporation rapturously explained his constant care, his carefully regulated play and exercise, and the diet prescribed for him by "famous specialists." As master of Sunny Ridge Farm, the Biddles' winter estate in North Carolina, young Livingston III had "enjoyed every luxury of social position and wealth, since the day he was born." Yet, by the grace of a...modern providence, it happened that Livingston's health was protected by "a simple plan every mother can use." Mrs. Biddle gave Cream of Wheat to the young heir for both breakfast and supper. The world's foremost child experts knew of no better diet; great wealth could procure no finer nourishment. Cream of Wheat summarized the central point of the advertisement by claiming that "every mother can give her youngsters the fun and benefits of a Cream of Wheat breakfast just as do the parents of these boys and girls who have the best that wealth can command."

While enjoying this glimpse of childrearing among the socially distinguished, *Ladies Home Journal* readers found themselves drawn in by one of the most pervasive of all advertising strategies of the 1920's—the concept of the Democracy of Goods. According to this idea, the wonders of modern mass production and distribution enabled everyone to enjoy society's most desirable pleasures, conveniences, or benefits. The particular pleasure, benefit, or convenience varied, of course, with each advertiser who used the formula. But the cumulative effect of the constant reminders that "any woman can..." and "every home can afford..." was to publicize an image of American society in which concentrated wealth at the top of a hierarchy of social classes restricted no family's opportunity to acquire the most desirable products. By implicitly defining "democracy" in terms of equal access to consumer products, these advertisements offered Americans an inviting vision of their society as one of incontestable equality.

In its most common advertising formula, the concept of the Democracy of Goods asserted that although the rich enjoyed a great variety of luxuries, the acquisition of their *one* most precious luxury would provide anyone with the ultimate in satisfaction. For instance, a Chase and Sanborn's Coffee advertisement, with an elegant butler serving a family in a dining room with a sixteen-foot ceiling, reminded Chicago families that although "compared with the riches of the more fortunate, your way of life may seem modest indeed," yet no one—"king, prince, statesman, or capitalist"—could enjoy better coffee.

The Association of Soap and Glycerine Producers proclaimed that the charm of cleanliness was as readily available to the poor as to the rich, and Ivory Soap reassuringly related how one young housewife, who couldn't afford a $780-a-year maid like her neighbor, still maintained "nice hands" by using Ivory. The C. F. Church Manufacturing Company epitomized this feature of the Democracy of Goods technique in an ad entitled "a bathroom luxury everyone can afford": "If you lived in one of those palatial apartments on Park Avenue, in New York City, where you have to pay $2,000 to $7,000 a year rent, you still couldn't have a better toilet seat in your bathroom than they have—the Church Sani-white Toilet Seat, which you can afford to have right now."

Thus, according to the concept of the Democracy of Goods, no differences in wealth could prevent the humblest citizens, provided they chose their purchases wisely, from coming home to a setting in which they could contemplate their essential equality, through possession of a particular product, with the nation's millionaires. In 1929, Howard Dickinson, a contributor to *Printers' Ink,* concisely expressed the social psychology behind Democracy of Goods advertisements: "'With whom do the mass of people think they want to foregather?' asks the psychologist in advertising. 'Why, with the wealthy and socially distinguished, of course!' If we can't get an invitation to tea for our millions of customers, we can at least present the fellowship of using the same brand of merchandise. And it works."

ELEMENTS OF AN EFFECTIVE LAYOUT
Dorothy Cohen

This selection originally appeared in Dorothy Cohen's textbook Advertising (1988).

Fundamentally a good layout should attract attention and interest and should provide some control over the manner in which the advertisement is read. The message to be communicated may be sincere, relevant, and important to the consumer, but because of the competitive "noise" in the communication channel, the opportunity to be heard may depend on the effectiveness of the layout. In addition to attracting attention, the most important requisites for an effective layout are balance, proportion, movement, utility, clarity, and emphasis.

Balance

Balance is a fundamental law in nature and its application to layout design formulates one of the basic principles of this process. Balance is a matter of weight distribution; in layout it is keyed to the *optical center* of an advertisement, the point which the reader's eye designates as the center of an area. In an advertisement a vertical line which divides the area into right and left halves contains the center; however the optical center is between one-tenth and one-third the distance above the mathematical horizontal center line. . . .

In order to provide good artistic composition, the elements in the layout must be in equilibrium. Equilibrium can be achieved through balance, and this process may be likened to the balancing of a seesaw. The optical center of the advertisement serves as the fulcrum or balancing point, and the elements may be balanced on both sides of this fulcrum through considerations of their size and tonal quality.

The simplest way to ensure formal balance between the elements to the right and left of the vertical line is to have all masses in the left duplicated on the right in size, weight, and distance from the center....Formal balance imparts feelings of dignity, solidity, refinement, and reserve. It has been used for institutional advertising and suggests conservatism on the part of the advertiser. Its major deficiency is that it may present a static and somewhat unexciting appearance; however, formal balance presents material in an easy-to-follow order and works well for many ads.

5   To understand informal balance, think of children of unequal weight balanced on a seesaw; to ensure equilibrium it is necessary to place the smaller child far from the center and the larger child closer to the fulcrum. In informal balance the elements are balanced, but not evenly, because of different sizes and color contrast. This type of a symmetric balance requires care so that the various elements do not create a lopsided or top-heavy appearance. A knowledge or a sense of the composition can help create the feeling of symmetry in what is essentially asymmetric balance.

Informal balance presents a fresh, untraditional approach. It creates excitement, a sense of originality, forcefulness, and, to some extent, the element of surprise. Whereas formal balance may depend on the high interest value of the illustration to attract the reader, informal balance may attract attention through the design of the layout....

Proportion

Proportion helps develop order and creates a pleasing impression. It is related to balance but is concerned primarily with the division of the space and the emphasis to be accorded each element. Proportion, to the advertising designer, is the relationship between the size of one element in the ad to another, the amount of space between elements, as well as the width of the total ad to its depth. Proportion also involves the tone of the ad: the amount of light area in relation to dark area and the amount of color and noncolor.*

As a general rule unequal dimensions and distances make the most lively design in advertising. The designer also places the elements on the page so that each element is given space and position in proportion to its importance in the total advertisement and does not look like it stands alone.

Movement

If an advertisement is to appear dynamic rather than static, it must contain some movement. *Movement* (also called *sequence*) provides the directional flow for the advertisement, gives it its follow-through, and provides coherence. It guides the reader's eye from one element to another and makes sure he or she does not miss anything.

---

*Roy Paul Nelson, *The Design of Advertising,* 4th ed. (Dubuque, IA: Brown, 1981): 18.

10   Motion in layout is generally from left to right and from top to bottom—the direction established through the reading habits of speakers of Western language. The directional impetus should not disturb the natural visual flow but should favor the elements to be stressed, while care should be taken not to direct the reader's eye out of the advertisement. This can be done by the following:

- *Gaze motion* directs the reader's attention by directing the looks of the people or animals in an ad. If a subject is gazing at a unit in the layout, the natural tendency is for the reader to follow the direction of that gaze; if someone is looking directly out of the advertisement, the reader may stop to see who's staring.

- *Structural motion* incorporates the lines of direction and patterns of movement by mechanical means. An obvious way is to use an arrow or a pointed finger....

Unity

Another important design principle is the unification of the layout. Although an advertisement is made up of many elements, all of these should be welded into a compact composition. Unity is achieved when the elements tie into one another by using the same basic shapes, sizes, textures, colors, and mood. In addition, the type should have the same character as the art.

A *border* surrounding an ad provides a method of achieving unity. Sets of borders may occur within an ad, and, when they are similar in thickness and tone, they provide a sense of unity.

Effective use of white space can help to establish unity....*White space* is defined as that part of the advertising space which is not occupied by any other elements; in this definition, white space is not always white in color. White space may be used to feature an important element by setting it off, or to imply luxury and prestige by preventing a crowded appearance. It may be used to direct and control the reader's attention by tying elements together. If white space is used incorrectly, it may cause separation of the elements and create difficulty in viewing the advertisement as a whole.

Clarity and Simplicity

The good art director does not permit a layout to become too complicated or tricky. An advertisement should retain its clarity and be easy to read and easy to understand. The reader tends to see the total image of an advertisement; thus it should not appear fussy, contrived, or confusing. Color contrasts, including tones of gray, should be strong enough to be easily deciphered, and the various units should be clear and easy to understand. Type size and design should be selected for ease of reading, and lines of type should be a comfortable reading length. Too many units in an advertisement are distracting; therefore, any elements that can be eliminated without destroying the message should be. One way in which clarity can be achieved is by combining the logo, trademark, tag line, and company name into one compact group.

Part Two ■ *Strategies*

6 ■ Writing as a Process

■ WRITING AS THINKING

Most of us regard writing as an activity that culminates in a finished product: a paper, an application letter, study notes, and the like. We focus on the result rather than on the process of getting there. But how *do* we produce that paper or letter? Does the thought you write down not exist until it appears on the page? Does thought precede writing? If so, is writing merely a translation of prior thought? The relationship between thinking and writing is complex and not entirely understood. But it is worth reflecting on, especially as you embark on your writing-intensive career as a college student. Every time you pick up a pen or sit down at a computer to write, you engage in a thinking process—and what and how and when you think both affects and is affected by your writing in a variety of ways. Consider the possibilities as you complete the following brief exercises:

> **A:** You find yourself enrolled in a composition class at a particular school. Why are you attending this school and not another? Write for five minutes on this question.
>
> **B:** What single moment in your freshman experience thus far has been most (a) humorous, (b) promising, (c) vexing, (d) exasperating? Choose *one* and write for five minutes on this topic.
>
> **C:** Select one page of notes from the presumably many you have taken in any of your classes. Reread the page and rewrite it, converting your first-pass notes into a well-organized study guide that would help you prepare for an exam. Devote five minutes to the effort.

Reflect on these exercises. Specifically, locate in your response to each one the point at which you believe your thinking took place. (Admittedly, this may be difficult, but give it a try.) Before completing Exercise A, you probably gave considerable thought to *where* you are or would like to be attending college. Examine your writing and reflect on your thinking: Were you in any way rethinking your choice of school as you wrote? Or were you explaining a decision you've already made—that is, reporting on *prior* thinking? Perhaps some combination of these?

Now turn to your work for Exercise B, for which you wrote (most likely) on a new topic. Where did thinking occur here? As you wrote? Moments prior to your writing, as you selected the topic and focused your ideas?

Last, consider Exercise C. Where did your thinking take place? How did revision change your first-draft notes? What makes your second draft a better study guide than your first draft?

Finally, consider the differences in the relationship between writing and thinking *across* Exercises A, B, and C as you wrote on a topic you'd previously thought (but not written) about, on a new topic, and on a topic you've written about and are revising. Note the changing relationship between writing and thinking. Note especially how rewriting is related to rethinking.

In completing and reflecting on these exercises, you have glimpsed something of the marvelous complexity of writing. The job of this chapter is to help you develop some familiarity and comfort with this mysterious but crucial process.

■ STAGES OF THE WRITING PROCESS

By breaking the process into stages, writers turn the sometimes overwhelming task of writing a paper into manageable chunks, each requiring different activities that, collectively, build to a final draft. Generally, the stages involve *understanding the task, gathering data, invention, drafting, revision,* and *editing.*

Broadly speaking, the six stages of the writing process occur in the order we've listed. But writing is *recursive;* the process tends to loop back on itself. You generally move forward as you write, toward a finished product. But moving forward is seldom a straight-line process.

The Writing Process

- *Understanding the task:* Read—or create—the assignment. Understand its purpose, scope, and audience.
- *Gathering data:* Locate and review information—from sources and from your own experience—and formulate an approach.
- *Invention:* Use various techniques (e.g., listing, outlining, freewriting) to generate promising ideas and a particular approach to the assignment. Gather more data if needed. Aim for a working thesis, a tentative (but well-reasoned and well-informed) statement of the direction you intend to pursue.
- *Drafting:* Sketch the paper you intend to compose and then write all sections necessary to support the working thesis. Stop if necessary to gather more data. Typically, you will both follow your plan and

(continues)

revise and invent a new (or slightly new) plan as you write. Expect to discover key parts of your paper as you write.

- *Revision:* Rewrite in order to make the draft coherent and unified.

    Revise at the *global* level, reshaping your thesis and adding to, rearranging, or deleting paragraphs in order to support the thesis. Gather more data as needed to flesh out paragraphs in support of the thesis.

    Revise at the *local* level of paragraphs, ensuring that each is well reasoned and supports the thesis.

- *Editing:* Revise at the *sentence* level for style and brevity. Revise for correctness: grammar, punctuation, usage, and spelling.

■ STAGE 1: UNDERSTANDING THE TASK

Papers in the Academic Disciplines

Although most of your experience with academic papers in high school may have been in English classes, you should be prepared for instructors in other academic disciplines to assign papers with significant research components. Here is a sampling of topics that have been assigned recently in a broad range of undergraduate courses:

Art History: Discuss the main differences between Romanesque and Gothic sculpture, using the sculptures of Jeremiah (St. Pierre Cathedral) and St. Theodore (Chartres Cathedral) as major examples.

Physics: Research and write a paper on solar cell technology, covering the following areas: basic physical theory, history and development, structure and materials, types and characteristics, practical uses, state of the art, and future prospects.

Political Science: Explain the contours of California's referendum process in recent years and then, by focusing on one specific controversial referendum, explain and analyze the origins of this proposed measure, the campaign for and against it, its fate at the polls, and the political effects and legacy of this measure (whether it passed or failed).

Religious Studies: Select a particular religious group or movement present in the nation for at least twenty years and show how its belief or practice has changed since members of the group have been in America or, if the group began in America, since its first generation.

Some of these assignments allow students a considerable range of choice (within the general subject); others are highly specific in requiring students to address a particular issue. Most call for some library or online research; a few call for a combination of online, library, and field research; others may be based entirely on field research. As with all academic writing, your first task is to make sure you understand the assignment. Remember to critically read and analyze the specific task(s) required of you in a paper assignment. One useful technique for doing this is to locate the assignment's key verb(s), which will stipulate exactly what is expected of you.

Exercise 6.1

Analyze an Assignment

Reread the instructions for a recent assignment from another course.

1. Identify the key verb(s).
2. List the type of print, interview, or graphical data you were to gather to complete the assignment.
3. Reflect on your own experience to find some anecdote that might be appropriately included in a paper (or, absent that, a related experience that would provide a personal motivation for writing the paper).

■ STAGE 2: GATHERING DATA

When you begin a writing assignment, consider three questions:

1. What is the assignment?
2. What do I know about the subject?*
3. What do I need to know in order to begin writing?

These questions prompt you to reflect on the assignment and define what is expected. Taking stock of class notes, readings, and whatever resources are available, you survey what you already know. Having identified the gaps between what you know and what you need to know in order to write, you can begin to gather data—most likely in stages. You may gather enough, at first, to formulate initial ideas. You may begin to write, see new gaps, and realize you need more data.

Types of Data

Data is a term used most often to refer to quantitative information such as the frequencies or percentages of natural phenomena in the sciences (e.g., the rate at which glaciers melt) or of social phenomena in the social sciences (e.g., the average age of Americans when they first marry). But not all data is quantifiable. For example, interviews recorded by a social scientist are also considered to be *data*. In the humanities, *data* can refer to the qualitative

---

*Note: The terms *subject* and *topic* are often used interchangeably. In this chapter, we use *subject* to mean a broad area of interest that, once narrowed to a *topic*, becomes the focus of a paper. Within a thesis (the major organizing sentence of the paper), we speak of *topic*, not *subject*.

observations one makes of a particular art object that one is interpreting or evaluating. Generally, quantitative data encompasses issues of "how many?" or "how often?", whereas qualitative research accounts for such issues as "what kind?" and "why?"

Primary and Secondary Sources

Whether quantitative or qualitative, the kind of information that a researcher gathers directly by using the research methods appropriate to that particular field of study—experiments or observations in the sciences, surveys or interviews in the social sciences, close reading and interpretation of unpublished documents and literary texts or works of art in the humanities—is considered *primary* data. As an undergraduate, you will more commonly collect *secondary* data: information and ideas collected or generated by others who have performed their own primary and/or secondary research. The data gathering for most undergraduate academic writing involves library research and, increasingly, research conducted online via Internet databases and other resources.

Chapter 7 provides an in-depth discussion of locating and using secondary sources. Refer also to the material in Chapters 1 and 2 on summary, critical reading, and critique; the techniques of critical reading and assessment of sources will help you make the best use of your sources. And the material in Chapter 1 on avoiding plagiarism will help you conform to the highest ethical standards in your research and writing.

■ STAGE 3: INVENTION

Your preliminary data gathering completed, you can now frame your writing project: give it scope, develop your main idea, and create conditions for productive writing. You must define what you are writing about, after all, and you do this in the *invention* stage. This stage might also be termed "brainstorming" or "predrafting." Regardless of the name, invention is an important part of the process that typically overlaps with data gathering. The preliminary data you gather on a topic will inform the choices you make in defining (that is, in "inventing" ideas for) your project. As you invent, you will often return to gather more data.

Writers sometimes skip the invention stage, preferring to save time by launching directly from gathering data into writing a draft. This is a serious mistake. Time spent narrowing your ideas to a manageable scope at the beginning of a project will pay dividends all through the writing process. Papers head down the wrong track when writers choose topics that are too broad (resulting in the superficial treatment of subtopics), or too narrow (resulting in writers "padding" their work to meet a length requirement).

The Myth of Inspiration

Some people believe that good writing comes primarily from a kind of magical—and unpredictable—formation of ideas that occurs as one sits down in front of a blank page or computer screen. According to this myth, a writer must be inspired in order to write, as if receiving his or her ideas from some muse. While some element of inspiration may inform your writing, most of the time it is hard work—especially in the invention stage—that gets the job done. The old adage attributed to Thomas Edison—"Invention is one part inspiration and ninety-nine parts perspiration"—applies here.

Choosing and Narrowing Your Subject

Suppose you have been assigned a ten-page paper in an introductory course on environmental science. The assignment is open ended, so not only do you need to choose a subject, you also need to narrow it sufficiently and formulate your thesis.

Where will you begin?

First, you need to select broad subject matter from the course and become knowledgeable about its general features. But what if no broad area of interest occurs to you?

- Work through the syllabus or your textbook(s). Identify topics that sparked your interest.

- Review course notes and pay especially close attention to lectures that held your interest.

- Scan recent newspapers and newsmagazines that bear on your coursework.

Assume for your course in environmental science that you've settled on the broad subject of energy conservation. At this point, the goal of your research is to limit this subject to a manageable scope. A subject can be limited in at least two ways. First, you can seek out a general article (perhaps an encyclopedia entry, though it would not typically be accepted as a source in a college-level paper). A general article may do the work for you by breaking the larger topic down into smaller subtopics that you can explore and, perhaps, limit even further. Second, you can limit a subject by asking questions about it:

Who?

Which aspects?

Where?

(continues)

When?

How?

Why?

These questions will occur to you as you conduct your research and notice the ways in which various authors have focused their discussions. Having read several sources on energy conservation and having decided that you'd like to use them, you might limit the subject by asking *which aspects* and deciding to focus on energy conservation as it relates to motor vehicles.

The Myth of Talent

Many inexperienced writers believe that you either have writing talent or you don't; and that if you don't, you are fated to go through life as a "bad writer." But again, hard work, rather than talent, is what leads to competent writing. Yes, some people have more natural verbal ability than others—we all have our areas of strength and weakness. But in any endeavor, talent alone can't ensure success, and with hard work, writers who don't yet have much confidence can achieve impressive results. Not everyone can be a brilliant writer, but everyone *can* be a competent writer.

Certainly, "energy-efficient vehicles" offers a more specific focus than does "energy conservation." Still, the revised focus is too broad for a ten-page paper. (One can easily imagine several book-length works on the subject.) So again, you try to limit your subject by posing other questions from the same list. You might ask which types of energy-efficient vehicles are possible and feasible and how auto manufacturers can be encouraged to develop them. In response to these questions, you may jot down preliminary notes:

- Types of energy-efficient vehicles

    All-electric vehicles

    Hybrid (combination of gasoline and electric) vehicles

    Fuel-cell vehicles

- Government action to encourage development of energy-efficient vehicles

    Mandates to automakers to build minimum quantities of energy-efficient vehicles by certain deadlines

    Additional taxes imposed on high-mileage vehicles

    Subsidies to developers of energy-efficient vehicles

Focusing on any *one* of these aspects as an approach to encouraging the use of energy-efficient vehicles could provide the focus of a ten-page paper.

Practice Narrowing Subjects

In groups of three or four classmates, choose one of the following subjects and collaborate on a paragraph or two that explores the questions we listed for narrowing subjects: Who? Which aspects? Where? When? How? Why? See if you can narrow the subject.

- Downloading music off the Internet
- Internet chat rooms
- College sports
- School violence or bullying
- America's public school system

Invention Strategies

You may already be familiar with a variety of strategies for thinking through your ideas. Here are four of these strategies:

Directed Freewriting

To freewrite is to let your mind go and write spontaneously, often for a set amount of time or a set number of pages. The process of "just writing" can often free up thoughts and ideas about which we aren't even fully conscious, or that we haven't articulated to ourselves. In *directed freewriting*, you focus on a subject and let what you think and know about the subject flow out of you in a focused stream of ideas. As a first step in the invention stage, you might sit down with an assignment and write continuously for fifteen minutes. If even one solid idea comes through, you've succeeded in using freewriting to help "free up" your thinking. As a second step, you might take that one idea and freewrite about it, shift to a different invention strategy to explore that one idea, or even begin to draft a thesis and then a rough draft, depending on how well formed your idea is at this stage.

Listing

Some writers find it helpful to make *lists* of their ideas, breaking significant ideas into sublists and seeing where they lead. Approach this strategy as a form of freewriting; let your mind go, and jot down words and phrases that are related. Create lists by pulling related ideas out of your notes or your course readings. *A caution:* The linear nature of lists can lead you to jump prematurely into planning your paper's structure before working out your ideas. Instead, list ideas as a way of brainstorming, and then generate another list that works out the best structure for your points in a draft.

Outlining

A more structured version of a list, an *outline* groups ideas in hierarchical order, with main points broken into subordinate points, sometimes indicating evidence in support of these points. Use outlines as a first stage in generating ideas during your invention process, or as a second step in invention. After freewriting and/or listing, refine and build on your ideas by inserting them into an outline for a workable structure in which you can discuss the ideas you've brainstormed. (See the example of an outline on pp. 148–149.)

Clustering and Branching

These two methods of invention are more graphic, nonlinear versions of listing and outlining. With both clustering and branching, you start with an assignment's main topic, or with an idea generated by freewriting or listing, and you brainstorm related ideas that flow from that main idea. *Clustering* involves writing an idea in the middle of a page and circling it; you then draw lines leading from that circle, or "bubble," to new bubbles containing subtopics of the central idea. Picking the subtopics that interest you most, draw lines leading to more bubbles in which you note important aspects of the subtopics. (See illustration below.)

Branching follows the same principle, but instead of placing ideas in bubbles, you write them on lines that branch off to other lines that, in turn, contain the related subtopics of your larger topic.

Clustering and branching are useful first steps in invention, for each helps isolate the topics about which you are most knowledgeable. As you branch off into the subtopics of a main paper topic, the number of ideas you generate in relation to these topics will help show where you have the most knowledge and/or interest.

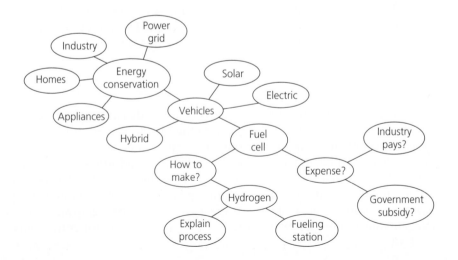

You can modify and combine invention techniques in a number of ways. There is no one right way to generate ideas—or to write a paper—and every writer will want to try different methods to find those that work best. What's important to remember is that regardless of the method, the time spent on invention creates the conditions for writing a solid first draft.

Exercise 6.3

Practice Invention Strategies

After completing the group exercise (Exercise 6.2, p. 223) in which you narrowed a subject, work individually to brainstorm ideas about the subject your group chose. Use one of the invention strategies listed above—preferably one that you haven't used before. After brainstorming on your own, meet with your group again to compare the ideas you each generated.

■ STAGE 4: DRAFTING

It's usually best to begin drafting a paper after you've settled on at least a working or preliminary thesis. While consulting the fruits of your efforts during invention (notes, lists, outlines, and so on), you'll face a number of choices about how to proceed with drafting your paper. Let's consider some of those choices, including the crucial step of drafting the thesis.

Strategies for Writing the Paper

Some people can sit down very early in the process and put their ideas into an orderly form as they write. This drafting method results in a completed *rough draft*. But even professional writers rarely produce an adequate piece of writing the first time around. Most need to plan the structure of a paper before they can sit down to write a first draft. Even if this initial structure proves to be little more than a sketch that changes markedly as the paper develops, some sort of scaffolding usually helps in taking the step from planning to writing a first draft.

Ultimately, *you* will decide how best to proceed. And don't be surprised if you begin different writing projects differently. Whether you jump in without a plan, plan rigorously, or commit yourself to the briefest preliminary sketch, ask yourself:

- What's the main point of my paper?
- What subpoints do I need to address in order to develop and support my main point?
- In what order should my points be arranged? (Do certain subpoints lead naturally to others?)

At Stage 3, as you clarify the direction in which you believe your paper is heading, you ought to be able to formulate at least a *preliminary thesis* (see below). Your thesis can be quite rough, but if you don't have some sense of your main point, writing the first draft won't be possible. In this case, you would have to consider what you've written a preliminary or *discovery draft* (more of an invention strategy than an actual draft)—which is a perfectly sensible way to proceed if you're having difficulty clarifying your thoughts. Even if you begin with what you regard as a clearly stated point, don't be surprised if by the end of the draft—just at the point where you are summing up—you discover that the paper you have in fact written differs from the paper you intended to write. However firm your ideas may be when you begin, the act of writing a draft will usually clarify matters for you.

As we've suggested, the drafting and invention stages overlap. How much planning you do after working out your ideas and before drafting your paper is a matter of personal preference. Try different methods to see which work best for you, and keep in mind that different assignments may require different methods for invention and drafting.

Writing a Thesis

A thesis, as we have seen, is a one- or two-sentence summary of a paper's content. Whether explanatory, mildly argumentative, or strongly argumentative, the thesis is an assertion about that content—for instance, what the content is, how it works, what it means, if it is valuable, if action should be taken, and so on. A paper's thesis is similar to its conclusion, but it lacks the conclusion's concern for broad implications and significance. The thesis is the product of your thinking; it therefore represents *your* conclusion about the topic on which you're writing. So you have to have spent some time thinking about this conclusion (that is, during the invention stage) in order to arrive at the thesis that will govern your paper.

For a writer in the drafting stages, the thesis establishes a focus, a basis on which to include or exclude information. For the reader of a finished product, the thesis forecasts the author's discussion. A thesis, therefore, is an essential tool for both writers and readers of academic papers.

The Components of a Thesis

Like any other sentence, a thesis includes a subject and a predicate that makes an assertion about the subject. In the sentence "Lee and Grant were different kinds of generals," "Lee and Grant" is the subject and "were different kinds of generals" is the predicate. What distinguishes a thesis from any other sentence with a subject and a predicate is that *the thesis presents the controlling idea of the paper.* The subject of a thesis, and the assertion about it, must present the right balance between the general and the specific to allow for a thorough discussion within the allotted length of the paper. The discussion might include definitions, details, comparisons, contrasts—whatever is needed to illuminate a subject and support the assertion. (If the sentence about Lee and Grant were a thesis, the reader would assume that the rest of the paper contained comparisons and contrasts between the two generals.)

Bear in mind when writing theses that the more general your subject and the more complex your assertion, the longer your discussion must be to cover the subject adequately. The broadest theses require book-length treatments, as in this case:

> Meaningful energy conservation requires a shrewd application of political, financial, and scientific will.

You couldn't write an effective ten-page paper based on this thesis. The topic alone would require pages just to define what you mean by "energy conservation" and "meaningful." Energy can be conserved in homes, vehicles, industries, appliances, and power plants, and each of these areas would need consideration. Having accomplished this first task of definition, you would then turn your attention to the claim, which entails a discussion of how politics, finance, and science individually and collectively influence energy conservation. Moreover, the thesis requires you to argue that "shrewd application" of politics, finance, and science is required. The thesis may very well be accurate and compelling. Yet it promises entirely too much for a ten-page paper.

So to write an effective thesis and therefore a controlled, effective paper, you need to limit your subject and your claims about it. We discussed narrowing your subject during the invention stage (pp. 220–222); this narrowing process should help you arrive at a manageable topic for your paper. You will convert that topic to a thesis when you make an assertion about it—a *claim* that you will explain and support in the paper.

Making an Assertion

Thesis statements make an assertion or claim *about* your paper's topic. If you have spent enough time reading and gathering information, and brainstorming ideas about the assignment, you'll be knowledgeable enough to have something to say based on a combination of your own thinking and the thinking of your sources.

If you have trouble coming up with such an assertion, devote more time to invention strategies: Try writing your subject at the top of a page and then listing everything you now know and feel about it. Often from such a list you'll venture an assertion you can then use to fashion a working thesis. One good way to gauge the reasonableness of your claim is to see what other authors have asserted about the same topic. Keeping good notes on the views of others will provide you with a useful counterpoint to your own views as you write and think about your claim, and you may want to use those notes in your paper.

Next, make several assertions about your topic, in order of increasing complexity, as in the following:

1. Fuel-cell technology has emerged as a promising approach to developing energy-efficient vehicles.
2. To reduce our dependence on nonrenewable fossil fuel, the federal government should encourage the development of fuel-cell vehicles.
3. The federal government should subsidize the development of fuel-cell vehicles as well as the hydrogen infrastructure needed to support them; otherwise, the United States will be increasingly vulnerable to recession and other economic dislocations resulting from our dependence on the continued flow of foreign oil.

Keep in mind that these are *working theses*. Because you haven't begun a paper based on any of them, they remain *hypotheses* to be tested. You might choose one and use it to focus your initial draft. After completing a first draft, you would revise it by comparing the contents of the paper to the thesis and making adjustments as necessary for unity. The working thesis is an excellent tool for planning broad sections of the paper, but—again—don't let it prevent you from pursuing related discussions as they occur to you.

Starting with a Working Thesis

As a student, you are not yet an expert on the subjects of your papers and therefore don't usually have the luxury of beginning writing tasks with a definite thesis in mind. But let's assume that you *do* have an area of expertise, that you are in your own right a professional (albeit not in academic matters). We'll assume that you understand some nonacademic subject—say, backpacking—and have been given a clear purpose for writing: to discuss the relative merits of backpack designs. Your job is to write a recommendation for the owner of a sporting-goods chain, suggesting which line of backpacks the chain should carry. Because you already know a good deal about backpacks, you may have some well-developed ideas on the subject before you start doing additional research.

Yet even as an expert in your field, you will find that crafting a thesis is challenging. After all, a thesis is a summary, and it is difficult to summarize a presentation yet to be written—especially if you plan to discover what you want to say during the process of writing. Even if you know your material well, the best you can do at first is to formulate a working thesis—a hypothesis of sorts, a well-informed hunch about your topic and the claim you intend to make about it. After completing a draft, you can evaluate the degree to which your working thesis accurately summarizes the content of your paper. If the match is a good one, the working thesis becomes the final thesis. But if sections of the paper drift from the focus of the working thesis, you'll need to revise the thesis and the paper itself to ensure that the presentation is unified. (You'll know that the match between content and thesis is good when every paragraph directly refers to and develops some element of the thesis.) Later in this chapter we'll discuss useful revision techniques for establishing unity in your work.

This model works whether dealing with a subject in your area of expertise—backpacking, for example—or one that is more in your instructor's territory, such as government policy or medieval poetry. The difference is that when approaching subjects that are less familiar to you, you'll likely spend more time gathering data and brainstorming in order to make assertions about your subject.

Using the Thesis to Plan a Structure

A working thesis will help you sketch the structure of your paper because an effective structure flows directly from the thesis. Consider, for example, the third thesis (see p. 228) on fuel-cell technology:

> The federal government should subsidize the development of fuel-cell vehicles as well as the hydrogen infrastructure needed to support them; otherwise, the United States will be increasingly vulnerable to recession and other economic dislocations resulting from our dependence on the continued flow of foreign oil.

This thesis is *strongly argumentative*, or *persuasive*. The economic crises mentioned suggest urgency in the need for the solution recommended: the federal subsidy of a national hydrogen infrastructure to support fuel-cell vehicles. A well-developed paper based on this thesis would require you to commit yourself to explaining (1) why fuel-cell vehicles are a preferred alternative to gasoline-powered vehicles; (2) why fuel-cell vehicles require a hydrogen infrastructure (i.e., you must explain that fuel cells produce power by mixing hydrogen and oxygen, generating both electricity and water in the process); (3) why the government needs to subsidize industry in developing fuel-cell vehicles; and (4) how continued reliance on fossil fuel technology could make the country vulnerable to economic dislocations.

How Ambitious Should Your Thesis Be?

Writing tasks vary according to the nature of the thesis.

- The *explanatory thesis* is often developed in response to short-answer exam questions that call for information, not analysis (e.g., "How does James Barber categorize the main types of presidential personality?").

- The *mildly argumentative thesis* is appropriate for organizing reports (even lengthy ones), as well as for essay questions that call for some analysis (e.g., "Discuss the qualities of a good speech").

(continues)

> • The *strongly argumentative thesis* is used to organize papers and exam
>   questions that call for information, analysis, *and* the writer's force-
>   fully stated point of view (e.g., "Evaluate the proposed reforms of
>   health maintenance organizations").
>
> The strongly argumentative thesis, of course, is the riskiest of the
> three because you must state your position forcefully and make it appear
> reasonable—which requires that you offer evidence and defend against
> logical objections. But such intellectual risks pay dividends; and if you
> become involved enough in your work to make challenging assertions,
> you will provoke challenging responses that enliven classroom discus-
> sions as well as your own learning.

This thesis therefore helps you plan the paper, which should include a
section on each of the four topics. Assuming that the argument follows the organizational plan we've proposed, the working thesis would become the final
thesis. Based on this thesis, a reader could anticipate sections of the paper to
come. A focused thesis therefore becomes an essential tool for guiding readers.

At this stage, however, your thesis is still provisional. It may turn out that
as you do research or begin drafting, the paper to which this thesis commits
you looks to be too long and complex. You may therefore decide to drop
the second clause of the thesis (concerning the country's vulnerability to
economic dislocations) and focus instead on the need for the government to
subsidize the development of fuel-cell vehicles and a hydrogen infrastructure, relegating the economic concerns to your conclusion (if at all). With
such a change, your final thesis might read: "The federal government should
subsidize the development of fuel-cell vehicles as well as the hydrogen infrastructure needed to support them."

This revised thesis makes an assertive commitment to the subject even
though the assertion is not as complex as the original. Still, it is more argumentative than the second proposed thesis:

> To reduce our dependence on nonrenewable fossil fuel energy sources,
> the federal government should encourage the development of fuel-cell
> vehicles.

Here we have a *mildly argumentative* thesis that enables the writer to express
an opinion. We infer from the use of the words "should encourage" that the
writer endorses the idea of the government's promoting fuel-cell development. But a government that "encourages" development is making a lesser
commitment than one that "subsidizes," which means that it allocates funds
for a specific policy. So the writer who argues for mere encouragement
takes a milder position than the one who argues for subsidies. Note also the
contrast between the second thesis and the first one, in which the writer is

committed to no involvement in the debate and suggests no government involvement whatsoever:

> Fuel-cell technology has emerged as a promising approach to developing energy-efficient vehicles.

This, the first of the three thesis statements, is *explanatory*, or *informative*. In developing a paper based on this thesis, the writer is committed only to explaining how fuel-cell technology works and why it is a promising approach to energy-efficient vehicles. Given this thesis, a reader would *not* expect to find the writer strongly recommending, for instance, that fuel-cell engines replace internal combustion engines in the near future. Neither does the thesis require the writer to defend a personal opinion; he or she need only justify the use of the relatively mild term "promising."

In sum, for any topic you might explore in a paper, you can make any number of assertions—some relatively simple, some complex. On the basis of these assertions, you set yourself an agenda for your writing—and readers set for themselves expectations for reading. The more ambitious the thesis, the more complex will be the paper and the greater the readers' expectations.

To review: A thesis (a one-sentence summary of your paper) helps you organize your discussion, and helps your reader anticipate it. Theses are distinguished by their carefully worded subjects and predicates, which should be just broad and complex enough to be developed within the length limitations of the assignment. Both novices and experts typically begin the initial draft of a paper with a working thesis—a statement that provides writers with sufficient structure to get started but latitude enough to discover what they want to say as they write. Once you have completed a first draft, you test the "fit" of your thesis with what you have written. If the fit is good, every element of the thesis will be developed in the paper that follows. Discussions that drift from your thesis should be deleted, or the thesis revised to accommodate the new discussions. These revision concerns will be more fully addressed when we consider the revision stage of the writing process.

Exercise 6.4

Drafting Thesis Statements

After completing the group exercise in narrowing a subject (Exercise 6.2, p. 223) and the individual invention exercise (Exercise 6.3, p. 225), work individually or in small groups to draft three theses based on your earlier ideas: one explanatory thesis, one mildly argumentative thesis, and one strongly argumentative thesis.

Writing Introductions and Conclusions

Writing introductions and conclusions is usually difficult. How to start? What's the best way to approach your topic? With a serious tone, a light touch, an anecdote? And how to end? How to leave the reader feeling satisfied, intrigued, provoked?

Often, writers avoid such decisions by putting them off—and productively so. Bypassing careful planning for the introduction and conclusion, they begin writing the body of the piece. Only after they've finished the body do they go back to write the opening and closing paragraphs. There's a lot to be said for this approach: Because you've presumably spent more time thinking and writing about the topic itself than about how you're going to introduce or conclude it, you're in a better position to set out your ideas. Often it's not until you've actually seen the text on paper or on screen and read it over once or twice that a natural or effective way of introducing or concluding it occurs to you. Also, you're generally in better psychological shape to write both the introduction and the conclusion after the major task of writing is behind you and you've already set down the main body of your discussion or argument.

Introductions

An effective introduction prepares the reader to enter the world of your paper. It makes the connection between the more familiar world inhabited by the reader and the less familiar world of the writer's topic; it places a discussion in a context that the reader can understand. If you find yourself getting stuck on an introduction at the beginning of a first draft, skip over it for the moment. State your working thesis directly and move on to the body of the paper.

Here are some of the most common strategies for opening a paper:

Quotation   Consider the two introductory paragraphs to an article titled "The Radical Idea of Marrying for Love," from Stephanie Coontz's *Marriage: A History.*

> George Bernard Shaw described marriage as an institution that brings together two people "under the influence of the most violent, most insane, most delusive, and most transient of passions. They are required to swear that they will remain in that excited, abnormal, and exhausting condition continuously until death do them part."
>
> Shaw's comment was amusing when he wrote it at the beginning of the twentieth century, and it still makes us smile today, because it pokes fun at the unrealistic expectations that spring from a dearly held cultural ideal—that marriage should be based on intense, profound love and a couple should maintain their ardor until death do them part. But for thousands of years the joke would have fallen flat.*

---

*"The Radical Idea of Marrying for Love," from *Marriage: A History,* by Stephanie Coontz, copyright 2005 by the S.J. Coontz Company. Published by Viking Penguin, a division of Penguin Group (USA), Inc.

Coontz uses the provocative quotation by Shaw to puncture our romantic assumptions about the role of love and passion in marriage. She follows the quotation with an explanation of why Shaw's statement "makes us smile" before setting out on her main undertaking in this article—as indicated in the final sentence of the second paragraph—a historical survey demonstrating that for most of the last few thousand years, love and marriage have had little to do with one another. Quoting the words of others offers many points of departure for your paper: You can agree with the quotation. You can agree and expand. You can sharply disagree. You can use the quotation to set a historical context or establish a tone.

Historical Review   Often the reader will be unprepared to follow the issue you discuss without some historical background. Consider this introduction to a paper on the film-rating system:

> Sex and violence on the screen are not new issues. In the Roaring Twenties there was increasing pressure from civic and religious groups to ban depictions of "immorality" from the screen. Faced with the threat of federal censorship, the film producers decided to clean their own house. In 1930, the Motion Picture Producers and Distributors of America established the Production Code. At first, adherence to the Code was voluntary; but in 1934 Joseph Breen, newly appointed head of the MPPDA, gave the Code teeth. Henceforth all newly produced films had to be submitted for approval to the Production Code Administration, which had the power to award or withhold the Code seal. Without a Code seal, it was virtually impossible for a film to be shown anywhere in the United States, since exhibitors would not accept it. At about the same time, the Catholic Legion of Decency was formed to advise the faithful which films were and were not objectionable. For several decades the Production Code Administration exercised powerful control over what was portrayed in American theatrical films. By the 1960s, however, changing standards of morality had considerably weakened the Code's grip. In 1968, the Production Code was replaced with a rating system designed to keep younger audiences away from films with high levels of sex or violence. Despite its imperfections, this rating system has proved more beneficial to American films than did the old censorship system.

The paper examines the relative benefits of the rating system. By opening with some historical background on the rating system, the writer helps readers understand his arguments. (Notice the chronological development of details.)

Review of a Controversy   A particular type of historical review provides the background on a controversy or debate. Consider this introduction:

> The *American Heritage Dictionary*'s definition of civil disobedience is rather simple: "the refusal to obey civil laws that are regarded as unjust, usually by employing methods of passive resistance." However,

despite such famous (and beloved) examples of civil disobedience as the movements of Mahatma Gandhi in India and the Reverend Martin Luther King, Jr., in the United States, the question of whether or not civil disobedience should be considered an asset to society is hardly clear cut. For instance, Hannah Arendt, in her article "Civil Disobedience," holds that "to think of disobedient minorities as rebels and truants is against the letter and spirit of a constitution whose framers were especially sensitive to the dangers of unbridled majority rule." On the other hand, a noted lawyer, Lewis Van Dusen, Jr., in his article "Civil Disobedience: Destroyer of Democracy," states that "civil disobedience, whatever the ethical rationalization, is still an assault on our democratic society, an affront to our legal order and an attack on our constitutional government." These two views are clearly incompatible. I believe, though, that Van Dusen's is the more convincing. On balance, civil disobedience is dangerous to society.*

The case against civil disobedience, rather than Van Dusen's article, is the topic of this paper. But to introduce this topic, the writer has provided quotations and references that represent opposing sides of the controversy over civil disobedience. By focusing at the outset on the particular rather than on the abstract qualities of the topic, the writer hopes to secure the attention of her readers and involve them in the controversy that forms the subject of her paper.

From the General to the Specific   Another way of providing a transition from the reader's world to the less familiar world of the paper is to work from a general subject to a specific one. The following introduction begins a paper on improving air quality by urging people to trade the use of their cars for public transportation.

While generalizations are risky, it seems pretty safe to say that most human beings are selfish. Self-interest may be part of our nature, and probably aids the survival of our species, since self-interested pursuits increase the likelihood of individual survival and genetic reproduction. Ironically, however, our selfishness has caused us to abuse the natural environment upon which we depend. We have polluted, deforested, depleted, deformed, and endangered our earth, water, and air to such an extent that now our species' survival is gravely threatened. In America, air pollution is one of our most pressing environmental problems, and it is our selfish use of the automobile that poses the greatest threat to clean air, as well as the greatest challenge to efforts to stop air pollution. Very few of us seem willing to give up our cars, let alone use them less. We are spoiled by the individual freedom afforded us when we can hop into our gas-guzzling vehicles and go where we want, when we want. Somehow, we as a nation will

*Michele Jacques, "Civil Disobedience: Van Dusen vs. Arendt," unpublished paper, 1993, 1. Used by permission.

have to wean ourselves from this addiction to the automobile, and we can do this by designing alternative forms of transportation that serve our selfish interests.*

Anecdote and Illustration: From the Specific to the General   The following two paragraphs offer an anecdote in order to move from the specific to a general subject:

> The night of March 24, 1989, was cold and calm, the air crystalline, as the giant *Exxon Valdez* oil tanker pulled out of Valdez, Alaska, into the tranquil waters of Prince William Sound. In these clearest of possible conditions the ship made a planned turn out of the shipping channel and didn't turn back in time. The huge tanker ran aground, spilling millions of gallons of crude oil into the sound. The cost of the cleanup effort was over $2 billion. The ultimate cost of continuing environmental damage is incalculable. Furthermore, when the civil trial was finally over in the summer of 1995, the Exxon Corporation was assessed an additional $5 billion in punitive damages. Everyone I query in my travels vividly recalls the accident, and most have the impression that it had something to do with the master's alcohol consumption. No one is aware of the true cause of the tragedy. In its final report, the National Transportation Safety Board (NTSB) found that sleep deprivation and sleep debt were direct causes of the accident. This stunning result got a brief mention in the back pages of the newspapers.
>
> Out of the vast ocean of knowledge about sleep, there are a few facts that are so important that I will try to burn them into your brain forever. None is more important than the topic of sleep debt. If we can learn to understand sleep indebtedness and manage it, we can improve everyday life as well as avoid many injuries, horribly diminished lives, and premature deaths.†

The previous introduction about pollution went from the general (the statement that human beings are selfish) to the specific (how to decrease air pollution). This one goes from the specific (a calamitous oil spill by a giant oil tanker in Alaskan waters) to the general (the enormous financial and human costs of "sleep debt," or not getting enough sleep). The anecdote is one of the most effective means at your disposal for capturing and holding your reader's attention. It is also one of the most commonly used types of introduction in popular articles. For decades, speakers have begun their remarks with a funny, touching, or otherwise appropriate story. (In fact, plenty of books are nothing but collections of such stories, arranged by subject.)

---

*Travis Knight, "Reducing Air Pollution with Alternative Transportation," unpublished paper, 1998, 1. Used by permission.
†From "The Promise of Sleep," copyright 1999 by William C. Dement. Used by permission of Dell Publishing, a division of Random House, Inc.

Question Frequently you can provoke the reader's attention by posing a question or a series of questions:

> Which of the following people would you say is the most admirable: Mother Teresa, Bill Gates, or Norman Borlaug? And which do you think is the least admirable? For most people, it's an easy question. Mother Teresa, famous for ministering to the poor in Calcutta, has been beatified by the Vatican, awarded the Nobel Peace Prize and ranked in an American poll as the most admired person of the 20th century. Bill Gates, infamous for giving us the Microsoft dancing paper clip and the blue screen of death, has been decapitated in effigy in "I Hate Gates" Web sites and hit with a pie in the face. As for Norman Borlaug...who the heck is Norman Borlaug?
>
> Yet a deeper look might lead you to rethink your answers. Borlaug, father of the "Green Revolution" that used agricultural science to reduce world hunger, has been credited with saving a billion lives, more than anyone else in history. Gates, in deciding what to do with his fortune, crunched the numbers and determined that he could alleviate the most misery by fighting everyday scourges in the developing world like malaria, diarrhea and parasites. Mother Teresa, for her part, extolled the virtue of suffering and ran her well-financed missions accordingly: their sick patrons were offered plenty of prayer but harsh conditions, few analgesics and dangerously primitive medical care.
>
> It's not hard to see why the moral reputations of this trio should be so out of line with the good they have done....*

In this introduction to "The Moral Instinct," Steven Pinker asks a question that appears to be easy; but the answer turns out to be more complex than the average reader would have suspected. Pinker uses the rest of the first paragraph to explain why the question appears to be so easy. (After all, no one was more widely admired than Mother Teresa; and for many people—especially Apple partisans!—former Microsoft CEO Bill Gates was an emblem of capitalist greed.) In the second paragraph, Pinker overturns these assumptions as he begins his exploration of the moral sense. Opening your paper with a question is provocative because it forces the reader to take an active role. Put on the spot by the author, he or she must consider answers—in this case, Who *is* the most admirable? What kind of qualities or activities *should* we admire? An opening question, chosen well, will engage readers and launch them into your paper.

Statement of Thesis Perhaps the most direct method of introduction is to begin immediately with the thesis:

> The contemporary American shopping mall is the formal garden of late twentieth-century culture, a commodified version of the great

---

*Steven J. Pinker, "The Moral Instinct," *New York Times Magazine* 12 Jan. 2008.

garden styles of Western history with which it shares fundamental characteristics. Set apart from the rest of the world as a place of earthly delight like the medieval walled garden; filled with fountains, statuary, and ingeniously devised machinery like the Italian Renaissance garden; designed on grandiose and symmetrical principles like the seventeenth-century French garden; made up of the fragments of cultural and architectural history like the eighteenth-century irregular English garden; and set aside for the public like the nineteenth-century American park, the mall is the next phase of this garden history, a synthesis of all these styles that have come before. But it is now joined with the shopping street, or at least a sanitized and standardized version of one, something that never before has been allowed within the garden.*

This selection begins with a general assertion—that the American shopping mall is analogous to the great formal gardens of Western history. This idea is Richard Keller Simon's thesis for an article titled "The Formal Garden in the Age of Consumer Culture," which he begins to develop in his second sentence with comparisons between the modern shopping mall and various types of gardens throughout history. In the paragraphs following this introduction, Simon draws correspondences between contemporary shopping malls in Houston, Philadelphia, and Palo Alto and such classic formal gardens as Henry VIII's Hampton Court. The "promenades, walls, vistas, mounts, labyrinths, statues, archways" of classic gardens, he writes, all have their analogs in the modern mall. Beginning with a thesis statement (as opposed to a quotation, question, or anecdote) works well when you want to develop an unexpected, or controversial, argument. The mall as a formal garden? Who would think so? We read on.

Or perhaps you open with the provocative assertion that "Reading is dead" in a paper examining the problem of declining literacy in the digital age. The reader sits up and takes notice, perhaps even protesting ("No, it's not—I read all the time!"). This strategy "hooks" a reader, who is likely to want to find out how you will support such an emphatic thesis.

One final note about our model introductions: They may be longer than introductions you have been accustomed to writing. Many writers (and readers) prefer shorter, snappier introductions. The ideal length of an introduction depends on the length of the paper it introduces, and it may also be a matter of personal or corporate style. There is no rule concerning the correct length of an introduction. If you feel that a short introduction is appropriate, use one. Conversely, you may wish to break up what seems like a long introduction into two paragraphs.

Excerpted from "The Formal Garden in the Age of Consumer Culture: A Reading of the Twentieth-Century Shopping Mall," copyright 1992 by Richard Keller Simon. Reprinted from Mapping the American Culture, ed. Wayne Franklin and Michael Steiner. Published by the University of Iowa Press.

Exercise 6.5

Drafting Introductions

Imagine that you are writing a paper using the topic, ideas, and thesis you developed in the exercises in this chapter. Conduct some preliminary research on the topic, using an Internet search engine such as *Google* or *Bing* or an article database available at your college. Choose one of the seven types of introductions we've discussed—preferably one you have never used before—and draft an introduction that would work to open a paper on your topic. Use our examples as models to help you draft your introduction.

Conclusions

You might view your conclusion as an introduction in reverse: a bridge from the world of your paper back to the world of your reader. The simplest conclusion is a summary of the paper, but at this point you should go beyond mere summary. You might begin with a summary, for example, and then extend it with a discussion of the paper's significance or its implications for future study, for choices that individuals might make, for policy, and so on. You could urge readers to change an attitude or modify behavior. Certainly, you're under no obligation to discuss the broader significance of your work (and a summary, alone, will satisfy the formal requirement that your paper have an ending); but the conclusions of effective papers often reveal that their authors are "thinking large" by placing their limited subject into a larger social, cultural, or historical context.

Two words of advice: First, no matter how clever or beautifully executed, a conclusion cannot salvage a poorly written paper. Second, by virtue of its placement, the conclusion carries rhetorical weight: it is the last statement a reader will encounter before turning from your work. Realizing this, writers who expand on the basic summary conclusion often wish to give their final words a dramatic flourish, a heightened level of diction. Soaring rhetoric and drama in a conclusion are fine as long as they do not unbalance the paper and call attention to themselves. Having labored long hours over your paper, you may be inclined at this point to wax eloquent. But keep a sense of proportion and timing. Make your points quickly and end crisply.

Statement of the Subject's Significance   One of the more effective ways to conclude a paper is to discuss the larger significance of your subject. Here you move from the specific concern of your paper to the broader concerns of the reader's world. A paper on the Wright brothers might end with a discussion of air travel as it affects economies, politics, or families; a paper on contraception might end with a discussion of its effect on sexual mores, population, or the church. But don't overwhelm your reader with the importance of your remarks. Keep your discussion focused.

In this paragraph, June J. Pilcher and Amy S. Walters conclude a paper on how "sleep debt" hurts college students:

> In sum, our findings suggest that college students are not aware of the extent to which sleep deprivation impairs their ability to complete cognitive tasks successfully because they consistently overrate their concentration and effort, as well as their estimated performance. In addition, the current data suggest that 24 hours of sleep deprivation significantly affects only fatigue and confusion and does not have a more general effect on positive or negative mood states. The practical implication of these findings is that many college students are unknowingly sabotaging their own performance by choosing to deprive themselves of sleep [while] they complete complex cognitive tasks.*

The first sentence (as the initial phrase indicates) summarizes the chief finding of the study on which the authors have written. They expand on this conclusion before ending with a statement of the subject's significance ("The practical implication of these findings is that..."). Ending a paper in this way is another way of saying, "The conclusions of this paper matter." If you have taken the trouble to write a good paper, the conclusions *do* matter. Don't be bashful: State the larger significance of the point(s) you have made. Just don't claim too great a significance for your work, lest by overreaching you pop the balloon and your reader thinks, "No, the paper's not *that* important."

Call for Further Research Scientists and social scientists often end their papers with a review of what has been presented (as, for instance, in an experiment) and the ways in which the subject under consideration needs to be further explored. *A word of caution:* If you raise questions that you call on others to answer, make sure you know that the research you are calling for hasn't already been conducted.

The following conclusion ends a sociological report on the placement of elderly men and women in nursing homes.

> Thus, our study shows a correlation between the placement of elderly citizens in nursing facilities and the significant decline of their motor and intellectual skills over the ten months following placement. What the research has not made clear is the extent to which this marked decline is due to physical as opposed to emotional causes. The elderly are referred to homes at that point in their lives when they grow less able to care for themselves—which suggests that the drop-off in skills may be due to physical causes. But the emotional stress of being

---

*"How Sleep Deprivation Affects Psychological Variables Related to College Students' Cognitive Performance" by June J. Pilcher and Amy S. Walters, from *Journal of American College Health*, Vol. 46, issue 3, November 1997, pp. 121–126. Published by the Helen Dwight Reid Educational Foundation, Heldref Publications.

placed in a home, away from family and in an environment that confirms the patient's view of himself as decrepit, may exacerbate—if not itself be a primary cause of—the patient's rapid loss of abilities. Further research is needed to clarify the relationship between depression and particular physical ailments as these affect the skills of the elderly in nursing facilities. There is little doubt that information yielded by such studies can enable health care professionals to deliver more effective services.*

Notice how this call for further study locates the author in a larger community of researchers on whom he depends for assistance in answering the questions that emerge from his own work. The author summarizes his findings (in the first sentence of the paragraph), states what his work has not shown, and then extends his invitation.

Solution/Recommendation   The purpose of your paper might be to review a problem or controversy and to discuss contributing factors. In such a case, after summarizing your discussion, you could offer a solution based on the knowledge you've gained while conducting research, as in the following conclusion. Of course, if your solution is to be taken seriously, your knowledge must be amply demonstrated in the body of the paper.

The major problem in college sports today is not commercialism—it is the exploitation of athletes and the proliferation of illicit practices which dilute educational standards.

Many universities are currently deriving substantial benefits from sports programs that depend on the labor of athletes drawn from the poorest sections of America's population. It is the responsibility of educators, civil rights leaders, and concerned citizens to see that these young people get a fair return for their labor both in terms of direct remuneration and in terms of career preparation for a life outside sports.

Minimally, scholarships in revenue-producing sports should be designed to extend until graduation, rather than covering only four years of athletic eligibility, and should include guarantees of tutoring, counseling, and proper medical care. At institutions where the profits are particularly large [and the head football coach earns a multi-million-dollar salary], scholarships should also provide salaries that extend beyond room, board, and tuition. The important thing is that the athlete be remunerated fairly and have the opportunity to gain skills from a university environment without undue competition from a physically and psychologically demanding full-time job. This may well require that scholarships be extended over five or six years, including summers.

Such a proposal, I suspect, will not be easy to implement. The current amateur system, despite its moral and educational flaws, enables universities to hire their athletic labor at minimal cost. But solving

*Adam Price, "The Crisis in Nursing Home Care," unpublished paper, 2001. Used by permission.

> the fiscal crisis of the universities on the backs of America's poor and minorities is not, in the long run, a tenable solution. With the support of concerned educators, parents, and civil rights leaders, and with the help from organized labor, the college athlete, truly a sleeping giant, will someday speak out and demand what is rightly his—and hers—a fair share of the revenue created by their hard work.*

In this conclusion, the author summarizes his article in one sentence: "The major problem in college sports today is not commercialism—it is the exploitation of athletes and the proliferation of illicit practices which dilute educational standards." In paragraph 2 he continues with an analysis of the problem just stated and follows with a general recommendation that "educators, civil rights leaders, and concerned citizens" be responsible for the welfare of college athletes. In paragraph 3 he makes a specific proposal, and in the final paragraph, he anticipates resistance to the proposal. He concludes by discounting this resistance and returning to the general point, that college athletes should receive a fair deal.

Anecdote   As we've seen in our discussion of introductions, an anecdote is a briefly told story or joke, the point of which is to shed light on your subject. The anecdote is more direct than an allusion. With an allusion, you merely refer to a story ("We would all love to go floating down the river like Huck…"); with the anecdote, you retell the story. The anecdote allows readers to discover for themselves the significance of a reference to another source— an effort most readers enjoy because they get to exercise their creativity.

The following anecdote concludes a political-philosophical essay. After the author sums up her argument in a paragraph, she continues—and concludes—with a brief story.

> Ironically, our economy is fueled by the very thing that degrades our value system. But when politicians call for a return to "traditional family values," they seldom criticize the business interests that promote and benefit from our coarsened values. Consumer capitalism values things over people; it thrives on discontent and unhappiness since discontented people make excellent consumers, buying vast numbers of things that may somehow "fix" their inadequacies. We buy more than we need, the economy chugs along, but such materialism is the real culprit behind our warped value systems. Anthony de Mello tells the following story:
>
>> Socrates believed that the wise person would instinctively lead a frugal life, and he even went so far as to refuse to wear shoes. Yet he constantly fell under the spell of the marketplace and would go there often to look at the great variety and magnificence of the wares on display.

---

*Mark Naison, "Scenario for Scandal," *Commonweal* 109.16 (1982).

A friend once asked him why he was so intrigued with the allures of the market. "I love to go there," Socrates replied, "to discover how many things I am perfectly happy without."*

The writer could, at this point, have offered an interpretation instead of an anecdote, but this would have spoiled the dramatic value for the reader. The purpose of an anecdote is to make your point with subtlety, to resist the temptation to interpret. When selecting an anecdote, keep in mind four guidelines: The anecdote should fit your content; it should be prepared for (readers should have all the information they need to understand it); it should provoke the readers' interest; and it should not be so obscure as to be unintelligible.

Quotation   A favorite concluding device is the quotation—the words of a famous person or an authority in the field on which you are writing. By quoting another, you link your work to that person's, thereby gaining authority and credibility. The first criterion for selecting a quotation is its suitability to your thesis. But consider carefully what your choice of sources says about you. Suppose you are writing a paper on the American work ethic. If you could use a line either by the comedian Jon Stewart or by the current secretary of labor to make the final point of your conclusion, which would you choose and why? One source may not be inherently more effective than the other, but the choice would affect the tone of your paper. The following paragraph concludes an article on single-sex education:

> But schools, inevitably, present many curriculums, some overt and some subtle; and critics argue that with Sax's[†] model comes a lesson that our gender differences are primary, and this message is at odds with one of the most foundational principles of America's public schools. Given the myriad ways in which our schools are failing, it may be hard to remember that public schools were intended not only to instruct children in reading and math but also to teach them commonality, tolerance and what it means to be American. "When you segregate, by any means, you lose some of that," says Richard Kahlenberg, a senior fellow at the Century Foundation. "Even if one could prove that sending a kid off to his or her own school based on religion or race or ethnicity or gender did a little bit better job of raising the academic skills for workers in the economy, there's also the issue of trying to create tolerant citizens in a democracy."**

In the article leading up to this conclusion, Elizabeth Weil takes a somewhat skeptical view of the virtues of "teaching boys and girls separately."

---

*Frances Wageneck, "Family Values in the Marketplace," unpublished paper, 2000. Used by permission.
[†]Leonard Sax is a psychologist and physician who gave up medicine to devote himself to promoting single-sex public education.
**Elizabeth Weil, "Teaching Boys and Girls Separately," *New York Times Magazine* 2 Mar. 2008.

She concludes with an apt quotation by Richard Kahlenberg, who, while conceding some value for single-sex education, supports Weil's own skepticism by suggesting that single-sex education may not create citizens as tolerant as those who have been through classes that include both genders.

Using quotations poses one potential problem, however: If you end with the words of another, you may leave the impression that someone else can make your case more effectively than you. The language of the quotation will put your own prose into relief. If your prose suffers by comparison—if the quotations are the best part of your paper—you need to spend time revising.

Question Just as questions are useful for opening papers, they are useful for closing them. Opening and closing questions function in different ways, however. The introductory question promises to be addressed in the paper that follows. But the concluding question leaves issues unresolved, calling on the readers to assume an active role by offering their own answers. Consider the following two paragraphs, written to conclude an article on genetically modified (GM) food:

> Are GM foods any more of a risk than other agricultural innovations that have taken place over the years, like selective breeding? Do the existing and potential future benefits of GM foods outweigh any risks that do exist? And what standard should governments use when assessing the safety of transgenic crops? The "frankenfood" frenzy has given life to a policy-making standard known as the "precautionary principle," which has been long advocated by environmental groups. That principle essentially calls for governments to prohibit any activity that raises concerns about human health or the environment, even if some cause-and-effect relationships are not fully established scientifically. As Liberal Democrat MP [Member of Parliament] Norman Baker told the BBC: "We must always apply the precautionary principle. That says that unless you're sure of adequate control, unless you're sure the risk is minimal, unless you're sure nothing horrible can go wrong, you don't do it."
>
> But can any innovation ever meet such a standard of certainty—especially given the proliferation of "experts" that are motivated as much by politics as they are by science? And what about those millions of malnourished people whose lives could be saved by transgenic foods?*

Rather than end with a question, you may choose to *raise* a question in your conclusion and then answer it, based on the material you've provided

---

*"Frankenfoods Frenzy," *Reason* 13 Jan. 2000.

in the paper. The answered question challenges a reader to agree or disagree with you and thus places the reader in an active role. The following brief conclusion ends a student paper titled "Is Feminism Dead?"

> So the answer to the question "Is the feminist movement dead?" is no, it's not. Even if most young women today don't consciously identify themselves as "feminists"—due to the ways in which the term has become loaded with negative associations—the principles of gender equality that lie at feminism's core are enthusiastically embraced by the vast number of young women, and even a large percentage of young men.

Speculation   When you speculate, you consider what might happen as well as what has happened. Speculation involves a spinning out of possibilities. It stimulates readers by immersing them in your discussion of the unknown, implicitly challenging them to agree or disagree. The following paragraph concludes the brief article "The Incandescent Charisma of the Lonely Light Bulb" by Dan Neil. The author laments the passing of the familiar electric light bulb (in favor of lower-wattage compact fluorescent lights) as one more indication of the end of the analog age and the triumph of the digital: "The demise of the light bulb marks the final transition from electrics to electronics":

> The passing of any technology provokes nostalgia. I'm sure someone bemoaned the rise of the push-button phone and eulogized the rotary dialer. (*What a beautiful sound, the "shickity-shick" of a well-spun number....*) But the Edisonian light bulb is a more fundamental thing—so much the proverbial better idea that it came to symbolize the eureka moment, the flash of insight, when it appeared over a cartoon character's head. The fact is, how we light the world inevitably affects how we see the world. I predict we're going to miss the soft, forgiving light of the incandescent bulb with its celestial geometry. *I predict a more harshly lighted future.**

The author's concluding speculation may not be entirely serious (though a few people do lament the passing of the manual typewriter and the phonograph record), but it does highlight what is often lost, and subsequently missed, in the relentless journey of technological progress. If you have provided the necessary information prior to a concluding speculation, you will send readers back into their lives (and away from your paper) with an implicit challenge: Do they regard the future as you do? Whether they do or not, you have set an agenda. You have got them thinking.

---

*Dan Neil, "The Incandescent Charisma of the Lonely Light Bulb," *Los Angeles Times Magazine* 3 Feb. 2008: 70.

Exercise 6.6

Drafting Conclusions

Imagine that you have written a paper using the topic, ideas, and thesis you developed in the earlier exercises in this chapter. Conduct some preliminary research on the topic, using an Internet search engine such as *Google* or *Bing* or an article database available at your college library. Choose one of the seven types of conclusions we've discussed—preferably one you have never used before—and draft a conclusion that would work to end your paper. Use our examples as models to help you draft your conclusion.

■ STAGE 5: REVISION

Perhaps it's stating the obvious to say that rough drafts need revision, yet too often students skimp on this phase of the writing process. The word *revision* can be used to describe all modifications one makes to a written document. But it's useful to distinguish among three kinds of revision:

Global revisions focus on the thesis, the type and pattern of evidence employed, the overall organization, the match between thesis and content, and the tone. A global revision may also emerge from a change in purpose.

Local revisions focus on paragraphs: topic and transitional sentences; the type of evidence presented within a paragraph; evidence added, modified, or dropped within a paragraph; and logical connections from one sentence (or set of sentences) within a paragraph to another.

Surface revisions deal with sentence style and construction as well as word choice. Sentence editing involves correcting errors of grammar, mechanics, spelling, and citation form.

Global and local revisions fall within Stage 5 of the writing process; surface revisions are covered in Stage 6, editing.

We advise separating large-scale (global and local) revision from later (sentence-editing) revision as a way of keeping priorities in order. If you take care of larger, global problems, you may find that in the process, you have fixed or simply dropped awkward sentences. Get the large components in place first: *content* (your ideas), *structure* (the arrangement of your paragraphs), and *paragraph structure* (the arrangement of ideas within your paragraphs). Then tend to the smaller elements, much as you would in building a house. You wouldn't lay the carpet before setting the floor joists.

Think of revision as re-vision, or "seeing anew." In order to re-see, it's often useful to set your paper aside for a time and come back later to view your rough draft with a fresh eye. Doing so will better allow you to determine whether your paper effectively deals with its subject—whether it comes across as unified, coherent, and fully developed.

Characteristics of Good Papers

Apply these principles of *unity, coherence,* and *development* to the whole revision process. Let's start with unity, which we've already discussed in the context of the thesis.

Unity

A paper is unified when it is focused on a main point. As we've noted, the chief tool for achieving paper unity is the thesis: It's hard to achieve unity in a paper when its central point remains unstated. But unity doesn't stop at the thesis; the body paragraphs that follow must clearly support and explain that thesis. To determine unity, therefore:

1. examine your introduction and make sure you have a clear, identifiable thesis;
2. check your paper's interior paragraphs to make sure that all your points relate to that thesis; and
3. ask yourself how your conclusion provides closure to the discussion.

Coherence

Coherence means "logical interconnectedness." When things cohere, elements come together and make a whole. Coherence is closely related to unity: Good papers cohere. They hold together logically and stay focused on a main point. All subordinate points in the body of the paper clearly relate to the main point expressed in the thesis. Moreover, all those subpoints, examples, and supporting quotations are presented in a logical order so that connections between them are clear. You could write a highly unified paper, but the reader will have a hard time following your argument or staying focused on your point if your points are discussed in haphazard order. Guide readers along with your writing. Show them not only how subpoints relate to the main point, but also how they relate to one another.

Development

Good papers are also well developed, meaning that their points are fully explained and supported. Readers do not live inside your head. They will not fully understand your points unless you adequately explain them. A reader may also not be persuaded that your paper's main point is valid unless you provide support for your arguments by using examples, the opinions of authorities on the subject, and your own sound logic to hold it all together.

Use the three principles of unity, coherence, and development to analyze what you have written, and make necessary revisions. Does your paper stay focused on the main point? Do your paper's points clearly relate to each other? Do you need better transitions between some paragraphs to help the ideas flow more logically and smoothly? Have you fully explained and given adequate support for all your points?

These three principles for good papers also apply to the composition of good paragraphs. Paragraphs are "minipapers": they should stick to a main point (the topic sentence) and fully develop that point in an orderly fashion. Transitional words or phrases such as *however, thus, on the other hand,* and *for example* help clarify for a reader how the sentences within individual paragraphs are related.

The Reverse Outline

The *reverse outline* is a useful technique for refining a working thesis and for establishing unity between your thesis statement and the body of your paper. When you outline a paper you intend to write, you do so *prospectively*— that is, before the fact of writing. In a reverse outline you outline the paper *retrospectively*—after the fact. The reverse outline is useful for spotting gaps in logic or development as well as problems with unity or coherence. Follow these steps to generate a reverse outline:

1. On a fresh sheet of paper (or electronic document), restate your thesis, making certain that the thesis you began with is the thesis that in fact governs the logic of the paper. (Look for a competing thesis in your conclusion. In summing up, you may have clarified for yourself your *actual* governing idea, as opposed to the idea you thought would organize the paper.)

2. In the margin of your draft, summarize *each* paragraph in a phrase. If you have trouble writing a summary, place an asterisk by the paragraph as a reminder to summarize it later.

3. Beneath your thesis, write your paragraph-summary phrases, one to a line, in outline format.

4. Review the outline you have just created. Is the paper divided into readily identifiable major points in support of the thesis? Have you sufficiently supported each major point? Do the sections of the outline lead logically from one to the next? Do all sections develop the thesis?

5. Be alert for uneven development. Add or delete material as needed to ensure a balanced presentation.

■ STAGE 6: EDITING

Only after revising a paper's large-scale elements—its unity, coherence, and content development; its overall structure; and its paragraph structure—are you ready to polish your paper by editing its sentences for style and correctness. At this stage you may be tired and strongly tempted to merely correct the obvious mistake here and there. Resist that impulse! Don't risk ruining a thoughtful, well-developed paper with sentence-level errors like incorrect word choice and faulty parallelism. After all your work, you don't want readers distracted by easily correctible mistakes in grammar, punctuation, and spelling.

Editing for Style

Developing an engaging writing style takes long practice. It's beyond the scope of this book to teach you the nuances of writing style, but you can consult many other fine books for help. (See, for example, William Zinsser's *On Writing Well.*) Here we'll focus on just one common stylistic problem: short, choppy sentences.

Perhaps out of fear of making common sentence errors like run-ons or comma splices, some writers avoid varying their sentence types, preferring strings of simple sentences. The result is usually unsatisfying. Compare, for instance, two versions of the same paragraph on a study of the human genome:

> Scientists have finally succeeded in decoding the human genome. This accomplishment opens up a whole new field of study. Researchers now have new ways to understand human biological functioning. We may also be able to learn new perspectives on human behavior. For centuries people have wondered about how much we are shaped by genetics. They have also wondered how much environment shapes us. The age-old questions about nature vs. nurture may now be answered. Each individual's genetic heritage as well as his or her genetic future will be visible to geneticists. All of these discoveries may help us to improve and extend human life. Many diseases will be detectable. New treatments will be developed. These new discoveries open up a new area of ethical debate. Scientists and the public are going to have to decide how far to take this new genetic technology.

This paragraph illustrates the problems with choppy, repetitive sentences. First, the writer hasn't connected ideas, and sentences don't flow smoothly from one to the next. Second, the same sentence structure (the simple sentence) appears monotonously, each following the simple subject-predicate form. The result, while grammatically correct, taxes the reader's patience. Compare the preceding version to this revision (which represents just one way the paragraph could be rewritten):

> Scientists have opened a whole new field of study following their recent decoding of the human genome. Armed with new ways of understanding human biological and behavioral functioning, researchers may someday sort out the extent to which we are shaped by our genes and by our environment. When geneticists can examine an individual's genetic past and future, they may also be able to alter these things, with the goal of improving and extending human life

through early disease detection and the development of new treatments. However, such promise is not without its pitfalls: genetic research must be scrutinized from an ethical standpoint, and scientists and the public will have to decide the uses and the limits of this new technology.

Not only is the revised version of this paragraph easier to read, it's also more concise, clear, and coherent. Sentences with related content have been combined. Brief sentences have been converted to clauses or phrases and incorporated into the structure of other sentences to form more complex units of meaning.

Guard against strings of short, choppy sentences in your own writing. Learn strategies for sentence-level revision by learning how different sentence structures work. You can link related ideas with subordinating conjunctions (*because, since, while, although,* etc.); commas and coordinating conjunctions (*for, and, nor, but, or, yet, so*); and semicolons and coordinating adverbs (*however, thus, therefore,* etc.).

Editing for Correctness

On matters of sentence style, there is no "correct" approach. Often, personal style and taste influence sentence construction, paragraph and sentence length, and word choice. Grammar and punctuation, on the other hand, follow more widely accepted, objective standards. Of these, we (and your instructors) can speak in terms of "correctness"—of agreed-upon conventions, or rules, that people working in academic, professional, and business environments adopt as a standard of communication. You will find the rules (for comma placement, say, or the use of "amount" versus "number" and "affect" versus "effect") in up-to-date writing handbooks. Review the list in the Common Sentence-level Errors box, and eliminate such errors from your papers before submitting them.

The Final Draft

When you have worked on a paper for days (or weeks), writing and revising several drafts, you may have trouble knowing when you're finished. Referring to the writing of poetry, the Pulitzer Prize–winning poet Henry Taylor once remarked that a writer is done when revisions begin to move the project sideways instead of forward. We think the same distinction applies to academic writing. Assuming you have revised at the sentence level for grammar and punctuation, when you get the impression that your changes *do not actively advance* the main point with new facts, arguments, illustrations, or supporting quotations, you are probably done. Stop writing and prepare a clean draft. Set it aside for a day or two (if you have that luxury), and read it one last time to catch remaining sentence-level errors.

Common Sentence-level Errors

ERRORS IN GRAMMAR

Sentence fragments—word groups lacking a subject or a predicate

Run-on sentences—two independent clauses joined without the proper conjunction (connecting word) or punctuation

Comma splices—two independent clauses joined by a comma alone when they need stronger linkage such as a coordinating conjunction, a conjunctive adverb, a semicolon, or a period

Subject-verb agreement errors—the verb form doesn't match the plural or singular nature of the subject

Pronoun usage—pronoun reference errors, lack of clarity in pronoun reference, or errors of pronoun-antecedent agreement

ERRORS IN PUNCTUATION

Misplaced commas, missing commas, improper use of semicolons or colons, missing apostrophes, and the like

ERRORS IN SPELLING

Misspelled words

Most difficult will be deciding when the paper is done stylistically, especially for the papers you care most deeply about. With respect to style, one could revise endlessly—and many writers do because there is no one correct way (stylistically speaking) to write a sentence. As long as a sentence is grammatical, you can write it numerous ways. Still, if a given sentence is dull, you will want to improve it, for an excessively dull style will bore the reader and defeat the paper as surely as a flawed argument or a host of grammatical errors. But having devoted time to polishing your sentences, you will at some point need to pronounce yourself finished. When your changes make your work merely different, not better, stop.

Your instructor will (likely) return the paper with comments and suggestions. Read them carefully. If you or the instructor feels that a revision is appropriate, think through the options for recasting the paper. Instructors generally respond well when you go into a conference with an action plan.

At some point, instructor's comments or no, the paper will be done and graded. Read it through one last time, and learn from it. Once you have determined what you did well and what you could improve on for the next effort, it is time to move on.

WRITING ASSIGNMENT: PROCESS

Choose either of the following writing assignments.

1. Write a paper following the process outlined in this chapter. As a guide, you may want to complete Exercises 6.1–6.6, which will serve as prompts. As you write, keep a log in which you record brief observations about each stage of the writing process. Share the log with your classmates and discuss the writing process with them.

2. In this chapter you have learned to approach writing as a task divided into stages that blend together and loop back on one another: data gathering, invention, drafting, revision, and editing. Write a one- or two-page statement in which you compare your writing process *prior* to taking a composition course to the process you've learned from this text and from your instructor. What are the main differences? similarities? At the end of your statement, speculate on the ways you might alter this process to better suit you.

7. Locating, Mining, and Citing Sources

■ SOURCE-BASED PAPERS

Research extends the boundaries of your knowledge and enables you to share your findings with others. The process of locating and working with multiple sources draws on many of the skills we have discussed in this book:

1. taking notes;

2. organizing your findings;

3. summarizing, paraphrasing, and quoting sources accurately and ethically;

4. critically evaluating sources for their value and relevance to your topic;

5. synthesizing information and ideas from several sources that best support your own critical viewpoint; and

6. analyzing topics for meaning and significance.

The model argument synthesis in Chapter 4, "Balancing Privacy and Safety in the Wake of Virginia Tech" (pp. 150–159), is an example of a research paper that fulfills these requirements. The quality of your research and the success of any paper on which it is based is directly related to your success in locating relevant, significant, reliable, and current sources. This chapter will help you in that process.

Where Do We Find Written Research?

Here are just a few of the types of writing that involve research:

ACADEMIC WRITING

- **Research papers** investigate an issue and incorporate results in a written or oral presentation.

- **Literature reviews** research and review relevant studies and approaches to a particular science, social science, or humanities topic.

(continues)

- **Experimental reports** describe primary research and may draw on previous studies.
- **Case studies** draw upon primary and sometimes secondary research to report on or analyze an individual, a group, or a set of events.
- **Position papers** research approaches to an issue or solutions to a problem in order to formulate and advocate a new approach.

WORKPLACE WRITING

- **Reports** in business, science, engineering, social services, medicine
- **Market analyses**
- **Business plans**
- **Environmental impact reports**
- **Legal research:** memoranda of points and authorities

Writing the Research Paper

Here is an overview of the main steps involved in writing research papers. Keep in mind that, as with other writing projects, writing such papers is a recursive process. For instance, you will gather data at various stages of your writing, as the list below illustrates.

DEVELOPING THE RESEARCH QUESTION

- *Find a subject.*
- *Develop a research question.* Formulate an important question that you propose to answer through your research.

LOCATING SOURCES

- *Conduct preliminary research.* Consult knowledgeable people, general and specialized encyclopedias, overviews and bibliographies in recent books, the *Bibliographic Index,* and subject-heading guides.
- *Refine your research question.* Based on your preliminary research, brainstorm about your topic and ways to answer your research question. Sharpen your focus, refining your question and planning the sources you'll need to consult.
- *Conduct focused research.* Consult books, electronic databases, general and specialized periodicals, biographical indexes, general

(continues)

and specialized dictionaries, government publications, and other appropriate sources. Conduct interviews and surveys, as necessary.

MINING SOURCES

- *Develop a working thesis.* Based on your initial research, formulate a working thesis that responds to your research question.
- *Develop a working bibliography.* Keep track of your sources, either on paper or electronically, including both bibliographic information and key points about each source. Make this bibliography easy to sort and rearrange.
- *Evaluate sources.* Determine the veracity and reliability of your sources; use your critical reading skills; check *Book Review Digest;* look up biographies of authors.
- *Take notes from sources.* Paraphrase and summarize important information and ideas from your sources. Copy down important quotations. Note page numbers from sources of this quoted and summarized material.
- *Develop a working outline and arrange your notes according to your outline.*

DRAFTING; CITING SOURCES

- *Write your draft.* Write the preliminary draft of your paper, working from your notes and according to your outline.
- *Avoid plagiarism.* Take care to cite all quoted, paraphrased, and summarized source material, making sure that your own wording and sentence structure differ from those of your sources.
- *Cite sources.* Use in-text citations and a Works Cited or References list, according to the conventions of the discipline (e.g., MLA, APA, CSE).

REVISING (GLOBAL AND LOCAL CHANGES)

- *Revise your draft.* Consider global, local, surface revisions. Check that your thesis still reflects your paper's focus. Review topic sentences and paragraph development and logic. Use transitional words and phrases to ensure coherence. Make sure that the paper reads smoothly and clearly from beginning to end.

EDITING (SURFACE CHANGES)

- *Edit your draft.* Check for style, combining short, choppy sentences and ensuring variety in your sentence structures. Check for grammatical correctness, punctuation, and spelling.

■ THE RESEARCH QUESTION

Pose a question to guide your research, one that interests you and allows you to fulfill the requirements of an assignment. In time, the short answer to this research question will become the thesis of your paper. By working with a question (as opposed to a thesis) early in the research process, you acknowledge that you still have ideas and information to discover before reaching your conclusions and beginning to write.

Research questions can be more or less effective in directing you to sources. Here are three suggestions for devising successful questions.

1. Pose neutral questions that open you to a variety of ideas and information. Avoid biased questions that suggest their own answers.

   EFFECTIVE How do musicians use computers to help them create songs?

   LESS EFFECTIVE Are musicians who rely on computers to compose and produce music cheating the creative process? [The use of "cheating" suggests that the researcher has already answered the question.]

2. Emphasize *how/why/what* questions that open discussion. Avoid yes or no questions that end discussion.

   EFFECTIVE How do software engineers create algorithms that map patterns in music?

   LESS EFFECTIVE Does music lend itself to mathematical analysis? [The yes or no question yields less information and leads to less understanding than the *how* question.]

3. Match the scope of your question to the scope of your paper. Avoid too-broad topics for brief papers; avoid too-narrow topics for longer papers.

   EFFECTIVE How has the use of computers affected both the production and the consumption of popular music in America?

   LESS EFFECTIVE How has the use of computers affected American popular culture? [Assuming a brief paper, the topic is too broad.]

Narrowing the Topic via Research

If you need help narrowing a broad subject, try one or more of the following:

- Search by subject in an electronic database to see how the subject breaks down into components.

(continues)

• Search the subject heading in an electronic periodical catalog such as *InfoTrac®* or in a print catalog such as the *Readers' Guide to Periodical Literature.*

• Search the *Library of Congress Subject Headings* catalog (see Subject-Heading Guides, p. 261, for details).

Exercise 7.1

Constructing Research Questions

Moving from a broad topic or idea to the formulation of precise research questions can be challenging. Practice this skill by working with small groups of your classmates to construct research questions about the following topics (or come up with topics of your own). Write at least one research question that narrows each topic listed; then discuss these topics and questions with the other groups in class.

Racial or gender stereotypes in television shows

Drug addiction in the U.S. adult population

Global environmental policies

Employment trends in high-technology industries

U.S. energy policy

■ LOCATING SOURCES ■

Once you have a research question, find out what references are available. In your preliminary research, familiarize yourself quickly with basic issues and generate a preliminary list of sources. This will help narrow your investigations before moving to focused research.

Types of Research Data (see also Chapter 6, pp. 219–220)

PRIMARY SOURCES

• Data gathered using research methods appropriate to a particular field

   sciences: experiments, observations

   social sciences: experiments, observations, surveys, interviews

   humanities: diaries, letters, and other unpublished documents; close reading, observation, and interpretation

(continues)

SECONDARY SOURCES

- Information and ideas collected or generated by others who have conducted their own primary and/or secondary research

  library research: books, periodicals, etc.

  online research

■ PRELIMINARY RESEARCH

Effective search strategies often begin with the most general reference sources: encyclopedias, bibliographic listings, biographical works, and dictionaries. Such sources are designed for people who need to familiarize themselves relatively quickly with the basic information about a particular topic. Authors of general sources assume that their readers have little or no prior knowledge of the subjects covered and of the specialized terminology of the field. By design, they cover a subject in less depth than do specialized sources. So review such comprehensive sources relatively early in your search even though you probably won't refer to them or cite them in your paper because they are so general.

Consulting Knowledgeable People

When you think of research, you may immediately think of libraries and print and online sources. But don't neglect a key reference: other people. Your *instructor* can probably suggest fruitful areas of research and some useful sources. Try to see your instructor during office hours, however, rather than immediately before or after class, so that you'll have enough time for a productive discussion.

Once you get to the library, ask a *reference librarian* which reference sources (e.g., bibliographies, specialized encyclopedias, periodical indexes) might be fruitful for your particular area of research. Librarians won't do your research for you, but they'll be glad to suggest ways to conduct research efficiently and systematically.

Locating Preliminary Sources

- Ask your instructor to recommend sources on the subject.
- Scan the "Suggestions for Further Reading" sections of your textbooks. Ask your college librarian for useful reference tools in your subject area.
- Read an encyclopedia article on the subject and use the bibliography following the article to identify other sources.

(continues)

> - Read the introduction to a recent book on the subject and review that book's bibliography to identify more sources.
> - Consult the annual *Bibliographic Index* (see p. 261 for details).
> - Use an Internet search engine to explore your topic. Type in different keyword or search term combinations and browse the sites you find for ideas and references to sources you can look up later (see the box on pp. 264–265 for details).

Encyclopedias

Reading an encyclopedia entry about your subject will give you a basic understanding of the most significant facts and issues. Whether the subject is American politics or the mechanics of genetic engineering, the encyclopedia article—written by a specialist in the field—offers a broad overview that may serve as a launching point to more specialized research in a particular area. The article may illuminate areas or raise questions that motivate you to pursue further. Equally important, the encyclopedia article frequently concludes with an *annotated bibliography* describing important books and articles on the subject. Encyclopedias have limitations, however.

1. Most professors don't accept encyclopedia articles as legitimate sources for academic papers. You should use encyclopedias primarily to familiarize yourself with (and to select a particular aspect of) the subject area and as a springboard for further research.

2. Because new editions of encyclopedias appear only once every five or ten years, the information they contain—including bibliographies—may not be current. Some print encyclopedias are now also available online—*Britannica Online,* for example—and this may mean, but not guarantee, that their information is up to date.

Consider consulting some of these general encyclopedias:

Academic American Encyclopedia

Columbia Encyclopedia

Encyclopedia Americana

New Encyclopaedia Britannica (or *Britannica Online*)

Wikipedia (online) [But see "Let the Buyer Beware" note below.]

Keep in mind that the library also contains a variety of more *specialized* encyclopedias, such as the *Grove* encyclopedias of art and architecture, the *Encyclopedia of Biology,* and the *Encyclopedia of Psychology.* Specialized encyclopedias restrict themselves to a particular disciplinary area, such as chemistry, law, or film, and are considerably more detailed in their treatment of a subject than are general encyclopedias.

Wikipedia: Let the Buyer Beware

One of the Web's most popular sites for general information is *Wikipedia* <http://www.wikipedia.org>. Launched in 2001 by the Internet entrepreneur Jimmy Wales, *Wikipedia* bills itself as "the free encyclopedia that anyone can edit." This site is thoroughly democratic: not only can anyone write articles for *Wikipedia,* anyone can edit articles others have written.

At the same time, and for the same reasons, these articles can be of doubtful accuracy and reliability. Authors of *Wikipedia* articles need no qualifications to write on their chosen subject, and their entries are subject to no peer review or fact-checking. (On numerous occasions, vandals have written or rewritten defamatory articles.)

The bottom line on *Wikipedia?* Caveat emptor: Let the buyer beware—but note: even if researchers can't always be sure of the reliability of *Wikipedia* articles, many of these articles conclude with a section of "External Links." These links often provide access to sources of established reliability, such as government agencies or academic sites.

Exercise 7.2

Exploring Specialized Encyclopedias

Go to the reference section of your campus library and locate several specialized encyclopedias within your major or area of interest. Look through the encyclopedias, noting their organization, and read entries on topics that interest you. Jot down some notes describing the kinds of information you find. You might also use this opportunity to look around at the other materials available in the reference section, including the *Bibliographic Index* and the *Book Review Digest.*

Biographical Sources

Your preliminary research may prompt you to look up information on particular people. In these cases, consult biographical sources, which can be classified in several ways: by person (living or dead), geography, subject area, gender, race, or historical period. Here are examples of biographical sources:

Black Americans in Congress

Contemporary Authors

Current Biography

Notable American Women

Who's Who in America

Who's Who in the Arab World

These online biographical sources are included in the database collections of many academic libraries:

American National Biography
Biography and Genealogy Master Index
Biography Reference Bank Select
Biography Resource Center
Contemporary Authors
Dictionary of Literary Biography

Almanacs and Yearbooks

Once you settle on a broad topic still in need of narrowing, you may want to consult almanacs and yearbooks, which are generally issued annually and provide facts, lists of data, and chronologies of events. Titles include the following:

Almanac of American Politics
Congressional Quarterly Almanac
State of the World's Children
World Almanac
World Trade Annual

Literature Guides and Handbooks

Guides to the literature of a certain subject area or handbooks can help you to locate useful sources. Pay particular attention to how these guides break broad topics into subtopics—a matter of particular interest to researchers in the early stages of their work. You may become interested in a particular subtopic for your research paper. Here are examples:

*American Historical Associations' Guide to
    Historical Literature*
*Bearing Witness: A Resource Guide to Literature
    and Videos by Holocaust Victims and Survivors*
Encyclopedia of Business Information Sources
Fine Arts: A Bibliographic Guide
Gallup Poll: Public Opinion
Guide to Economic Statistics
Handbook of Chemistry and Physics

Overviews and Bibliographies

If your professor or a bibliographic source directs you to an important recent book on your topic, skim the introductory (and possibly concluding) material, along with the table of contents, for an overview of key issues. Check also for a bibliography, Works Cited, and/or References list. These lists are extremely valuable resources for locating material for research. For example, Robert Dallek's 2003 book, *An Unfinished Life: John Fitzgerald Kennedy, 1917–1963*, includes a seven-page bibliography of reference sources on President Kennedy's life and times.

Bibliographic Index

The *Bibliographic Index* is a series of annual volumes that enables you to locate bibliographies on a particular subject. The bibliographies referred to in the *Index* generally appear at the end of book chapters or periodical articles, or they may themselves be book or pamphlet length. Browsing through the *Bibliographic Index* in a general subject area may give you ideas for further research in particular aspects of your subject, in addition to specific references.

Subject-Heading Guides

Seeing how a general subject (e.g., education) is broken down (e.g., into math instruction/public schools/Massachusetts/K8) in other sources also could stimulate research in a particular area. In subject-heading guides, general subjects are divided into secondary subject headings. The most well-known subject-heading guide is the *Library of Congress Subject Headings* catalog. You might also consult the *Propaedia* volume of the *Encyclopaedia Britannica* (2007). Online, look for these subject directories:

Internet Public Library
<http://ipl.sils.umich.edu/index.text.html>

Librarians' Index to the Internet
<http://lii.org>

WWW Virtual Library
<http://www.vlib.org> (for general subject directory)

Yahoo!
<http://www.yahoo.com>

Having used such tools to narrow the scope of your research to a particular topic, and having devised an interesting research question, you're ready to undertake more focused investigations.

■ FOCUSED RESEARCH

Once you have completed preliminary research, your objective becomes learning as much as you can about your topic. By the end of your inquiries, you'll have read enough to become something of an expert on your topic—or, if that's not possible, given time constraints, you will at least have become someone whose critical viewpoint is based solidly on the available evidence. The following pages will suggest how to find sources for this kind of focused research.

In most cases, your research will be *secondary* in nature, based on (1) books; (2) print and online articles found through electronic databases; and (3) specialized reference sources. In certain cases, you may gather your own *primary* research, using (perhaps) interviews, surveys, structured observations, diaries, letters, and other unpublished sources.

Databases

Much of the information that is available in print—and a good deal that is not—is also available in electronic form. Today, researchers typically access magazine, newspaper, and journal articles and reports, abstracts, and other forms of information through *online databases* (many of them on the Internet) and (to a lesser extent) through databases on *CD-ROMs*. One great advantage of using databases (as opposed to print indexes) is that you can search several years' worth of different periodicals at the same time.

Your library may offer access to hundreds of general and subject-specific databases, including the following:

CSA Illumia	*JSTOR*
EBSCOhost	*LexisNexis*
InfoTrac	*ProQuest*

Also look for common subject-specific and individual title databases, including these:

ERIC (education)
Historical New York Times
MEDLINE (medicine)
MLA International Bibliography (literature)
PsycARTICLES (psychology)
Wall Street Journal

Web Searches

The *World Wide Web* offers print, graphic, and video content that can be enormously helpful to your research. Keep in mind, however, that search engines like *Google* and *Bing* are only tools and that your own judgment in devising a precise search query will determine how useful these tools will be to your inquiries. Good queries yield good results; poor queries, poor results.

Constructing an Effective Search Query

Effective Web searches are built on well-chosen keywords or phrases that you enter into a search engine's query box before clicking the Search button. A well-constructed query will return a list of useful Web sites. Use the following tips.

1. **Focus on a noun: a person, place, or thing.** The most important terms in your query should be *objects*—that is, tangible "things." The thing (or person or place) you want to learn more about is the center of your search, your subject.

2. **Narrow the search with another noun or a modifier.** When you qualify your search terms by combining them in meaningful ways, Internet searches become more pointed and useful. You could create a more productive search by narrowing the keyword "computers" to "computers AND music" or "computers" AND "music" AND "culture."

3. **Try substituting words if the search is not working.** When a search does not yield useful information, change your search terms. Think of synonyms for keywords in your query. For nonacademic topics, you might use a thesaurus to locate synonyms. For example, you might substitute "cardiac" for "heart" and "aircraft" for "plane."

4. **Use "advanced" features to refine your search.** Search engines typically provide a "refine" function—sometimes called an "advanced" or "power" search tool—that allows you to narrow a search by date, type of publication, and type of Web site. You might instruct the engine to search only the sites of organizations, the government, or the military. You can also search in fields such as title, author, industry code, reviews, and so on. Refining your searches is easy: Locate the advanced feature option and fill in (or, in some cases, click to check) a box.

Search Engines

The Internet provides access to hundreds of millions of Web sites, and ill-formed searches can yield hundreds of thousands of hits (Web page links) that have nothing to do with your topic. You should therefore avoid using a search engine until you have narrowed your topic sufficiently to make the results list meaningful. *Google, Bing,* and *Ask.com* are three popular search engines.

As a rule of thumb, use *several* search services—both search engines and subject directories (such as Internet Public Library, WWW Virtual Library, and Yahoo!)—in any given search to ensure that you don't miss important sites and sources of information. Because each service uses a different method to catalog Web sites, each service will return a different results list for searches on the same term.

Using Keywords and Boolean Logic to Refine Online Searches

You'll find more—and more relevant—sources on Internet search engines and library databases if you carefully plan your search strategies. *Note:* Some search engines and online databases have their own systems for searching, so review the "Help" section of each search engine, and use "Advanced Search" options where available. The following tips are general guidelines, and their applicability in different search engines may vary somewhat.

1. *Identify multiple keywords:*

   Write down your topic and/or your research question, and then brainstorm synonyms and related terms for the words in that topic/question.

   Sample topic: Political activism on college campuses

   Sample research question: What kinds of political activism are college students involved in today?

   Keywords: Political activism; college students

   Synonyms and related terms: politics; voting; political organizations; protests; political issues; universities; colleges; campus politics

2. *Conduct searches using different combinations of synonyms and related terms.*

3. *Find new terms in the sources you locate and search with them.*

4. *Use quotation marks around words you want linked:* "political activism"

5. *Use "Boolean operators" to link keywords:*

   The words AND, OR, and NOT are used in "Boolean logic" to combine search terms and get more precise results than using keywords alone.

   AND: Connecting keywords with AND narrows a search by retrieving only those sources that contain *both* keywords:

   political activism AND college students

(continues)

> **OR:** Connecting keywords with OR broadens a search by retrieving all sources that contain at least one of the search terms. This operator is useful when you have a topic/keyword for which there are a number of synonyms. Linking synonyms with OR will lead you to the widest array of sources:
>
>> political activism OR protests OR political organizing OR voting OR campus politics
>>
>> college OR university OR campus OR students
>
> **AND** and **OR:** You can use these terms in combination, by putting the OR phrase in parentheses:
>
>> (political activism OR protests) AND (college OR university)
>
> **NOT:** Connecting keywords with NOT (or, in some cases, AND NOT) narrows a search by excluding certain terms. If you want to focus on a very specific topic, NOT can be used to limit what the search engine retrieves; however, this operator should be used carefully as it can cause you to miss sources that may actually be relevant:
>
>> college students NOT high school
>>
>> political activism NOT voting

Metasearch Engines

A metasearch engine searches multiple search engines simultaneously, combining the results from each into one listing. Metasearch provides a quick way to access the varying results on your topic found in different search engines. Consult these engines:

Clusty
<http://www.clusty.com>

Dogpile
<http://www.dogpile.com>

MetaCrawler
<http://www.metacrawler.com>

Evaluating Web Sources

The Web makes it possible for people at home, work, or school to gain access to corporate, government, and personal Web pages. Academic researchers are obligated to read Web-based material just as critically as they read print-based material. Chapter 2, Critical Reading and Critique, offers criteria for evaluating the quality and reliability of information and ideas in *any* source (pp. 51–62). Web sources are no exception, particularly self-published Web pages that are not subject to editorial review.

In their useful site *Evaluate Web Resources* (see <http://www.widener. edu/libraries/wolfgram/evaluate>), reference librarians Jan Alexander and Marsha Tate offer guidelines for helping researchers assess Web sources. First, they point out, it's important to determine what *type* of Web page you are dealing with. Web pages generally fall into one of five types, each with a different purpose:

1. business/marketing
2. reference/information
3. news
4. advocacy of a particular point of view or program
5. personal page

The purpose of a Web site—to sell, persuade, entertain—has a direct bearing on the objectivity and reliability of the information presented. When evaluating a site and determining its reliability for use in a research project, apply the same general criteria that you apply to print sources: (1) accuracy, (2) authority, (3) objectivity, (4) currency, (5) coverage. You might pose these questions in an effort to assess reliability:

- What's the likelihood that the information has been checked by anyone other than the author?
- What are the author's qualifications to write on the subject?
- What is the reputation of the publisher?
- Who is the author?
- What are the biases—stated or unstated—of the Web site?
- How current is the site?
- Which topics are included (and not included) in the site? To what extent are the topics covered in depth?

Pose these questions and determine, as you would for any non-Web source, reliability and suitability for your research project.

Other Pitfalls of Web Sites

Because reliable sites may include links to other sites that are inaccurate or outdated, users cannot rely on the link as a substitute for evaluating the five criteria just outlined. Web pages are also notoriously unstable, frequently changing and even disappearing without notice.

Remember: as a researcher working in an academic setting, you should apply the same critical reading skills to all your sources—no matter what types they are or where you found them, including on the Web.

Exercise 7.3

Exploring Electronic Sources

Go online and access one of the search engines or academic/professional databases discussed in this chapter. Select a topic/research question that interests you. Review the box on pages 264–265 and try different combinations of keywords and Boolean operators to see what sources you can find for your topic. Jot down notes describing the kinds of sources you find and which terms seem to yield the best results.

Exercise 7.4

Practice Evaluating Web Sources

To practice applying the evaluation criteria discussed in the section on Web sources, go to an Internet search engine and look for sources addressing a topic of interest to you (perhaps after completing Exercise 7.3). Try to locate one source representing each of the five types of Web pages (business/ marketing, reference/information, news, advocacy, and personal). Print the home page of each source and bring the copies to class. In small groups of classmates, look over the sites each student found and make notes on each example's (1) accuracy, (2) authority, (3) objectivity, (4) currency, and (5) coverage.

Periodicals: General

Because many more periodical articles than books are published every year, you are likely (depending on the subject) to find more information in periodicals than in books. General periodicals are the magazines and newspapers that are usually found on newsstands or in bookstores, such as the *New York Times*, *Newsweek*, and the *New Yorker*. By their nature, recent general periodical articles are more current than books. For example, the best way to find out about a political party's position on Social Security reform is to look for current articles in periodicals and newspapers. But periodical articles may have less critical distance than books, and like books, they may become dated, to be superseded by more recent articles.

Magazines

General periodicals such as *Time*, the *New Republic*, and the *Nation* are intended for nonspecialists. Their articles, which tend to be highly readable, may be written by staff writers, freelancers, or specialists. But they usually don't provide citations or other indications of sources, so they're of limited usefulness for scholarly research. Increasingly, texts and abstracts of articles in general sources are available in online databases.

Newspapers

News stories, feature stories, and editorials (even letters to the editor) may be important sources of information. Your college library will certainly have the *New York Times* index, and it may have indexes to other important newspapers such as the *Washington Post,* the *Los Angeles Times,* the *Chicago Tribune,* the *Wall Street Journal,* and the *Christian Science Monitor.*

Periodicals: Specialized

Some professors will expect at least some of your research to be based on articles in specialized periodicals or scholarly journals. So instead of (or in addition to) relying on an article from *Psychology Today* (considered a general periodical even though its subject is somewhat specialized) for an account of the effects of crack cocaine on mental functioning, you might also rely on an article from the *Journal of Abnormal Psychology.* If you are writing a paper on the satirist Jonathan Swift, in addition to a recent reference to him that may have appeared in the *New Yorker,* you may need to locate a relevant article in *Eighteenth-Century Studies.*

Articles in such journals are normally written by specialists and professionals in the field rather than by staff writers or freelancers, and the authors will assume that their readers already understand the basic facts and issues concerning the subject. Other characteristics of scholarly journals:

- They tend to be heavily researched, as indicated by their numerous notes and references.
- They are generally published by university presses.
- Most of the authors represented are university professors.
- The articles, which have a serious, formal, and scholarly tone, are generally peer reviewed by other scholars in the field.

To find articles in specialized periodicals, you'll use specialized indexes— that is, indexes for particular disciplines, such as the *Anthropological Index* and the *Education Index.* You also may find it helpful to refer to *abstracts.* Like specialized indexes, abstracts list articles published in a particular discipline over a given period, but abstracts also provide summaries of the articles listed. They can save you a lot of time in determining which articles you should read and which ones you can safely skip. Don't treat abstracts alone as sources for research, however; when you find useful material in an abstract, locate the article to which it applies and use that as the source you reference.

Exercise 7.5

Exploring Specialized Periodicals

Visit your campus library and locate the print-based or (more likely) computer-based specialized periodical indexes for your major or area of interest (ask a reference librarian for help). Note the call numbers for specialized periodicals (also called academic journals) in your field, and visit the section of the library where recent editions of academic journals are usually housed. Locate the call numbers you've noted and look through the specialized periodicals in your field. The articles you find in these journals represent some of the most recent scholarship in the field—the kind of scholarship many of your professors are busy conducting. Write half a page or so describing the articles you find interesting and why.

Books

Books are useful for providing both breadth and depth of coverage of a subject. Because they are generally published at least a year or two after the events treated, they also tend to provide the critical distance that is sometimes missing from articles. Conversely, this delay in coverage means that the information in books won't be as current as the information you find in periodicals. Any piece of writing, books included, may be inaccurate, outdated, or biased; for help in determining the reliability of a book, see *Book Review Digest*, discussed below. You can locate relevant books through a library's electronic catalog, which you may search in four ways:

- by author
- by title
- by subject
- by keyword

Entries include the call number, publication information, and, frequently, a summary of the book's contents.

Book Review Digest

Perhaps the best way to determine the reliability and credibility of a book you may want to use is to look it up in the *Book Review Digest* (also available online and issued monthly and cumulated annually). These volumes list (alphabetically by author) the most significant books published during the year, supply a brief description of each, and, most important, provide excerpts from (and references to) reviews. If a book receives bad reviews, you don't necessarily have to avoid it (the book may still have something useful to offer, and the review itself may be unreliable). But you should take any negative reaction into account when using that book as a source.

Government Publications and Other Sources

For statistical and other basic reference information on a subject, consult a *handbook* (such as *Statistical Abstracts of the United States*). For current information on a subject as of a given year, consult an *almanac* (such as *World Almanac*). For annual updates of information, consult a *yearbook* (such as *The Statesman's Yearbook*). For maps and other geographic information, consult an *atlas* (such as *New York Times Atlas of the World*). Often, simply browsing through the reference shelves for data on your general subject—such as biography, public affairs, psychology—will reveal valuable sources of information. And of course, much reference information is available on government sites on the Web.

In addition, many libraries keep pamphlets in a *vertical file* (i.e., a file cabinet). For example, a pamphlet on global warming might be found in the vertical file rather than in the library stacks. Such material is accessible through the *Vertical File Index* (a monthly subject-and-title index to pamphlet material).

Finally, the U.S. government regularly publishes large quantities of useful information. Among the indexes to government publications are:

American Statistics Index
Congressional Information Service

Interviews and Surveys

Depending on the subject of your paper, you may want to *interview* your professors, your fellow students, or other individuals knowledgeable about your subject. Additionally, or alternatively, you may wish to conduct *surveys* via *questionnaires* (see the related box). When well prepared and insightfully interpreted, such tools can produce valuable information about the ideas or preferences of a group of people.

Guidelines for Conducting Interviews

- Become knowledgeable about the subject before the interview so that you can ask intelligent questions. Prepare most of your questions beforehand.

- Ask "open-ended" questions designed to elicit meaningful responses, rather than "forced-choice" questions that can be answered with a word or two, or "leading questions" that presume a particular answer. For example, instead of asking, "Do you think that male managers should be more sensitive to women's concerns for equal pay in the workplace?", ask, "To what extent do you see evidence that male managers are insufficiently sensitive to women's concerns for equal pay in the workplace?"

- Ask follow-up questions to elicit additional insights or details.

- If you record the interview (in addition to or instead of taking notes), get your subject's permission, preferably in writing.

■ MINING SOURCES ■

Having located your sources (or at least having begun the process), you'll proceed to "mining" them—that is, extracting from them information and ideas that you can use in your paper. Mining sources involves three important tasks:

- Compiling a working bibliography to keep track of what information you have and how it relates to your research question.

- Taking notes on your sources and evaluating them for reliability and relevance.

- Developing some kind of *outline*—formal or informal—that allows you to see how you might subdivide and organize your discussion and at which points you might draw on relevant sources.

Guidelines for Conducting Surveys and Designing Questionnaires

- Determine your *purpose* in conducting the survey: what kind of *information* you seek and *whom* (i.e., what subgroup of the population) you intend to survey.

- Decide whether you want to collect information on the spot or have people send their responses back to you. (You will get fewer responses if they are sent back to you, but those you do get will likely be more complete than surveys conducted on the spot.)

- Devise and word questions carefully so that they (1) are understandable and (2) don't reflect your own biases. For example, for a survey on attitudes toward capital punishment, if you ask, "Do you believe that the state should endorse legalized murder?", you've loaded the question to influence people to answer in the negative.

- Devise short-answer or multiple-choice questions; open-ended questions encourage responses that are difficult to quantify. (You may want to leave space, however, for "additional comments.") Conversely, yes or no responses or rankings on a 5-point scale are easy to quantify.

- It may be useful to break out the responses by as many meaningful categories as possible—for example, gender, age, ethnicity, religion, education, geographic locality, profession, and income.

Critical Reading for Research

- *Use all the critical reading tips we've suggested thus far.* The tips contained in the boxes Critical Reading for Summary on page 5, Critical Reading for Critique on pages 76–77, Critical Reading for Synthesis on pages 120–121, and Critical Reading for Analysis on page 190 are all useful for the kinds of reading engaged in when conducting research.

- *Read for relationships to your research question.* How does the source help you formulate and clarify your research question?

(continues)

- *Read for relationships among sources.* How does each source illustrate, support, expand upon, contradict, or offer an alternative perspective to those of your other sources?
- *Consider the relationship between your source's form and content.* How does the form of the source—specialized encyclopedia, book, article in a popular magazine, article in a professional journal—affect its content, the manner in which that content is presented, and its relationship to other sources?
- *Pay special attention to the legitimacy of Internet sources.* Consider how the content and validity of the information on the Web page may be affected by the purpose of the site. Assess Web-based information for its (1) accuracy, (2) authority, (3) objectivity, (4) currency, and (5) coverage (see p. 266).

■ THE WORKING BIBLIOGRAPHY

As you conduct your research, keep a *working bibliography,* a record of bibliographic information on all the sources you're likely to use in preparing the paper. If you are careful to record *full* bibliographic information—e.g., author(s), title, publisher—you'll spare yourself the frustration of hunting for it during the composition of your paper.

Now that library catalogs and databases are available online, it's easy to copy and paste your sources' (or potential sources') bibliographic information into a document or to e-mail citations to yourself for cutting and pasting later. A more traditional but still very efficient way to compile bibliographic information is on 3" × 5" cards. (Note, also, that certain software programs allow you to create sortable electronic records.) Using any of these methods, you can easily add, delete, and rearrange individual bibliographic records as your research progresses. Whether you keep bibliographic information on 3" × 5" cards or in an electronic document, be sure to record the following:

- The author or editor (last name first) and, if relevant, the translator
- The title (and subtitle) of the book or article
- The publisher and place of publication (if a book) or the title of the periodical
- The date and/or year of publication; if a periodical, volume and issue number
- The date you accessed the source (if you are working with a Web site)
- The edition number (of a book beyond its first edition)
- The inclusive page numbers (if an article)
- The specific page number of a quotation or other special material you might paraphrase

You'll also find it helpful to include this additional information:

- A brief description of the source (to help you recall it later in the research process)
- The library call number or the URL, so that you can readily return to the source
- A code number, which you can use as a shorthand reference to the source in your notes (see the sample note records below)

Here's an example of a working bibliography record:

> Gorham, Eric B. *National Service, Political Socialization, and Political Education*. Albany: SUNY P, 1992.
>
> Argues that the language government uses to promote national service programs betrays an effort to "reproduce a postindustrial, capitalist economy in the name of good citizenship." Chap. 1 provides a historical survey of national service.

Here's an example of a working bibliography record for an article:

> Gergen, David. "A Time to Heed the Call." *U.S. News & World Report* 24 Dec. 2001: 60-61.
>
> Argues that in the wake of the surge of patriotism that followed the September 11 terrorist attacks, the government should encourage citizens to participate in community and national service. Supports the McCain-Bayh bill.

Here's an example of a working bibliography record for an online source:

> Bureau of Labor Statistics. "Table 1: Volunteers by Selected Characteristics, September 2009." 27 Jan. 2010. Web. 17 Feb. 2011. <http://www.bls.gov/news.release/ volun.t01.htm>.
>
> Provides statistical data on volunteerism in the U.S.

Some instructors may ask you to prepare—either in addition to or instead of a research paper—an *annotated bibliography.* This is a list of relevant works on a subject, with the contents of each work briefly described or assessed. The sample bibliography records above could become the basis for three entries in an annotated bibliography on national service. Annotations differ from abstracts in that annotations aren't comprehensive summaries; rather, they indicate how the items may be useful to the researcher.

Note-Taking

People have their favorite ways of note-taking. Some use legal pads or spiral notebooks; others type notes into a laptop or tablet computer, perhaps using a database program. Some prefer 4" × 6" cards for note-taking. Such cards have some of the same advantages that 3" × 5" cards have for working bibliographies: They can easily be added to, subtracted from, and rearranged to accommodate changing organizational plans. Also, discrete pieces of information from the same source can easily be arranged (and rearranged) into subtopics. Whatever your preferred approach, consider including the following along with the note:

- a topic or subtopic label corresponding to your outline (see below)
- a code number, corresponding to the number assigned the source in the working bibliography
- a page reference at the end of the note

Here's a sample note record for the table "Volunteers by Selected Characteristics, September 2009" from the Bureau of Labor Statistics (bibliographic record above):

<u>Pervasiveness of Volunteerism</u> (I)   7

Shows that 26.8 percent of Americans age 16 and older, 63.3 million in all, devote time to community service.

Here's a note record for the periodical article by Gergen (see bibliography note on the previous page):

<u>Beneficial Paid Volunteer Programs</u> (II)   12

Says that both the community and the individual benefit from voluntary service programs. Cites Teach for America, Alumni of City Year, Peace Corps as programs in which participants receive small stipends and important benefits (60). "Voluntary service when young often changes people for life. They learn to give their fair share." (60)

Both note records are headed by a topic label followed by the tentative location (indicated by a Roman numeral) in the paper outline where the information may be used. The number in the upper right corner corresponds to the number you assigned to the source in your bibliography note. The note in the first record uses *summary*. The note in the second record uses *summary* (sentence 1), *paraphrase* (sentence 2), and *quotation* (sentence 3). Notice the inclusion of page references, which the writer will reference in the paper itself (if the note is used). For hints on when to choose summary, paraphrase, and quotation, see Chapter 1, pages 43–44.

Remember: use quotation marks to distinguish between your language and the source author's language. Cite page references when you note an author's exact language *or* ideas. If you're careful to keep the distinctions between your language and that of authors clear, you'll avoid plagiarizing your sources. See the discussion of plagiarism on pages 46–47 and later in this chapter for more details.

■ | **Guidelines for Evaluating Sources**

- *Skim the source.* With a book, look over the table of contents, the introduction and conclusion, and the index; zero in on passages that your initial survey suggests are important. With an article, skim the introduction and the headings.

- *Be alert for references* in your sources to other important sources, particularly to sources that several authors treat as important.

- Other things being equal, the *more recent* the source, the better. Recent work usually incorporates or refers to important earlier work.

- If you're considering making multiple references to a book, look up the reviews in the *Book Review Digest* or the *Book Review Index*. Also, check the author's credentials in a source such as *Contemporary Authors* or *Current Biography*.

■ ARRANGING YOUR NOTES: THE OUTLINE

You won't use all the notes you take during the research process. Instead, you'll need to do some selecting, which requires you to distinguish more important from less important (and unimportant) material. Using your original working thesis (see Chapter 6 on theses)—or a new thesis that you have developed during the course of data gathering and invention—you can begin constructing a *preliminary outline* of your paper. This outline will indicate which elements of the topic you intend to discuss, and in what order. You can then arrange relevant note cards (or electronic files) accordingly and remove, to a separate location, notes that will not likely find their way into the paper.

Some people prefer not to develop an outline until they have more or less completed their research. At that point they look over their notes, consider the relationships among the various pieces of evidence, possibly arrange notes or cards into separate piles, and then develop an outline based on their perceptions and insights about the material. Subsequently, they rearrange and code the notes to conform to their outline—an informal outline indicating just the main sections of the paper and possibly one level below that.

The model paper on student privacy and campus safety (see Chapter 4) could be informally outlined as follows:

> Introduction
> > Recap of Virginia Tech shooting
> > Officials did not act on available info re: shooter
> > Review federal rules on privacy

Thesis statement:
> In responding to the Virginia Tech killings, we should resist rolling back federal rules protecting student privacy; for as long as college officials effectively respond to signs of trouble, these rules already provide a workable balance between privacy and public safety.

History of privacy on campus
> *In loco parentis*
> Court cases and law
> Recent developments on campus

Argument *against* student privacy
> Current responses—federal, university, public opinion
> Cornell response to Va. Tech: extreme, favoring safety

Argument *for* student privacy
> M.I.T. response to Va. Tech: extreme, favoring privacy
> Va. Tech the result of failed enforcement, not failed policy
> U of Kentucky a reasonable middle ground

Conclusion

Such an outline will help you organize your research and should not be an unduly restrictive guide to writing.

The *formal outline* is a multilevel plan with Roman and Arabic numerals and uppercase and lowercase lettered subheadings that can provide a useful blueprint for composition as well as a guide to revision. See pages 148–149 in Chapter 4 for a formal outline of the paper on balancing student privacy and public safety. Here is one section of that outline. Compare its level of detail with the level of detail in the informal outline immediately above:

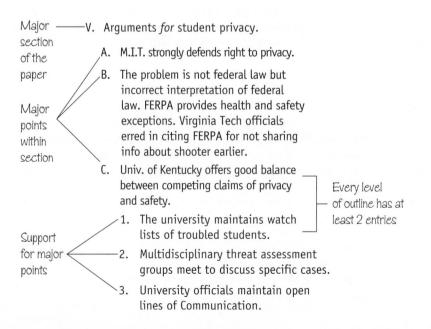

Major section of the paper —— V. Arguments *for* student privacy.

A. M.I.T. strongly defends right to privacy.

Major points within section

B. The problem is not federal law but incorrect interpretation of federal law. FERPA provides health and safety exceptions. Virginia Tech officials erred in citing FERPA for not sharing info about shooter earlier.

C. Univ. of Kentucky offers good balance between competing claims of privacy and safety.

Every level of outline has at least 2 entries

Support for major points

1. The university maintains watch lists of troubled students.

2. Multidisciplinary threat assessment groups meet to discuss specific cases.

3. University officials maintain open lines of Communication.

Outlining your draft after you have written it may help you discern structural problems: illogical sequences of material, confusing relationships between ideas, poor unity or coherence, or unevenly developed content. (See the discussion of *reverse outlines* in Chapter 6, p. 247.)

Instructors may require that a formal outline accompany the finished research paper. Formal outlines are generally of two types: *topic outlines* and *sentence outlines.* In the topic outline, headings and subheadings are words or phrases. In the sentence outline, each heading and subheading is a complete sentence. Both topic and sentence outlines are typically preceded by the thesis.

■ RESEARCH AND PLAGIARISM

All too easily, research can lead to plagiarism. See Chapter 1, pages 46–47, for a definition and examples of plagiarism. The discussion here will suggest ways of avoiding plagiarism.

None of the situations that lead to plagiarism discussed below assumes the plagiarist is a bad person. All kinds of pressures can cause someone to plagiarize. By understanding those pressures, you may come to recognize them and take corrective action before plagiarism seems like a reasonable option.

Time Management and Plagiarism

The problem: You do not allocate time well and face crushing deadlines. Work, sports, and family responsibilities are the kinds of commitments that can squeeze the time needed to conduct research and write.

A solution: Learn time management. If you do not manage time well, admit that and seek help (it will be a further asset when you graduate). Consider taking three steps:

1. Begin the paper on the day it is assigned. Work on the paper for a set amount of time each day.

2. Visit the on-campus learning-skills center and enroll in a time management class. (Most schools offer this on a noncredit basis. If your school has no such class, you can readily find one online.)

3. When (despite your best efforts) you discover that you will not make a deadline, explain the situation to your instructor and seek an extension *before* the paper is due. State that you are seeking help and do not expect the problem to recur. Do not ask for a second extension.

Confidence and Plagiarism

The problem: You lack the confidence to put forward your ideas.

A solution: Understand that knowledge about your topic, and your confidence to present it in your own words, will increase in direct proportion to your research. Suggestions:

1. Stop worrying and begin. The longer you wait, the greater will be the pressure to plagiarize.

2. Seek out the on-campus writing center and let a trained tutor help you to break the assignment into manageable parts. Then you can sit down to research or write one part of your paper at a time. Complete enough parts, and you will have finished the assignment.

Note-Taking and Plagiarism

The problem: Inaccurate note-taking results in plagiarism: You neglect to place quotation marks around quoted language and later copy the note into the paper without using quotation marks.

A solution: Develop careful note-taking skills. Some useful approaches and techniques:

1. Enroll in a study skills class on working with sources, in which you will learn techniques for improving the accuracy and efficiency of note-taking.

2. Make certain to gather bibliographic information for every source and to link every note with a source.

3. Photocopy sources when possible, making sure to include publication information. When you use a source in a paper, check your language against the original language. Make corrections and add quotation marks as needed.

4. Learn the difference between quotation, summary, and paraphrase (see Chapter 1).

Digital Life and Plagiarism

The problem: Plagiarism has never been easier, given the volume of information on the Internet and the ease of digital copying and pasting.

A solution: Recall some of the reasons you are in college:

1. to improve your ability to think critically

2. to learn how to think independently

3. to discover your own voice as a thinker and writer

Borrowing the work of others without giving due credit robs you of an opportunity to pursue these goals. Don't allow the ease of plagiarism in the digital age to compromise your ethics. Easily managed or not, plagiarism is cheating.

■ DETERMINING COMMON KNOWLEDGE

Note one exception to the rule that you must credit sources: when ideas and information are considered common knowledge. You can best understand common knowledge through examples:

General Lee commanded the Confederate forces during the Civil War.
Mars is the fourth planet from the sun.
Ernest Hemingway wrote *The Sun Also Rises.*

These statements represent shared, collective information. When an idea or item of information is thus shared, or commonly known, you do not need to cite it even though you may have learned of that information in a source. What is considered common knowledge changes from subject area to subject area. When in doubt, ask your instructor.

The key issue underlying the question of common knowledge is the likelihood of readers' mistakenly thinking that a certain idea or item of information originated with you when, in fact, it did not. If there is *any* chance of such a mistake occurring, cite the source.

A Guideline for Determining Common Knowledge

If the idea or information you intend to use can be found unattributed (that is, *not* credited to a specific author) in three or more sources, then you can consider that material common knowledge. But remember: If you quote a source (even if the material could be considered common knowledge), you must use quotation marks and give credit.

Here is an example of a paragraph in which the writer summarizes one source, quotes another, and draws on common knowledge twice. Only the summary and the quotation need to be cited.

Summarized source is cited.
⎧ Very soon, half of America will communicate via e-mail, according
⎩ to analysts (Singh 283). We can only assume that figure will grow—

rapidly—as children who have matured in the Internet era move to

Common knowledge
⎧ college and into careers. With e-mail becoming an increasingly common
⎨ form of communication, people are discovering and conversing with
⎩ one another in a variety of ways that bring a new twist to old, familiar

Quoted source is cited.
⎧ patterns. Using e-mail, people meet "to exchange pleasantries and argue,
⎨ engage in intellectual discourse, conduct commerce, exchange knowledge,
⎩ share emotional support, make plans, brainstorm, gossip, feud, [and] fall

Common knowledge
⎧ in love" (Chenault). That is, through e-mail, people do what they have
⎨ always done: communicate. But the medium of that communication has
⎩ changed, which excites some people and concerns others.

In both places where the writer draws on common knowledge, sources that could have been cited were not because evidence for the statements appeared in at least three sources.

■ PLAGIARISM, THE INTERNET, AND FAIR USE

The Internet is a medium like paper, television, or radio. Intellectual property (stories, articles, pictures) is transmitted through the medium. *The same rules that apply to not plagiarizing print sources also apply to not plagiarizing Internet sources.* Any content posted on the Internet that is not your original work is the intellectual property of others. Doing either of the following constitutes plagiarism:

- Copying and pasting electronic content from the Internet into your document without citing the source.
- Buying a prewritten or custom-written paper from the Internet.*

Internet Paper Mills

Online "paper mills" merit special attention, for they make available prewritten papers on almost any topic. Remember that instructors know how to use Internet search engines to find the same papers and identify cases of plagiarism.

■ Fair Use and Digital Media

U.S. copyright law permits "fair use" of copyrighted materials—including print (paper- and digital-based), images, video, and sound—for academic purposes. As long as you fully credit your sources, you may quote "excerpts in a review or criticism for purposes of illustration or comment; [and]…short passages in a scholarly or technical work."[†] The key to fair use of any material relies on the extent to which you have "transformed" the original work for your purposes. Thus:

- It is illegal for a student to copy a song from a CD and place it on a peer-to-peer file sharing network.
- It would be legal to "transform" that same song by including it as the background track to a digital movie or podcast, which includes other media elements created by the student, so long as it is created for educational purposes and cited on a bibliography page.

---

*Buying or using any part(s) of a paper written by another person is considered plagiarism regardless of its source.
[†]"Fair Use." U.S. Copyright Office. May 2009. Web. 23 Mar. 2010.

■ CITING SOURCES ■

When you refer to or quote the work of another, you are obligated to credit or cite your source properly. There are two types of citations—*in-text citations* in the body of a paper and *full citations* (Works Cited or References) at the end of the paper—and they work in tandem.

Types of Citations

- In-text citations indicate the source of quotations, paraphrases, and summarized information and ideas. These citations, generally limited to author's last name, relevant page number, and publication date of source, appear *in the text,* within parentheses.
- Full citations appear in an alphabetical list of "Works Cited" (MLA) or "References" (APA) *at the end of the paper,* always starting on a new page. These citations provide full bibliographical information on the source.

If you are writing a paper in the humanities, you will probably be expected to use the Modern Language Association (MLA) format for citation. This format is fully described in the *MLA Handbook for Writers of Research Papers,* 7th ed. (New York: Modern Language Association of America, 2009). A paper in the social sciences will probably use the American Psychological Association (APA) format. This format is fully described in the *Publication Manual of the American Psychological Association,* 6th ed. (Washington, D.C.: American Psychological Association, 2010).

In the following section, we will focus on MLA and APA styles. Keep in mind, however, that instructors often have their own preferences. Check with your instructor for the preferred documentation format if this is not specified in the assignment.*

Examples of the most commonly used citations in MLA and APA formats are shown below. For a more complete listing, consult the current edition of the MLA *Handbook,* the APA *Publication Manual,* or whatever style guide your instructor has specified. If you have no ready access to these manuals, conduct a *Google* or *Bing* search. Many college writing centers maintain online guides to MLA and APA citation formats.

---

*Some instructors require the documentation style specified in the *Chicago Manual of Style,* 16th ed. (Chicago: University of Chicago Press, 2010). This style is similar to the American Psychological Association style, except that publication dates are not placed within parentheses. Instructors in the sciences often follow the Council of Science Editors (CSE) formats, one of which is a number format: Each source listed on the bibliography page is assigned a number, and all text references to the source are followed by the appropriate number within parentheses. Some instructors prefer the old MLA style, which called for footnotes and endnotes.

■ MLA STYLE: IN-TEXT CITATIONS

The general rule for in-text citation is to include only enough information to alert the reader to the source of the reference and to the location within that source. In MLA style, this information normally includes the author's last name and the page number (for instance, "Behrens and Rosen 282"). Here are sample in-text citations using the MLA system:

> From the beginning, the AIDS antibody test has been "mired in controversy" (Bayer 101).

If you have already mentioned the author's name in the text—in a *signal phrase* (e.g., "According to...")—do not repeat it in the citation:

> According to Bayer, from the beginning, the AIDS antibody test has been "mired in controversy" (101).

Notice that in the MLA system, no date or punctuation comes between the author's name and the page number in parentheses. Notice also that the parenthetical reference is placed *before* the final punctuation of the sentence because the reference is considered part of the sentence. In MLA format, you must supply page numbers for summaries and paraphrases of print sources as well as for quotations:

> According to Bayer, the AIDS antibody test has been controversial from the outset (101).

Use a block, or indented form, for quotations of five lines or more. Introduce the block quotation with a full sentence followed by a colon. Indent one inch or ten spaces (that is, double the normal paragraph indentation). Place the parenthetical citation *after* the final period:

> Robert Flaherty's refusal to portray primitive people's contact with civilization arose from an inner conflict:
>
>> He had originally plunged with all his heart into the role of explorer and prospector; before Nanook, his own father was his hero. Yet as he entered the Eskimo world, he knew he did so as the advance guard of industrial civilization, the world of United States Steel and Sir William Mackenzie and railroad and mining empires. The mixed feeling this gave him left his mark on all his films. (Barnouw 45)

Again, were Barnouw's name mentioned in the sentence leading into the quotation, the parenthetical reference would be simply "(45)."

Usually parenthetical citations appear at the end of your sentences; however, if the reference applies only to the first part of the sentence, the parenthetical information is inserted at the appropriate point *within* the sentence:

> While Baumrind argues that "the laboratory is not the place to study degree of obedience" (421), Milgram asserts that such arguments are groundless.

At times, you must modify the basic author and page number reference. Depending on the nature of your source(s), you may need to use one of the following citation formats:

Source quoted by another source

(qtd. in Garber 211)

An anonymous work

("Obedience" 32)

Two authors

(Bernstein and Politi 208)

One of two or more works by the same author in the list of Works Cited

(Toffler, *Wave* 96-97)

Two or more sources as the basis of your statement

(Butler 109; Carey 57)

Location of a passage in a literary text

for example, Hardy's *The Return of the Native* (224; ch. 7)

[Page 224 in the edition used by the writer; the chapter number, "7," is provided for the convenience of those referring to another edition.]

A multivolume work

(3: 7-12)

[volume number: page numbers; note the space between the colon and the page numbers]

Location of a passage in a play

(1.2.308-22)

[act.scene.line number(s)]

The Bible

(John 3.16)

(Col. 3.14)

[book. chapter.verse]

In-Text Citation of Electronic Sources

Web sites, CD-ROM data, and e-mail generally do not have numbered pages. In addition, different browsers may display and printers may produce differing numbers of pages for any particular site. You should therefore omit both page numbers and paragraph numbers from in-text citations to electronic sources, unless those page or paragraph numbers are provided within the source itself. For these in-text citations, cite the entire work.

■ MLA STYLE: CITATIONS IN THE WORKS CITED LIST

In MLA format, the complete list of sources, with all the information necessary for a reader to locate a source, starts on a new page headed "Works Cited." The Works Cited list includes only those sources for which you have included in-text citations in your paper. A more comprehensive list of references—one that includes every source you consulted in preparing your paper—would be titled "Bibliography" or "Works Consulted." Prepare the Works Cited list as follows:

- Double-space entries.
- Indent second and subsequent lines of each entry ("hanging indent" style) five spaces or one-half inch.
- Follow a period with a single space.
- Alphabetize the list by author's last name.

Not every possible variation of Works Cited entries is presented in the examples that follow. In formatting a complicated entry for your own list, you may need to combine features from two or more examples. Your guiding consideration should be to include information that will help the interested reader find the documented source.

Periodicals (Articles Available via Print, Downloaded File, Database, and Web)

A *periodical* is a publication that appears regularly—for example, a daily or weekly newspaper, a magazine, or a scholarly or professional journal. Periodicals may be accessed in a variety of media: in a print edition, online via the Web or in a subscription database, or as a downloaded digital file. Every entry in your Works Cited list for a periodical should consist of four parts: the author's name, the title of the article (in quotation marks), the title of the periodical (in italics), and details of publication—including the page range for the entire article, not just the portion you cite in your paper. For months, use the following abbreviations: *Jan., Feb., Mar., Apr., Aug., Sept., Oct., Nov.,* and *Dec.* May, June, and July are not abbreviated.

For periodicals located on the Web, follow the word "Web" with the date you accessed the selection.

Article from a magazine

MAGAZINE ARTICLE ACCESSED VIA PRINT

Kurlantzick, Joshua. "The World Is Bumpy: Deglobalization and Its Dangers." *New Republic* 15 July 2009: 27-31. Print.

MAGAZINE ARTICLE ACCESSED VIA DOWNLOADED DIGITAL FILE

Kurlantzick, Joshua. "The World Is Bumpy: Deglobalization and Its Dangers." *New Republic* 15 July 2009: 27-31. PDF file.

MAGAZINE ARTICLE ACCESSED VIA DATABASE

Kurlantzick, Joshua. "The World Is Bumpy: Deglobalization and Its Dangers." *New Republic* 15 July 2009: 27-31. *EBSCOhost.* Web. 8 Nov. 2010.

MAGAZINE ARTICLE ACCESSED VIA WEB

Kurlantzick, Joshua. "The World Is Bumpy: Deglobalization and Its Dangers." *New Republic*. The New Republic, 15 July 2009. Web. 8 Nov. 2010.

MAGAZINE ARTICLE WITH NO PRINT EQUIVALENT ACCESSED VIA WEB (EXISTS ONLY ON WEB)

Greenwald, Glenn. "Eric Holder, Jack Quinn and the Rich Pardon." *Salon.com*. Salon Media Group, 3 Dec. 2008. Web. 12 Jan. 2009.

Note: Include a URL in a citation only if readers could not otherwise locate the source through a standard search query or from the home page of the Web site you are referencing. Enclose the URL in angle brackets. If the URL does not fit on one line, break the address only after a slash. Add no hyphen or other punctuation where you break the URL.

Peterson, Paul. Interview by Gary James. *ClassicBands.com*. Classic Bands, 12 Feb. 2000. Web. 8 Jan. 2008. <http://www.classicbands.com/PaulPetersonInterview.html>.

Article (signed or unsigned) from a newspaper

NEWSPAPER ARTICLE ACCESSED VIA PRINT: SIGNED

Hook, Janet, and Noam N. Levey. "Senate Compromise Removes 'Public Option' Obstacle." *Los Angeles Times* 9 Dec. 2009, late ed.: A1+. Print.

Note: In the page number citation "(A1+)," "A" indicates the section of the newspaper, "1" indicates the page on which the article begins, and "+" indicates that the article continues on other pages. For small-town newspapers with generic names (like the *Examiner* or the *Sun-Times*), include the name of the newspaper's city of publication in brackets immediately after the title.

NEWSPAPER ARTICLE ACCESSED VIA DOWNLOADED DIGITAL FILE

> Hook, Janet, and Noam N. Levey. "Senate Compromise Removes 'Public
> Option' Obstacle." *Los Angeles Times* 9 Dec. 2009, late ed.: A1+.
> AZW file.

NEWSPAPER ARTICLE ACCESSED VIA DATABASE

> Hook, Janet, and Noam N. Levey. "Senate Compromise Removes 'Public
> Option' Obstacle." *Los Angeles Times* 9 Dec. 2009, late ed.: A1+.
> *LexisNexis*. Web. 12 Dec. 2009.

NEWSPAPER ARTICLE ACCESSED VIA WEB

> Hook, Janet, and Noam N. Levey. "Senate Compromise Removes 'Public
> Option' Obstacle." *Los Angeles Times*. Tribune Company, 9 Dec.
> 2009. Web. 9 Dec. 2009.

The Hook and Levey article is authored, or signed, so the authors' names begin the entry. When an article is unsigned, begin with the title of the article, in quotation marks.

NEWSPAPER ARTICLE ACCESSED VIA PRINT: UNSIGNED

> "The World's Meeting Place." *New York Times* 6 Sept. 2000, natl. ed.:
> A11. Print.

Article from a scholarly journal   Journals are published with volume and issue numbers. Some journals begin pagination anew with each issue; others maintain running pagination throughout the year, across multiple issues. Cite volume and issue numbers ("89" and "11," respectively, in the next example) when they are provided.

SCHOLARLY ARTICLE ACCESSED VIA PRINT (INCLUDE VOLUME AND ISSUE NUMBERS)

> Takimoto, Gaku, David A. Spiller, and David M. Post. "Ecosystem Size,
> but Not Disturbance, Determines Food-Chain Length on Islands of
> the Bahamas." *Ecology* 89.11 (2008): 3001-07. Print.

SCHOLARLY ARTICLE ACCESSED VIA DATABASE

> Takimoto, Gaku, David A. Spiller, and David M. Post. "Ecosystem Size,
> but Not Disturbance, Determines Food-Chain Length on Islands

of the Bahamas." *Ecology* 89.11 (2008): 3001-07. *JSTOR*. Web. 11
Dec. 2010.

SCHOLARLY ARTICLE ACCESSED VIA WEB

Takimoto, Gaku, David A. Spiller, and David M. Post. "Ecosystem Size,
but Not Disturbance, Determines Food-Chain Length on Islands of
the Bahamas." *Ecology*. Ecological Society of America, Nov. 2008.
Web. 11 Dec. 2010.

SCHOLARLY ARTICLE WITH NO PRINT EQUIVALENT ACCESSED VIA WEB (ELECTRONIC JOURNAL EXISTS ONLY ON WEB)

Peterson, Karen. "Teens, Literature, and the Web." *Alan Review* 31.3
(2004): n. pag. Web. 3 Mar. 2009.

Note: When publication details are not available, cite as much of the pertinent detail about publication that is available. On occasion, a text may not
provide key information. Use the following abbreviations to note omissions:
"n.p." for no place of publication or no publisher, "n.d." for no date of publication, and "n. pag." for no pagination.

Editorial An editorial reference follows its publication type. The editorial
illustrated in the following example appeared originally in a newspaper. If
you are citing an editorial from a magazine or journal, use those formats.

"Cultural Revolution in the GOP." Editorial. *Boston Globe* 8 Dec. 2009:
A18. Print.

Letter to the editor A letter to the editor reference follows its publication
type. The letter to the editor illustrated in the following example appeared
originally in a magazine.

LETTER TO THE EDITOR ACCESSED VIA WEB

Williams, Bryan. "The Stain of Torture." Letter. *The Atlantic.com*.
Atlantic Monthly Group, Dec. 2009. Web. 21 Jan. 2010.

Review A review reference follows its publication type. The review illustrated in the following example appeared originally in a magazine.

Barber, Benjamin R. "The Crack in the Picture Window." Rev. of *Bowling Alone: The Collapse and Revival of American Community*, by
Robert D. Putnam. *Nation* 7 Aug. 2000: 29-34. Print.

Books (Available via Print, Downloaded File, Database, and Web)

Every book entry consists of three parts: the author's name, the italicized
title of the book, and the publication information. Books can be accessed

via print or electronically, and your reference citations must provide all information necessary for readers to locate the books you cite. MLA style abbreviates the names of university presses (e.g., "Oxford UP" for "Oxford University Press"). Commercial publishers' names are also shortened by dropping such endings as "Co." and "Inc." Here are several commonly used abbreviations. Capitalize the first letter of an abbreviation when it follows a period; otherwise, begin with a lowercase letter: "ed." for "editor" or "edited by"; "eds." for "editors"; "dir." for "director"; "trans." for "translator"; and "comp." for "compiler."

One author   Complete publication information for a Works Cited book entry includes author's name, italicized title of book, place of publication and publisher, year of publication, and medium of access.

BOOK, ONE AUTHOR, ACCESSED VIA PRINT

> Lowengard, Sarah. *The Creation of Color in Eighteenth-Century Europe*. New York: Columbia UP, 2007. Print.

BOOK, ONE AUTHOR, ACCESSED VIA DOWNLOADED DIGITAL FILE

If you accessed a book through a digital format, arrange the entry as you would for a print publication but omit "Print" as the medium and insert the name of the file format and the word "file." In the following example, a book available in print was read on an e-book reader (an Amazon Kindle).

> Thomas, Michael. *Man Gone Down*. New York: Black Cat-Grove Atlantic, 2007. AZW file.

BOOK, ONE AUTHOR, ACCESSED VIA WEB OR DATABASE

The entry for a print book you accessed via the Web or an online database retains most details of print publication but does not conclude with "Print." Instead, you do the following:

- Place the name of the Web site or database in italics.
- Give "Web" as the medium of publication.
- Conclude with your date of access: day month (abbreviated) and year.

> Lowengard, Sarah. *The Creation of Color in Eighteenth-Century Europe*. New York: Columbia UP, 2007. *ACLS Humanities E-Book*. Web. 14 Feb. 2010.

Two or more books by the same author   In place of the author's name for the second (and subsequent) titles, place three hyphens, followed by a period. List works alphabetically in order of title (ignore *A, An,* and *The* when alphabetizing).

BOOKS, SAME AUTHOR, ACCESSED VIA PRINT

Steinbeck, John. *The Grapes of Wrath*. New York: Viking-Penguin, 1939. Print.

---. *Of Mice and Men*. New York: Collier, 1937. Print.

BOOKS, SAME AUTHOR, ACCESSED VIA WEB

Steinbeck, John. *The Grapes of Wrath*. New York: Viking-Penguin, 1939. *librarything.com*. Web. 17 Jan. 2010.

---. *Of Mice and Men*. 1937. New York: Viking-Penguin, 1994. *Google Book Search*. Web. 22 Apr. 2009.

Two or three authors

BOOK, TWO AUTHORS, ACCESSED VIA DATABASE

Francis, Daniel, and Toby Morantz. *Partners in Furs: A History of the Fur Trade in Eastern James Bay, 1600-1870*. Montreal: McGill-Queen's UP, 1983. *ACLS Humanities E-Book Collection*. Web. 3 Dec. 2010.

BOOK, THREE AUTHORS, ACCESSED VIA PRINT

Campbell, Neil A., Jane B. Reece, and Martha R. Taylor. *Student Study Guide for Biology*. 8th ed. San Francisco: Benjamin-Cummings, 2008. Print.

More than three authors   You have the choice of listing all the authors or, after listing the first author, using the Latin abbreviation for "and others": "et al."

Tan, James, et al. *Expert Guide to Infectious Diseases*. Philadelphia: Amer.Coll. of Physicians, 2008. *Rittenhouse Digital Library*. Web. 14 May 2010.

An anthology: A collection of readings, with an editor   When citing the anthology as a whole, begin with the name of the editor(s). In this example, the abbreviation would read "ed." if there were only one editor.

Daley, Caroline, and Melanie Nolan, eds. *Suffrage and Beyond: International Feminist Perspectives*. New York: New York UP, 1994. Print.

A selection in an anthology   Begin your reference to a specific selection in an anthology with the author and title of the selection, followed by the title of the anthology. Continue with publication details for the anthology itself. In the examples below, "Ed." is an abbreviation of "edited by," not "editors."

SELECTION IN AN ANTHOLOGY ACCESSED VIA DATABASE

> Cott, Nancy F. "Early-Twentieth-Century Feminism in Political Context: A Comparative Look at Germany and the United States." *Suffrage and Beyond: International Feminist Perspectives*. Ed. Caroline Daley and Melanie Nolan. New York: New York UP, 1994. 234-51. *ACLS History E-Book*. Web. 21 Jan. 2010.

Second or subsequent edition   When a book appears in a second or subsequent edition, include the edition number in your entry.

> LeBlond, Richard F., Richard L. DeGowin, and Donald D. Brown. *DeGowin's Diagnostic Examination*. 9th ed. New York: McGraw Medical, 2009. Print.

Corporation or other organization as author   A corporation or other organization may publish a book under its own name rather than under a specific writer's name.

> University of Chicago Press. *Chicago Manual of Style*. 16th ed. Chicago: U of Chicago P, 2010. Print.

BOOK, CORPORATE AUTHOR, ACCESSED VIA WEB

> University of Chicago Press. *Chicago Manual of Style*. 16th ed. Chicago: U of Chicago P, 2010. *Chicagomanualofstyle.org*. Web. 14 Aug. 2010.

Anonymous author   Begin the entry with the title of the work.

> *Everyman: A Morality Play*. London: Philip Lee Warner, 1911. Print.

Translation   If you cite the translator's work more than the author's work, begin your citation with the name of the translator. Otherwise, begin your citation with the name of the author. You have the option of adding original publication information to the Works Cited entry.

> De Beauvoir, Simone. *The Second Sex*. Trans. H. M. Parshley. New York: Penguin, 1972. *marxists.org*. Web. 3 Apr. 2009.

Government publication   Cite as author the name of the government or governing body, such as "United States," "United Nations," or "Alabama." Follow, as appropriate for your source, with a legislative designation (such as "Cong." for "Congress," followed by "Senate" or "House"); an agency or committee name (use abbreviations, such as "Dept."); and the italicized title of the document. If appropriate, identify the legislative session that generated the document (e.g., "82nd Cong., 2nd sess.") and any other identifying information (such as Resolution or Report number or number of volumes).

GOVERNMENT PUBLICATION ACCESSED VIA PRINT

United States. Natl. Inst. of Child Health and Human Development. *Closing the Gap: A National Blueprint to Improve the Health of Persons with Mental Retardation*. Washington: GPO, 2002. Print.

GOVERNMENT PUBLICATION ACCESSED VIA DATABASE

United States. Natl. Inst. of Child Health and Human Development. *Closing the Gap: A National Blueprint to Improve the Health of Persons with Mental Retardation*. Washington: GPO, 2002. *National Center for Biotechnology Information*. Web. 21 Oct. 2010.

Religious text List the text by its name (ignoring *A, An,* and *The*) and follow with publication details. End with medium of publication and the version used.

RELIGIOUS TEXT ACCESSED VIA PRINT

The Holy Bible. Grand Rapids: Zondervan, 1976. Print. New Intl. Vers.

RELIGIOUS TEXT ACCESSED VIA WEB

The Holy Bible. Grand Rapids: Zondervan, 1976. *BibleGateway.com*. Web. 13 Nov. 2010. New Intl. Vers.

DISSERTATION

Vlachos, Chris A. *The Law and the Knowledge of Good and Evil*. Diss. Wheaton Coll. Graduate School, 2006. Eugene: Wipf and Stock, 2009. Print.

Web-Only Sources

For sources found *only* on the Web such as wikis and blogs, include as much of the following information as is available:

1. Name of the author, editor, translator, or compiler (as provided).
2. Title, in quotation marks, of a work (such as an article or a story) that is part of a larger work. Italicize the titles of larger works like books or films.
3. Name of the Web site, in italics, if different from the title of the work.
4. Edition or version used, abbreviated (e.g., "4th ed.").
5. Publisher or sponsor of the site. If none is provided, use the abbreviation "N.p."
6. Publication information (day, abbreviation of month, year). If this is not provided, use "n.d."
7. Publication medium: the word "Web."

8. Access information: day, abbreviation of month, year; URL in angle brackets *only* if readers would have difficulty locating the reference using a search engine.

The following are published only on the Web, without equivalents in print or other media.

ARTICLE, CREATED FOR AND PUBLISHED ON WEB

> McGirt, Ellen. "The Minneapolis Bridge Collapse: Our Crumbling Infra-
> structure." *Fast Company*. Mansueto Ventures LLC, 2 Aug. 2007.
> Web. 12 Sept. 2008.
>
> "Thriving Small Businesses Still Struggling to Get Loans." *CNN.com*.
> Cable News Network, 13 Dec. 2009. Web. 15 Dec. 2009.

BOOK, CREATED FOR AND PUBLISHED ON WEB

> Haffly, Corrie. *The Photoshop Anthology: 101 Web Design Tricks, Tips,
> and Techniques*. *SitePoint.com*. Sitepoint Australia, 2006. Web.
> 12 Nov. 2009.

HOME PAGE ON WEB

> West, Tim, dir. Home page. *Southern Historical Collection*. U of North
> Carolina, 30 Nov. 2009. Web. 14 Dec. 2009.

WIKI

> "Garden Bridge, Shanghai." *CC-Wiki*. Travellerspoint Travel Community,
> 2008. Web. 15 Nov. 2009.

BLOG

> O'Toole, Randal. "New Study Questions Cause of Wildfires." *The Com-
> mons: Markets Protecting the Environment*. The Commons Blog, 11
> July 2006. Web. 12 Mar. 2009.

AUDIO AND VIDEO (INCLUDING *YOUTUBE* AND PODCASTS)

> Brown, John. "How to Change a Flat Tire on a Bicycle." *Expert Village*.
> YouTube, 19 Nov. 2007. Web. 12 Dec. 2010.

E-MAIL COMMUNICATION

> Mendez, Michael R. "Re: Solar Power." Message to Edgar V. Atamian.
> 11 Sept. 2008. E-mail.

BIBLIOGRAPHY

> Pfaff, Steve, comp. *Globalization References*. N.p., n.d. Web. 5 May
> 2008.

■ APA STYLE: IN-TEXT CITATIONS

The general rule for in-text citation is to include only enough information to alert the reader to the source of the reference and to the location within that source. In APA style, you include last name, year of publication, and page number (for example, "Behrens & Rosen, 2012, p. 293"). In-text citations using the APA system take this form:

> A good deal of research shows that rather than inducing any lasting changes in a child's behavior, punishment "promotes only momentary compliance" (Berk, 2002, p. 383).

If you have already mentioned the author's name in the text, do not repeat it in the citation:

> According to Berk (2002), a good deal of research shows that rather than inducing any lasting changes in a child's behavior, punishment "promotes only momentary compliance" (p. 383).

The APA system requires a comma between the author's name and the date and another comma between the date and the page number, which is preceded by "p." or "pp." Notice also that the parenthetical reference is placed *before* the final punctuation of the sentence.

> According to Berk, a good deal of research shows that rather than inducing any lasting changes in a child's behavior, punishment "promotes only momentary compliance" (2002, p. 383).

APA encourages you to provide page numbers in your citations when paraphrasing or summarizing a source. Any time you borrow the idea of another, help your readers to locate that idea in the original source material. If you do not refer to a specific page, simply indicate the date:

> Berk (2002) asserts that many research findings view punishment as a quick fix rather than a long-term solution to behavior problems in children.

For quotations of forty words or more, use block (indented) quotations. In these cases, place the parenthetical citation *after* the concluding period:

> Various strategies exist for reducing children's tendency to view the world in a gender-biased fashion:
>
> > Once children notice the vast array of gender stereotypes in their society, parents and teachers can point out exceptions. For example, they can arrange for children to see men and women pursuing nontraditional careers. And they can reason with children, explaining that interests and skills, not sex, should determine a person's occupation and activities. (Berk, 2002, p. 395)

Again, were Berk's name mentioned in the sentence leading into the quotation, the parenthetical reference would be simply "(2002, p. 395)."

If the reference applies only to the first part of a sentence, the parenthetical reference is inserted at the appropriate point *within* the sentence:

> Shapiro (2002) emphasizes the idea that law firms are "continually in flux" (p. 32), while Sikes (2003)focuses on their stability as institutions.

At times you must modify the basic author/date/page number reference. Depending on the nature of your source(s), you may need to use one of the following citation formats:

Quoted material appearing in another source

> (as cited in Garber, 2000, p. 211)

An anonymous work

> ("Obedience," 2003, p. 32)

Two authors

> (Striano & Rochat, 2000, p. 257)

> [Note use of ampersand.]

Two or more sources (arrange entries in alphabetic order of surname)

> (Ehrenreich, 2001, p. 68; Hitchens, 2001, p. 140)

A multivolume work

> (Brown, 2003, vol. 2, p. 88)

In-Text Citation of Electronic Sources

Direct your readers as closely as possible to the location of quoted material. When available, cite the author, year, and page number of your source. For digital sources without page numbers, provide a section heading (abbreviating long section titles) and follow with the appropriate paragraph number, abbreviating "paragraph" as "para." Do not abbreviate "chapter" or "section" (or variants such as "Results section") when pointing readers to your source:

> In her investigation of adolescent purchasing patterns, Jones (2009) reviews "the steep rise in advertising dollars devoted to the youth market" (Introduction section, para. 3).

■ APA STYLE: CITATIONS IN THE REFERENCES LIST

In APA format the complete list of sources, with all publication details, starts on a new page titled "References." Include in the References list only those sources you cite in your paper.

- Entries in the References list should be double-spaced and alphabetized by the author's last name. The last name is followed by first and middle initials.
- Second and subsequent lines of each entry should be indented five spaces or one-half inch.
- A single space should follow a period.
- Use a DOI, or digital object identifier, to identify all sources, digital and print, when available. Otherwise, use details of print publication or, for Web sites, the URL of the source home page introduced by "Retrieved from."
- Use a detailed URL only if the source is likely to change (as with a wiki) or if the source would be difficult to locate by searching from the home page or by using standard search engines.
- Do not list the names of databases in your reference entries.

The examples that follow do not show every possible variation of entries in the References list. For entries in your own list, you may need to combine elements from two or more examples. Generally, include any information that will help a reader locate the documented source.

Periodicals

Any publication that appears on a regular basis—a scholarly or professional journal, a daily or weekly newspaper, a magazine—is a *periodical.* An entry for a periodical has four parts: the author's name; the date of publication (if none is provided, write "n.d.") in parentheses; the titles of the article and the periodical, and the facts of publication.

JOURNAL ARTICLE: PRINT OR DATABASE, WITH DOI

When it is available, provide the digital object identifier (DOI), the article's unique reference locator. (Note that there is no space following the colon after the abbreviation "doi.")

> Alpers, G. W. (2009). Ambulatory assessment in panic disorder and specific phobia. *Psychological Assessment, 21*(4), 476–485. doi:10.1037/a0017489

In the example above, "21" is the volume number of the periodical and "4" is the issue number. When no issue number is available, place a comma after the italicized volume number. Include the entire page range in the reference (not just the pages you cited). Do *not* list the database in which you have located a source. (*An exception:* Provide the URL for the home page of an electronic archive/database when the material in question cannot be located elsewhere through other standard searches. Use the "Retrieved from" format.)

JOURNAL ARTICLE: PRINT OR DATABASE, NO DOI AVAILABLE

> Kimmel, J., Forster, W., & Tompkins, L. (2009). Resistance to sleep phase reset among adolescent males. *Quarterly Review of Adolescent Health, 11*(3), 14–22.

JOURNAL ARTICLE: DIGITAL, NO DOI AVAILABLE

When providing retrieval information for a Web site, begin with "Retrieved from" and follow with the URL.

- Break long URLs *before* punctuation marks such as a slash (but do not break "http://").
- Do not insert hyphens when breaking a URL, and do not place a period at the end of a URL.
- Do not include a retrieval date unless the material is likely to change—in which case, write "Retrieved Month day, year, from URL."

> Adler, A. B., Bliese, P. D., McGurk, D., Hoge, C. W., & Castro, C. A. (2009). Battlemind debriefing and battlemind training as early interventions with soldiers returning from Iraq: Randomization by platoon. *Journal of Consulting and Clinical Psychology, 77*(5), 928–940. Retrieved from http://www.apa.org

JOURNAL ARTICLE: PRINT OR DATABASE, EIGHT OR MORE AUTHORS

List the first six authors, followed by an ellipsis and the last author. The in-text citation for this example would be "(Kennard et al., 2009)."

> Kennard, B. D., Clarke, G. N., Weersing, V. R., Asarnow, J. R., Shamsed-deen, W., Porta, G.,...Brent, D. (2009). Effective components of TROIDA cognitive-behavioral therapy for adolescent depression: Preliminary findings. *Journal of Consulting and Clinical Psychology, 77*(6), 1033–1041. doi:10.1037/a0017411

MAGAZINE ARTICLE: PRINT OR DATABASE, WITH VOLUME AND ISSUE NUMBERS

Notice the placement of year and month within parentheses:

> Karis, E. (2009, March). Words about water. *Parabola, 34*(3), 18–21.

MAGAZINE ARTICLE: DIGITAL

Provide the URL of the magazine's home page, but do not cite the name of an online database.

> Sandel, M. J. (2004, April). The case against perfection: What's wrong with designer children, bionic athletes, and genetic engineering. *The Atlantic, 293*. Retrieved from http://www.theatlantic.com

MAGAZINE ARTICLE: PRINT OR DATABASE, NO AUTHOR LISTED

> Spain and the Basques: Dangerous stalemate. (2003, July 5). *The Economist, 368*, 44–45.

NEWSPAPER ARTICLE: PRINT OR DATABASE

Place the year, month, and day of publication in parentheses. Note also the use of an abbreviation for "pages" and the complete page range of the article:

> Hook, J., & Levey, N. (2009, December 9). Senate compromise removes "public option" obstacle. *The Los Angeles Times,* pp. A1, A6.

NEWSPAPER ARTICLE: DIGITAL

Provide the URL of the newspaper's home page. If you have located the newspaper via an online database, do not include the database name in your entry.

> Hook, J., & Levey, N. (2009, December 9). Senate compromise re-moves "public option" obstacle. *The Los Angeles Times*. Retrieved from http://www.latimes.com

EDITORIAL (UNSIGNED)

> Cultural revolution in the GOP [Editorial]. (2009, December 8). *The Boston Globe*. Retrieved from http://www.boston.com

Note: In this entry the bracketed information ("[Editorial]") *precedes* the parenthetical date of publication because no author is listed. The next entry is a more typical placement of the brackets.

EDITORIAL (SIGNED)

> Mahrt, W. (2009). Saying and singing [Editorial]. *Sacred Music, 136*(1), 3–7.

LETTER TO THE EDITOR

> Williams, B. (2009, December). The stain of torture [Letter to the edi-tor]. *The Atlantic, 363*. Retrieved from http://www.theatlantic.com

Books

A book entry has four parts: the author's name; the year of publication (if none is provided, write "n.d."); the title of the book; and the publication information. A References entry for a book will take one of five forms; in the following, "I" refers to the initial(s) of the author's first and middle names:

Author, I. (year of publication). *Book title*. City of print publication, State: Publisher.

Author, I. (year of publication). *Book title*. Retrieved from URL

Author, I. (year of publication). *Book title*. doi:number

Author, I. (year of publication). Article or chapter title. In I. Editor & I. Editor (Eds.), *Book title* (pp. 00–00). Place of publication: Publisher *or* Retrieved from URL *or* DOI

Editor, I. (Ed.). (year of publication). *Book title*. Place of publication: Publisher *or* Retrieved from URL *or* DOI

PRINT BOOK: TWO TO SEVEN AUTHORS

List from two to seven authors as follows. Note the use of commas, author initials, and the ampersand.

> Mandelbrot, B., & Hudson, R. L. (2004). *The (mis)behavior of markets: A fractal view of risk, ruin, and reward*. New York, NY: Basic Books.

PRINT BOOK: EIGHT OR MORE AUTHORS

For eight or more authors, list the first six, follow with an ellipsis, and conclude with the last author.

> Vaughn, L. J., Estes, D., Lloyd, F. N., Wallace, J., Tosler, R., Abrams, W. S.,...Brand, M. (2006). *Simulation environments: Case studies*. New York, NY: Halcyon.

DIGITAL VERSION OF A PRINT BOOK

> Dayme, M. B. (Ed.). (2009). *Dynamics of the singing voice* (5th ed.). doi:10.1007/978-3-211-88729-5

> Dayme, M. B. (Ed.). (2009). *Dynamics of the singing voice* (5th ed.) [AZW Reader version]. Retrieved from http://www.amazon.com

DIGITAL BOOK WITH NO PRINT EQUIVALENT

> Haffly, C. (2006). *The Photoshop anthology: 101 web design tricks, tips, and techniques*. Retrieved from http://www.sitepoint.com /books/photoshop

BOOK WITH AN EDITOR (AN ANTHOLOGY OR AN EDITED COLLECTION): PRINT

> Daley, C., & Nolan, M. (Eds.). (1994). *Suffrage and beyond: International feminist perspectives*. New York: New York University Press.

Note: If a publisher is a university press and the name of that press includes the state name in which the press is located, omit the abbreviation of the state in the publisher location part of your citation.

BOOK WITH AN EDITOR (AN ANTHOLOGY OR AN EDITED COLLECTION): DIGITAL

> Daley, C., & Nolan, M. (Eds.). (1994). *Suffrage and beyond: International feminist perspectives*. Retrieved from http://hdl.handle.net/2027/heb.02496

SELECTION FROM AN ANTHOLOGY OR AN EDITED COLLECTION: PRINT

> Cott, N. F. (1994). Early-twentieth-century feminism in political context: A comparative look at Germany and the United States. In C. Daley & N. Nolan (Eds.), *Suffrage and beyond: International feminist perspectives* (pp. 234–251). New York: New York University Press.

SELECTION FROM AN ANTHOLOGY OR AN EDITED COLLECTION: DIGITAL

> Cott, N. F. (1994). Early-twentieth-century feminism in political context: A comparative look at Germany and the United States. In C. Daley & N. Nolan (Eds.), *Suffrage and beyond: International feminist perspectives* (pp. 234–251). Retrieved from http://hdl.handle.net/2027/heb.02496

Note: The exact URL is provided, not the home page URL, because this source is difficult to locate.

BOOK WITH A CORPORATE AUTHOR: PRINT

When the publisher is the same as the listed author, write "Author" in the entry's publisher position.

> Alcoholics Anonymous World Services. (2001). *Alcoholics anonymous: The story of how many thousands of men and women have recovered from alcoholism* (4th ed.). New York, NY: Author.

BOOK WITH A CORPORATE AUTHOR: DIGITAL

> Encyclopaedia Britannica. (2008). *Technology and inventions* (2nd ed.). [Adobe Digital Editions version]. Retrieved from http://www.ebooks.com

BOOK OR REPORT WITH A GOVERNMENT AUTHOR: PRINT

> U.S. Department of Health and Human Services, National Institutes of Health, National Institute of Child Health and Human Development. (2002). *Closing the gap: A national blueprint to improve*

> *the health of persons with mental retardation.* Washington, DC:
> Government Printing Office.

BOOK OR REPORT WITH A GOVERNMENT AUTHOR: DIGITAL

> U.S. Department of Labor, Mine Safety and Health Administra-
> tion. (2004). *Evaluation of electronic detonators—require-
> ments for shunting and circuit testing* (MSHA Publication
> No. PAR0088857A10). Retrieved from http://www.msha.gov

LATER EDITION: PRINT

Note in parentheses, after the title of the work, a numbered edition, a revised edition, a translation, or a multivolume work.

> Quine, W. V. (1992). *Pursuit of truth* (Rev. ed.). Cambridge, MA: Har-
> vard University Press.

> LeBlond, R. F., DeGowin, R. L., & Brown, D. D. (2009). *DeGowin's diag-
> nostic examination* (9th ed.). New York, NY: McGraw Medical.

TRANSLATION: PRINT

> De Beauvoir, S. (1972). *The second sex* (H. M. Parshley, Trans.).
> New York, NY: Penguin. (Original work published 1949)

TWO OR MORE WORKS BY THE SAME AUTHOR

Works by the same author are listed in chronological order of publication
year, earliest first.

> Gubar, S. (1997). *Racechanges: White skin, black face in American
> culture.* New York, NY: Oxford University Press.

> Gubar, S. (2000). *Critical condition: Feminism at the turn of the cen-
> tury.* New York, NY: Columbia University Press.

TWO OR MORE WORKS BY THE SAME AUTHOR IN THE SAME YEAR

Alphabetize by title multiple works by the same author in the same
year. Then attach a lowercase letter to the year to distinguish each work:
"(2002a)," "(2002b)," and so on.

> Merikangas, K. R. (2002a). Genetic epidemiology of substance-use
> disorders. In H. D'haenen, J. A. Den Boer, & P. Willner (Eds.),
> *Biological psychiatry* (Vol. 1, pp. 537–546). Chichester, United
> Kingdom: Wiley.

> Merikangas, K. R. (2002b). Implications of genetic epidemiology
> for classification. In J. E. Helzer & J. J. Hudziak (Eds.), *Defin-
> ing psychopathology in the 21st century: SSM-V and beyond*
> (pp. 195–209). Washington, DC: American Psychiatric Press.

Other Sources

ABSTRACT

> Briesch, A. M., & Chafouleas, S. M. (2009). Review and analysis of literature on self-management interventions to promote appropriate classroom behaviors (1988–2008) [Abstract]. *School Psychology Quarterly, 24*(2), 106–118. doi:10.1037/a0016159

ADVERTISEMENT

> The Royal Thai Government. (2009, November 16). Thailand shining through [Advertisement]. *Newsweek,* 30.

WIKI

Include the retrieval date for wikis and other Web pages that are likely to change.

> Kiff, J. (2006, March 31). Genetic determinism [Wiki]. *The psychology wiki*. Retrieved January 12, 2010, from http://psychology.wikia.com

PODCAST

> Reid, H., & Francica, J. (2007, January 7). *Accurate 3D geometry for the automotive industry* [Video podcast]. Retrieved from http://lbs360.directionsmag.com

> Ulaby, N. (Producer). (2009, December 23). *Culturetopia* [Audio podcast]. Retrieved from http://www.npr.org/blogs

DIGITAL POSTING: BLOG, ONLINE FORUM, MAILING LIST

> Murray, T. (2009, December 30). Iberdrola completes wind farm [Web log post]. Retrieved from http://greenenergyreporter .com/2009/12/iberdrola-completes-rugby-wind-farm

Note: The exact URL is provided, not the home page URL, because this source is difficult to locate. To create an entry for a blog comment, substitute "comment" for "post" in the bracketed information; all other elements remain the same. If your source is an online forum, place "Online forum comment" within the brackets. If you located your source on an electronic mailing list, use "Electronic mailing list message." For a video blog, substitute the words "Video file."

PHOTOGRAPH

> Adams, A. (1941). Mount Moran and Jackson Lake from Signal Hill [Photograph]. Retrieved from http://www.archives.gov/research /ansel-adams/images/aag07.jpg

Note: The exact URL is provided, not the home page URL, because this source is difficult to locate.

MOTION PICTURE

> Polanski, R. (Director). (2002). *The pianist* [Motion picture]. United States: Focus Features and Universal.

LECTURE

> Baldwin, J. (2009, January 11). *The self in social interactions.* Sociology 2 lecture, University of California, Santa Barbara.

DISSERTATION, RETRIEVED FROM COMMERCIAL DATABASE

> Sheahan, M. T. (1999). *Living on the edge: Ecology and economy in Willa Cather's "Wild Land": Webster county, Nebraska, 1980–1900* (Doctoral dissertation). Available from ProQuest Dissertations and Theses database. (UMI No. 1298A)

Note: Include the title of the database (capitalize significant words) and the reference number, as shown.

WRITING ASSIGNMENT: SOURCE-BASED PAPER

Using the methods we have outlined in this chapter—and incorporating the skills covered in this textbook as a whole—conduct your own research on a topic and research question that fall within your major or your area of interest. Your research process should culminate in a 1500- to 1700-word paper that draws upon your sources to present an answer to your research question.

Practicing ∎ *8*
Academic Writing

∎ THE CHANGING LANDSCAPE OF WORK IN THE TWENTY-FIRST CENTURY

You attend college for many reasons, but perhaps none is so compelling as the hope and expectation that higher education offers a passport to a better future. If you already devote long hours to supporting your family or paying your way through school, then you know *exactly* why so many pursue a degree: the conviction that a diploma will ensure better, more meaningful, and more secure employment. Learn, apply yourself, and succeed: This has always been the formula for achieving the American dream.

The times, however (to paraphrase Bob Dylan), are changing.

In the second half of the twentieth century, the labor market rewarded the educated, conferring on those who attended college an "education premium." Even as the forces of globalization reshaped the American economy and workers began losing manufacturing jobs to competitors offshore in China and India, college-educated workers were generally spared severe disruptions. Today, however, education no longer promises such protection. In the wake of the severe economic downturn that began in 2008, the unemployment rate for college graduates under age 25 was, at 9.2% (as compared to 5.2% for college graduates overall), no lower than the unemployment rate for those with only a high school education. In addition, the relentless search for cheap labor and plentiful raw materials, together with advances in technology, have opened the information-based service economy to foreign competition. According to economists and other analysts, the American, college-educated workforce will increasingly face the same relentless pressures that decades ago so unsettled the automotive and manufacturing sectors. Employers are already offshoring computer coding, certain types of accounting, and medical consultation (the reading of X-rays, MRIs, CT scans, and such)—services that require extensive training.

Experts predict that more American jobs will be lost to foreign competition and that fewer will entail a lifelong commitment between employer and employee. (Pensions, for instance, are fast disappearing.) What are the implications of these developments for you and your intended career? How will they affect the courses you take, the major (and minors) you choose, the summer jobs and internships you pursue? Could you investigate *now* how to anticipate and avoid major disruptions to your working life tomorrow?

This chapter provides an opportunity to learn what economists, policy analysts, and educators are thinking about the world of work in the twenty-first century. We open with five selections that set a broad context for the discussion. First, Richard Judy and Carol D'Amico, analysts at the Hudson Institute, offer a "map" of the vastly changed employment landscape, with clear winners and losers among American workers. Next, in an excerpt from his best-selling *The World Is Flat*, the *New York Times* columnist Thomas Friedman urges young people contemplating future work to become "untouchable"—that is, to take on jobs that cannot be easily outsourced. In much the same vein, the Princeton economist and former presidential advisor Alan S. Blinder distinguishes between "personal services" workers and "impersonal services" workers and leaves no room for doubt as to which you should want to be. We follow with an article from *The Economist*, "Into the Unknown," which assures us that even as jobs are lost to computerization and automation, and even as overseas competitors siphon off jobs and create concern for the future of the American workforce, the economy will nevertheless grow. Technologies we cannot imagine today will emerge to service the needs and desires of tomorrow, in the process creating jobs for you and your grandchildren.

These selections are followed by five other readings that consider the future of employment in specific career fields: engineering, business, technology/services industries, law, and medicine. They offer a glimpse of what experts are saying about the future of work in areas that may touch on your intended career. Prior to this second set of readings is a summary by the Bureau of Labor Statistics of its "Employment Projections: 2008–2018," with links to ten detailed tables on the BLS Web site.

Your main assignment in this practice chapter is to write an argument that synthesizes your own insights with what various authors have written on the topic. In preparation, you will complete several briefer exercises that require you to draw on your sources. During this progression of assignments, you will write a combination of summaries, paraphrases, critiques, and explanations that will prepare you for—and that will produce sections of—your more ambitious argument synthesis. In this respect, the assignments here are typical of other writing you will do in college: While at times you will be called on to write a stand-alone critique or a purely explanatory paper, you will also write papers that blend the basic forms of college writing that you have studied in this text. Both your critiques and your explanations will rely in part on summaries—or partial summaries—of specific articles. Your arguments may rely on summaries, critiques, *and* explanations. The assignments in this chapter will therefore help prepare you for future academic research tasks while broadening your understanding of the world of employment that you are preparing to enter.

■ THE ASSIGNMENTS

Read: Prepare to Write

In this chapter, you'll read a variety of sources on "The Changing Landscape of Work in the Twenty-first Century." At the outset, a series of assignments prompts you to write papers based on these sources. We suggest that you read these assignments before you read the selections themselves. Knowing what you are expected to write will help prepare you to read. As you read, mark up the texts: write notes to yourself in the margins and comment on what the authors have said.

To prepare for the most ambitious of the assignments that follow—the explanatory and argumentative syntheses—consider drawing up a topic list of your sources as you read. For each topic about which two or more authors have something to say, jot down notes and page references. Here is a sample entry:

> Who will succeed/Who will fail in the twenty-first-century workplace?
>
> Thomas Friedman: untouchables, fungible vs. non-fungible work,
>   p. 320
> Alan Blinder: personal services jobs vs. impersonal services jobs,
>   pages 7–12
> Victoria Reitz: innovators vs. commodities, page 329
> Tom Peters: specialists vs. generalists, page 330

A topic list keyed to your sources will spare you the frustration of reading thirty or more pages and flipping through them later saying, "Now, where did I read that?" In the sample entry, we see that four authors speak to the likely success and failure of different types of work in the coming decades. At this early point, you don't need to know how you might write a paper based on this or any other topic. But a robust list with multiple topics and accurate notes for each lays the groundwork for your own discussion later and puts you in a good position to write a synthesis.

As it happens, the sample entry above should come in handy when you're preparing to write your explanatory and argumentative syntheses on the changing landscape of work in the twenty-first century. Creating a topic list with multiple entries will take you a bit more time as you read, but will save you time as you write.

Group Assignment #1: Make Topic Lists

> **Create two topic list entries for the selections in this chapter, making sure to jot down notes and page references for each. Create one topic on your own, based on your own careful reading of the selections. Choose your second topic from the list that follows.**

- importance of a global perspective
- effects of globalization, positive and negative
- protecting jobs from outsourcing/offshoring
- effects of (high) technology/automation in general
- disappearance of/changes in traditional jobs/careers/professions
- emergence of new jobs/opportunities, entrepreneurial and otherwise
- thinking "outside the box" of traditional jobs/careers/ways of making money
- "revolution in services" (see Lohr)—implications
- role of education (secondary, postsecondary)
- importance of retraining and continuing education
- effects of aging boomer generation on consumer market/labor market
- effects of changing demographics of workforce—e.g., growing Hispanic population
- role of innovation, technology
- role of telecommunications, telecommuting
- the new business mentality needed for getting ahead, remaining competitive
- changing nature of leadership, teamwork
- "survival of the fittest" economy
- clashes of old and new business models/professional cultures
- personal qualities needed to succeed

Meet in groups of three or four to exchange notes on your topics. As a group, discuss which source authors write about each topic. (Note that not all authors will discuss all topics.) Working together, develop the entries: Create the most comprehensive notes you can for each topic. As a class, generate a master list of topics and notes. This list should include all topics suggested above and all topics created by individual class members. At the conclusion of this exercise, all class members should have a comprehensive guide to key topics in the source readings. For ease of completing Assignment #2 below, use a separate sheet of paper for each topic and its accompanying notes.

Group Assignment #2: Create a Topic Web

> Working in groups of three or four, create a network, or web, of connections among topics. That is, determine which topics relate or "speak" to other topics.

Articulate these connections. For instance, draw a line from one topic (say, the importance of maintaining a global perspective) to another (say, the role of innovation and technology). How are these topics related? As a group, generate as many connections as possible. At the conclusion of this session, you will have in hand not only the fruits of Assignment #1—multiple authors discussing common topics—you will also have a potential connection *among* topics—basically, the necessary raw material for writing your syntheses.

Note that one synthesis—a single paper—couldn't possibly refer to every topic, or every connection among topics, that you have found. Your proficiency in preparing and writing a synthesis depends on your ability to *discern* and *select* closely related topics and then to make and develop a claim that links and is supported by those topics.

Summary

Summary Assignments #1 and #2: Summarizing Text

> **#1: Summarize either "Work and Workers in the Twenty-first Century" by Judy and D'Amico or "The Untouchables" by Thomas Friedman. Make careful notes on the selection as you prepare your summary. Follow the guidelines in Chapter 1, particularly the Guidelines for Writing Summaries box on pages 6–7. Also, consult the advice on note-taking (pp. 12–15). For the selection you are *not* summarizing, read it carefully and highlight the text *as if* you were preparing to write a summary of it.**

> **#2: In preparation for writing a critique, summarize "Into the Unknown," pages 321–323. As with Summary #1, make careful notes on the selection as you read and then follow the advice for writing summaries in Chapter 1. Before writing, read the assignment for Critique below. Your summary will become an important section of that critique.**

Summary Assignment #3: Summarizing Tables

> **#3: Review (online) the ten tables presented by the Bureau of Labor Statistics (see the titles and URLs on p. 327). Before selecting a BLS table for this assignment, read the assignments for Argument below. To the extent that you are able, decide on the argument you will be writing and choose a table to summarize accordingly. Use your summary of the BLS table to support your argument.**

Note: In each table, the BLS presents far too much information for you to summarize in its entirety. Therefore, write a *partial* summary—keeping in mind the argument you expect to write. First, decide which table will be most useful to that argument; then decide on a *subset* of information that will best advance your argument's claim. For advice on summarizing tables (and parts of tables), see pages 23–32.

Critique

> **Write a critique of "Into the Unknown" (pp. 321–323).**

You'll find the thesis of the article in the first sentence of paragraph 4: "What the worriers always forget is that the same changes in production technology that destroy jobs also create new ones." This thesis rests on the assumption that the economy will "take care of its own consequences."* That is, without any meddling by well-intentioned policymakers, the economy will, in the long term, create opportunities for workers in new areas even as it eliminates opportunities in other areas. Left alone to operate, market forces will in the end create the best outcomes for the economy as a whole. Individuals may win or lose, but overall the economy remains stable and healthy. In this chapter you'll find others working with this same assumption: See, for instance, the footnote on page 314 explaining the term "creative destruction." See also Alan Blinder's essay, paragraph 8, on page 9.

To write this critique, you don't need to be an economics major or even to have taken an introductory course in economics. Rather, in developing your critical evaluation of the piece, rely on your own experience. Probe the assumption; do not feel pressured to agree or disagree with it. Pose questions such as these:

- Have you witnessed the economy treat one group of workers harshly? Have friends or relatives been treated harshly?

- Considering the experiences of people you know, do new jobs created by the economy necessarily aid the workers who have lost their jobs? Would you expect the economy to operate in this way? Think of examples.

- Do you believe that the economy takes care of its own consequences? Think of the winners and losers in our evolving economy. Who provides for the losers? How?

- What happens to the main argument of "Into the Unknown" if this key assumption turns out not to be true—if the economy does *not* take care of its own consequences?

Because the writing you do for this assignment will be incorporated into a larger argument with its own introduction and conclusion, you needn't write an introduction or conclusion to this critique. Instead, write an *abbreviated* critique consisting of three parts:

1. a summary of the selection (your response to Summary Assignment #2)
2. an evaluation of the presentation for accuracy, clarity, logic, and/or fairness
3. a statement of your agreement and/or disagreement with the author

For parts 2 and 3, be sure to support your evaluation with reasons. Refer to the selection, summarizing or quoting key elements as needed. See Chapter 2 for advice on critical reading. See particularly the Guidelines for Writing Critiques box on pages 68–69, along with the hints on incorporating quoted material into your own writing, pages 36–46.

---

*Jonathan Sacks, *Dignity of Difference* (London: Continuum, 2003): 88.

Explanation

> Based on the reading selections in this chapter, write three expla-
> nations you might use in a broader argument on the subject of the
> changing American workplace. The explanations should each consist
> of two to four well-developed paragraphs on the following topics:
> (1) the developments responsible for the accelerating changes in the
> American workplace, (2) the jobs that are most—and least—at risk
> from these changes, and (3) why an American worker has reasons for
> both optimism and pessimism regarding these changes.

Key requirements for each explanation:

- Consider each explanation to be a paper in miniature with its own thesis: a single statement that will guide the writing of the paragraphs of
  explanation that follow.

- Begin each paragraph of explanation that follows the explanatory thesis with a clear topic sentence.

- Refer in each paragraph of explanation to *at least two* different sources.
  Be sure to set up the references (which can be summaries, paraphrases,
  or quotations) with care, using an appropriate citation format, most
  likely MLA (see pp. 282–292).

- To develop your explanation, draw on facts, examples, statistics, and
  expert opinions from your sources, as needed.

Analysis

> Select a principle or definition discussed in one of the readings on
> "The Changing Landscape of Work in the Twenty-first Century"
> and apply this principle or definition to (1) a particular situation
> relating to work of which you have personal knowledge, or (2) a
> work-related situation involving a particular individual or group of
> individuals that you have read about in an article you found in the
> course of research.

First, review the master list of topics and the notes that you generated for
Group Assignment #1 (pp. 305–306) to determine possible analytic principles
or definitions. For example, under the topic of technology/automation, you
may be most interested in Judy and D'Amico's contention that "automation
will continue to displace low-skilled or unskilled workers in America's manufacturing firms and offices." In the area of globalization, you may be intrigued
by Friedman's concept of making yourself "untouchable" or his distinction
between "fungible" and "nonfungible" work. Other possibilities: Blinder's
urging young people to prepare for high-end "personal services" jobs or
Lohr's quoting the assertion that " 'We need a revolution in services.' " Any of
these—and numerous other principles or terms introduced in the readings—
could serve as a lens through which to study a work-related situation.

In writing your analysis, follow the Guidelines for Writing Analyses on pages 185–186. Use the fruits of your earlier assignments involving summary and explanation. Consider using the following structure for your analysis:

- An introductory paragraph that sets a context for the topic you will be analyzing and presents the claim you are going to support. Your claim—your thesis—may appear at the end of this paragraph (or introductory section).

- A paragraph or two explaining the developments responsible for the accelerating changes in the American workplace. See the Explanatory Synthesis assignment and the assignment for your first or second Summary. You may be able to import one or both into this analysis. See also the Alan Blinder Summary on page 321.

- A paragraph or two explaining the jobs that are most—and least—at risk from these changes. See the Explanatory Synthesis assignment and the assignment for your first or second Summary; you may be able to import them into your argument. See also the example topic under "Read: Prepare to Write," page 305.

- *Claims and support:* (Re)state your analytical claim at the end of a paragraph that sets a work-related experience you know well (or the experience of an individual or group you have researched) into the context of the changing workplace of the twenty-first century.

- A paragraph defining the key term or principle you will be using in your analysis—the term borrowed, with attribution, from one of the source authors in this chapter.

- A systematic inquiry into the work-related experience that your analysis seeks to illuminate. *This is the main section of the paper.* It should consist of several paragraphs, each focused on revealing a specific element of the topic.

- A paragraph of supporting data from the Bureau of Labor Statistics.

- A conclusion in which you argue, based on the insights gained through your analysis, that the work-related experience in question can now be more fully or clearly understood. See Chapter 6, pages 238–244, for pointers on concluding your paper.

Argument

Having carefully read the selections in this chapter, develop an argument about the changing landscape of work in the twenty-first century. Adopt *one* of these statements as your claim:

> *Claim #1*
> **Faced with the changing landscape of work, many students will need to adjust their career plans and modify their assumptions about how best to succeed after college.**

Or:

Claim #2
The workplace is likely to undergo profound changes in the coming decades; however, enough current occupations will remain in demand that not many students should need to adjust their career plans or modify their assumptions about how best to succeed after college.

In planning your synthesis, review the master list of topics and notes that you and your classmates generated for Group Assignments #1 and #2 (pp. 305–307); and in developing your outline, draw on what the authors of the passages have written about these topics. Devise a thesis that summarizes your argument and plan to support it with facts, opinions, and statistics from the passages.

Note that one synthesis—a single paper—could not possibly refer to every topic, or every connection among authors, that you have found. Writing an effective synthesis depends on your ability to *select* closely related topics and then to make and develop a claim that links and can be supported by those topics. You needn't refer to *all* of the selections in this chapter while developing your paper, though you will likely want to refer to many of them. You may even want to research additional sources.

In writing your argument, follow the Guidelines for Writing Syntheses on pages 88–89. Use the products of your earlier assignments involving summary and explanation. Consider using the following structure for your argument.

• An introductory paragraph that sets a context for the topic and presents the claim you are going to support in the argument that follows. Your claim—that is, your thesis—may appear at the end of this paragraph (or introductory section).

• A paragraph or two explaining the developments responsible for the accelerating changes in the American workplace. See the Explanatory Synthesis assignment and the assignment for your first or second Summary. You may be able to import one or both into this argument. See also the Alan Blinder Summary on pages 320–321.

• A paragraph or two explaining the jobs that are most—and least—at risk from these changes. See the Explanatory Synthesis assignment and the assignment for your first or second Summary; you may be able to import them into your argument. See also the example topic under "Read: Prepare to Write" on page 305.

• An analysis of one job or profession and the importance of considering examples such as this for students preparing to enter the workplace. See the Analysis assignment, paragraphs of which may help you support the claim of this argument.

• Reasons for optimism if students can adapt their thinking—or not, depending on which claim you develop. See the Explanatory Synthesis assignment and consider importing paragraphs into this argument.

- The dangers if students do not take into account the opinions, facts, and statistics available.

- Counterargument and rebuttal: Consider developing one or both of two counterarguments for Claim #1:

> College years are not only a preparation for the world of work, they are also a safe harbor from it—a time to think broadly, impractically even, and look beyond the narrow needs of the workplace.
>
> Because no one can predict the future with certainty, a college student is best served by training broadly, developing core skills (such as critical thinking, writing, and speaking), and later meeting the challenges of the future workplace as they arise.

Possible counterarguments for Claim #2:

> 1. A favorite uncle or aunt tells you: "You'd better be realistic about your studies. Changes are coming, and you need to be prepared."
> 2. A college education is expensive. It's unconscionable to spend all that money and not get the training you need for a good job immediately after graduation.

- A paragraph or two of conclusion. See Chapter 6, pages 238–244, for advice on concluding your paper.

It's up to you to decide *where* you place the individual elements of this argument synthesis. It's also up to you to decide which sources to use and what logic to present in defense of your claim. See pages 145–150 and pages 164–170 for help in thinking about structuring and supporting your argument.

A Note on Incorporating Quotations and Paraphrases   Identify those sources that you intend to use in your synthesis. Working with a phrase, sentence, or brief passage from each, use a variety of the techniques discussed in the Incorporating Quotations into Your Sentences section (pp. 40–46) to advance your argument. Some of these sentences should demonstrate the use of ellipses and brackets. (See pp. 42–43 in Chapter 1.) Paraphrase passages as needed, incorporating the paraphrases into your paragraphs.

■ THE READINGS

Read the following passages, and then complete each writing assignment above.

Note well! When writing source-based papers, it is all too easy to become careless in giving proper credit. Before drafting your paper, review the section on Avoiding Plagiarism (pp. 46–47) and the relevant sections on citing sources in Chapter 7.

WORK AND WORKERS IN THE TWENTY-FIRST CENTURY

Richard W. Judy and Carol D'Amico

The selection that follows forms the opening section of the Hudson Institute's Workforce 2020, *which appeared twenty years after its predecessor,* Workforce 2000. *That book challenged policymakers and employers to consider and respond to trends that were revolutionizing the landscape of work at the end of the twentieth century. In this update, Hudson analysts Richard Judy and Carol D'Amico similarly ask us to project current trends into the near future so that we can respond to them meaningfully. The Hudson Institute describes itself as "a non-partisan policy research organization dedicated to innovative research and analysis that promotes global security, prosperity, and freedom."*

You have before you a map, one that describes the journey America's labor force is now beginning. It lays out the general contours of the employment landscape, not the fine details or the specific landmarks, depicting the many roads to what we call "Workforce 2020." Some will be superhighways and some will be dead ends for American workers. Although immense forces shape the employment landscape, we believe that we know the difference between the superhighways and the dead ends.

Skilled cartographers in the guise of economists, education experts, and policy researchers at Hudson Institute helped prepare this map. It offers our best ideas about what lies ahead and what Americans—collectively and individually, in large and small firms, in federal agencies and in small-town development commissions—should do to prepare for the journey to Workforce 2020.

Our map is needed because American workers at the threshold of the twenty-first century are embarking on mysterious voyages. They seek glittering destinations but travel along roads with numerous pitfalls and unexpected diversions. Many workers—more than at any time in America's history—will reach the glittering destinations. They will enjoy incomes unimaginable to their parents, along with working and living conditions more comfortable than anyone could have dreamed of in centuries past. But many other workers will be stymied by the pitfalls along the road or baffled by the diversions. Their standard of living may stagnate or even decline. Much is already known today about what will divide the hopeful from the anxious along these roads, and we will share that knowledge here.

What makes America's voyage to the workforce of 2020 unique is not merely the heights to which some will climb or the difficulties others will endure. Two qualities give a truly unprecedented character to the roads ahead. First, the gates have lifted before almost every American who wishes to embark on the journey of work. Age, gender, and race barriers to employment opportunity have broken down. What little conscious discrimination remains will be swept away soon—not by government regulation but by the enlightened self-interest of employers. Second, more and more individuals now undertake their own journeys through the labor force, rather than "hitching rides" on the traditional mass transportation provided by unions, large corporations, and government bureaucracies. For most workers, this "free agency" will be immensely liberating. But for others, it will provoke anxiety and anger. For all workers, the premium on education, flexibility, and foresight has never been greater than it will be in the years ahead.

5   What explains the immense satisfactions and dangers ahead? What makes possible the unprecedented expansion of opportunities in the labor force? What forces conspire, for better or worse, to demand that we compete as individuals and contend with ever-changing knowledge and skill requirements? We highlight four forces in particular.

First, the pace of technological change in today's economy has never been greater. It will accelerate still further, in an exponential manner. Innovations in biotechnology, computing, telecommunications, and their confluences will bring new products and services that are at once marvelous and potentially frightening. And the "creative destruction"* wrought by this technology on national economies, firms, and individual workers will be even more powerful in the twenty-first century than when economist Joseph Schumpeter coined the phrase fifty years ago. We cannot know what innovations will transform the global economy by 2020, any more than analysts in the mid-1970s could have foreseen the rise of the personal computer or the proliferation of satellite, fiber-optic, and wireless communications. However, the computer and telecommunications revolutions enable us to speculate in an informed manner on the implications of today's Innovation Age for the American workforce:

• Automation will continue to displace low-skilled or unskilled workers in America's manufacturing firms and offices. Indeed, machines will substitute for increasingly more sophisticated forms of human labor. Even firms that develop advanced technology will be able to replace some of their employees with technology (witness the "CASE tools" that now assist in writing routine computer code) or with lower-paid workers in other countries (witness the rise of India's computer programmers and data processors).

• However, experience suggests that the development, marketing, and servicing of ever more sophisticated products—and the use of those products in an ever richer ensemble of personal and professional services—almost certainly will create more jobs than the underlying technology will destroy. On the whole, the new jobs will also be safer, more stimulating, and better paid than the ones they replace.

• The best jobs created in the Innovation Age will be filled by Americans (and workers in other advanced countries) to the extent that workers possess the skills required to compete for them and carry them out. If jobs go unfilled in the U.S., they will quickly migrate elsewhere in our truly global economy.

• Because the best new jobs will demand brains rather than brawn, and because physical presence in a particular location at a particular time will become

---

*In *Capitalism, Socialism and Democracy* (1942), Joseph Schumpeter coined the term "creative destruction" to describe the process by which capitalism, operating through "new consumers, goods, the new methods of production or transportation, the new markets, [and] the new forms of industrial organization,…incessantly revolutionizes the economic structure *from within,* incessantly destroying the old one, incessantly creating a new one" (New York, Harper: 1975, pp. 82–85; <http://transcriptions.english.ucsb.edu/archive/courses/liu/english25/materials/schumpeter.html>).

increasingly irrelevant, structural barriers to the employment of women and older Americans will continue to fall away. Americans of all backgrounds will be increasingly able to determine their own working environments and hours.

Second, the rest of the world matters to a degree that it never did in the past. We can no longer say anything sensible about the prospects for American workers if we consider only the U.S. economy or the characteristics of the U.S. labor force. Fast-growing Asian and Latin American economies present us with both opportunities and challenges. Meanwhile, communications and transportation costs have plummeted (declining to almost zero in the case of information exchanged on the Internet), resulting in what some have called "the death of distance." Whereas the costs of shipping an automobile or a heavy machine tool remain consequential, the products of the world's most dynamic industries—such as biological formulas, computers, financial services, microchips, and software—can cross the globe for a pittance. Investment capital is also more abundant and more mobile than ever before, traversing borders with abandon in search of the best ideas, the savviest entrepreneurs, and the most productive economies. The implications of this globalization for U.S. workers are no less complex than the implications of new technology:

- Manufacturing will continue to dominate U.S. exports. Almost 20 percent of U.S. manufacturing workers now have jobs that depend on exports; that figure will continue to escalate. America's growing export dependence in the early twenty-first century will benefit most of America's highly productive workers, because many foreign economies will continue to expand more rapidly than our own, thereby generating massive demand for U.S. goods. Skilled workers whose jobs depend on exports are better paid than other U.S. manufacturing workers as a rule, because the U.S. enjoys a comparative advantage in the specialized manufacturing and service sectors that create their jobs. These workers also tend to earn more than similar workers in other countries.

- But globalization will affect low-skilled or unskilled American workers very differently. They will compete for jobs and wages not just with their counterparts across town or in other parts of the U.S., but also with low-skilled workers around the globe. As labor costs become more important to manufacturers than shipping costs, the U.S. will retain almost no comparative advantage in low-skilled manufacturing. Jobs in that sector will disappear or be available only at depressed wages. Second or third jobs and full-time employment for both spouses—already the norm in households headed by low-skilled workers—will become even more necessary.

- Manufacturing's share of total U.S. employment will continue to decline, due to the combined effects of automation and globalization. But the millions of high-productivity manufacturing jobs that remain will be more highly skilled and therefore better paid than at any other time in U.S. history. Employment growth, meanwhile, will remain concentrated in services, which also will benefit increasingly from export markets and will offer high salaries for skilled workers.

- Globalization and technological change will make most segments of the U.S. economy extremely volatile, as comparative advantages in particular market segments rise and then fall away. Small- and medium-sized firms will be well situated to react to this volatility, and their numbers will grow. Labor unions will cope badly with this rapidly evolving economy of small producers, and their membership and influence will shrink. Individual workers will change jobs frequently over time. For those who maintain and improve their skills, the changes should bring increasing rewards. But the changes may be traumatic for those who fall behind the skills curve and resist retraining.

Third, America is getting older. At some level, all of us are aware of this. Our parents and grandparents are living longer, and we are having fewer children. But U.S. public policy as well as many employers have yet to come to grips with the full implications of America's aging. The oldest among America's so-called baby boomers—the massive cohort born between 1945 and 1965—will begin to reach age 65 in 2010. By 2020, almost 20 percent of the U.S. population will be 65 or older. There will be as many Americans of "retirement age" as there are 20–35-year-olds. America's aging baby boomers will decisively affect the U.S. workforce, through their departure from and continued presence in it, and as recipients of public entitlements and purchasers of services:

• America's taxpayer-funded entitlements for its aging population—Medicare and Social Security—are likely to undergo profound changes in the next two decades. The tax rates necessary to sustain the current "pay-as-you-go" approach to funding these programs as the baby boomers retire will rise, perhaps precipitously, unless the expectations of retirees regarding their benefits become more modest, the economy grows more strongly than expected, or the programs receive fundamental overhauls.

• Depending on how the funding of entitlement programs is resolved and how well individual baby boomers have prepared for retirement, some who reach age 65 will continue to require outside income and will be unable to retire. Many others will not want to retire and will seek flexible work options. As average life expectancies extend past 80 years of age, even many of the well-heeled will conclude that twenty years on golf courses and cruise ships do not present enough of a challenge.

• Whether they continue working or simply enjoy the fruits of past labors, America's aging baby boomers will constitute a large and powerful segment of the consumer market. Their resulting demand for entertainment, travel, and other leisure-time pursuits; specialized health care; long-term care facilities; and accounting, home-repair, and other professional services will fuel strong local labor markets throughout the U.S., but particularly in cities and regions that attract many retirees. The jobs created by this boom in the service sector in local economies may replace many of the low-skilled or unskilled manufacturing jobs the U.S. stands to lose, though not always at comparable wages.

Fourth, the U.S. labor force continues its ethnic diversification, though at a fairly slow pace. Most white non-Hispanics entering America's early twenty-first century workforce simply will replace exiting white workers; minorities will constitute slightly more than half of net new entrants to the U.S. workforce. Minorities will account for only about a third of total new entrants over the next decade.

Whites constitute 76 percent of the total labor force today and will account for 68 percent in 2020. The share of African-Americans in the labor force probably will remain constant, at 11 percent, over the next twenty years. The Asian and Hispanic shares will grow to 6 and 14 percent, respectively. Most of this change will be due to the growth of Asian and Hispanic workforce representation in the South and West. The changes will not be dramatic on a national scale. The aging of the U.S. workforce will be far more dramatic than its ethnic shifts.

10   In summary, Hudson Institute's *Workforce 2020* offers a vision of a bifurcated U.S. labor force in the early twenty-first century. As we envision the next twenty-plus years, the skills premium appears even more powerful to us than it did to our predecessors who wrote *Workforce 2000*. Millions of Americans with proficiency in math, science, and the English language will join a global elite whose services will be in intense demand. These workers will command generous and growing compensation. Burgeoning local markets for services in some parts of the U.S. will continue to sustain some decent-paying, low-skill jobs. But other Americans with inadequate education and no technological expertise—how many depends in large part on what we do to improve their training—will face declining real wages or unemployment, particularly in manufacturing.

THE UNTOUCHABLES

Thomas L. Friedman

Thomas Friedman, an investigative reporter and a columnist for the New York Times, *has won the National Book Award for* From Beirut to Jerusalem *(1989) and three Pulitzer Prizes for international reporting and commentary. Most recently he has written* Hot, Flat, and Crowded *(2008). The selection that follows appears in his best seller* The World Is Flat: A Brief History of the Twenty-First Century *(2005), in which Friedman explores the opportunities and dangers associated with globalization. Friedman uses the word "flat" to describe "the stunning rise of middle classes all over the world." In this newly flat world, "we are now connecting all the knowledge centers on the planet together into a single global network, which—if politics and terrorism do not get in the way—could usher in an amazing era of prosperity, innovation, and collaboration, by companies, communities, and individuals."*

If the flattening of the world is largely (but not entirely) unstoppable, and if it holds out the potential to be as beneficial to American society in general as past market evolutions have been, how does an individual get the best out of it? What do we tell our kids?

My simple answer is this: There will be plenty of good jobs out there in the flat world for people with the right knowledge, skills, ideas, and self-motivation to seize them. But there is no sugar-coating the new challenge: Every young American today would be wise to think of himself or herself as competing against every young Chinese, Indian, and Brazilian. In Globalization 1.0, countries had to think globally to thrive, or at least survive. In Globalization 2.0, companies had to think globally to thrive, or at least survive. In Globalization 3.0, individuals have to think globally to thrive, or at least survive. This requires not only a new level of technical skills but also a certain mental flexibility, self-motivation, and psychological mobility. I am certain that we Americans can indeed thrive in this world. But I am also certain that it will not be as easy as it was in the last fifty years. Each of us, as an individual, will have to work a little harder and run a little faster to keep our standard of living rising.

"Globalization went from globalizing industries to globalizing individuals," said Vivek Paul, the Wipro president.* "I think today that people working in most jobs can sense how what they are doing integrates globally: 'I am working with someone in India. I am buying from someone in China. I am selling to someone in England.' As a result of the ability to move work around, we have created an amazing awareness on the part of every individual that says: 'Not only does my work have to fit into somebody's global supply chain, but I myself have to understand how I need to compete and have the skill sets required to work at a pace that fits the supply chain. And I had better be able to do that as well or better than anyone else in the world.'" That sense of responsibility for one's own advancement runs deeper than ever today. In many global industries now, you have got to justify your job every day with the value you create and the unique skills you contribute. And if you don't, that job can fly away farther and faster than ever.

In sum, it was never good to be mediocre in your job, but in a world of walls, mediocrity could still earn you a decent wage. You could get by and then some. In a flatter world, you *really* do not want to be mediocre or lack any passion for what you do. You don't want to find yourself in the shoes of Willy Loman in *Death of a Salesman,* when his son Biff dispels his idea that the Loman family is special by declaring, "Pop! I'm a dime a dozen, and so are you!" An angry Willy retorts, "I am not a dime a dozen! I am Willy Loman, and you are Biff Loman!"

5   I don't care to have that conversation with my girls, so my advice to them in this flat world is very brief and very blunt: "Girls, when I was growing up, my parents used to say to me, 'Tom, finish your dinner—people in China and India are starving.' My advice to you is: Girls, finish your homework—people in China and India are starving for your jobs." And in a flat world, they can have them, because in a flat world there is no such thing as an American job. There is just a job, and in more cases than ever before it will go to the best, smartest, most productive, or cheapest worker—wherever he or she resides.

The New Middle

It is going to take more than just doing your homework to thrive in a flat world, though. You are going to have to do the *right kind* of homework as well. Because the companies that are adjusting best to the flat world are not just making minor changes, they are changing the whole model of the work they do and how they do it—in order to take advantage of the flat-world platform and to compete with others who are doing the same. What this means is that students also have to

---

*Wipro is a global technology company that provides "integrated business, technology, and process solutions" in North and South America, Europe, the Middle East, Asia, and Australia.

fundamentally reorient what they are learning and educators how they are teaching it. They can't just keep the same old model that worked for the past fifty years, when the world was round. This set of issues is what I will explore in this...chapter: What kind of good middle-class jobs are successful companies and entrepreneurs creating today? How do workers need to prepare themselves for those jobs, and how can educators help them do just that?

Let's start at the beginning. The key to thriving, as an individual, in a flat world is figuring out how to make yourself an "untouchable." That's right. When the world goes flat, the caste system gets turned upside down. In India, untouchables are the lowest social class, but in a flat world everyone should want to be an untouchable. "Untouchables," in my lexicon, are people whose jobs cannot be outsourced, digitized, or automated. And remember, as analyst David Rothkopf notes, most jobs are not lost to outsourcing to India or China—most lost jobs are "outsourced to the past." That is, they get digitized and automated. *The New York Times*'s Washington bureau used to have a telephone operator–receptionist. Now it has a recorded greeting and voice mail. That reception job didn't go to India; it went to the past or it went to a microchip. The flatter the world gets, the more anything that can be digitized, automated, or outsourced will be digitized, automated, or outsourced. As Infosys CEO Nandan Nilekani likes to say, in a flat world there is "fungible and nonfungible work." Work that can be easily digitized, automated, or transferred abroad is fungible. One of the most distinguishing features of the flat world is how many jobs—not just blue-collar manufacturing jobs but now also *white-collar service jobs*—are becoming fungible. Since more of us work in those service jobs than ever before, more of us will be affected.

. . .

[W]ho will the untouchables be? What jobs are not likely to become fungible, easy to automate, digitize, or outsource? I would argue that the untouchables in a flat world will fall into three broad categories. First are people who are really "special or specialized." This label would apply to Michael Jordan, Madonna, Elton John, J. K. Rowling, your brain surgeon, and the top cancer researcher at the National Institutes of Health. These people perform functions in ways that are so special or specialized that they can never be outsourced, automated, or made tradable by electronic transfer. They are untouchables. They have a global market for their goods and services and can command global wages.

Second are people who are really "localized" and "anchored." This category includes many, many people. They are untouchables because their jobs must be done in a specific location, either because they involve some specific local knowledge or because they require face-to-face, personalized contact or interaction with a customer, client, patient, colleague, or audience. All these people are untouchables because they are anchored: my barber, the waitress at lunch, the chefs in the kitchen, the plumber, nurses, my dentist, lounge singers, masseurs, retail sales clerks, repairmen, electricians, nannies, gardeners, cleaning ladies, and divorce lawyers. Note that these people can be working in high-end jobs (divorce lawyer, dentist), vocational jobs (plumber, carpenter), or low-end jobs (garbage collector, maid). Regardless of that worker's level of sophistication, their wages will be set by the local market forces of supply and demand.

10   That then brings me to the third broad category. This category includes people in many formerly middle-class jobs—from assembly line work to data entry to securities analysis to certain forms of accounting and radiology—that were once deemed nonfungible or nontradable and are now being made quite fungible and tradable thanks to the ten flatteners.* Let's call these the "old middle" jobs. Many of them are now under pressure from the flattening of the world. As Nandan Nilekani puts it: "The problem [for America] is in the middle. Because the days when you could count on being an accounts-payable clerk are gone. And a lot of the middle class are where that [old] middle is.... This middle has not yet grasped the competitive intensity of the future. Unless they [do], they will not make the investments in reskilling themselves and you will end up with a lot of people stranded on an island."

That is not something we want. The American economy used to look like a bell curve, with a big bulge in the middle. That bulge of middle-class jobs has been the foundation not only of our economic stability but of our political stability as well. Democracy cannot be stable without a broad and deep middle class. We cannot afford to move from a bell curve economy to a barbell economy—with a big high end and a bigger low end and nothing in the middle. It would be economically unfair and politically unstable. As former Clinton national economic adviser Gene Sperling rightly argues, "We either grow together or we will grow apart."

So if the next new thing is the automation and outsourcing of more and more old middle-class jobs, then the big question for America—and every other developed country—is this: What will be the jobs of the new middle, and what skills will they be based on? In the United States, new middle jobs are coming into being all the time; that is why we don't have large-scale unemployment, despite the flattening of the world. But to get and keep these new middle jobs you need certain skills that are suited to the flat world—skills that can make you, at least temporarily, special, specialized, or anchored, and therefore, at least temporarily, an untouchable. In the new middle, we are all temps now.

WILL YOUR JOB BE EXPORTED?

Alan S. Blinder

Alan S. Blinder is the Gordon S. Rentschler Memorial Professor of Economics at Princeton University. He has served as vice chairman of the Federal Reserve Board and was a member of President Clinton's original Council of Economic Advisers. This article first appeared in The American Prospect *in November 2006. The following summary of "Will Your Job Be Exported?" appears in Chapter 1, in the context of a discussion on how to write summaries. See pages 7–12 for the complete text of this important article.*

---

*In *The World Is Flat,* Friedman argues that ten forces have "flattened" the world. These forces include the fall of the Berlin Wall (November 1989), the emergence of Internet connectivity, and the outsourcing of work.

In "Will Your Job Be Exported?" economist Alan S. Blinder argues that the quality and security of future jobs in America's services sector will be determined by how "offshorable" those jobs are. For the past twenty-five years, the greater a worker's skill or level of education, the better and more stable the job. No longer. Advances in technology have brought to the services sector the same pressures that forced so many manufacturing jobs offshore to China and India. The rate of offshoring in the service sector will accelerate, and jobs requiring both relatively little education (like call-center staffing) and extensive education (like software development) will increasingly be lost to workers overseas.

These losses will "eventually exceed" losses in manufacturing, but not all services jobs are equally at risk. While "personal services" workers (like barbers and surgeons) will be relatively safe from offshoring because their work requires close physical proximity to customers, "impersonal services" workers (like call-center operators and radiologists), regardless of their skill or education, will be at risk because their work can be completed remotely without loss of quality and then delivered via phone or computer. "[T]he relative demand for labor in the United States will [probably] shift away from impersonal services and toward personal services."

Blinder recommends three courses of action. He advises young people to plan for "a high-end personal services occupation that is not offshorable." He urges educators to prepare the future workforce by anticipating the needs of a personal services economy and redesigning classroom instruction and vocational training accordingly. Finally, he urges the government to adopt policies that will improve existing personal services jobs by increasing wages for low-wage workers; retraining workers to take on better jobs; and increasing opportunities in high-demand, well-paid areas like nursing and carpentry. Ultimately, Blinder wants America to prepare a new generation to "lead and innovate" in an economy that will continue exporting jobs that require "following and copying."

INTO THE UNKNOWN

The Economist

The following piece first appeared in The Economist *(November 13, 2004).*

Where will the jobs of the future come from?

"Has the machine in its last furious manifestation begun to eliminate workers faster than new tasks can be found for them?" wonders Stuart Chase, an American writer. "Mechanical devices are already ousting skilled clerical workers and replacing them with operators.... Opportunity in the white-collar services is being steadily undermined." The anxiety sounds thoroughly contemporary. But Mr. Chase's publisher, MacMillan, "set up and electrotyped" his book, *Men and Machines,* in 1929.

The worry about "exporting" jobs that currently grips America, Germany and Japan is essentially the same as Mr. Chase's worry about mechanization 75 years ago. When companies move manufacturing plants from Japan to China, or call-center workers from America to India, they are changing the way they produce things. This change in production technology has the same effect as automation: some workers in America, Germany and Japan lose their jobs as machines or foreign workers take over. This fans fears of rising unemployment.

What the worriers always forget is that the same changes in production technology that destroy jobs also create new ones. Because machines and foreign workers can perform the same work more cheaply, the cost of production falls. That means higher profits and lower prices, lifting demand for new goods and services. Entrepreneurs set up new businesses to meet demand for these new necessities of life, creating new jobs.

5   As Alan Greenspan, [former] chairman of America's Federal Reserve Bank, has pointed out, there is always likely to be anxiety about the jobs of the future, because in the long run most of them will involve producing goods and services that have not yet been invented.* William Nordhaus, an economist at Yale University, has calculated that under 30% of the goods and services consumed at the end of the 20th century were variants of the goods and services produced 100 years earlier. "We travel in vehicles that were not yet invented that are powered by fuels not yet produced, communicate through devices not yet manufactured, enjoy cool air on the hottest days, are entertained by electronic wizardry that was not dreamed of and receive medical treatments that were unheard of," writes Mr. Nordhaus. What hardy late 19th-century American pioneer would have guessed that, barely more than a century later, his country would find employment for (by the government's latest count) 139,000 psychologists, 104,000 floral designers and 51,000 manicurists and pedicurists?

Even relatively short-term labor-market predictions can be hazardous. In 1988, government experts at the Bureau of Labor Statistics confidently predicted strong demand in America over the next 12 years for, among others, travel agents and [gas]-station attendants. But by 2000, the number of travel agents had fallen by 6% because more travellers booked online, and the number of pump attendants was down to little more than half because drivers were filling up their cars themselves. Of the 20 occupations that the government predicted would suffer the most job losses between 1988 and 2000, half actually gained jobs. Travel agents have now joined the government's list of endangered occupations for 2012. Maybe they are due for a modest revival. You never know.

The bureau's statisticians are now forecasting a large rise in the number of nurses, teachers, salespeople, "combined food preparation and serving workers, including fast food" (a fancy way of saying burger flippers), waiters, truck drivers and security guards over the next eight years. If that list fails to strike a chord with recent Stanford graduates, the bureau also expects America to create an extra 179,000 software-engineering jobs and 185,000 more places for computer-systems analysts over the same period.

Has the bureau forgotten about Bangalore? Probably not. Catherine Mann of the Institute for International Economics points out that the widely quoted number of half a million for [Information Technology] jobs "lost" to India in the past couple of years takes as its starting point the year 2001, the top of the industry's cycle. Most of the subsequent job losses were due to the recession in the industry

---

*Alan Greenspan served as chairman of the Federal Reserve Bank from 1987 to 2006.

rather than to an exodus to India. Measured from 1999 to 2003, the number of IT-related white-collar jobs in America has risen....

Ms. Mann thinks that demand will continue to grow as falling prices help to spread IT more widely through the economy, and as American companies demand more tailored software and services. Azim Premji, the boss of Wipro,[†] is currently trying to expand his business in America. "IT professionals are in short supply in America," says Mr. Premji. "Within the next few months, we will have a labor shortage."

10   If that seems surprising, it illustrates a larger confusion about jobs and work. Those who worry about the migration of white-collar work abroad like to talk about "lost jobs" or "jobs at risk." Ashok Bardhan, an economist at the University of California at Berkeley, thinks that 14 [million] Americans, a whopping 11% of the workforce, are in jobs "at risk to outsourcing." The list includes computer operators, computer professionals, paralegals and legal assistants. But what Mr. Bardhan is really saying is that some of this work can now also be done elsewhere.

What effect this has on jobs and pay will depend on supply and demand in the labor market and on the opportunity, willingness and ability of workers to retrain. American computer professionals, for instance, have been finding recently that certain skills, such as maintaining standard business-software packages, are no longer in such demand in America, because there are plenty of Indian programmers willing to do this work more cheaply. On the other hand, IT firms in America face a shortage of skills in areas such as tailored business software and services. There is a limited supply of fresh IT graduates to recruit and train in America, so companies such as IBM and Accenture are having to retrain their employees in these sought-after skills.

Moreover, Mr. Bardhan's list of 14 [million] jobs at risk features many that face automation anyway, regardless of whether the work is first shipped abroad. Medical transcriptionists, data-entry clerks and a large category of 8.6 [million] miscellaneous "office support" workers may face the chop as companies find new ways of mechanizing paperwork and capturing information.

Indeed, the definition of the sort of work that Indian outsourcing firms are good at doing remotely—repetitive and bound tightly by rules—sounds just like the sort of work that could also be delegated to machines. If offshoring is to be blamed for this "lost" work, then mechanical diggers should be blamed for usurping the work of men with shovels. In reality, shedding such lower-value tasks enables economies to redeploy the workers concerned to jobs that create more value.

Stuart Chase understood the virtuous economics of technological change, but he still could not stop himself from fretting. "An uneasy suspicion has gathered that the saturation point has at last been reached" he reflected darkly. Could it be that, with the invention of the automobile, central heating, the phonograph and the electric refrigerator, entrepreneurs had at long last emptied the reservoir of human desires? He need not have worried. Today's list of human desires includes instant messaging, online role-playing games and internet dating services, all unknown in the 1920s. And there will be many more tomorrow.

[†]See footnote on page 318.

EMPLOYMENT PROJECTIONS: *2008–2018* SUMMARY

Bureau of Labor Statistics

The Bureau of Labor Statistics, a division of the U.S. Department of Labor, releases ten-year employment projections, updated every two years, as part of a "60-year tradition of providing information to individuals who are making education and training choices, entering the job market, or changing careers." What follows is a summary of the data released by the BLS on December 11, 2009. At the end of this selection, you will be referred to ten tables (available online) accompanying this summary.

Employment Projections — 2008–18

Total employment is projected to increase by 15.3 million, or 10.1 percent, during the 2008–18 period, the U.S. Bureau of Labor Statistics reported today.

The projections show an aging and more racially and ethnically diverse labor force, and employment growth in service-providing industries. More than half of the new jobs will be in professional and related occupations and service occupations. In addition, occupations where a postsecondary degree or award is usually required are expected to account for one-third of total job openings during the projection period. Job openings from replacement needs—those which occur when workers who retire or otherwise leave their occupations need to be replaced—are projected to be more than double the number of openings due to economic growth.

The projected growth for the 2008–18 period is larger than the increase of 10.4 million over the 1998–2008 period, or 7.4 percent. The relatively slow growth rate for the earlier 10-year period was affected by the recession which began in December 2007, and the projected growth rate is higher than would otherwise be expected because the 2008 starting point is a recession year.

This news release focuses on four areas for which BLS develops projections—labor force, industry employment, occupational employment, and education and training.

Labor Force

5   The civilian labor force is projected to grow by 12.6 million between 2008 and 2018, to 166.9 million persons. Slower population growth and a decreasing overall labor force participation rate are expected to contribute to a slowdown in labor force growth. The projected 8.2-percent increase for the 2008–18 period is less than the 12.1-percent growth that occurred between 1998 and 2008. (See Table 1.*)

As the members of the large baby boom generation grow older and continue their trend of increased labor force participation, the number of persons age 55 years and older in the labor force is expected to increase by 12.0 million, or 43.0 percent, during the 2008–18 period. Persons in the 55 years and older age group are projected to make up nearly one-quarter of the labor force in 2018. Young people (age 16–24) are expected to account for 12.7 percent of the labor force in 2018, and persons in the prime-age working group (age 25 to 54) to account for 63.5 percent of the 2018 labor force.

---

*The URLs for Tables 1–10 can be found on page 327.

The labor force in 2018 will be more diverse. As a result of higher population growth among minorities—due to higher birth rates and increased immigration, along with higher labor force participation rates by Hispanics and Asians—the share of the labor force held by minorities is projected to increase significantly. Whites will remain the largest race group in the labor force in 2018 (79.4 percent) despite growing by just 5.5 percent between 2008 and 2018. The number of Asians in the labor force is projected to increase by 29.8 percent and the number of blacks by 14.1 percent. In 2018, Asians are projected to comprise 5.6 percent of the labor force and blacks to make up 12.1 percent.

Hispanics (who can be of any race) will join the labor force in greater numbers than non-Hispanics. The number of Hispanics in the labor force is projected to grow by 7.3 million or 33.1 percent. Their share of the labor force will expand from 14.3 percent in 2008 to 17.6 percent in 2018. In contrast, the number of persons in the labor force not of Hispanic origin is expected to grow by 4.0 percent, and their share of the labor force to decline to 82.4 percent.

Industry Employment

Projected employment growth is concentrated in the service-providing sector, continuing a long-term shift from the goods-producing sector of the economy. From 2008 to 2018, service-providing industries are projected to add 14.6 million jobs, or 96 percent of the increase in total employment. The 2 industry sectors expected to have the largest employment growth are professional and business services (4.2 million) and health care and social assistance (4.0 million).

10   Goods-producing employment, as a whole, is expected to show virtually no growth. While employment in the construction industry is projected to increase by 1.3 million, declines in manufacturing (–1.2 million) and mining (–104,000) will nearly offset this growth. By 2018, the goods-producing sector is expected to account for 12.9 percent of total jobs, down from 17.3 percent in 1998 and 14.2 percent in 2008. (See Table 2.)

Three of the 10 detailed industries projected to have the most employment growth are in professional and business services: management, scientific, and technical consulting; computer systems design; and employment services. Altogether, these 3 industries are expected to add 2.1 million jobs. Four of the top 10 gainers are in health care and social assistance industries. Employment in offices of physicians, home health care, services for the elderly and persons with disabilities, and nursing care facilities is expected to grow by 2.0 million. (See Table 3.)

Of the 10 detailed industries with the largest projected employment declines, 4 are in the manufacturing sector and 2 each are within retail trade and information. The largest decline among the detailed industries is expected to be in department stores, with a loss of 159,000 jobs, followed by manufacturers of semiconductors (–146,000) and motor vehicle parts (–101,000). (See Table 4.)

Occupational Employment

Two major occupational groups—professional and related occupations and service occupations—are projected to provide more than half of the total employment growth during the 2008–18 period. Production occupations are projected to decline.

The 30 detailed occupations with the largest gains in employment are expected to account for nearly half of all new jobs, and 17 of these occupations are professional and related occupations and service occupations. The detailed occupation projected to add the most jobs is registered nurses (582,000), followed by home health aides (461,000) and customer service representatives (400,000). All but 3 of the top 30 fastest-growing detailed occupations are found within professional and related occupations and service occupations. Seventeen of these rapidly growing occupations are related to healthcare or medical research. (See Tables 5, 6, and 7.)

Of the 30 detailed occupations projected to have the largest employment declines, 12 are production occupations and 11 are office and administrative support occupations. (See Table 8.)

Education and Training

15   Occupations that usually require a postsecondary degree or award are expected to account for nearly half of all new jobs from 2008 to 2018 and one-third of total job openings. Among the education and training categories, the fastest growth will occur in occupations requiring an associate degree. (See Table 9.)

Short- and moderate-term on-the-job training are the most significant sources of postsecondary education or training for 17 of the 30 detailed occupations projected to have the largest employment growth. However, in terms of percent growth, 14 of the 30 fastest- growing detailed occupations have a bachelor's degree or higher as the most significant source of postsecondary education or training. (See Tables 6 and 7.)

Of the 30 detailed occupations projected to have the largest employment declines, 17 are classified as having short-term on-the-job training as the most significant source of education and training, and 10 are in the moderate-term on-the-job training category. (See Table 8.)

Total job openings during the 2008–18 period are projected to be 50.9 million, and 19.6 million of these jobs are expected to be in the short-term on-the-job training category. Sixteen of the 30 detailed occupations with the most job openings will have short-term on-the-job training as the most significant source of education and training. (See Tables 9 and 10.)

A Note on Labor Shortages in the Context of Long-Term Economic Projections

Users of these data should not assume that the difference between the projected increase in the labor force and the projected increase in employment implies a labor shortage or surplus. Employment and labor force measures differ in concept. Employment is a count of jobs, and persons who hold more than one job would be counted for each job. Labor force is a count of individuals, and a person is counted only once regardless of how many jobs he or she holds. In addition, the BLS projections assume a labor market in equilibrium, that is, one where labor supply meets labor demand except for some degree of frictional unemployment. For a discussion of the basic projection methodology, see "Employment projections, 2008–18," Kristina Bartsch, November 2009, *Monthly Labor Review*.

[Editors' note: If the links listed below do not work, search on the title of the table, in quotation marks, followed by "BLS."]

- Table 1. Civilian labor force by age, sex, race, and Hispanic origin, 1998, 2008, and projected 2018

  [http://www.bls.gov/news.release/ecopro.t01.htm]

- Table 2. Employment by major industry sector, 1998, 2008, and projected 2018

  [http://www.bls.gov/news.release/ecopro.t02.htm]

- Table 3. The 10 industries with the largest wage and salary employment growth, 2008–18 (1)

  [http://www.bls.gov/news.release/ecopro.t03.htm]

- Table 4. The 10 industries with the largest wage and salary employment declines, 2008–18 (1)

  [http://www.bls.gov/news.release/ecopro.t04.htm]

- Table 5. Employment by major occupational group, 2008 and projected 2018

  [http://www.bls.gov/news.release/ecopro.t05.htm]

- Table 6. The 30 occupations with the largest employment growth, 2008–18

  [http://www.bls.gov/news.release/ecopro.t06.htm]

- Table 7. The 30 fastest-growing occupations, 2008–18

  [http://www.bls.gov/news.release/ecopro.t07.htm]

- Table 8. The 30 occupations with the largest employment declines, 2008–18

  [http://www.bls.gov/news.release/ecopro.t08.htm]

- Table 9. Employment and total job openings by postsecondary education or training category, 2008–18

  [http://www.bls.gov/news.release/ecopro.t09.htm]

- Table 10. The 30 occupations with the largest number of total job openings due to growth and replacements, 2008–18

  [http://www.bls.gov/news.release/ecopro.t10.htm]

■ LOOKING FORWARD: FIVE PROFESSIONS ■

The selections that follow explore the contours of future work in engineering, business, technology, law, and medicine. As you read, apply the observations of writers from the previous selections to the particulars of these five professions. Questions to consider:

- To what extent do the observations of Judy and D'Amico, Friedman, Blinder, and *The Economist* ring true?

- What features do you find most striking about future employment in each profession?

- What features generalize across professions?

- To what extent do you find yourself encouraged or discouraged by what you read?
- To what extent does the Bureau of Labor Statistics data confirm what the authors report (or project) about each profession?

Read actively. For each selection, make marginal notes that both summarize and evaluate. Also, create connections among sources: List topics and assign authors and page references to each, as appropriate.

ENGINEERING
Victoria Reitz

The selection that follows, originally titled "Want to Outsourceproof Your Career? Don't Become a Commodity," first appeared in Machine Design *(April 26, 2007).*

We asked over 1,500 engineers what they thought about their careers, what keeps them in their jobs, and what the future of engineering will look like. Sixty-four percent of them feel secure or very secure in their current positions, and 24% say engineers have been laid off from their companies in the last year. And best of all, salaries are up. The average annual wage is $76,900, up from $73,300 last year. For 65% of survey takers this was an increase of 1 to 5% over last year.

Sixty-two percent received a bonus, overtime, or special incentive compensation, based mainly on company profit sharing and personal performance. About 40% received 1 to 5% of their annual pay as bonus.

Most respondents, 78%, would recommend engineering as a career to friends and family, and 61% believe the job has gotten better during their careers. Of the 71% whose companies outsource, 78% farm out manufacturing, 44% outsource mechanical design, and 30% contract CAD work.

Is There a Future for Engineers?

Many survey takers expressed concern about the future of technology and innovation in the U.S., feeling that as more manufacturing jobs head overseas, there will be less demand for technical skills. But experts say just the opposite. "There is a high, unmet demand for engineering talent," says Scott Kingdom, a senior client partner and global managing director at Korn/Ferry International. Kingdom oversees recruiting at the executive search firm. "Employers I talk to say they would hire more engineers if they could find them." He also adds, "Because engineering skills are in such demand, other countries are busy training citizens to fill these roles."

5   Why the shortage of talent? "One reason might be that our educational system doesn't foster and promote science and engineering," Kingdom adds. "Another is that the economy is moving more and more into the service sector. Some of our best minds get pulled into service-related organizations such as banking and consulting, that might otherwise have gone into engineering."

Make Yourself Valuable

What can you do to ensure a successful career? "Sharp, intelligent engineers with leadership and business skills can just about write their own career path," says Kingdom. "Make sure your technical skills are cutting edge and develop management skills. Get involved in jobs that put you in leadership roles," he adds. Also, consider accepting projects and responsibilities outside the U.S.

Innovation is the key to keeping technical jobs in the U.S., according to Kingdom. Businesses that manufacture commodities will likely go offshore, "and probably should go offshore. But where there is real innovation, there is real demand for engineering services and skills."

The same can be said of your career. If your skills and talent are a commodity, you're easily replaced. Make sure you add value and innovation. "There's no one in this economy that can sit still and decide they don't want to change. The world is evolving around us so fast, you'll be irrelevant quickly."

BUSINESS

Tom Peters

The selection that follows, originally titled "The New Wired World of Work: A More Transparent Workplace Will Mean More White-collar Accountability and Less Tolerance for Hangers-on," first appeared in Business Week *(April 9, 2008).*

You're hiking along near the Grand Canyon in August, 2000, but fretting about the progress your virtual partner in Kuala Lumpur has made in the past 24 hours? No problem! Your local Kampgrounds of America campsite now has Internet access.

Call it the new wired world of work. Depending on how you view it, it's intrusive, pervasive, or merely ubiquitous. But it's definitely not your dad's office. And this perpetually plugged-in existence is just the beginning of the changes we'll see in the 21st century white-collar workplace.

Work in the '50s and '60s meant trudging to the same office for decades. Same colleagues. Same processes, mostly rote. Former MCI Communications Chief Bill McGowan called yesterday's middle managers "human message switches." And the information was laughably dated. Closing the account books at month's end could drag on for weeks. Customer data were nonexistent, or hopelessly unreliable.

But in the next few years, whether at a tiny company or behemoth, we will be working with an eclectic mix of contract teammates from around the globe, many of whom we'll never meet face-to-face. Every project will call for a new team, composed of specially tailored skills. Info that's more than hours old will be viewed with concern.

5   Every player on this team will be evaluated—pass by pass, at-bat by at-bat—for the quality and uniqueness and timeliness and passion of her or his contribution. And therein lies the peril, and the remarkable opportunity, of this weird, wired, wild new age of work. White-collar accountability has until now been mostly an oxymoron.

Show up, suck up, process your paper flow with a modicum of efficiency, and you could count on a pretty decent end-of-year evaluation, a cost-of-living-plus raise, and a sure-as-death-and-taxes 40-year tenure at Desk No. 263.

Now you are like a New York Yankees or Los Angeles Dodgers closer. A couple of blown saves following a night on the town and your pressured and performance-driven teammates, more than your manager, are ready to show you the exit. This will hold for the freshly minted University of Wisconsin grad as well as the 56-year-old who had envisioned himself on a pain-free coast toward retirement. There may be a tight labor market for stellar performers, but the flip side is much less tolerance for hangers-on.

As enterprise resource-planning software and other such systems wreak havoc on the vast majority of staff jobs in the next decade, what will it take for you and me to navigate and win? Here's a list of minimal survival skills for the 21st century office worker:

• Mastery: To thrive in tomorrow's transparent team environment, the typical white-collar worker will have to be noticeably good at something the world values. "HR guy" doesn't cut it. Nor does "CPA." What subset of, say, techie recruiting skills or international accountancy excellence makes you a clearly valued contributor? I firmly believe that if you can't describe your distinction in the space of a one-sixteenth-page Yellow Pages ad, you will be doomed.

• Who Do You Know?: The new Rolodex will deemphasize bosses and traditional power figures, focusing more on peers (future project mates!) who appreciate your clear-cut contributions. I consider my own electronic Rolodex to be my Extended Global University, colleagues I can call upon (and who can call upon me) to further my current and future projects.

• Entrepreneurial Instinct: You do not have to start your own business. But as I see it, all these projects are entrepreneurial. So you must act as if you were running your own business. Think of yourself as Maggie Inc., who happens to be at General Electric Capital Services Inc. at the moment. And speaking of which, I fully expect women to dominate managerial roles. I think they tend to handle ambiguity better than we guys do. The new world is a floating crap game, with new projects, new teammates, and a constant need to adjust. Those who can operate in the absence of laid-out bounds will be the leaders.

• Love of Technology: Technology is changing everything. Believe the hype—if anything, it's understated. You need not be a technologist per se, but you must embrace technology. "Coping" with it is not enough.

• Marketing: You do not have to become a shameless self-promoter, a la Martha Stewart. But you must get your story out on the airwaves. Do it via your personal Web site. Do it by telling your project's story at a trade show.

• Passion for Renewal: You've got to constantly improve and, on occasion, reinvent yourself. My bread and butter—at age 57—are my lectures. But I imagine that the Internet will devour many conventional meetings in a few years. Hence I am madly working with several groups that will deliver my message via the new technologies.

I love to read Dilbert and usually choke with laughter. But I have a problem with the subtext: My company stinks, my boss stinks, my job stinks. If that's your take—at this moment of monumental change and gargantuan opportunity—then I can only feel sad for you. We get to reinvent the world. I feel so damn lucky!

TECHNOLOGY AND SERVICES
Steve Lohr

The selection that follows, originally titled "Creating the Jobs of the Future" first appeared in the New York Times (April 17, 2006).

On his Asian trip last month, President George W. Bush urged Americans to not fear the rise toward prosperity of emerging economies like India. Education, Bush said, was the best response to globalization, climbing further up the ladder of skills to "fill the jobs of the 21st century."

But a ladder to where? That is, where are educated young Americans likely to find good jobs that will not be shipped off to India or China?

The answer, according to a growing number of universities, corporations and government agencies, is in what is being called services science. The hybrid field seeks to use technology, management, mathematics and engineering expertise to improve the performance of service businesses like transportation, retailing and health care—as well as service functions like marketing, design or customer service that are also crucial in manufacturing industries.

A couple of dozen universities—including the University of California at Berkeley, Arizona State, Stanford, North Carolina State, Rensselaer Polytechnic Institute and Georgia Tech—are experimenting with courses or research programs in the field.

5   The push for services science is partly a game of catch-up, a belated recognition that services now account for 70 percent of the U.S. economy, so education, research and policy should reflect the shift. "Services is a drastically understudied field," said Matthew Realff, director of a new program at the National Science Foundation to finance university research in the field. "We need a revolution in services."

Kurt Koester, a 24-year-old graduate student in engineering at Berkeley, is eager to take part. Yet engineering alone, he observes, can often be outsourced to lower-cost economies overseas.

Koester's special interest is in biomedical engineering, which combines engineering and biology. And he is also taking the services science course at the Haas School of Business at Berkeley. He figures it should help him someday better manage teams of technologists, spot innovations and new markets, and blend products and services.

"I love engineering, but I want a much broader and more diverse background," he said. "Hopefully, that will be my competitive advantage."

His personal strategy, according to economists, is the best way to prepare for an increasingly global labor market.

10   "This is how you address the global challenge," said Jerry Sheehan, a senior economist at the Organization for Economic Cooperation and Development. "You have to move up to do more complex, higher-value work."

Representatives from technology companies including International Business Machines, Accenture, Electronic Data Systems and Hewlett-Packard, a few universities and government agencies met in Washington in December to discuss how to raise interest in services science. A further step is a conference on education in services science being held Tuesday at the National Academy of Sciences.

IBM is a leading corporate proponent of services science, sponsoring workshops, awarding research grants and helping develop course materials.

IBM itself is a striking example of the shift toward services over the past decade or two. Once known as a computer maker, the company now gets half its revenue from services. And increasingly, IBM is moving into sophisticated technology services, by working with corporate customers to automate and streamline business tasks like purchasing, human relations and customer relations programs.

In recent years, IBM has shopped the global labor market, expanding significantly in India, especially for software programming work. But it has also reoriented and retrained its existing work force to support the swing to services.

15   The researchers in its laboratories were dubious at first. "The response here was there is no science in services," recalled Paul Horn, the senior vice president in charge of the IBM labs. "But as people got into it, they got excited by working on the fascinating problems in services."

Baruch Schieber, 48, is one of the converts. After joining IBM in 1987, Schieber did basic research and published articles in scholarly journals mostly on algorithms that optimize computing calculations. Yet the math techniques used to make work flow efficiently through a computer—a complex system—can be applied to other complex systems in business. That is what Schieber did, first in manufacturing and later in services.

One recent assignment had Schieber studying drivers and dispatchers at Boston Coach, a limousine service that operates in 10 cities. His job was to create a computerized optimization system to improve the utilization of vehicles and drivers in Boston and New York, where the company handles more than 1,000 rides a day.

The system gathered real-time data on car locations, reservations, travel times, traffic patterns, airport conditions and flight times. The system generated recommendations to the dispatchers about which car and driver to send for each ride. The car utilization rate rose 20 percent, and revenue increased 10 percent.

An accumulation of technological advances is behind the growing interest in services science. The spread of high-speed Internet access, low-cost computing, wireless networks, electronic sensors and ever-smarter software are the tools for building a "globalized services economy," said Anatole Gershman, director of research at Accenture Technology Labs. "That's what is new here."

20   The current wave of technology, according to Gershman, is the digital equivalent of national railways and electric motors in the 19th century. They paved the way for new companies and new kinds of industrial organization, from national retailers like Sears to assembly-line mass production.

He points to projects his company is doing as examples of services made possible by new technology. In transportation, networked sensors and analytic software are being used to diagnose the condition of engines. The goal is to make the mechanical upkeep of everything from jets to municipal buses more intelligent, shifting from regimented maintenance schedules to as-needed maintenance, which can reduce repair and maintenance costs by 50 percent, he said.

In health care, Gershman said, it should be possible to use tiny implants to monitor a person's biological functions, whisk reports wirelessly to personalized databases, automatically analyze the results, and send alerts and updates to patients and doctors.

"Just what will be done with this technology we don't know," Gershman said. "But the significant thing is that we now have the underpinnings for the construction of new services."

Even in manufacturing, the competitive edge of many American companies lies in the intangible realm of service work. Look at the iPod. Apple Computer farms out the manufacturing of its popular music player to Asian subcontractors. But Apple designed the iPod and wrote the software for easily finding, storing and playing music. It built the iPod brand, and guided its advertising and marketing. In short, Apple keeps for itself the most intellectually challenging, creative work, which adds the most value and pays the highest wages.

25   The high-end work, experts say, typically taps several disciplines, requires conceptual thinking and pattern recognition. Such work cannot be easily reduced to a simple step-by-step recipe. "Those are the jobs that are very hard to automate or ship to India," said Frank Levy, a labor economist at the Massachusetts Institute of Technology.

LAW

Tom McGrath

The selection that follows, originally titled "The Last Days of the Philadelphia Lawyer," first appeared in Philadelphia *magazine (April 2008). While nominally the writer investigates changes in the legal profession in Philadelphia, the changes he observes are occurring nationwide, throughout the profession.*

Lawyers, it probably goes without saying, like to argue, but the one thing they all agree on is that over the past two decades, their once high-minded profession has been transformed into a high-stakes business. "A revolution has occurred," says Michael Coleman, one of the city's preeminent legal recruiters. That revolution may only be a prologue to an even bigger transformation now taking place: the high-stakes business slamming head-on into the fast-moving, and generally unforgiving, 21st-century global economy.

"The world is flat," Alderman tells his Penn Law students one day, as they're seated around a seminar table. Alderman's course is called "The Law of Law Firms," and in contrast to the legal-reasoning courses that make up the bulk of a law student's education, this class attempts to give the next generation of lawyers a realistic view of the business they're getting themselves into.

...[T]he technological and economic changes affecting all of us are certainly making an impact on lawyers—particularly on the dozen or so largest, most prestigious firms in Philadelphia. For starters, the pressure is on firms to be bigger and broader—to open offices in all the places around the world where their clients are doing business....

Even more important, though, is that the market for legal services has been, if not globalized, at least nationalized—which means that Philly firms are now competing for clients with firms in New York and Chicago and Charlotte and anywhere else easily reachable with a BlackBerry and some frequent-flier miles.

5   The heightened competition—combined with the bottom-line mentality that began taking hold at least 15 years ago—has spun off its own consequences. While lawyers at big firms make more money than ever, there's a certain sense of ennui among many in the profession. Previous generations of attorneys had the sense that in practicing law, they were serving the public good. A fair number of lawyers today fret that what they do has no more value than selling used cars. "It can suck the soul out of you," one lawyer complains of the constant focus on billable hours and client development and all the other things lawyers now do that aren't actually practicing law. Says another, of the pressure to make more and more profits, "How much is enough?"

The answer to...the broader question of why the legal profession in America currently operates the way it does—can be traced back to changes that started in the 1980s....

The impact of the *American Lawyer* rankings [of law firms according to how much money they earned] over the past two decades is tough to overestimate. For starters, they've transformed the mind-sets of many lawyers—or at least those who run large law firms. Twenty years ago, a partner at a Philadelphia firm might have been very happy making $150,000 per year—until he saw that lawyers at a firm in, say, Boston were making $250,000 per year. Telling competitive people like lawyers how much their peers were making was like giving someone with an addictive personality his first hit on a crack pipe.

Just as important, though, is that over the years, large firms have come to realize that the Am Law rankings are their best marketing tool when it comes to attracting the best law-school graduates and, now, the best partners from other firms—partners who bring with them books of clients that contribute handsomely to the bottom line. After all, why stay at a firm with profits per partner of only $400,000 per year when folks at the firm down the road are making 20 percent more?

...[T]he Am Law rankings—both literally, in the sense that firms care enormously about where they fall on them, and figuratively, in the sense that they represent a legal world all about the Benjamins—have become the dominant measuring stick in the legal industry.

10   If there's an irony in law having become a business, it's that law, it turns out, isn't a very *good* business—or at least doesn't have a very efficient business model. While manufacturers typically make money through economies of scale, and other service professionals, like investment bankers or architects, make

money by taking a percentage of a deal or the cost of a project, lawyers for the most part still work for an hourly wage. In short, they're in the business of selling their time.

The problem, of course, is that time is finite, so even if you're selling those hours for an exorbitantly high rate—a handful of lawyers in Philadelphia can charge up to $1,000 an hour—it can be tough to build a successful, globally competitive business.

To compensate for that labor-intensive business model, firms have adopted various strategies. Strategy number one: Make young lawyers—associates—bill as many hours as humanly possible. In the 1960s and '70s, associates at big firms were expected to bill between 1,600 and 1,800 per year; today, the expectation is generally around 2,200 hours per year. And since not every hour you spend at the office can be billed to a client, associates typically end up putting in 80-to-90-hour weeks. With starting associate salaries approaching $150,000 at Philly's biggest firms, this might not be so bad—if the work was consistently challenging intellectually, and if the path to becoming a partner was as fast as it used to be. But some associates complain that they spend their days locked in the office, pushing through paper. As for partnership, it's a reward that takes longer and longer to realize these days.

But associates aren't the only ones for whom the rules of the game have changed. While once it was enough for a partner at a firm simply to be a smart practitioner who understood the law and served his clients well, today the focus is less on what you do in the courtroom or boardroom than on what kind of business you bring in the door. In the past, becoming a partner at a big firm was pretty much like becoming a tenured college professor—you were there for as long as you wanted to be. Today, it's not unheard-of for a partner to be de-equitized—essentially, pushed back to being a salaried employee—or driven out completely. "I know some lawyers in their 50s who have been asked to leave their firms because they don't have a book of business," says Steve Cozen, of Cozen O'Connor. "The problem is, they were never told they *had* to have a book of business. It used to be enough for them just to be good lawyers."

In some firms, it's no longer enough even to have clients—they must be clients who can pay hourly rates hefty enough to support an insatiable appetite for profits. Over the past few years, Dechert [Philadelphia's most profitable law firm] has rid itself of several practice areas that simply didn't command high enough rates from clients, including media law, which was led by respected First Amendment attorney Amy Ginensky, who last year moved to Pepper Hamilton after 28 years at Dechert. Ginensky says she could have stayed, but she didn't like the constraints the firm's economic strategy placed on her. "I didn't want to decide what cases to take based solely on how much money they would make," she says. Dechert's strategy is one any businessman would understand instantly—if a product line isn't profitable enough, you discontinue it and move on to something else. But for the lawyers involved, who were asked to practice a different type of law or simply to leave, it's a tough adjustment to make. "We're dealing with human capital, not widgets," says legal recruiter Michael Coleman. "I don't know if when you're 45, you want to be retooled."

MEDICINE

Matt Richtel

The selection that follows, originally titled "Young Doctors and Wish Lists: No Weekend Calls, No Beepers," first appeared in the New York Times *(January 7, 2004).*

Jennifer C. Boldrick lights up when the topic turns to blisters, eczema and skin cancer. She is also a big fan of getting a full night of sleep. And the combination of these interests has led Dr. Boldrick to become part of a marked shift in the medical profession.

Dr. Boldrick, 31, a graduate of Stanford University Medical School, is training to become a dermatologist. Dermatology has become one of the most competitive fields for new doctors, with a 40 percent increase in students pursuing the profession over the last five years, compared with a 40 percent drop in those interested in family practice.

The field may have acquired its newfound chic from television shows like "Nip/Tuck" and the vogue for cosmetic treatments like Botox, but for young doctors it satisfies another longing. Today's medical residents, half of them women, are choosing specialties with what experts call a "controllable lifestyle." Dermatologists typically do not work nights or weekends, have decent control over their time and are often paid out of pocket, rather than dealing with the inconveniences of insurance.

"The surgery lifestyle is so much worse," said Dr. Boldrick, who rejected a career in plastic surgery. "I want to have a family. And when you work 80 or 90 hours a week, you can't even take care of yourself."

5   Other specialties also enjoying a surge in popularity are radiology, anesthesiology and even emergency-room medicine, which despite their differences all allow doctors to put work behind them when their shifts end, and make medicine less all-encompassing, more like a 9-to-5 job.

What young doctors say they want is that "when they finish their shift, they don't carry a beeper; they're done," said Dr. Gregory W. Rutecki, chairman of medical education at Evanston Northwestern Healthcare, a community hospital affiliated with the Feinberg School of Medicine at Northwestern University.

Lifestyle considerations accounted for 55 percent of a doctor's choice of specialty in 2002, according to a paper in the *Journal of the American Medical Association* in September by Dr. Rutecki and two co-authors. That factor far outweighs income, which accounted for only 9 percent of the weight prospective residents gave in selecting a specialty.

Many of the brightest students vie for several hundred dermatology residency spots. The National Residency Matching Program, which matches medical school graduates to residency openings, reported that in 2002, 338 medical school seniors were interested in dermatology, up from 244 in 1997—though the 2002 figure still represented only 2.3 percent of the potential doctor pool.

In 2002, 944 seniors wanted to pursue anesthesiology, compared with 243 five years earlier—while the interest in radiology almost doubled, to 903 from 463, according to the matching program's figures.

10   Numerous medical educators noted that the growth of interest in these fields coincided with a drop in students drawn to more traditional—and all-consuming—fields. In 2002, the number of students interested in general surgery dropped to 1,123 from 1,437, for example.

And that has many doctors and educators concerned. "There's a brain drain to dermatology, radiology and anesthesia," Dr. Rutecki said. He said that students who are not selected for residencies in these lifestyle-friendly specialties are choosing internal medicine by default.

"Not only are we getting interest from people lower in the class, but we're getting a number of them because they have nowhere else to go," Dr. Rutecki said.

This notion of a "brain drain" to subspecialties from the bread and butter fields of medicine is not new. But in recent years it has come to be associated with a flight to more lucrative fields. What is new, say medical educators, is an emphasis on way of life. In some cases, it even means doctors are willing to take lower-paying jobs—say, in emergency room medicine—or work part time. In other fields, like dermatology and radiology, doctors can enjoy both more control over their time and a relatively hefty paycheck.

According to the American Medical Association, a dermatologist averages $221,000 annually for 45.5 hours of work per week. That's more lucrative—and less time-consuming—than internal medicine or pediatrics, where doctors earn around $135,000 and spend more than 50 hours a week at work. A general surgeon averages $238,000 for a 60-hour week, while an orthopedist makes $323,000 for a 58-hour week. The number of dermatology residencies has been steadily growing. The American Academy of Dermatology says there are 343 dermatology residents in their third year, 377 in their second year, and 392 in their first.

15   The trend comes as the medical profession is already struggling to balance the demands of patient care with the strain put on doctors from overwork. Since last year, new rules have limited a resident's hours to 80 hours a week.

Some medical careers, like radiology, entail working long hours but not responding to patient emergencies on nights and weekends.

Educators point to a number of factors to explain the newfound emphasis on lifestyle. Dr. Elliott Wolfe, director of professional development for medical students at Stanford, cites the growing proportion of medical students who are women; in the 2002–3 year they made up 49.1 percent of entering students, according to the American Medical Association. Dermatology offers more control and income than, say, pediatrics and family medicine, which have traditionally drawn women.

Lee Ann Michelson, director of premedical and health care advising at Harvard University, said undergraduates considering a future in medicine are extremely concerned about whether they can have a life outside of medicine. She said she talks to numerous children of physicians who are concerned they will be as absent in the lives of their children, as their parents were.

The symbol for "controllable lifestyle" is dermatology. And when residents graduate they can count on plenty of faces and bodies to heal and reconstruct, thanks to an aging, and affluent, population. One-stop dermatology spas seem to open weekly in Manhattan, offering lunchtime visitors quick-fix lip fillers, laser procedures and face peels. It's not fast food, it's fast facial.

20   "You make your own hours. You can see 15 patients a day, or 10 patients a day. There are very few emergencies. It's not an acute situation, ever," said Dr. Dennis Gross, a Manhattan dermatologist. Plus, he said the procedures dermatologists perform can be lucrative; a 12-minute Botox treatment can cost a patient $400, with the doctor keeping half, for instance.

And the procedures often are elective, meaning that patients pay out of their own pockets. "It's cash, check or credit card," said Dr. Wolfe of Stanford.

The difference in lives is well illustrated by the experience of Z. Paul Lorenc and Marek M. Lorenc, 48-year-old twin brothers who chose careers on different ends of the spectrum.

Marek is a dermatologist in Santa Rosa, Calif., north of San Francisco. He gets into work at 8 a.m., leaves at 6 p.m., and is rarely called to the hospital at night, giving him ample time to spend with his wife and two children. "When I'm done," he said, "I'm a husband and a father. I go to soccer games. I coach soccer games."

His brother is a plastic surgeon in Manhattan. He arrives at work before 7, kissing his two sleeping children before he leaves the house. He performs face lifts, breast augmentations, brow lifts and liposuction, intensive surgical procedures that demand round-the-clock availability at the hospital. He often does not get home until after 9 p.m., and he goes into the office on Saturday. He doesn't see his children nearly as much as he would like, but he said that is what the pursuit of excellence in his specialty requires.

25   He is bothered by what he sees as a lack of devotion by today's medical students. A faculty member at New York University's medical school, he said the interest in way of life is across the board.

"When residents come looking for jobs, they ask, 'How often do I have to take night calls,' " he said. "There's less intensity, less determination and less devotion."

But Dr. Boldrick said she is not trying to avoid hard work. While she intends to have two children, she still plans to work full time.

What she wants to avoid is chaos and uncertainty and the lack of control that comes with other specialties. "I see people around me who like to do those things, and I think, 'Thank God,' " said Dr. Boldrick, who added that she feels she can make a contribution without taking on the meat and potatoes of say, internal medicine. "If I force myself to do something that didn't make me happy in order to pay a debt to society, that wouldn't do anyone any good," she said.

The reasoning resonates with Dr. Clara Choi, 32, a resident in radiation oncology at Stanford. Dr. Choi finds her field fascinating but pointed out that it also demands few unexpected calls to the hospital.

30   Married, she plans to have a family. "I'd have to get someone to take care of the baby if I spent every third or fourth night in the hospital," Dr. Choi said.

Dr. Rutecki says he completely understands, having missed out on a lot in the lives of his own two children.

"I missed a lot because I was on call three to five days a week," he said. "Rather than take this data as an opportunity to criticize, I think we recognize that this is the way medicine is moving."

CREDITS ∎

TEXT CREDITS

CHAPTER 1

Blinder: Reprinted with permission from Alan S. Blinder, "Outsourcing: Bigger Than You Thought," *The American Prospect,* Volume 17, Number 11: November, 2006. http://www.prospect.org. *The American Prospect,* 1710 Rhode Island Avenue, NW, 12th Floor, Washington, DC 20036. All rights reserved.

Klare: "The US and China Are Over a Barrel" by Michael Klare. *Los Angeles Times,* Apr 28, 2008, p. 17. Used by permission of Michael T. Klare.

Isaacson: Reprinted with the permission of Simon & Schuster, Inc. from *Einstein: His Life and Universe* by Walter Isaacson. Copyright © 2007 by Walter Isaacson.

Goodwin: Reprinted with the permission of Simon & Schuster, Inc. and Penguin Books Ltd. from *Team of Rivals: The Political Genius of Abraham Lincoln* by Doris Kearns Goodwin. Copyright © 2005 by Blithedale Productions, Inc. All rights reserved.

CHAPTER 2

Krauthammer: "The Moon We Left Behind" by Charles Krauthammer. *Washington Post,* July 17, 2009: A17. Used by permission of *The Washington Post.*

Beres: "The Common App Fallacy" by Damon Beres. Used by permission of Damon Beres, *Washington Square News.*

CHAPTER 3

Moss: "While Warning About Fat, U.S. Pushes Cheese Sales" by Michael Moss. *The New York Times,* November 6, 2010. Copyright © 2010 The New York Times. All rights reserved. Used with permission.

Jackson: "Got too much cheese?" by Derrick Z. Jackson. *The Boston Globe,* November 9, 2010. Copyright © 2010 The Boston Globe. All rights reserved. Used with permission.

U.S. Department of Energy: "Genetically Modified Foods and Organisms." Human Genome Project, U.S. Department of Energy, November 5, 2008.

GM Freeze Campaign: "Why a GM Freeze?" GM Freeze, © September 9, 2009. http://www.gmfreeze.org. Reprinted with permission from GM Freeze.

Edwards: "The Space Elevator" by Bradley C. Edwards. National Institute for Advanced Concepts, Phase II Final Report, March 1, 2003.

Lemley: "Going Up" by Brad Lemley. *Discover* magazine, July 2004. Reprinted by permission of the author. Brad Lemley is Contributing Editor, *Discover* magazine.

Swan and Swan: "Why We Need a Space Elevator" by Cathy W. Swan and Peter A. Swan. *Space Policy* 22.2 (May 2006): 86–91. Reprinted by permission of the publisher, Elsevier.

Kent: "Getting into Space on a Thread: Space Elevator as Alternative Access to Space" by Jason R. Kent, Maxwell AFB, Air War College, April, 2007.

CHAPTER 4

Review Panel: Summary of Key Findings from "Mass Shootings at Virginia Tech, April 16, 2007," Report of the Review Panel, Presented to Governor Kaine, Commonwealth of Virginia.

Gammage and Burling: "Laws Limit Schools Even After Alarms" by Jeff Gammage and Stacey Burling. *Philadelphia Inquirer,* April 19, 2007: A01. Used by permission.

Christian Science Monitor: "Perilous Privacy at Virginia Tech." Reprinted with permission from the September 4, 2007, issue of *The Christian Science Monitor* (www.csmonitor.com). © 2007 The Christian Science Monitor.

McMurray: "Colleges Are Watching Troubled Students" by Jeffrey McMurray. Associated Press. March 28, 2008. Used with permission.

Gordon: "Campus Stabbing Student Sues UC Regents" by Larry Gordon in *Los Angeles Times,* December 8, 2010. Used with permission.

Associated Press: "Virginia Tech Massacre Has Altered Campus Mental Health Systems." Attributed to the Associated Press; appeared in the *Los Angeles Times,* April 14, 2008. Used by permission.

FERPA: *The Family Educational Rights and Privacy Act* (FERPA). United States Code, Title 20. Education. Ch. 31, General Provisions Concerning Education. Section 1232g.

CHAPTER 5

Winn: "A Changed State of Consciousness" from *The Plug-In Drug, Revised and Updated—25th Anniversary Edition* by Marie Winn. Copyright © 1977,

CHAPTER 6

Pilcher and Waters: Excerpt from "How Sleep Deprivation Affects Psychological Variables Related to College Students" by June J. Pilcher and Amy S. Waters in *Journal of American College Health,* Volume 46, Issue 3, November 1997, 121–126. Published by the Helen Dwight Reid Educational Foundation, Heldref Publications.

Price: Excerpt from "The Crisis in Nursing Home Care" by Adam Price, unpublished paper, 2001. Used by permission.

Naison: Excerpt from "Scenario for Scandal" by Mark Naison. *Commonweal,* 109.16, 1982.

Wageneck: Excerpt from "Family Values in the Marketplace" by Frances Wageneck, unpublished paper, 2000. Used by permission.

Weil: Excerpt from "Teaching Boys and Girls Separately" by Elizabeth Weil. *The New York Times Magazine,* March 2, 2008.

Reason: Excerpt from "Frankenfoods Frenzy." *Reason,* January 13, 2000.

Neil: Excerpt from "The Incandescent Charisma of the Lonely Light Bulb" by Dan Neil. *The Los Angeles Times Magazine,* February 2008, p. 70.

CHAPTER 8

Sacks: Excerpt from *Dignity of Difference* by Jonathan Sacks. Published by Continuum, 2003, p. 88.

Judy and D'Amico: Executive Summary in *Workforce 2020: Work and Workers in the Twenty-First Century* by Richard W. Judy and Carol D'Amico. Indianapolis: Hudson Institute, 1998. Used by permission.

Friedman: Excerpt from *The World Is Flat: A Brief History of the Twenty-First Century, Updated and Expanded Edition* by Thomas L. Friedman. Copyright © 2005, 2006, 2007 by Thomas L. Friedman. Reprinted by permission of Farrar, Straus and Giroux, LLC.

The Economist: "Into the Unknown." *The Economist,* November 13, 2004: p. 17. Reproduced with permission of Economist Newspaper Ltd.

Bureau of Labor Statistics, U.S. Department of Labor: Employment Projections: 2008–2018 Summary. Bureau of Labor Statistics, U.S. Department of Labor.

Reitz: "Want to Outsource Proof Your Career? Don't Become a Commodity" by Victoria Reitz. *Machine Design,* April 26, 2007.

Peters: "The New Wired World of Work: A more transparent workplace will mean more white-collar accountability and less tolerance for hangers-on" by Tom Peters. *Business Week,* April 9, 2008. Used by permission of Business Week.

Lohr: "Creating the Jobs of the Future" by Steve Lohr. *The New York Times,* April 17, 2006, p. C1. Copyright © 2006 The New York Times. All rights reserved. Used with permission.

McGrath: "The Last Days of the Philadelphia Lawyer" by Tom McGrath. As first appeared in *Philadelphia Magazine.* Copyright © 2008 Metro Corp. Reprinted with permission.

Richtel: "Young Doctors and Wish Lists: No weekend calls, no beepers" by Matt Richtel. *The New York Times,* January 7, 2004. Copyright © 2004 The New York Times. All rights reserved. Used with permission.

PHOTO CREDITS

Pages 94, 95, 114, and 115: Images created by Alan Chan with permission from Dr. Brad Edwards.

Page 208: Fancy Feast ad: "The Best the World Has to Offer Now Presents the Best of the Sea," 2003, Nestle Purina Pet Care. Reprinted by permission of McCann Erickson.

Page 210: GE Monogram appliance ad: Reprinted by permission of General Electric Appliances.

INDEX